MARC GOERGEN

CORPORATE GOVERNANCE

A GLOBAL PERSPECTIVE

T0334058

CENGAGE

Australia • Brazil • Mexico • Singapore • United Kingdom • United States

CENGAGE

Corporate Governance: A Global Perspective, 1st edition
Marc Goergen

Publisher: Annabel Ainscow

List Manager: Abbie Coppin

Content Project Manager:
Phillipa Davidson-Blake

Manufacturing Manager: Elaine Bevan

Marketing Manager: Sophie Clarke

Typesetter: MPS Limited

Text Designer: MPS Limited

Cover Designer: Simon Levy Associates

Cover Image: © Malchev/Shutterstock Inc

For product information and technology assistance, contact us at
emea.info@cengage.com

For permission to use material from this text or product and for permission queries, email **emea.permissions@cengage.com**

British Library Cataloguing-in-Publication Data

A catalogue record for this book is available from the British Library.

ISBN: 978-1-4737-5917-6

Cengage Learning, EMEA
Cheriton House, North Way
Andover, Hampshire, SP10 5BE
United Kingdom

Cengage Learning is a leading provider of customized learning solutions with employees residing in nearly 40 different countries and sales in more than 125 countries around the world. Find your local representative at:
www.cengage.co.uk.

Cengage Learning products are represented in Canada by Nelson Education, Ltd.

For your course and learning solutions, visit
www.cengage.co.uk.

Purchase any of our products at your local college store or at our preferred online store **www.cengagebrain.com.**

Printed in the United Kingdom by Ashford Colour Press Ltd.
Print Number: 06   Print Year: 2024

Contents

Preface to Cengage edition

Since the publication of the Pearson edition of this textbook in 2012, the consequences of the 2008 financial crisis or the 'Great Recession' have become much more obvious. For example, Western societies are now much more divisive, with certain parts of society emerging as the main victims from the crisis whereas others have suffered much less or have even benefitted from the crisis. Nevertheless, increasing inequality within society cannot just be attributed to the Great Recession. Some argue that globalization and neoliberalism, phenomena whose origins can be traced back to the 1970s, are also to blame. What matters is that this increasing inequality, which can also be observed in emerging economies such as China that was left relatively unscathed by the Great Recession, has refuelled the debate about the design of capitalist systems. Fortunately, the public debate has benefitted from the input of academics such as Dani Rodrik and Thomas Piketty. However, more recently the debate has been dominated by populist arguments, and rising inequality has been blamed on various social groups such as immigrants and refugees who have little or no voice in society. Hence, there is a clear need to revisit capitalist systems, including the design of corporate governance.

I do hope that this textbook will convey to the reader a sense that corporate governance is much more than boards of directors and compliance with codes of best practice. This textbook goes back to basics by attempting to answer a number of important questions which also feed into the ongoing debate about the design of capitalist systems. Who controls and owns stock-market listed corporations across the world? How can we ensure that these corporations create wealth for their shareholders and other stakeholders? What types of financial systems are there and what are their advantages and disadvantages? Should corporations be (more) socially responsible and, if the answer to this question is affirmative, how can this be achieved?

Changes to Cengage edition

The structure of the textbook has changed to improve the flow throughout the book. Part II, which used to be entitled 'International corporate governance', is now called 'Macro corporate governance'. Parts III and IV have been swapped around to improve progression through the book. Chapter 8 (formerly Chapter 5) on 'Incentivizing managers and the disciplining of badly performing managers', which used to be in Part II, has been moved to Part III. A new chapter, Chapter 7 on 'Boards of directors', including some of the material which used to be in old Chapter 5, has also been added to Part III. Throughout the book, many of the case studies in the textboxes have been replaced with more up-to-date material. In addition, errors, omissions and inaccuracies that were spotted by the author and various users of the text have also been corrected. The glossary has also been updated to include terminology used in the new material.

While it is not feasible to provide an exhaustive list of all the changes made, in what follows I provide a summary of the main changes made to each chapter. The definition of corporate governance in Chapter 1 – which is used throughout this book – now distinguishes between four types of conflicts of interests rather than just three. Indeed, the conflicts of interests between the providers of finance and the managers has been broken up into the conflicts between the shareholders and the managers and the conflicts between the shareholders and the debtholders. The definitions of ownership and control have also been clarified and the discussion of the agency problem of debt has been improved. Finally, an appendix has been added to Chapter 1. The appendix contains an extensive discussion of the theoretical framework underlying the Jensen and Meckling (1976) paper.[1] Chapter 2 has benefitted from extensive updating wherever feasible and pedagogically defensible. Importantly, a trade-off had to be made between reporting the most recent figures on corporate control for each region on the one side and ensuring that the figures are detailed enough and are based on ultimate control to enable a comparison with other studies on the other. The case studies in Chapter 3 have been updated. The statistics in Chapter 4 have been updated to the latest figures available. Section 5.5 in Chapter 5 (which used to be Chapter 6) has been renamed to reflect the section's focus on country trust. Chapter 6 on corporate governance regulation has been extensively updated to reflect recent developments and changes in regulation and codes of best practice. It also now includes a new section (Section 6.5) with brief summaries of the regulatory approach and focus in China, Japan, Germany and India. The section on positive action has been moved to the new Chapter 7 on boards of directors in Part III. This material, which has been extensively updated, can now be found in Section 7.6 on board gender balance and board diversity. Finally, a new section, Section 7.5, on the market for directors has been added to the same chapter. Chapter 8 (old Chapter 5) now focuses on all previously included corporate governance mechanisms, except for the board of directors which again is now the focus of new Chapter 7. Chapter 11 on IPO firms (old Chapter 14) has now an additional section (Section 11.7) on the specific corporate governance needs of IPO firms and how these differ from those of more mature firms. Various sections of this chapter have also been updated to reflect recent developments in academic research. The Chapter Aims and Learning Outcomes of Chapter 12 on the behavioural biases (old Chapter 15) have been rewritten to make the link between behavioural biases and corporate governance more obvious. Section 12.7 has been extensively updated to reflect recent advances in research on the effects of gender and age on corporate governance. Chapter 13 (old Chapter 8) on CSR and SRI has also benefitted from a number of fairly major updates (see Sections 13.2 and 13.4). The chapter also now summarizes the United Nations' Principles of Responsible Investment. Finally, Section 15.5 on employee board representation in Chapter 15 (old Chapter 10) now includes a discussion of the most recent literature on the subject.

---

[1]Jensen, M. and Meckling, W. (1976), 'Theory of the Firm: Managerial Behavior, Agency Costs and Capital Structure', *Journal of Financial Economics* 3, 305–60.

Acknowledgements for Cengage edition

I would like to thank Øyvind Bøhren at BI Norwegian Business School for his very thorough reading of the Pearson edition of the book and his many comments which have helped to improve this edition. Thanks are also due to the four anonymous reviewers who read the draft for the Cengage edition of the book and who provided many helpful comments. Finally, I am grateful to Jie Chen at Cardiff University and Wei Song at Swansea University for kindly updating Figure 8.1 in Chapter 8.

Marc Goergen

Cardiff, June 2017

The publisher would like to thank the following reviewers for their helpful comments on the development of this edition:

André Betzer, Schumpeter School of Business and Economics, Germany

Mark Billings, University of Exeter Business School, UK

Peter Limbach, University of Cologne, Germany

Inga van den Bongard, University of Mannheim, Germany

Preface to Pearson edition

I had been toying with the idea of writing a textbook on corporate governance for a long time, but until recently I did not have the courage to undertake this venture. I had been teaching corporate governance as part of other modules, such as modules on corporate finance, financial management and international finance at UMIST and Manchester Business School. However, it is only when I joined Cardiff Business School that I was given the opportunity to teach an entire module on corporate governance. While I was very excited about this opportunity, I also found the task of designing an entire module on corporate governance somewhat daunting. The main reason was the lack of a suitable text on corporate governance. I felt that the existing textbooks had too narrow a view of corporate governance. They seemed mainly to equate corporate governance to regulation and disclosure whereas I believe that corporate governance is much more wide-ranging than this.

I hope that the readers of this textbook will get a feel for how rich the field of corporate governance is and that it is more than just regulation and codes of best practice. I have tried to make a conscious effort in this book to reflect the diversity of not just the field of corporate governance research, but also that of corporate governance arrangements and settings across countries. The one lesson I wish readers to draw from this book is that diversity is not necessarily bad. While over the last few decades national and cross-national policy makers have endeavoured to harmonize and even standardize national systems, the recent financial crisis has taught us an important lesson. No single system of corporate governance is infallible. More generally, there are still a lot of unanswered questions about corporate governance, in particular the effectiveness of various arrangements. Hence, it seems rather premature to favour one system over all the other ones.

One of the challenges I was facing while writing this textbook, which also made this task so exciting, was that it can be very difficult to keep an arm's length from one's political convictions, in particular those relating to the distribution and redistribution of wealth, income and power in society. Indeed, ultimately corporate governance is not just about 'how companies are governed', but also about the design of much broader societal institutions. Finally, I do hope that the readers of this textbook will find this book fun to read and that it will awaken their interest in the field of corporate governance.

Acknowledgements for Pearson edition

I would like to thank the eight anonymous referees who kindly commented on the initial book proposal as well as some of the draft chapters. I am also indebted to several of my colleagues and friends who read all or part of the manuscript: Christian Andres (Otto Beisheim School of Management), André Betzer (University of Wuppertal), Salim Chahine (American University of Beirut), Mahmoud Ezzamel (Cardiff University), William Forbes (Loughborough University), David Hillier (University of Strathclyde), Vanessa Jones (Institute of Chartered Accountants in England and Wales), Luc Renneboog (Tilburg University), Noel O'Sullivan (Loughborough University) and Geoff Wood (University of Sheffield). A special thank you goes to Chris Bell for his encouragement during the writing of this book. I am also grateful to my cats for making the write-up of this book so much more fun: Teddy Pompom for moving parts of the manuscript around the house and then leaving them all over the house, making the whole place look like a bomb site, and Misi Nounou for being so much fun to play with. Finally, I would like to thank Russell Curnow and the whole team at Pearson Education for their encouragement during the write-up of this textbook.

Marc Goergen

Cardiff, June 2011

Introduction

Corporate governance concerns us all. While some of us hold shares directly in stock-exchange listed firms, most of the working population holds shares indirectly via pension funds, mutual funds or unit trusts. Even those of us who do not invest directly in the stock market and are not members of a pension fund have been hit by the recent corporate scandals as well as the subprime mortgage crisis. One of the examples discussed in this book (see Chapter 1) concerns the failure of Icelandic banks. One of these failed Icelandic banks is Glitnir. To date it still owes British local councils £200m which the councils deposited with the bank. Partly as a result of the loss of these funds, British local councils had to cut back the services they provide to their communities. Glitnir was controlled by the Icelandic businessman Jon Asgeir Johannesson. During the peak of his empire, Mr Johannesson had control via his holding company Baugur over large chunks of the UK high street, including names such as House of Fraser, Woolworths, All Saints and French Connection, as well as the supermarket chain Iceland Foods. Baugur also had a stake in the US chain of department stores Saks Inc. Mr Johannesson, who at the time of the filing of the case with a court in New York was still on the board of House of Fraser and the chairman of Iceland Foods, stood trial and was accused, alongside other investors of 'a sweeping conspiracy to wrest control of Iceland's Glitnir Bank to fill [his] pockets and prop up [his] own failing companies'. He was also served with a global asset-freeze order forcing him to hand over all his assets. The case was eventually thrown out by the judge on the basis that most of the key players were Icelanders and that the case concerned the failure of Icelandic banks. The case was then taken to Iceland, but the plaintiffs eventually lost their case in 2014. While the case was eventually unsuccessful, the losses made by Glitnir and some of the other Icelandic banks are nevertheless real. As this example illustrates, corporate failures in one country can have wide-ranging consequences which hit not just the shareholders of the failing corporations, but also remote economic actors that have no direct links with the former. Hence, we should all be concerned about the governance of stock-exchange listed firms and, in particular, the behaviour of the managers of these firms.

Philosophy of the book

Existing textbooks on corporate governance tend to have a strong focus on UK and/or US corporate governance. This focus is somewhat surprising as the UK and US corporate governance systems have features which clearly set them apart from pretty much the rest of the world. Indeed, the typical British and American stock-market listed firm is widely held (by many shareholders) and control therefore lies with the management rather than the shareholders. In contrast, most stock-exchange listed firms from the rest of the world have a large shareholder whose control is substantial enough to have a significant influence over the firm's affairs. Given these marked differences in ownership and control, corporate governance issues emerging in non-UK and non-US firms tend to be very different from those that may affect British and American companies. Hence, it is important for a textbook to bear in mind the diversity of ownership and control in order to provide a holistic overview of corporate governance issues across the world. Indeed, there is no single way of – or system for – ensuring good corporate governance. Further, while national and cross-national regulators since the late 1990s have advocated the superiority of the Anglo-American approach to corporate governance, the 2008 financial crisis highlights that there is no perfect system and that each system has shortcomings which may result in spectacular corporate failures.

Importantly, this global perspective is adopted throughout the entire book and is not just limited to a particular part of the book or individual chapters. The adoption of a global perspective is not only important given the nature and diversity of corporate governance, but is also paramount given the increasingly international character of student bodies in most universities (including MBA programmes).

Rather than focusing on corporate governance regulation as some of the established textbooks do, this book builds on existing academic research, but without ignoring practice. The adoption of a strong theoretical framework is important as it sets the basis for a critical analysis of existing corporate governance practice and regulation. Frequently, existing textbooks consider corporate governance regulation to be set in stone, failing to question the premises it is built on as well as its effectiveness. For example, successive UK codes of best practice have been based on the premise that independent, non-executive directors are key to good corporate governance despite the lack of academic evidence on the effectiveness of non-executive directors. Even more worryingly, as suggested by recent research on director networks, independent directors are often only independent by name.

The book also adopts a multidisciplinary perspective which is important given that corporate governance relates to a range of issues such as economic, organisational, financial, accounting, legal, ethical and behavioural issues. Again, existing textbooks frequently have too narrow a focus, such as on corporate governance regulation, environmental accounting and corporate social responsibility.

Finally, an effort has been made to convey to the reader the leading edge of knowledge in a given area of corporate governance in an objective and unbiased way. For some areas, the evidence is as yet inconclusive. Rather than proposing unfounded conjectures or taking the approach adopted by regulators as the (only) way forward, this book clearly spells out the lack of knowledge in a particular area. While in some cases this lack of knowledge may be frustrating to the reader, the alternative of lulling the reader into a false sense of security is perceived to be worse.

To summarize, this book adopts a global perspective, reflects the multidisciplinary nature of the area and provides a critical review of existing institutional and legal arrangements.

Synopsis of the subject matter of the book

The book is divided into the following five parts:

- Part I – Introduction to corporate governance
- Part II – Macro corporate governance
- Part III – Improving corporate governance
- Part IV – Corporate governance and stakeholders
- Part V – Conclusions

Part I introduces corporate governance. Lecturers who wish to cover the basics of corporate governance, without going into too much detail, may concentrate on this part. This part reviews the various definitions of corporate governance and discusses the main theories, including the principal-agent model. It also reviews the patterns of corporate control across the world, highlighting the differences between the UK and USA on one side and the rest of the world on the other. While in the UK and the USA there is normally no or little difference between control and ownership, in the rest of the world there is often a major difference between the two. It is important to be aware of such deviations between control and ownership as they generate particular conflicts of interests which would not otherwise emerge. Both the differences in corporate control and deviations between ownership and control create conflicts of interests in most corporations which are very different from the conflicts of interests at the basis of the principal-agent model. Hence, the principal-agent theory has only limited applicability across the world.

Part II contains an in-depth review of the macro-level aspects of corporate governance. Rather than describing the various systems of corporate governance via a lengthy list of fairly concise sections devoted to individual countries as some texts do, the approach that is adopted here is a comparative one. The focus will be on the characteristics shared across the various systems as well as those characteristics that make them distinct. This part will begin with a review of the various taxonomies of corporate governance systems after discussing the economic and political context in which global capitalism has risen. It will then review the evidence on the link between corporate governance, the development of financial markets and growth. The last chapter of this part will be on corporate governance regulation, with the focus being on the main national regulatory approaches (e.g. prescriptive rules versus codes of best practice) as well as their advantages and shortcomings.

Part III focuses on the ways to enable good corporate governance within countries as well as within individual corporations. This part starts with a chapter on the board of directors. Given the importance that various regulators and codes of best practices – as well as academic research – have attached to this corporate governance mechanism, it deserves its own chapter. The following chapter focuses on the other corporate governance devices that are employed across the world to ensure that managers create shareholder value. The next chapter deals with corporate governance in emerging markets. Emerging economies are often dominated by crony capitalism such as inherited wealth and political interference in corporate affairs, both of which make improvements in corporate governance particularly challenging. This chapter will also discuss the role of stock markets in economic development. The following chapter then reviews the ways and means by which individual companies can deviate from their national corporate governance standards by offering their shareholders and other stakeholders better protection against expropriation by the management and large shareholders. Such means include cross-listing on foreign stock markets, cross-border mergers and (re)incorporations in foreign countries or other federal states of the same country. This part also includes a chapter on corporate governance issues faced by firms that are in the process of going public and/or have recently gone public. These firms suffer from issues such as the pronounced asymmetry of information between insiders and outsiders. They also have stakeholders, such as venture capitalists, that are not normally present in more mature firms, as well as CEOs that are typically more powerful than their counterparts in more mature firms. The final chapter covers behavioural issues, such as excessive loyalty of the board members to the CEO (or the major shareholder) and managerial overconfidence or hubris.

Part IV covers issues relating to corporate stakeholders other than the shareholders. These issues include corporate social responsibility and socially responsible investment, debtholder related issues (the positive role of debtholders in corporate governance as well as the conflicts of interests that debtholders may be subject to), the rights and the voice of employees across the various corporate governance systems, and the role and responsibilities of gatekeepers (such as auditors, credit-rating agencies and stock-exchange regulators) in corporate governance.

Part V concludes the book by drawing the lessons from the previous chapters, identifying the challenges that those concerned with improving corporate governance face and by proposing ways forward. To be effective, markets need good governance. Recent events have shown that bad market governance – in particular bad corporate governance – has not only negative effects for the markets concerned, but has also much more wide-ranging and devastating effects on wealth distribution and social justice for society as a whole. In other words, corporate governance failures tend to not only result in the expropriation of the shareholders of the immediate corporations concerned, but also affect other economic actors and stakeholders such as debtholders, taxpayers, consumers and job-market participants.

New theories and developments covered by this book

The book covers a range of emerging topics in corporate governance, including contractual corporate governance and behavioural issues, which are not typically covered by the established textbooks in the area. Contractual corporate governance is an important and fast-emerging area of corporate governance. It refers to the ways and means by which individual companies can deviate from their national corporate governance standards by increasing (or reducing) the level of protection they offer to their shareholders and other stakeholders. Such ways include cross-listing on foreign stock markets and cross-border mergers. While some of these new issues are covered by existing *finance* textbooks, they are frequently only covered in isolation and also with little reference to corporate governance. This book intends to fill this gap. Finally, behavioural issues, such as those relating to the management and employees, are receiving increased attention from various constituencies. For example in the UK, the Financial Reporting Council published a document entitled 'Corporate Culture and the Role of Boards. Report of Observations' in July 2016. On p.11, the report states the following:

> The key challenge for boards is to understand what in practice drives the behaviour of employees and management and to shape and influence those drivers in a way that will foster greater sustainability and improved performance over time.

Hence, given the interest of professional bodies and practitioners as well as regulators in behavioural issues, it is important that a textbook on corporate governance covers this topic. This book aims to do exactly this.

Target audience for the book, their learning needs and challenges

The book targets advanced undergraduates, Master's students and MBA students. The book can be used as the main text for an entire module devoted to corporate governance or can be used as one of the textbooks for a module with significant coverage of corporate governance issues (such as a module on (international) corporate finance). As a reflection of the diversity of audiences that may use this book, there is an extensive glossary explaining the main technical terms.

The teaching challenges for the lecturer

One of the main challenges of teaching corporate governance is its multidisciplinary nature. Hence, the study of corporate governance assumes a generalist background in management and a familiarity with the basic concepts of accounting, economics, finance and corporate law. While an effort is being made in the book to present the concepts of corporate governance – and other relevant subjects – in a non-technical way, there are nevertheless limits to achieving this. Whenever a chapter relies on particular background knowledge, this will be made clear to the reader from the start and readers who do not possess this knowledge will be directed to appropriate readings.

Courses for which the book would be suitable

The book is suitable as the main textbook for a module devoted to corporate governance. Such modules are typically aimed at final year undergraduates in management or a related discipline. The book is also suitable for use on a specialist Master's programme (such as a Master's programme in accounting, finance or management) or an MBA course.

Key features of the book

The book and its web-based resources include the following:

- Textboxes containing case studies illustrating the theoretical concepts covered in the chapter
- Discussion questions at the end of each chapter and exercises for the chapters introducing quantitative concepts of corporate governance
- A test bank consisting of more than 100 multiple-choice questions of varying degrees of difficulty testing student knowledge and comprehension
- A section with key readings as well as further (more advanced) readings at the end of each chapter
- A link to third-party web resources where appropriate
- A glossary with the technical terms used in this book, reflecting the diversity of audiences that may use this book
- Microsoft® Office PowerPoint® slides for each chapter
- An instructor's manual with teaching notes for the discussion questions and exercises
- A regular internet blog which will comment on recent news on corporate governance, recent developments, etc.

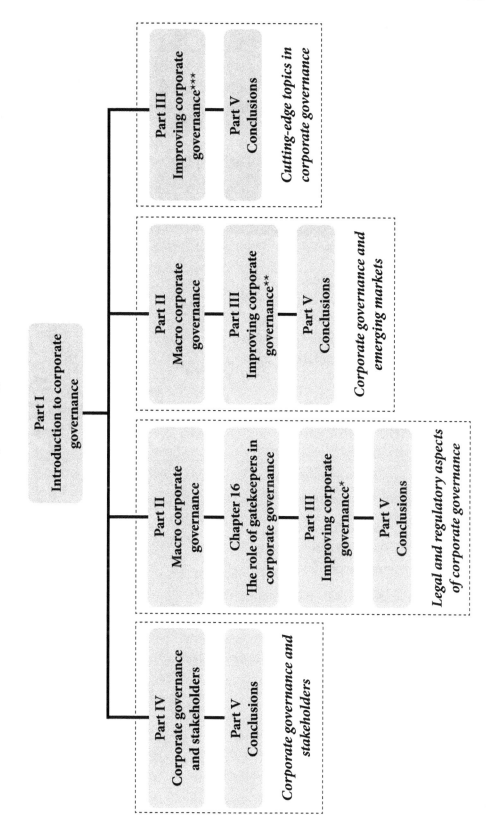

Possible paths through this book

Notes:

*with or without Chapter 11 – Corporate governance in initial public offerings, and Chapter 12 – Behavioural biases and corporate governance

**with or without Chapter 12 – Behavioural biases and corporate governance

***with or without Chapter 7 – Boards of directors, and Chapter 8 – Incentivizing managers and the disciplining of badly performing managers

CENGAGE

Teaching & Learning Support Resources

Cengage's peer reviewed content for higher and further education courses is accompanied by a range of digital teaching and learning support resources. The resources are carefully tailored to the specific needs of the instructor, student and the course. Examples of the kind of resources provided include:

- A password protected area for instructors with, for example, a testbank, PowerPoint slides and an instructor's manual.

- An open-access area for students including, for example, useful weblinks and glossary terms.

Lecturers: to discover the dedicated lecturer digital support resources accompanying this textbook please register here for access: login.cengage.com.

Students: to discover the dedicated student digital support resources accompanying this textbook, please search for **CORPORATE GOVERNANCE** on: cengagebrain.co.uk.

BE UNSTOPPABLE

Learn more at cengage.co.uk/education

Introduction to corporate governance

PART I

1 Defining corporate governance and key theoretical models

Chapter Aims

This chapter aims to introduce you to the subject area of corporate governance. The chapter discusses the various definitions of corporate governance, reviews the debate on the main objective of the corporation and explains how corporate governance problems change across different levels of ownership and control. The chapter also introduces the main theories underpinning corporate governance. While the book focuses on stock-exchange listed corporations, this chapter also discusses alternative forms of organizations, i.e. mutual organizations and partnerships.

Learning Outcomes

After reading this chapter, you should be able to:

1 Contrast the different definitions of corporate governance

2 Critically review the principal-agent model

3 Compare the agency problems of equity and debt

4 Explain the corporate governance problem that prevails in countries where corporate ownership and control are concentrated

5 Distinguish between ownership and control

1.1 Introduction

While this chapter will briefly review alternative forms of organization and ownership, the focus of this book is on stock-exchange listed firms. These firms are typically in the form of stock corporations, i.e. they have equity stocks or shares outstanding which trade on an officially recognized stock exchange. Stocks or shares are certificates of ownership and they also frequently have control rights, i.e. voting rights which enable their holders, the shareholders, to vote at the annual general shareholders' meeting (AGM). One of the important rights that voting shares confer to their holders is the right to appoint the members of the board of directors. The board of directors is the ultimate governing body *within* the corporation. Its duty, and in particular the duty of the non-executive directors, is to look after the interests of all the shareholders as well as sometimes those of other stakeholders such as the corporation's employees or banks. More precisely, the non-executives have two main roles. First, to monitor the firm's top management, including the executive directors which are the other type of directors sitting on the firm's board.[1] Second, to provide advice such as strategic direction. While in the US non-executives are referred to as (independent or outside) directors and

[1]As we shall see in Part II of the book, there is great diversity in terms of corporate governance arrangements. While UK and US corporations have a single board on which both the executive directors and the non-executive directors sit, corporations from some countries (such as China and Germany) have two boards. Corporate governance systems with two-tier boards have a supervisory board

executives are referred to as officers, this book adopts the internationally used terminology of non-executive and executive directors.

1.2 Defining corporate governance

Most definitions of corporate governance are based on implicit, if not explicit assumptions about what should be the main objective of the corporation. However, there is no universal agreement as to what the main objective of a corporation should be, and this objective is likely to depend on a country's culture and electoral system, its government's political orientation as well as the country's legal system. Chapter 4 of Part II will shed more light on how these cultural, political and institutional factors may explain differences in corporate governance and control across countries.

Andrei Shleifer and Robert Vishny define corporate governance as:

> [t]he ways in which suppliers of finance to corporations assure themselves of getting a return on their investment.[2]

Basing themselves on Oliver Williamson's work,[3] Shleifer and Vishny's definition clearly assumes that the main objective of the corporation is to maximize the returns to the shareholders (as well as the debtholders). They justified their focus by the argument that investments in the firm by the providers of finance are typically sunk funds, i.e. funds that the latter are likely to lose if the corporation runs into trouble. On the contrary, the corporation's other stakeholders, such as its employees, suppliers and customers, can easily walk away from the corporation without losing their investments. For example, an employee should be able to find a job in another firm which values her human capital. While the providers of finance lose the capital they have invested in the corporation, the employee does not lose her human capital in case the firm fails. Another perspective does not focus on the firm being in financial distress, but rather focuses on who has the strongest incentive for the firm to be run efficiently. That is the most junior claimant in the firm. The claims of employees, customers and suppliers, etc. have to be met first before any monies can be paid to the providers of finance, in particular the shareholders. Put differently, the providers of finance can only eat once the other stakeholders have eaten.

Hence, the providers of finance, and in particular the shareholders, are the residual risk bearers or the residual claimants to the firm's assets. In other words, if the firm gets into financial distress, the claims of all the stakeholders other than the shareholders will be met first before the claims of the latter can be met. Typically when the firm is in financial distress, the firm's assets are insufficient to meet all of the claims it is facing and the shareholders will lose their initial investment. In contrast, the other claimants will walk away with all or at least some of their capital.

In contrast to Shleifer and Vishny, Sarah Worthington argued that there is nothing in the legal status of a shareholder that justifies the focus on shareholder value maximization.[4] Paddy Ireland went one step further arguing that corporate assets should no longer be considered to be the private property of the shareholders but rather as common property given that they are 'the product of the collective labour of many generations'

---

and a management board. The supervisory board is the board on which the non-executive directors sit. The role of the non-executives is to represent the shareholders. Some of the seats on the supervisory board may also be held by other stakeholder representatives such as employee and trade union representatives and bankers. The management board is the board on which the executive directors sit. The executive directors are the corporation's top management team.

[2]Shleifer, A. and Vishny, R.W. (1997), 'A Survey of Corporate Governance', *Journal of Finance* 52, 737–83.

[3]Williamson, O. (1984), 'Corporate Governance', *Yale Law Journal* 93, 1197–230.

[4]See Worthington, S. (2001a), 'Shares and Shareholders: Property, Power and Entitlement: Part I', *Company Lawyer* 22, 258–66; and Worthington, S. (2001b), 'Shares and Shareholders: Property, Power and Entitlement: Part II', *Company Lawyer* 22, 307–14.

(p.56).[5] Marc Goergen and Luc Renneboog suggested a definition which allows for differences across firms in terms of the actors or stakeholders whose interests the corporation focuses on. According to their definition,

> [a] corporate governance system is the combination of mechanisms which ensure that the management (the agent) runs the firm for the benefit of one or several stakeholders (principals). Such stakeholders may cover shareholders, creditors, suppliers, clients, employees and other parties with whom the firm conducts its business.[6]

While Shleifer and Vishny's definition largely reflected the focus of the typical American or British stock-exchange listed corporation, managers of most Continental European firms also tend to consider the interests of the corporation's other stakeholders when running the firm. Although this statement dates back to the 1970s and may now appear somewhat outdated, it nevertheless is a good illustration of what still is frequently managers' attitude outside the Anglo-American world. The chief executive officer (CEO) of the German car maker Volkswagen AG stated the following:

> Why should I care about the shareholders, who I see once a year at the general meeting? It is much more important that I care about the employees; I see them every day.[7]

Further, in Germany corporate law explicitly mentions other stakeholder interests. Indeed, the German Co-determination Law of 1976 requires firms with more than 2,000 workers to have 50 per cent of employee representatives on their supervisory board (see Chapter 15). In a questionnaire survey sent to managers of German, Japanese, UK and US companies, Masaru Yoshimori asked the question as to whose company it is.[8] While 89 per cent of both UK and US managers state that the company's objective is the shareholders, only a minority of French, German and Japanese managers do so. In fact, 97 per cent of Japanese managers believe that the company belongs to the stakeholders rather than the shareholders. Nevertheless, if this survey were to be repeated today, the views of French and German managers would likely be closer to those of their UK and US counterparts.

Hence, while Anglo-American firms tend to – or at least are expected to – pursue shareholder value maximization, firms from the rest of the world tend to cater for multiple stakeholders. However, since the late 1990s, the two camps have moved closer to each other. For example, in the UK, the recent Company Law Review resulted in the Companies Act 2006 which now states in its Section 172 that:

> Directors should also recognise, as the circumstances require, the company's need to foster relationships with its employees, customers and suppliers, its need to maintain its business reputation, and its need to consider the company's impact on the community and the working environment.

Nevertheless, company directors must act bona fide in accordance with what would most likely promote the success of the company for the benefit of the collective body of shareholders. In other words, while directors are expected to consider the interests of other stakeholders, they should only do so if this is in the long-term interest of the company, and ultimately its shareholders, i.e. its owners. Hence, the principle of shareholder primacy is still pretty much intact in the UK and also the USA. At the same time, Continental Europe has moved closer to the shareholder-oriented system of corporate governance. In particular, European Union (EU)

---

[5] Ireland, P. (1999), 'Company Law and the Myth of Shareholder Ownership', *Modern Law Review* 62, 32–57.

[6] Goergen, M. and Renneboog, l. (2006), 'Corporate Governance and Shareholder Value', in D. Lowe and R. Leiringer (eds), *Commercial Management of Projects: Defining the Discipline*, Blackwell Publishing, 100–31. See also Tirole, J. (2001), 'Corporate Governance', *Econometrica* 9, 1–35.

[7] Kohlhausen, M. (1994), 'Der Wettbewerb um Aktionäre und Eigenkapital', presented during the Börsen-Zeitung seminar on 23 February 1994 in Frankfurt, mimeo.

[8] Yoshimori, M. (1995), 'Whose Company Is It? The Concept of the Corporation in Japan and the West', *Long Range Planning* 28, 33–44.

law has moved the law of its (as of 2017) 28 member states closer to UK law. An example is the 2004 EU Takeovers Directive which was largely modelled on the UK City Code on Mergers and Takeovers (see Chapter 6 for details). In turn, recent pressure on (large) corporations to behave socially responsible has moved stakeholder considerations to the forefront.

A more neutral and less politically charged definition of corporate governance is that the latter deals with conflicts of interests, and their prevention or mitigation, between:

- the shareholders and the managers.
- the shareholders and the debtholders.
- the shareholders and the non-financial stakeholders.
- different types of shareholders (mainly the large shareholder and the minority shareholders).

This is the definition which is adopted in this book. Another important advantage of this definition is that it can be applied to a variety of corporate governance systems. More precisely, this definition does not assume that problems of corporate governance are limited to the failure of the management to look after the interests of the firm's shareholders, but it also covers other possible corporate governance problems which are more likely to emerge in countries where corporations are characterized by concentrated ownership and control. These corporate governance problems normally consist of conflicts of interests between the firm's larger shareholders and its minority shareholders.

One of the first codes of best practice on corporate governance, if not even the very first one, was the Cadbury Report which was issued in 1992 in the United Kingdom.[9] The Cadbury Report defines corporate governance as 'the system by which companies are directed and controlled'. However, in the following sentences, the Report then goes on to mention what it considers to be the crucial role of boards of directors in corporate governance:

> Boards of directors are responsible for the governance of their companies. The shareholders' role in governance is to appoint the directors and the auditors and to satisfy themselves that an appropriate governance structure is in place. The responsibilities of the board include setting the company's strategic aims, providing the leadership to put them into effect, supervising the management of the business and reporting to shareholders on their stewardship. The board's actions are subject to laws, regulations and the shareholders in general meeting.

Thus, this definition is less general than the one adopted in this book for at least two reasons. First, it is built on the premise that boards of directors have a crucial role in corporate governance. In Chapter 7 of this book, we shall see that there is as yet very little empirical evidence that boards of directors are an effective corporate governance mechanism. Second, the Cadbury definition also implicitly assumes that individual shareholders are not powerful enough to take actions when their company's management performs badly. In Chapter 2, we shall see that this is typically not the case in stock-exchange listed corporations outside the UK and the USA as these corporations tend to have large shareholders that have sufficient voting power to fire inefficient management.

1.3 Corporate governance theory

Corporate governance issues are not new. They date back to at least the eighteenth century when large stock corporations were emerging. In his treatise published in 1776, the Scottish economist Adam Smith wrote the following.[10]

---

[9]Cadbury, A. (1992), *Report of the Committee on the Financial Aspects of Corporate Governance*, London: Gee & Co Ltd.
[10]Smith, A. (1776), *An Inquiry into the Nature and Causes of the Wealth of Nations*, reprinted in K. Sutherland (ed.) (1993), World's Classics, Oxford, UK: Oxford University Press.

It is in the interest of every man to live as much at his ease as he can; and if his emoluments are to be precisely the same, whether he does, or does not perform some laborious duty, it is certainly his interest, at least as interest is vulgarly understood, either to neglect it altogether, or, if he is subject to some authority which will not suffer him to do this, to perform it in as careless and slovenly a manner as that authority will permit.

This statement clearly illustrates the conflicts of interests that may exist between a so-called agent and the agent's principal. These conflicts of interests were later formalized by Michael Jensen and William Meckling in their principal-agent theory or model which was introduced in their seminal 1976 paper.[11] While the agent has been asked by the principal to carry out a specific duty, the agent may not act in the best interest of the principal once the contract between the two parties has been signed and may prefer to pursue his own interests. This type of danger is what economists normally refer to as moral hazard. Moral hazard consists of the fact that once a contract has been signed it may be in the interests of the agent to behave badly or at least less responsibly, i.e. in ways that may harm the principal while clearly serving the interests of the agent. Cases of moral hazard are not just limited to corporate governance. Indeed, they are also a major issue for insurance companies. For example, as soon as you have taken out an insurance policy covering yourself against burglary you may change your behaviour and be less careful about locking the front door of your house in the mornings when you leave for college or work. Rather than walking back home if you happen to be unsure about whether you have locked the door as you would have done in the past, you may decide not to do so as you are now covered against burglary by the insurance company. If your front door happens to be unlocked and you get burgled, the cost will be (at least partially) borne by the insurance company. If you walk back home you will be late for college or work. Hence, you may just decide to act in your own interests, i.e. save yourself the bother of going all the way back home, rather than act as a responsible policy holder.

A potential way to mitigate or even avoid principal-agent problems is so-called complete contracts. Complete contracts are contracts which specify exactly what:

- the managers must do in each future contingency of the world and.
- what the distribution of profits will be in each contingency.

As first pointed out by Oliver Williamson,[12] in practice, however, contracts are unlikely to be complete as:

- it is impossible to predict all future contingencies of the world.
- such contracts would be too complex to write and.
- they would be difficult or even impossible to monitor and reinforce by outsiders such as a court of law.[13]

A necessary condition for moral hazard to exist and for complete contracts to be an impossibility is the existence of asymmetric information. Asymmetric information refers to situations where one party, typically the one that agrees to carry out a certain duty or agrees to behave in a certain way, i.e. the agent, has

---

[11]Jensen, M. and Meckling, W. (1976), 'Theory of the Firm. Managerial Behavior, Agency Costs and Capital Structure', *Journal of Financial Economics* 3, 305–60. This section as well as the following two sections provide a primer on corporate governance theory. Readers interested in a more detailed discussion of the theoretical framework underlying the principal-agent theory are referred to the appendix at the end of this chapter.

[12]Williamson, O. (1984), 'Corporate Governance', *Yale Law Journal* 93, 1197–230. See also Hart, O.D. (1988), 'Incomplete Contracts and the Theory of the Firm', *Journal of Law, Economics and Organization* 4, 119–39.

[13]See Grossman, S.J. and Hart, O.D. (1986), 'The Costs and Benefits of Ownership: A Theory of Vertical and Lateral Integration', *Journal of Political Economy* 94, 691–719; Hart, O.D. and Moore, J. (1988), 'Incomplete Contracts and Renegotiation', *Econometrica* 56, 755–85. Hart, O.D. (1995), *Firms, Contracts, and Financial Structure*, Oxford, UK: Clarendon Press.

more information than the other party, the principal. If both the agent and the principal had access to the same information at all times, there would be no moral hazard issue. In other words, moral hazard exists because the principal cannot keep track of the agent's actions at all times. Even ex post, it can be difficult for a principal to judge whether failure is due to the agent or due to circumstances that were outside the control of the agent.

Returning to Jensen and Meckling's principal-agent model, apart from the existence of asymmetric information, the model also assumes that there is a separation of ownership and control in the corporation. Adolf Berle and Gardiner Means were the first to highlight this separation of ownership and control in their 1932 book *The Modern Corporation and Private Property*.[14] They argued that at first a firm starts off as a small business which is fully owned by its founder, typically an entrepreneur. At this stage, there are no conflicts of interests within the firm as the entrepreneur both owns 100 per cent of the firm and runs the firm. Hence, if the entrepreneur decides to work harder, all of the additional revenue generated by this increased effort will go into his own pockets. This implies that the entrepreneur has the perfect incentive to work hard: all the additional revenue generated by working harder will always accrue to him.

As the firm grows, it becomes more and more difficult for the entrepreneur to provide all the capital needed. At some point the entrepreneur might need to take the firm to the stock market so that the latter can tap into external capital. Once the firm has raised external capital, the entrepreneur's incentives have significantly altered. As the entrepreneur no longer owns all the firm's capital, he may now be less inclined to work hard. In other words, if the entrepreneur works harder, some of the fruits from his efforts will go to the firm's new shareholders. As the firm becomes larger and larger, the separation of ownership and control is likely to become more pronounced. Once the entrepreneur has sold all his remaining shares, there will come a point where the firm will be run by professional managers who own none or very little of the firm's capital. These managers are the agents, who are expected to run the firm on behalf of the principals, the firm's owners or shareholders. Hence, there is a clear 'division of labour' in the modern corporation. On the one hand, the managers have the expertise to run the firm, but lack the required funds to finance its operations. On the other, the shareholders have the required funds, but typically are not qualified to run the firm. In other words, de facto control lies with the managers who run the day-to-day operations of the firm whereas the firm is owned by the shareholders: hence the separation of ownership and control.

This brings us back to situations of asymmetric information where a less (or even badly) informed principal asks an agent with expert knowledge to carry out a certain duty on his behalf. Given the asymmetry of information, once he has been appointed the agent may decide to run the firm in his interests rather than those of the principal. This is the so-called principal-agent problem or agency problem, first formalized by Jensen and Meckling. Agency costs are then the sum of the following three components. The first component consists of the monitoring expenses incurred by the principal. Monitoring not only consists of the principal observing the agent and keeping a record of the latter's behaviour, but also consists of intervening in various ways to constrain the agent's behaviour and to avoid unwanted actions. The second component is the bonding costs incurred by the agent. Bonding costs are costs incurred by the agent in order to signal credibly to the principal that they will act in the interests of the latter. One credible way for the agent to bond herself to the principal is to invest in the latter's firm. Finally, the third component is the residual loss. The residual loss is the loss incurred by the principal due to fact that the agent may still make some decisions that do not maximize the value of the firm for the former and which are not prevented by monitoring and bonding.

[14]Berle A. and Means, G. (1932), *The Modern Corporation and Private Property*, New York: Macmillan.

1.4 Agency problems between managers and shareholders

The two main types of agency problems are perquisites and empire building. Perquisites or perks – also called fringe benefits – consist of on-the-job consumption by the firm's managers. While the benefits from the perks accrue to the managers, their costs are borne by the shareholders. Perks can come in lots of different forms. They may consist of excessively expensive managerial offices, private use of corporate jets and CEO mansions, all financed by shareholder funds. They may also consist of giving jobs within the firm to the management's family members rather than to the most qualified candidates on the job market. Box 1.1 contains real-life examples of executive perks.

Box 1.1
Perquisites

One of the most extreme examples of perquisites consumed by a top executive concerns the former CEO of US conglomerate Tyco International. His perks ranged from a staggering US$1 million of company funds spent towards financing his wife's 40th birthday on the Italian island of Sardinia, to a more modest US$15,000 for an umbrella stand and US$6,000 for a shower curtain.

Source: Alex Berenson (2004), 'Executives' Perks Provoke Calls for Greater Disclosure', *The New York Times*, 23 February, Finance Section, p. 13.

The CEO of American Express, Ken Chenault, spent $405,375 on personal travel with the corporate jet, and $132,019 on personal use of his company car.

Ray R. Irani, the CEO and chairman of Occidental Petroleum, spent $562,589 worth of the company's funds on security services. In a year when his total pay amounted to $415 million, he charged the company $556,470 for tax and financial consulting services.

Richard Notebaert, the CEO of Qwest, spent $332,000 on personal use of the corporate jet, $62,000 on financial-planning and tax-preparation services, as well as $56,000 for office expenses, including the services of a personal assistant. Qwest paid him an additional $197,000 to cover the taxes he incurred on these perquisites.

Source: Greg Farrell and Barbara Hansen (2007), 'A Peek at the Perks of the Corner Office', *USA Today*, 16 April, Money Section, p. 1B.

On top of his salary of more than US$100 million, the chairman of Starbucks Corporation received perks for a total of US$1.23 million. The perks included life insurance contributions as well as security and personal use of a corporate jet. Amazon.com spent a total of US$1.1 million on security for its founder, Jeff Bezos. In comparison, his annual salary was a meagre US$81,840.

Source: Craig Harris and Andrea James (2007), 'Top Execs Rake in the Perks. Region's Biggest Companies Shell out for Jet Use, Security', *The Seattle Post* – Intelligencer, 26 February, News Section, p. A1.

Angela Ahrendts, CEO of designer Burberry, received cash, perks and shares worth GBP6.1 million. The perks, which amounted to a total of GBP432,000, included car and clothing benefits.

Source: Simon Bowers and Julia Finch (2010), 'Blue-Chip Companies Braced for the Great Boardroom Pay Rebellion: Shareholders Likely to Revolt at Four Meetings – Targets of Investor Anger Include M&S and Burberry', *The Guardian*, 12 July, no page number stated.

John Thain, the Former Merrill-Lynch CEO, spent $1.2 million on the renovation of his offices, including a $35,000 toilet.

In January 2009, Citigroup, which was rescued by the US government with a $45 billion bailout under the Troubled Assets Relief Program (TARP), cancelled its order for a corporate jet costing $50 million after public outrage over the purchase. Wells Fargo & Co., another bank that had been bailed out under TARP with a total of $25 billion of taxpayer money, cancelled a 12-night retreat for staff at 2 luxury Las Vegas resorts.

Source: Sheldon Alberts (2009), 'Obama Scolds Wall St. Titans for Taking Lavish Bonuses', *The Gazette* (Montreal), 5 February, Business Section, p. B1.

Andy Haste, CEO of British insurance company RSA, received a 14 per cent increase in his salary in 2009, raising his salary to GBP2.33 million. This included a bonus of GBP1.02 million and perks, including car and travel allowances of GBP42,000 and pension contributions of GBP309,000. During the same year, RSA's profit dropped to GBP544 million, a decrease of 27%!

Source: Nick Goodway (2010), 'Outrage at RSA Chief Haste's Pay Package', *Evening Standard*, 12 April, no page number stated.

While perquisites can cause public outrage as Box 1.1 illustrates, especially when they are combined with lacklustre performance or, even worse, corporate failure, the amount of shareholder funds they typically consume is relatively modest compared to the other main type of agency problem, which is empire building. Nevertheless, research by David Yermack suggested that when CEO perks are first disclosed, the stock price decreases by roughly one per cent.[15] Over the long run, firms that allow their CEO to use their jets for personal use underperform by four per cent, which is significantly more than the cost of the corporate resources the CEO consumes. Yermack justified this decline in the stock price by the fact that perks are typically disclosed *before* bad news is disclosed to the shareholders. Yermack concluded that CEOs postpone the disclosure of bad news until they have secured the perks. Funnily enough, Yermack found a strong correlation between personal use of corporate aircraft by CEOs and membership of long-distance golf clubs.

Empire building is also called the free cash flow problem following Michael Jensen's influential 1986 paper.[16] Empire building consists of the management pursuing growth rather than shareholder value maximization. While there is a link between the two, growth does not necessarily generate shareholder value and vice-versa. If managers are to act in the interests of the shareholders, they should only invest in so-called positive net present value (NPV) projects, i.e. projects whose future expected cash flows exceed their initial investment outlay.[17] Any cash flow that remains after investing in all available positive-NPV projects is the so-called free cash flow. Projects with negative NPVs are projects whose discounted future expected cash flows are lower than the initial investment outlay and hence destroy – rather than create – shareholder value. Empire building may come in various forms, but frequently consists of the management going on a shopping spree and acquiring other firms, sometimes even firms that operate in business sectors that are completely unrelated to the business sector the management's firm operates in. Again, empire building can be seen as the refusal of the company's management to pay out the free cash flow when there are no positive-NPV projects available. While a company may have limited investment opportunities, this is typically not the case for its shareholders, who have access to a wide range of investment opportunities. Hence, it makes sense for the company's management to pay out the free cash flows to its shareholders and give the latter the opportunity to reinvest the funds in positive-NPV projects. So why would managers be tempted to engage in empire building? Managers derive benefits from increasing the size of their firm. Such benefits include an increase in their power and social status from running a larger firm. As we shall see in Chapter 8, managerial compensation has also been reported to grow in line with company size. Hence, there are clear benefits that managers derive from engaging in growth strategies, whereas the costs are borne by the shareholders.

Other agency problems include managerial entrenchment, whereby managers shield themselves from hostile takeovers and internal disciplinary actions, which may also be a consequence of the principal-agent problem. However, managerial entrenchment may also exist in the presence of family control whereby top management posts within the family are passed onto the next generation of the family rather than being filled by the

[15]Yermack, D. (2006), 'Flights of Fancy: Corporate Jets, CEO Perquisites, and Inferior Shareholder Returns', *Journal of Financial Economics* 80, 211–42.
[16]Jensen, M.C. (1986), 'Agency Costs of Free Cash Flow, Corporate Finance, and Takeovers', *American Economic Review* 76, 323–9.
[17]In some situations, it may even make sense for the management to reduce the size of the firm by closing down unprofitable projects, thereby creating shareholder value.

most suitable candidate in the managerial labour market.[18] Managerial entrenchment may also manifest itself in the form of the 'quiet life'[19] or managerial shirking, whereby managers avoid cognitively difficult activities.[20] In other words, they underinvest, as well as avoid closing down unprofitable projects and stay clear of other improvements in firm efficiency. A related agency problem is managerial risk aversion, whereby managers are reluctant to invest in risky, but shareholder value enhancing projects. This reluctance stems from the fact that managers are heavily exposed to firm-specific risk as all their human capital is invested in the firm (i.e. if the firm fails, they lose their job) and they also typically hold undiversified investment portfolios, as a large part of their personal wealth tends to be invested in the firm. In other words, contrary to their shareholders who tend to hold diversified portfolios, managers tend to hold undiversified portfolios.

Finally, ways of mitigating agency problems include not only bonding and monitoring (see Section 1.3), but also managerial incentive setting. These ways will be discussed in more detail in Chapter 8.

1.5 The agency problems of debt and equity

So far, we have focused on the agency problem that may exist between the managers and the shareholders. However, there exists a second type of agency problem. This agency problem relates to the other main source of financing, which is debt. When a firm has very little equity financing left (such as when it is in financial distress), the shareholders may be tempted to gamble with the debtholders' money by investing the firm's funds into high-risk projects. If the risky projects fail, the major part of the costs will be borne by the debtholders. However, if these projects are successful and generate a massive payoff, most of this payoff will go to the shareholders. Figure 1.1 illustrates how this works. Remember that the debtholders' claims are more senior than

Figure 1.1 **Firm value**

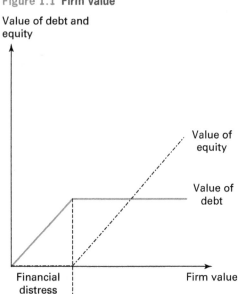

Value of debt and
equity

Value of
equity

Value of
debt

Financial
distress

Firm value

---

[18]See also nepotism in Section 1.6.
[19]John Hicks was the first to develop the so-called 'quiet life' hypothesis in the context of monopolies. See Hicks, J. (1935), 'Annual Survey of Economic Theory: The Theory of Monopoly', *Econometrica* 3, 1–20.
[20]Bertrand, M. and Mullainathan, S. (2003), 'Enjoying the Quiet Life? Corporate Governance and Managerial Preferences', *Journal of Political Economy* 111, 1043–75.

those of the shareholders. This implies that when the firm's assets are insufficient to meet all the claims it is facing, it will first have to meet the claims of the debtholders. Hence, the value of the debt increases as the value of the firm's assets increases until it hits an upper bound. This upper bound consists of the situation where the firm has at least sufficient assets to reimburse the debtholders and to pay the contractual interest payments on the debt. In other words, the value of the debtholders' claims has a limited upside. Conversely, the claims of the equity holders, i.e. the shareholders, have an unlimited upside. This difference in the upside of the two types of claims explains why it makes sense in certain situations for the shareholders to gamble with the money of the debtholders.[21]

Jensen and Meckling argued that given there are agency costs from both debt and equity, there is an optimal mix of debt and equity, i.e. a particular capital structure that minimizes total agency costs and hence maximizes firm value. Figure 1.2 shows that when all the firm's funding is in the form of debt, the agency costs of debt will be highest. The agency costs of debt then start to decrease as more and more funding comes in the form of equity financing. At the other extreme of the capital structure where all the funding is in the form of equity, the agency costs of equity will be highest. Put differently, Jensen's free cash flow problem, i.e. the agency problem of equity, will be most severe if the firm does not have any debt outstanding. Once the firm takes out debt, some of its cash flows will be committed to the servicing of the debt, thereby reducing the amount of free cash flows that managers can waste.

The total agency costs are the sum of the agency costs of debt and the agency costs of equity. As Figure 1.2 shows, the total agency costs have a curvilinear, convex, U-shaped relationship with the firm's capital structure. What is important to realize is that there is a capital structure or mix of debt and equity which minimizes the total agency costs. Again, this will also be the capital structure that maximizes firm value.

Figure 1.2 **Agency costs of debt and equity**

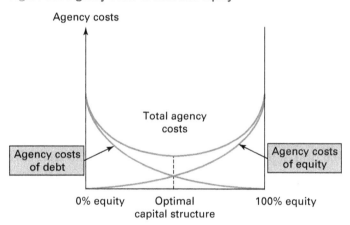

1.6 The classic agency problem versus the expropriation of minority shareholders

The principal-agent model is based on the Berle-Means premise that as firms grow, ownership eventually separates from control. Hence, corporations end up being run by professional managers with no or very little equity ownership on behalf of the owners or the shareholders. However, as we shall be seeing in Chapter 2,

---

[21]Another way of characterizing the payoff functions is that the value of equity corresponds to a long call option whereas the value of debt is equivalent to a short put option.

this is only an accurate description of the Anglo-American system of corporate governance. Indeed, in the rest of the world, most stock-exchange listed firms have large shareholders that have a substantial degree of control over the firm's affairs. Hence, in most quoted corporations across the world, control lies with one or a few shareholders and not with the management as in the UK and the USA. These controlling shareholders are frequently other corporations, families and governments, to name just a few types of large shareholders. However, as we shall see in what follows – and in great detail in Chapters 2 and 3 – there is still a separation of ownership and control in these corporations. However, the separation of ownership and control does not concern the managers and the body of the shareholders. In fact, it only concerns the shareholders. Put differently, these corporations have two types of shareholders: the controlling shareholder(s) and the minority shareholders. While the former type has enough control over the firm's affairs to dominate or at least influence its decision-making process, the latter lacks power to intervene. Thus, the main corporate governance problem in most corporations across the world is not the classic agency problem between the managers and the shareholders, but the potential expropriation of the minority shareholders by the controlling shareholder. Expropriation of the minority shareholders by the large shareholder can be in a variety of forms, the main forms being:

- Tunnelling.
- Transfer pricing.
- Nepotism.
- Infighting.

We shall illustrate the first two forms of expropriation, i.e. tunnelling and transfer pricing, by the example in Figure 1.3. The example is of a shareholder who holds shares in two firms, firm A and firm B. While the shareholder owns all of firm B's equity, he only owns 51 per cent of firm A's equity while the remainder of the equity is held by a large number of small shareholders. We assume that the large shareholder dominates the decision-making process in firm A via his majority stake and that his decisions cannot be vetoed by the minority shareholders of firm A. Hence, the large shareholder has enough power to steal the assets of firm A. If he steals one dollar of firm A's assets by transferring the assets in question to firm B, the gross gain from doing so will also be one dollar and the net gain will be $1 – $0.51, i.e. $0.49 or 49 cents. Transferring assets or profits from a firm to its large shareholder and thereby expropriating the former firm's minority shareholders is normally referred to as tunnelling.[22] The cost to the minority shareholders will be 49 cents. Hence, the large shareholder derives a net gain from stealing firm A's assets. The net gain stems from the fact that when the large shareholder steals a dollar from firm A, he effectively ends up stealing 49 cents from firm A's minority shareholders. The other main way of expropriating the minority shareholders is via transfer pricing. This consists of overcharging firm A for services or assets provided by firm B. Imagine that firm B

Figure 1.3 **Expropriation of the minority shareholders by the large shareholder**

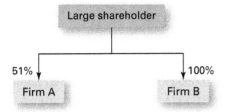

[22]Johnson, S., La Porta, R., Lopez-de-Silanes, F. and Shleifer, A. (2000). 'Tunneling', *American Economic Review* 90, 22–7.

provides secretarial services to firm A, but charges firm A above the market rate. The excess profits from providing the secretarial services to firm A will then go into the pockets of the large shareholders, at the cost of the minority shareholders. Both tunnelling and transfer pricing involving the large shareholder are also sometimes referred to as related-party transactions.[23]

The large shareholder may be able to have effective control over firm A by owning a smaller stake than a majority stake, possibly benefitting from the fact that average attendance at an AGM is about two-thirds of shareholders. In this case, the benefits he derives from stealing from firm A will be even greater. However, there is another, safer way for the large shareholder to increase his net gains from expropriating firm A's minority shareholders. This consists of leveraging control, i.e. of keeping control over firm A, but at the same time reducing his ownership stake in firm A. Such a situation is depicted in Figure 1.4. The large shareholder has leveraged control by transferring his 51 per cent stake to a holding company of which he owns 51 per cent of the equity. Similar to firm A, the remaining 49 per cent of the holding company's equity is held by a large number of small shareholders who are not powerful enough to veto the large shareholder's decisions. As the large shareholder has a majority stake in the holding firm, we again assume that he has control over the holding firm. In turn, the holding firm is the largest shareholder in firm A via its majority stake. Ultimately, the large shareholder is the controlling shareholder in firm A via the *intermediary* of the holding company as at each level of this ownership pyramid he has majority control. However, majority control in firm A is achieved with an ownership stake of only about 26.01 per cent, i.e. 51 per cent of 51 per cent. Returning to our previous example of tunnelling, if the large shareholder steals one dollar worth of assets from firm A by transferring them to firm B, he will still earn a gross gain of one dollar, but at a reduced cost of 26.01 cents. How is this possible? Well, remember that both firm A and the holding firm have minority shareholders. If the large shareholder now steals from firm A, the total cost or loss to the minority shareholders of both firms amounts to 73.99 cents, with firm A's minority shareholders bearing a cost of 49 cents (as in the example of Figure 1.3) and the minority shareholders of the holding company incurring a cost of 24.99 cents, generated by their 49 per cent stake in the holding company's 51 per cent stake in firm A. As a result of stealing from firm A, the large shareholder ends up expropriating not only the direct minority shareholders in firm A, but also the minority shareholders in the intermediate holding company. Box 1.2 lists related-party transactions linked to the collapse of Icelandic banks in the aftermath of the 2008 financial crisis.

Figure 1.4 **Leveraging control and increasing the potential for expropriation**

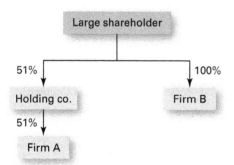

[23]See Levine, M.A., Fitzsimons, A.P. and Siegel, J.G. (1997), 'Auditing Related Party Transactions', *CPA Journal* 67, 46–50, for a detailed discussion of related-party transactions.

Box 1.2
Related-party transactions

One of the countries that has suffered substantially from the 'credit crunch' is one of Europe's smallest economies, Iceland. However, the collapse of Icelandic banks such as Glitnir, Kaupthing and Landsbanki is not just a mere consequence of a wider ranging, global problem. Indeed, the failure of the Icelandic banks seems to be inextricably linked to related-party transactions. All three of the collapsed banks were owned by private investors and each of these now stands accused of diverting shareholder funds.

For example, Glitnir, the smallest of the banks, was controlled by Jon Asgeir Johannesson. During the peak of his empire, the private equity investor – via his holding company Baugur – had control over large chunks of the UK high street, including names such as Debenhams, Woolworths, House of Fraser, Karen Millen and Hamleys, as well as the supermarket chain Iceland Foods. Baugur also had a stake in Saks Inc. Mr Johannesson, who is still on the board of House of Fraser and the chairman of Iceland Foods, now stands trial and is accused, alongside other investors of 'a sweeping conspiracy to wrest control of Iceland's Glitnir Bank to fill [his] pockets and prop up [his] own failing companies'. The case was filed in London, New York and Reykjavik by the board of Glitnir, which collapsed in October 2008 and still owes British local councils £200m. Johannesson has been served a global asset freeze order forcing him to hand over all his assets. The lawsuit also targets accountancy firm PwC in Iceland, accusing them of 'facilitating' the alleged fraud.

Kaupthing was controlled by the Gudmundsson brothers, Agust and Lydur, via a 23 per cent stake held by their holding company Exista. About €6bn, i.e. more than one-third of Kaupthing's loans, had been made to a small number of businessmen, including London-based property tycoon Robert Tchenguiz, with connections to the Gudmundsson brothers and the bank's management. Exista itself had borrowed a total of €1.86bn in loans from Kaupthing whereas Robert Tchenguiz had received loans amounting to €1.74bn to buy stakes in UK firms including the supermarket chain Sainsbury's and the Mitchells & Butlers pubs. These loans were being investigated after the bank's failure.

Similarly, Landsbanki has made loans of €300m to companies connected with members of its board of directors. Landsbanki's main shareholder was Bjorgolfur Gudmundsson who declared himself bankrupt shortly after the collapse of his bank.

Sources: Rowena Mason (2009), 'As the Country's Banks Stabilise, What Ugly Secrets Will Be Revealed, asks Rowena Mason, Puzzle of Iceland's Collapse', *The Sunday Telegraph*, 16 August, p. 6.

Rowena Mason (2009), 'Baugur Boss's Property Deal under Scrutiny', *The Daily Telegraph*, April 13, Newsbank, City, p. 1.

Rowena Mason (2010), 'Former Baugur Boss Jon Asgeir Johannesson Accused of $2bn Fraud', *The Daily Telegraph*, May 2010, Business, p. 3.

Jeanne Whalen and Charles Forelle (2008), 'Aftershocks Felt from Iceland. "Like Lehman", the Small Nation's Turmoil has Far-Reaching Economic Effects', *The Wall Street Journal*, 9 October, p. A4.

Another form of minority shareholder expropriation is nepotism. This form of expropriation consists of family shareholders appointing members of their family to top management positions within their firm, rather than the most competent candidate in the managerial labour market. Box 1.3 discusses a potential case of nepotism.

Finally, there is infighting which is not necessarily a wilful form of expropriating a firm's minority shareholders, but nevertheless is likely to deflect management time as well as other firm resources from value creation (see Box 1.4). A classic example of infighting is the case of the two German brothers Adolf and Rudolf Dassler who founded a shoe factory in 1924, but then as a result of a feud, which probably started because of political differences during the Second World War, set up two separate competing companies, Adidas and Puma, on either side of the river in the same Bavarian town in 1948.[24]

[24]See news.bbc.co.uk/1/hi/8262040.stm and about.puma.com, accessed on 17 May 2011.

Box 1.3
Nepotism

U ntil 2002, the British Sky Broadcasting Group plc (BSkyB) did not have a nomination committee. Rupert Murdoch was the main shareholder holding a 35.4 per cent stake and was also the chairman of the board of directors. In 2003, Rupert Murdoch's son, James, was to replace CEO Tony Ball. At the time, institutional investors, led by the National Association of Pension Funds (NAPF) and the Association of British Insurers (ABI), voiced their concerns about the appointment process. NAPF also criticized the company's senior non-executive director, Lord St John of Fawsley who had been in office for 12 years and was no longer considered to be independent. Rupert Murdoch eventually outvoted the disgruntled shareholders and on 4 November 2003 appointed his son James as BSkyB's CEO. However, to allay shareholder concerns, Rupert Murdoch agreed to appoint a deputy chairman, Lord Rothschild.

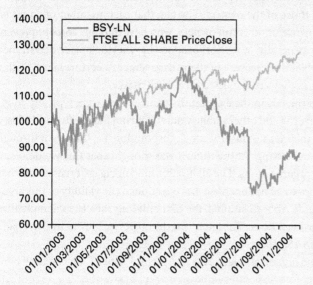

Sources: Saeed Shah (2003), 'BSkyB Chief Ball "preparing to leave Murdoch's empire"', *The Independent*, 16 September.

Neill Michael (2004), 'Nepotism Charges Cloud Murdoch BSyB Foray', *Financial Times*, 24 July, FT Money – Markets Week UK, p.22.

Share prices are from Thomson Datastream.

Box 1.4
Infighting

W hile some families at the head of large companies have done a rather good job, others have been haunted by infighting and in some cases even murder. The Gucci fashion empire was founded in 1921 by Guccio Gucci. Family infighting gradually drove all of the family members, apart from Guccio's grandson Maurizio, out of the company. Patrizia Reggiani Martinelli, the former wife of Maurizio, was arrested in 1997 and sentenced to 29 years in prison for her ex-husband's gangland killing in 1998. Martinelli's reason for killing her ex-husband was said to be her concern that the 'other woman' would inherit everything.

Sources: Various including Victoria Masterson (1999), 'When a Boardroom Battle is a Family Affair', *The Scotsman*, 29 June, no page number stated.

1.7 Alternative forms of organization and ownership

While this book focuses on stock corporations and the corporate governance issues affecting them, it is worth mentioning other types of organization and ownership. The main alternative to the stock corporation is the mutual organization. A mutual organization is owned by and run on behalf of its members. For example, the members of a mutual building society or bank are its savers as well as its borrowers. Such mutual banks exist all over the world: they include UK building societies such as Nationwide, the Dutch Rabobank and the Raiffeisen banks which exist across Europe – including Austria, Germany and Luxembourg. Other important types of mutual organizations include some insurance companies as well as mutual funds in the USA and units trusts in the UK.

Both stock corporations and mutual organizations are expected to suffer from the principal-agent problem. However, this problem may be much more severe in the latter given that the former benefit from a range of mechanisms that mitigate agency problems (see also Chapter 8). Such mechanisms include the threat of a hostile takeover, monitoring by large shareholders and ownership of stock options and stocks by the managers and employees which realign their interests with those of the owners. The fact that each member of a mutual organization has only one vote prevents the emergence of powerful owners, who have enough votes to prevent self-serving behaviour by the management. More generally, stock corporations have a stock price determined on an organized market which provides a more objective measure of their management's performance. Such a measure is not available for mutual organizations as they are not listed on a stock market.

The first building societies started emerging in the UK in the eighteenth century. They were typically cooperative savings societies whose members met in taverns and other public venues. During the 1980s and 1990s, a number of UK mutual building societies changed their legal status to a stock corporation, i.e. they went through a demutualization, and applied for a stock-exchange listing. At the time, it was thought that this would result in a major improvement in the efficiency of these organizations. The 2008 subprime mortgage crisis, which has caused a number of demutualized building societies to be nationalized, has questioned the validity of this argument. These demutualized building societies include Abbey National, the first building society to demutualize in 1989, Bradford & Bingley and, importantly, Northern Rock. The latter was the object in 2007 of the first bank run on a British financial institution for more than 150 years.

Nevertheless, it is still unclear which of these two organizational forms is superior.[25] One of the potential benefits of the mutual form is that it avoids conflicts of interests between owners and customers. These conflicts are likely to be severe for products and services involving long-term contracts, as they may tempt the shareholders to expropriate their customers. Examples of products and services involving long-term contracts are mortgages, life insurance and pension savings. For such products and services, the mutual organization is likely to be superior as it merges the functions of owners and customers, thereby avoiding any conflicts between the two.

While mutual organizations are not subject to the disciplinary function of the stock market, they nevertheless have their own disciplinary mechanism. Indeed, the members of a mutual organization can withdraw their funds at any time. Given that mutuals do not have access to the stock exchange, such withdrawals immediately reduce their financial basis. In contrast, although their stock price may fall, stock corporations do not see their funds shrink when their shareholders sell their shares. Hence, this disciplinary mechanism may substitute for large shareholder monitoring and keep managers on their toes.

Finally, some commercial organizations are in the form of partnerships which are owned by their employees. Some of these partnerships – which include the American investment bank Goldman Sachs, which for more

---

[25]Shinozawa, Y. (2010), 'Mutual versus Proprietary Ownership: An Empirical Study from the UK Unit Trust Industry with a Company-product Measure', *Annals of Public and Cooperative Economics* 81, 247–80.

than 100 years operated as a partnership, and the UK chain of department stores, John Lewis Partnership – have been very successful. More generally, Sanford Grossman, Oliver Hart and John Moore's theory of property rights addresses the issue as to when employees should have ownership of their firm.[26] Employees should be given property rights in their firm if they have to provide investments in human capital which are highly specific to the firm or *idiosyncratic*. Indeed, once the employees have made the investment in their human capital, it makes sense for the owners of the firm to expropriate them. For example, once a scientist working for a biotech firm has made a discovery about a new drug, it is tempting for the firm's owners to seize the rights to the new drug even if this results in breaking any contracts on intellectual property rights they had with the scientist. Hence, there may be a conflict of interests between the owners and the employees in firms where employees make substantial sunk investments in terms of their human capital. These conflicts of interests can be mitigated by making the employees owners of the firm.

As previously mentioned, this book will focus on stock corporations that are listed on an official stock exchange. However, this choice of focus does not imply that the author of this textbook believes that stock corporations are the only efficient form of organization. Indeed, as we shall see in more detail in Chapter 8, the fact that all these organizational forms operate in the same competitive product or service markets may render considerations relating to organizational structure of secondary importance. In other words, the disciplinary nature of competition will put pressure on managers from various organizational forms to perform well to survive in the market place.

1.8 Defining ownership and control

In Section 1.6, we discussed pyramids of ownership which enable a shareholder to have control over a firm despite holding a relatively small ownership stake. Pyramids are one of the mechanisms or devices that create a difference between the ownership and control held by a given shareholder. Chapter 3 will review other devices that create a wedge between ownership and control, or in the words of Sanford Grossman and Oliver Hart violate the rule of one-share one-vote.[27]

We have now reached the stage in this book where it is crucial to define ownership and control. Ownership is defined as cash flow rights. Cash flow rights give the holder a pro rata right to the firm's assets (after the claims of all the other stakeholders have been met) if the firm is liquidated and a pro rata right to the firm's earnings while it remains a going concern. Control is defined as control rights. Control rights typically stem from voting rights. Voting rights give the holder the right to make certain decisions about the firm and/or vote in favour or against specific agenda points at the AGM. Such agenda points may include the appointment or dismissal of members of the company's board of directors. However, there may be other channels for control. For example, the firm's articles of association may include a clause whereby the founder or his descendants have the right to appoint a specific number of board members as long as the founding family holds at least one share in the firm. Another channel consists of a so-called golden share, sometimes held by a government in a firm of national importance (e.g. an arms manufacturer) which enables the government to block the takeover of the firm by a foreign investor. Finally, the management of a firm may have de facto control in the absence of a large shareholder.

---

[26]Grossman, S.J. and Hart, O.D. (1986), 'The Costs and Benefits of Ownership: A Theory of Vertical and Lateral Integration', *Journal of Political Economy* 94, 691–719; Hart, O.D. and Moore, J. (1990), 'Property Rights and the Nature of the Firm', *Journal of Political Economy* 98, 1119–58. Hart, O.D. (1995), *Firms, Contracts, and Financial Structure*, Oxford, UK: Clarendon Press.
[27]Grossman, S.J. and Hart, O.D. (1988), 'One Share-One Vote and the Market for Corporate Control', *Journal of Financial Economics* 20, 175–202.

In the remainder of the book, we shall focus on control unless otherwise stated. There are two reasons for this focus. First, control determines the level and type of corporate governance problems that are likely to prevail in a company. Second, in most countries of the world it is a requirement for major shareholders to disclose their ownership of the firm's control rights, but no such requirement exists for cash flow rights. Hence, while it is easy to obtain data on corporate control, it can be challenging to obtain the equivalent data on ownership.

1.9 Conclusions

This first chapter has shown that the definition of corporate governance depends on the chosen objective of the corporation. Whereas in Anglo-Saxon countries the principle of shareholder primacy tends to prevail, in most other countries corporate governance refers to some or all of the firm's stakeholders and the preservation of their interests, rather than just those of the shareholders. The definition this book adopts is that corporate governance deals with conflicts of interests between the shareholders and the managers; the shareholders and the debtholders; the shareholders and the non-financial stakeholders; as well as between different types of shareholders (mainly the large shareholder and the minority shareholders); and the prevention or mitigation of these conflicts of interests.

The link between the objective of the firm and the definition of corporate governance

The chapter also discussed the main theoretical model of corporate governance which is the principal-agent model. This model or theory predicts that the main, potential conflict of interests within a corporation is between the managers and the shareholders. As a business grows there comes the stage where the founder is no longer able to provide all the financing, and external investors need to be approached to provide further financing for the firm. This stage results in a separation of ownership and control whereby there is a clear division of labour between the management that owns few or no shares in the firm and runs the firm on a day-to-day basis, and the owners or shareholders who provide the financing but are not directly involved with the running of the firm. While the management or the agent is expected to run the firm in the interests of the shareholders or the principals, the former may prefer to pursue their own objectives. This is the so-called principal-agent problem.

The principal-agent model

However, as most corporations outside the Anglo-Saxon world have large shareholders, they are unlikely to suffer from the principal-agent problem. The main corporate governance issue that is likely to afflict these corporations is the expropriation of the minority shareholders by the large controlling shareholder. The latter may be in various forms, including tunnelling and transfer pricing (so-called related-party transactions), nepotism and infighting.

The expropriation of minority shareholders

Returning to the definition of corporate governance adopted in this book, this definition is a more generalized version of the Jensen and Meckling principal-agent framework, as the former covers conflicts of interests not just between the management and the shareholders as well as between the latter and the debtholders, but also allows for conflicts of interests between the shareholders and non-financial stakeholders (such as customers) as well as conflicts of interests that may exist between large and small shareholders.

Conflicts of interests: the definition of corporate governance adopted in this book

Finally, we defined ownership and control. In the next chapter, we shall return to the case where there is a deviation between the control rights and the cash flow rights held by the shareholders. We shall also review patterns of corporate ownership and control across the world and provide a more nuanced discussion of the corporate governance problems that may prevail under different combinations of ownership and control.

Ownership versus control

1.10 Discussion questions

1 Discuss Andrei Shleifer and Robert Vishny's definition of corporate governance. What is their rationale for attributing a special status to the providers of finance compared to other corporate stakeholders?

2 Compare the principal-agent problem of equity with that of debt.

3 What are the differences between ownership and control? Why do differences between the two matter?

4 What are the potential weaknesses of mutual organizations compared to stock corporations in corporate governance?

1.11 Exercises

1 Calculate the percentage of ownership that Edwina Scissor holds in Sheffield Scissor Sisters Plc (see Figure 1.5). Assuming that Edwina Scissor has effective control of each of the firms in the ownership pyramid, including Sheffield Scissor Sisters Plc, what would be the percentage of shares that Edwina Scissor holds in Scissor Sisters Assets Ltd that would just about *not* make it worthwhile for her to steal from Sheffield Scissor Sisters Plc?

Figure 1.5 **Edwina Scissor**

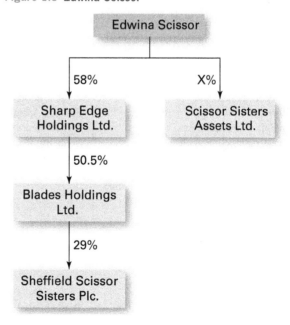

2   Based on Figure 1.6, calculate the losses to the minority shareholders of Mueller Holding Company Ltd. and those of Mueller Cake Factory Inc. if Arthur Mueller III senior were to transfer free oven equipment from the latter for a value of US$5m to Monaco-Mueller Investment Fund S.A. Assume that Arthur Mueller III senior has effective control of Mueller Cake Factory Inc. via the 25 per cent held by Mueller Holding Company Ltd.

Figure 1.6 **Holdings of Arthur Mueller III, senior**

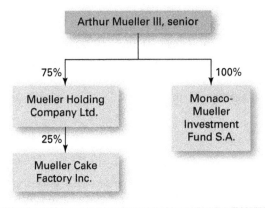

Reading list

Key reading

Grossman, S.J. and Hart, O.D. (1986), 'The Costs and Benefits of Ownership: A Theory of Vertical and Lateral Integration', *Journal of Political Economy* 94, 691–719.

Grossman, S.J. and Hart, O.D. (1988), 'One Share-One Vote and the Market for Corporate Control', *Journal of Financial Economics* 20, 175–202.

Hart, O.D. (1995), *Firms, Contracts, and Financial Structure*, Oxford, UK: Clarendon Press.

Hart, O.D. and Moore, J. (1988), 'Incomplete Contracts and Renegotiation', *Econometrica* 56, 755–85.

Jensen, M.C. (1986), 'Agency Costs of Free Cash Flow, Corporate Finance, and Takeovers', *American Economic Review* 76, 323–9.

Jensen, M. and Meckling, W. (1976), 'Theory of the Firm: Managerial Behavior, Agency Costs and Capital Structure', *Journal of Financial Economics* 3, 305–60.

Johnson, S. La Porta, R., Lopez-de-Silanes, F. and Shleifer, A. (2000). 'Tunneling', *American Economic Review* 90, 22–7.

Shleifer, A. and Vishny, R.W. (1997), 'A Survey of Corporate Governance', *Journal of Finance* 52, 737–83.

Williamson, O. (1984), 'Corporate Governance', *Yale Law Journal* 93, 1197–230.

Further reading

Alchian, A.A. and Demsetz, H. (1972), 'Production, Information Costs, and Economic Organization', *American Economic Review* 62, 777–95.

Berle A., and Means, G. (1932), *The Modern Corporation and Private Property*, New York: Macmillan.

Bertrand, M. and Mullainathan, S. (2003), 'Enjoying the Quiet Life? Corporate Governance and Managerial Preferences', *Journal of Political Economy* 111, 1043–75.

Bottenberg, K., Tuschke, A. and Flickinger, M. (2017), 'Corporate Governance between Shareholder and

Stakeholder Orientation', *Journal of Management Inquiry* 26, 165–80.

Goergen, M. and Renneboog, L. (2006), 'Corporate Governance and Shareholder Value', in D. Lowe and R. Leiringer (eds), *Commercial Management of Projects: Defining the Discipline*, Oxford, UK: Blackwell Publishing, 100–31.

Goergen, M., Mallin, C., Mitleton-Kelly, E., Al-Hawamdeh, A. and Chiu, I.H.Y. (2010), *Corporate Governance and Complexity Theory*, Cheltenham, UK: Edward Elgar.

Hansmann, H. (1996), *The Ownership of Enterprise*, Cambridge, MA: The Belknap Press of Harvard University Press.

Ireland, P. (1999), 'Company Law and the Myth of Shareholder Ownership', *Modern Law Review* 62, 32–57.

Levine, M.A., Fitzsimons, A.P. and Siegel, J.G. (1997), 'Auditing Related Party Transactions', *CPA Journal* 67, 46–50.

Worthington, S. (2001a), 'Shares and Shareholders: Property, Power and Entitlement: Part I', *Company Lawyer* 22, 258–66.

Worthington, S. (2001b), 'Shares and Shareholders: Property, Power and Entitlement: Part II', *Company Lawyer* 22, 307–14.

Appendix
The principal-agent model

This appendix is a supplement to Sections 1.3–1.5. It contains a detailed discussion of the theoretical framework underlying the Jensen and Meckling principal-agent theory.[28] Readers with a background in economics and who are interested in the development of the model itself are referred to the actual paper.

Jensen and Meckling effectively combine three theories – the theory of the firm, the theory on property rights and agency theory – to develop what they call the *theory of ownership structure for the firm* and what is commonly known as the principal-agent theory or model. The input of each of these theories to the principal-agent theory is as follows. First, the theory of the firm considers the firm to maximize its profit under input and output constraints. Jensen and Meckling retain this profit-maximizing objective for their theory. Second, the theory on property rights defines the firm as a nexus of contracts. The contracts specify how the costs and rewards generated by the firm are distributed across the individuals forming the organization. The characteristics of these contracts likely determine the behaviour of individuals within the organization. Finally, agency theory defines an agency relationship as a contract between a principal and an agent whereby the agent engages himself to perform a certain duty for the principal. If both the principal and agent are utility maximizers, then there is the risk that the agent may not act in the best interests of the principal. The principal may reduce this risk by offering appropriate incentives to the agent and by monitoring the latter. In addition, the agent may incur so-called bonding costs to assure the principal that he will act in her interests (see also Section 1.3).

More generally, Jensen and Meckling argue that agency problems can arise in any situation where individuals rely on the cooperation of others or where there is joint production and even though there may not be an obvious principal-agent relationship. An example of such a situation concerns a coursework assignment whereby students are required to form groups and to write a report on a case study. Some of the students may end up free-riding on the efforts of the other members of the group.[29] Returning to the context of the firm, Jensen and Meckling argue that the separation of ownership and control within the typical firm is strongly associated with the agency problem.

The British economist Ronald Coase is one of the pioneers of the theory of the firm and the theory on property rights. In a nutshell, he argues that the boundaries of the firm are dictated by the minimization of transaction fees within an economy. Typically, markets are better at allocating resources and effectuating exchanges. However, there

---

[28]Jensen, M. and Meckling, W. (1976), 'Theory of the Firm: Managerial Behavior, Agency Costs and Capital Structure', *Journal of Financial Economics* 3, 305–60.
[29]The author's own example.

may be situations that require authority and direction which firms provide. Put differently, these are the situations where firms generate lower transaction costs than markets. Jensen and Meckling critique Coase basing themselves on the 1972 paper by Armen Alchian and Harold Demsetz.[30] Alchian and Demsetz argue that the activities of the firm that involve joint production (e.g. production by teams of workers) are not governed by authority, but by contractual relationships and that these relationships require monitoring rather than authority. In turn, Jensen and Meckling critique Alchian-Demsetz. They argue that firms cannot be described merely in terms of the contracts they have with their workers. Indeed, firms also have contracts with, e.g. customers, suppliers and creditors. All of these contracts are subject to principal-agent problems and contracts relating to joint production can therefore only explain part of the workings of a firm.

Hence, Jensen and Meckling define the firm as 'simply one form of legal fiction *which serves as a nexus for contracting relationships and which is also characterized by the existence of divisible residual claims on the assets and cash flows of the organization which can generally be sold without permission of the other contracting individuals*'.[31] It is important to highlight that Jensen and Meckling avoid defining the firm as a legal *person* as defined by corporate law. They argue this implies that the question about what should be the firm's objective and the question whether the firm has social responsibility are irrelevant. In other words, as the firm is not an individual it should be treated similarly to a market, which just creates an equilibrium between demand and supply and nothing more.

[30]Alchian, A.A. and Demsetz, H. (1972), 'Production, Information Costs, and Economic Organization', *American Economic Review* 62, 777–95.
[31]See Jensen, M. and Meckling, W. (1976), 'Theory of the Firm: Managerial Behavior, Agency Costs and Capital Structure', *Journal of Financial Economics* 3, p.311. The italic is in the source.

2 Corporate control across the world

Chapter Aims

This chapter reviews the differences in corporate control patterns across the world. The chapter shows that corporate control and ownership in the UK and USA differ markedly from corporate control and ownership in the rest of the world. Whereas in the UK and the USA most stock-exchange listed companies are widely held, in the rest of the world control tends to be concentrated in the hands of one shareholder or a small number of shareholders. In addition to the differences in the concentration of control, there are also differences in terms of the types of shareholders that prevail across regions and countries.

Learning Outcomes

After reading this chapter, you should be able to:

1 Describe the differences in the levels of corporate control across the world

2 Be aware of differences in the importance of various types of shareholders across regions and countries

3 Explain why the Berle-Means hypothesis does not hold outside the UK and the USA

2.1 Introduction

In the previous chapter, we identified an important limitation of the principal-agent model. This limitation refers to the model's premise that once a firm has grown beyond a certain size and has raised outside finance, a separation of ownership and control emerges. As a result of this premise, the model focuses on the conflicts of interests that may exist between the management and the shareholders. However, Chapter 1 has already suggested that most corporations outside the UK and the USA have large shareholders that exercise a sizeable degree of control over their firm's management. Hence, conflicts of interests are more likely to emerge between the large shareholder(s) and the minority shareholders than between the shareholders and the managers.

This chapter will provide a guided tour of corporate control across the world. We start with Europe and the USA, and then move on to other regions and countries. However, before beginning this tour it is important to bear in mind that this book focuses on stock-exchange listed firms. Hence, the differences in control we shall observe are not due to comparing larger, stock-market quoted firms in the UK and the USA with unlisted firms in the rest of the world. In Chapter 4, we shall see that some countries have underdeveloped stock markets. Still, the focus here is exclusively on stock-exchange listed firms, independent of the size of a country's stock market.

In what follows, we shall also focus on control. The reasons for our focus on control were given in Section 1.8 of the previous chapter. Briefly, as a reminder, corporate governance concerns the distribution of power within the corporation and this power is a function of an economic actor's influence on the firm's decisions. Typically, this power stems from the votes held by a shareholder. In addition, in most countries it is compulsory for significant shareholders to disclose their ownership of voting rights, but there is no such requirement for the ownership of cash flow rights. Hence, data on control are widely available whereas those on ownership may be fairly limited.

Before looking at patterns of corporate control across the world, we shall first revisit Berle and Means's premise that as companies grow, they experience a separation of ownership and control. To test the validity of this premise, we shall analyze the evolution of control in firms after their initial public offering. The firms we shall look at are from the UK as well as a country which has a very different corporate governance system, i.e. Germany.

Finally, a trade-off had to be made between reporting recent figures on corporate control for a particular region on the one side and ensuring that the figures are detailed enough and are based on *ultimate control* rather than first-tier control to provide an accurate picture of corporate control and to enable a comparison with other studies on the other. Hence, in some cases the decision was made to report less recent, but more comparable figures.

2.2 The evolution of control after the initial public offering

Berle and Means stated in their 1932 book[1] that as companies grow, they experience a separation of ownership and control and that, in turn, this separation creates conflicts of interests between the managers and the owners, i.e. the shareholders. As a first step towards testing the validity of this hypothesis, it makes sense to focus on an important event in a firm's life, i.e. the firm's initial public offering (IPO). The IPO consists of the firm obtaining a listing on a recognized stock exchange and offering its shares to the general public for the very first time. The shares offered in an IPO may be of two types. First, they may consist of primary shares. These are new shares issued by the company itself. The proceeds from the sale of the primary shares go to the company, increasing its equity capital. There are various reasons why companies want to raise more capital, an important one being that internal funds, i.e. retained profits, and/or funds from the existing shareholders, are not sufficient to finance all of the available investment opportunities. Second, they may consist of secondary shares. These are the existing shares of the company, which are held by its incumbent shareholders. Indeed, an important reason why companies decide to undertake an IPO is to give their incumbent shareholders, typically the founders, the opportunity to sell some or all of their holdings. There may come a point in the lifetime of the company founder when she wants to exit from her company and diversify her investment portfolio. Of course, the proceeds from the sale of the secondary shares will accrue to the selling shareholder(s) and not to the company itself. Hence, selling secondary shares does not increase the company's equity base.

Most companies tend to offer a mix of both primary and secondary shares in their IPO. However, more importantly, both the sale of primary shares and the sale of secondary shares dilute the holdings of the existing shareholders. Imagine a company with 100 shares outstanding before the IPO and all the shares are held by the founder. Hence, before the IPO the founder owns all of the 100 shares, i.e. 100 per cent of the equity. The company now decides that it makes sense to have its IPO. The IPO will consist of the issue and the sale of 20 new shares, i.e. primary shares, as well as the sale of 10 secondary shares held by the founder. As a result of the IPO, the founder's holding has now dropped to 90 shares and the company has now 120 shares outstanding. The founder's stake has dropped from 100 per cent to 75 per cent (90/120).

---

[1] Berle, A. and Means, G. (1932), *The Modern Corporation and Private Property*, New York: Macmillan.

Why go through the workings of an IPO, you may wonder? During my PhD research, I conducted a simple experiment. I compared firms from two very different corporate governance systems, i.e. Germany and the UK, and tracked their control structure over the six years following their IPO. To ensure that I compared like with like, I started off with the list of German firms that had their IPO during the 1980s. I then focused on those firms that were controlled by a family or an individual before the IPO. My definition of a controlling shareholder was the largest shareholder in the firm holding at least 25 per cent of the voting rights. I then matched each German IPO firm with a UK IPO firm of a similar size (as measured by the market capitalization) which was also controlled by a family or individual. I then tracked each firm's control over the six years following the IPO by distinguishing between the old or initial shareholders, new shareholders (i.e. shareholders holding at least 25 per cent of the votes who emerged after the IPO) and the remainder of the shares which I considered to be the free float, i.e. widely held shares.

Table 2.1 shows the results from this experiment. Three important patterns emerge about the evolution of control after the IPO in the German and UK firms. First, if one defines control as majority control then the initial shareholders of the German IPOs lose control five years after the IPO. However, even in year 6 the initial shareholders still hold on average 45 per cent of the votes. In comparison, the initial shareholders of UK firms have already lost majority control two years after the IPO. Second, while new large shareholders take a bit longer to emerge in the German IPOs, six years after the IPO there is no significant difference between the two countries. Indeed, new large shareholders hold roughly one-third of the shares in both the German and UK IPOs. Third, there is a substantial difference in the free float between the German and UK IPOs. While the German IPOs have a free float of about 25 per cent, the UK IPOs have a much higher free float of roughly 40 per cent.

Table 2.1 **Percentage of free float and percentage of equity held by the initial shareholders and new large shareholders in German and UK IPOs**

Time after IPO (years)	German firms			UK firms		
	Initial shareholders (%)	Free float (%)	New large shareholders (%)	Initial shareholders (%)	Free float (%)	New large shareholders (%)
Immediately	76.4	22.2	1.5	62.8	37.2	0.1
1	73.7	24.0	2.4	51.4	43.1	5.5
2	69.6	25.0	5.4	47.3	39.5	13.3
3	64.9	25.3	9.8	37.7	36.0	26.4
4	59.4	25.0	15.5	33.6	37.6	28.8
5	50.7	26.3	23.1	31.4	36.5	32.1
6	45.0	24.8	30.2	30.0	40.8	29.2

Notes: Table 2.1 compares family controlled German IPOs from the 1980s to family controlled UK IPOs. Each German IPO is matched with a UK IPO by size (market capitalization). Control is tracked over the six years following the IPO. The percentages are the average percentages of voting rights held by the initial shareholders and the new large shareholders. The free float is the average residual percentage of the voting rights, i.e. the voting rights not held by the initial and new large shareholders.

Sources: Goergen, M. (1998), 'Corporate Governance and Financial Performance: A Study of German and UK Initial Public Offerings', Cheltenham: Edward Elgar Publishing. Goergen, M. and Renneboog, L. (2003), 'Why are the Levels of Control (So) Different in German and UK Companies? Evidence from Initial Public Offerings', *Journal of Law, Economics, and Organization* 19 (1), 141–75.

To summarize, there is evidence of a fairly rapid separation of ownership and control in UK firms after the IPO, whereas there is no such evidence for the German firms where a sizeable degree of control remains with the initial shareholders a long time after the IPO. Finally, the average age of the German firms at the time of the IPO was about 50 years compared to about 13 years for the UK firms.

We now move on to analyzing corporate control across a wider range of countries and for a more representative cross-section of firms listed on the stock market, i.e. not just firms that have recently had their IPO. We shall first look at corporate control in Continental Western Europe and contrast it with corporate control in the UK and the USA. In a second stage, we then move on to Asia and Eastern Europe.

2.3 Corporate control in Western Europe and the USA[2]

The first detailed study on corporate control across Western Europe was undertaken by the European Corporate Governance Network (ECGN), the predecessor of the European Corporate Governance Institute (ECGI).[3] The study was commissioned by the Directorate General for Industry of the European Commission. The study benefitted from the increased availability of data on corporate control caused by the Large Holdings Directive (88/627/EEC) that had harmonized disclosure rules across the EU member states. The results from this study were published in a book edited by Fabrizio Barca and Marco Becht.[4]

The ECGI study focuses on ultimate control. As previously defined, control typically stems from holding voting rights. As we shall see in this chapter, not all equity shares confer control or voting rights. The study not only focuses on control but also on ultimate control rather than direct control. Indeed, it is important to consider the shareholder that has ultimate control over a corporation, as control is not necessarily exercised directly, i.e. control is not necessarily located at the first tier. Figure 2.1 shows how ultimate control is defined

Figure 2.1 **Direct or first-tier control**

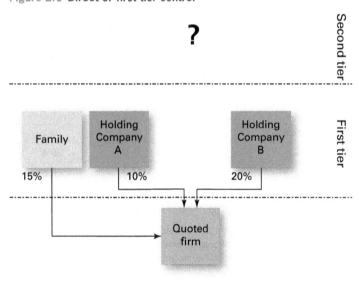

[2]Readers should refer to Basu, N., Paeglis, I. and Rahnamaei, M. (2016), 'Multiple Blockholders, Power, and Firm Value', *Journal of Banking and Finance* 66, 66–78, for more recent, detailed data on the distribution of blockholders and control in US firms.
[3]Another frequently cited study of corporate control in Europe is Faccio, M. and Lang, L.H.P. (2002), 'The Ultimate Ownership of Western European Corporations', *Journal of Financial Economics* 65, 365–95. However, a major limitation of this study is that it assumes that all unlisted firms are controlled families. The ECGI study found that this is not necessarily the case as other types of shareholders, such as industrial companies, also frequently hold their stakes via unlisted companies. Hence, the figures reported in Faccio and Lang for family control are likely to suffer from a significant upward bias.
[4]Barca, F. and Becht, M. (2001), *The Control of Corporate Europe*, Oxford, UK: Oxford University Press.

in the ECGI study. The study focuses on the quoted firm at the bottom of Figure 2.1. The quoted firm has three large shareholders, Holding Company A which holds 10 per cent of the votes, Holding Company B which holds 20 per cent and a family which holds 15 per cent of the votes. The two holding companies may be quoted on the stock exchange, but this is not essential. These three shareholders are the direct shareholders of the quoted firm or the shareholders with **first-tier control**. If the focus is on direct control, then the conclusion is that the quoted firm has three shareholders. Further, if one defines control as a **blocking minority**, i.e. 25 per cent of the votes, then the quoted firm in Figure 2.1 is widely held as none of its three shareholders holds such a blocking minority. What is a blocking minority? In most countries, while most motions at the AGM only require the approval of a simple **majority** of shareholder votes, motions that are likely to change the nature of the firm require a **supermajority** of 75 per cent.[5] Such motions include takeovers and mergers as well as the liquidation of the firm. Hence, while a blocking minority, i.e. a stake of at least 25 per cent, does not guarantee control it nevertheless confers a veto right upon its holder. In other words, a shareholder holding 25 per cent or more may not be able to push through a takeover offer if the other shareholders are against it, but has enough power to block the offer if he is opposed to it. As a result of the power obtained from both blocking minorities and majority stakes, the ECGI used both as alternative thresholds to identify large shareholders.

Returning to the example in Figure 2.1, as the ECGI study focused on ultimate control it would have investigated whether Holding Company A and Holding Company B had any controlling shareholders. In other words, it would have gone beyond the first tier of the control structure. Figure 2.2 shows the quoted firm's entire control structure. Both holding companies are controlled by the same family that has a direct stake of 15 per cent in the quoted firm. The family has full control over Holding Company A and majority control over Holding Company B. Whether control is defined as majority control or a blocking minority, both holding firms have a controlling shareholder, i.e. the family. Given that each of the holding companies has a stake in the quoted firm, the ECGI study then added up the two stakes, amounting to a total of 30 per cent of the votes in the quoted

Figure 2.2 Ultimate control

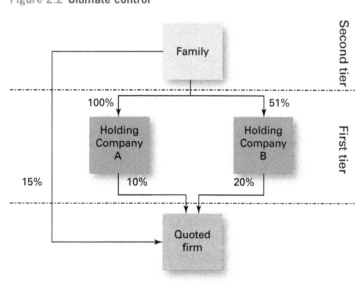

firm and attributed them to the family. Hence, the family's stake amounts to a total of 45 per cent. If control is defined as a blocking minority, then the quoted firm has a controlling shareholder, the family, as its 45 per cent stake exceeds the control threshold of 25 per cent. As a result, control over the quoted firm lies ultimately with the family, at the second tier of the control structure. However, if control is defined as majority control, then the quoted firm is widely held given that the aggregate first-tier stake of the family only adds up to 30 per cent. Although we shall return to this issue in more detail in Chapter 3, it is important to note that the family's ownership of the quoted firm is less than 45 per cent as it amounts to only 35.2 per cent (= 15% + 10% * 100% + 20% * 51%).

Returning to the ECGI study, this study covered the following nine EU member states: Austria, Belgium, France, Germany, Italy, the Netherlands, Spain, Sweden and the UK. The benchmark country in the study was the USA. For the USA, statistics were reported separately for the two main stock markets, which are the New York Stock Exchange (NYSE) and the Nasdaq (National Association of Securities Dealers Automated Quotations). While the former attracts mostly mature firms, the latter targets younger, high-growth and high-tech firms.

Figure 2.3 reports the percentage of companies that are ultimately controlled by a majority shareholder. It shows that apart from the UK and the two US stock markets, in all other countries a sizeable percentage of listed firms have a majority shareholder. At one extreme, roughly two-thirds of Austrian, Belgian and German firms have a single shareholder holding a majority of the voting rights. At the other extreme, only about 2 per cent of UK and US firms have a majority shareholder.

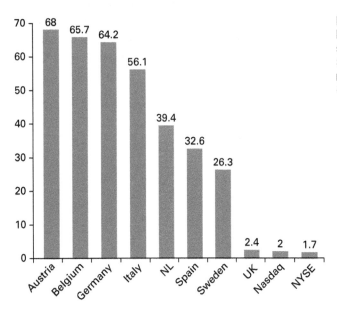

Figure 2.3
Percentage of listed firms with a majority shareholder in Europe and the USA
Source: Based on statistical data from table AIII.2, pp.319–320, in: Barca, F. and Becht, M. (2001), *The Control of Corporate Europe*, Oxford, UK: Oxford University Press.

Figure 2.4 uses the less stringent threshold for control, i.e. 25 per cent or a blocking minority. As expected, the country percentages of firms with a controlling shareholder have now substantially increased. Virtually all of the Belgian firms have a controlling shareholder and so do more than 80 per cent of the Austrian and German firms. However, the UK and the USA are still very different from all of the other countries. In both countries, stock-exchange listed firms with a controlling shareholder are still the exception rather than the norm.

While the above two figures have focused on the largest shareholder in each firm, i.e. the largest shareholder with a stake of at least 25 per cent and 50 per cent of the votes, respectively, it may also be worthwhile studying the distribution of all large shareholders across the stock-exchange listed firms. This exercise should tell us more about the distribution of power within each firm. Table 2.2 shows the results from this exercise. The average largest shareholder in the Continental Western European countries covered by Table 2.2 typically does not face any significant opposition from the other large shareholders and, importantly, the second largest shareholder. At the extreme, the largest shareholder in the average Austrian firm holds roughly 82 per cent of the votes compared to slightly under 10 per cent of the votes for the second largest. Hence, the second largest shareholder does not even have a blocking minority. While the situation is less extreme in the rest of Continental Europe, the same pattern still applies. For example, in France the largest shareholder holds 56 per cent of the voting rights, but the remaining ten or so large shareholders together hold substantially less than a blocking minority. Similar to what we have concluded before, the UK and the USA are very different. For example, in the UK the largest shareholder owns on average 14 per cent whereas the stake held by the second largest shareholder is only marginally smaller with about 8 per cent. However more importantly, the three largest shareholders would need to act together to have a sizeable degree of control, i.e. exercise slightly less than 30 per cent of the votes. A similar conclusion applies to the USA.

Figure 2.4 Percentage of listed firms with a shareholder holding a blocking minority in Europe and the USA
Source: Based on statistical data from table AIII.2, pp.319–320, in: Barca, F. and Becht, M. (2001), *The Control of Corporate Europe*, Oxford, UK: Oxford University Press.

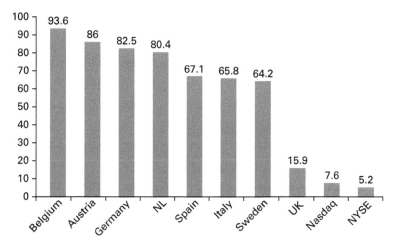

Hence, control lies with a single shareholder for most Continental Western European firms and this shareholder typically has uncontested control over the firm. Conversely, in the UK and the USA several large shareholders need to join forces to have any significant degree of influence over their firm's management.

Up to now, the focus has been on control, i.e. the concentration of votes. However, it is also important to investigate the nature of control, i.e. the type of shareholder who is in control. Table 2.3 provides the average total holdings of stakes of 5 per cent or more for the following types of shareholders: individuals and families, banks, insurance companies, investment funds, holding companies and industrial companies, governments and company directors. In broad terms, the most important type of large shareholder across Continental Western Europe is holding and industrial companies. However, another important type of shareholder in Continental Western European firms is families and individuals. Somewhat surprisingly, apart from France, the average percentage of votes held by banks is relatively low. However, it is likely that the figures of bank control in Table 2.3 are understated. The main reason is that banks in some countries, such as Germany, also hold **proxy votes**. Proxy votes are the votes from the shares held by the banks' customers that the banks exercise on behalf of their customers.

Table 2.2 Distribution of largest shareholders in Europe and the USA

Country	Sample	Shareholdings			
		Largest	2nd Largest	3rd	4–10th
Austria[a]	600	82.2	9.5	1.9	6.5
France[a]	403	56.0	16.0	6.0	5.0
Italy[a]	214	52.3	7.7	3.5	5.1
Netherlands[b]	137	28.2	9.2	4.3	7.1
Spain[a]	394	38.3	11.5	7.7	10.3
UK[b]	248	14.0	8.3	6.1	9.2
US-NYSE[b]	1 309	8.5	3.7	1.8	0.9
US-NASDAQ[b]	2 831	13.0	5.7	3.0	1.6
		Largest	2nd + 3rd	4th + 5th	6–10th
Belgium[a]	135	55.8	6.9	0.6	0.2
Germany[a]	402	59.7	8.6	2.6	0.3

Notes: This table gives the average size of the largest control stakes (stakes of voting equity) for European countries and the USA. For all countries, the data are for 1996 apart from Belgium (1994) and UK (1993). The Austrian sample consists of both listed and non-listed companies; the sample companies in all other countries are listed.

[a]Both direct and indirect shareholdings are considered.

[b]Only direct shareholdings.

Source: *Dividend Policy and Corporate Governance* (2004) by Luis Correia Da Silva and Marc Goergen, Oxford, UK: Oxford University Press.

Table 2.3 Distribution of control across types of large shareholders in Europe

Country	Sample	Individuals and families	Banks	Insurance companies	Investment funds	Holding and industrial companies	State	Directors
Austria[a]	600	38.6	5.6	0.0	0.0	33.9	11.7	0.0
Belgium[a]	155	15.6	0.4	1.0	3.8	37.5	0.3	0.0
France[a]	402	15.5	16.0	3.5	0.0	34.5	1.0	0.0
Germany[a]	402	7.4	1.2	0.2	0.0	21.0	0.7	0.0
Italy[b]	214	68.6	7.2	0.0	0.0	24.2	0.0[c]	0.0
The Netherlands[d]	137	10.8	7.2	2.4	16.1	10.9	1.3	0.0
Spain[a]	394	21.8	6.6	8.8	0.0	32.6	0.0	0.0
UK[d]	248	2.4	1.1	4.7	11.0	5.9	0.0	11.3

Notes: This table gives the total large shareholdings of voting rights (over 5%) held by different investor classes. For all countries the data cover the year 1996, except for Belgium (1994) and the UK (1993).

[a]Both direct and indirect shareholdings are considered.

[b]Numbers for Italy refer to both listed and non-listed companies.

[c]Of the listed Italian companies about 25% are directly and indirectly controlled by state holdings: this is classified in the table under 'Holdings and industrial companies'.

[d]Only direct shareholdings.

Source: *Dividend Policy and Corporate Governance* (2004) by Luis Correia Da Silva and Marc Goergen, Oxford, UK: Oxford University Press.

For example, in Germany small investors deposit their share certificates with their bank for safe-keeping. As a service to its customers, the bank checks the date of the AGM for each firm and then informs those of its customers that hold shares in a given firm about the impending AGM. Not only does the bank inform its customers about the annual shareholders meeting, but it also asks its customers whether they are happy for the bank to exercise their voting rights on their behalf. The letter the bank sends out states how it will vote for its customers' shares and, unless the customers reply to the bank stating that they do not want to transfer their voting rights to the bank, the bank will then exercise these votes at the AGM. This means that the percentage of votes that banks exercise at the AGM exceeds the percentage of votes they obtain from their direct holdings in listed firms. The fact that proxy votes are difficult to measure and are therefore not included in Table 2.3 may then explain why bank control is relatively low. Still, recent reforms – such as those in Germany[6] – have reduced the importance of banks as holders of equity in industrial and commercial firms (see Section 14.2 of Chapter 14).

From what we know so far, we expect the UK to be different from the rest of Europe. Table 2.3 shows that this is indeed the case. Contrary to the rest of Europe, the most important type of shareholder in the UK is institutional shareholders, i.e. banks, insurance companies and investment funds. Together, institutional shareholders hold on average 17 per cent (1.1% + 4.7% + 11.0%) of the shares. The second most important type of shareholder in British firms is the board of directors that in aggregate owns on average 11 per cent of the votes. In the rest of Europe, directors – unless they are members of the controlling family – do not normally hold shares in their firm. However, a closer look at Table 2.3 reveals that the Netherlands is more similar to the UK than the rest of Europe, given that control by institutional shareholders is also very important in this country.[7]

From what we have seen, we can summarize corporate control across Continental Western Europe as follows:

- In most firms, a majority of votes is held by one shareholder or a group of shareholders.
- Most firms have a shareholder with a blocking minority.
- The potential conflicts of interests are therefore those between the minority shareholders and the large shareholder.

Conversely, in the UK and the USA:

- Most firms are widely held.
- A coalition of the three largest shareholders votes for less than 30 per cent.
- The potential conflicts of interests are between the shareholders and the management, i.e. UK and US firms are likely to suffer from the classical principal-agent problem.

In terms of the nature of control:

- Industrial and holding firms are the most important type of shareholder in most of Continental Western Europe.
- Institutional shareholders are the main type of shareholder in the UK as well as the Netherlands.
- Family control is important in Continental Western Europe.
- Control by the management is important in the UK.
- Bank stakes are small as they range from 0.4 per cent in Belgium to 7.2 per cent in Italy and the Netherlands, except for France where banks control on average 16 per cent of the votes. However, these figures may underestimate control by banks as they exclude proxy votes exercised by the banks.

---

[6]In particular, the tax reform of 2002 enabled banks to sell their stakes in corporations without incurring capital gains tax.
[7]Section 4.2 of Chapter 4 reports recent trends in UK institutional ownership.

2.4 Corporate control in Asia

Richard Carney and Travers Child[8] have recently updated an earlier study by Stijn Claessens, Simeon Djankov and Harry Lang. The latter carried out a study similar to the ECGI for the East Asian countries of Hong Kong, Indonesia, Japan, Korea, the Philippines, Singapore, Taiwan and Thailand.[9] The thresholds used by both studies on Asia to measure control are somewhat different from those used in the ECGI study. They are 20 per cent and 10 per cent of the votes, respectively.

Figure 2.5 shows the percentage of listed firms in each country that have a shareholder with a stake of at least 20 per cent. Except for Japan and Taiwan, the majority of firms from all the other countries have a large shareholder. Apart from Japan and Taiwan, the percentage of firms with a 20 per cent shareholder is also relatively low in Korea and Thailand.

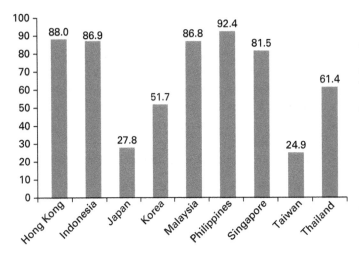

Figure 2.5

Percentage of listed East Asian firms with a 20% shareholder

Notes: Figure 2.5 is based on 1,386 publicly traded corporations in 2008, including both financial and non-financial institutions. Control rests with the institutional investors and the industrial corporations as these are widely held.

Source: Adapted from Carney, R.W. and Child, T.B. (2013), 'Changes to the Ownership and Control of East Asian Corporations between 1996 and 2008: The Primacy of Politics', *Journal of Financial Economics* 107, table 4.

Figure 2.6 is based on the lower control threshold of 10 per cent of the votes. As one would expect, virtually all of the companies now have a large shareholder. Even in Japan and Taiwan, more than 40 per cent of the firms have a shareholder controlling at least 10 per cent of the votes. Similar to Figure 2.5, Korea and Thailand also have a relatively low percentage of firms with a large shareholder. Carney and Child also looked at the distribution of control across shareholders. They found that the largest shareholder is typically the only large shareholder with a 10 per cent stake or more in the firms that are not widely held.

Table 2.4 is about the importance of the various types of large shareholders.[10] These are families, states, institutional investors, industrial companies and foreign states. Apart from Japan, Taiwan and Thailand, the majority of corporations from all other countries are controlled by families if control is defined as a voting stake of 10 per cent or more. Japan also sticks out in terms of control held by institutional shareholders and industrial corporations: roughly 7 per cent and 19 per cent of Japanese firms have an institutional shareholder and

[8]Carney, R.W. and Child, T.B. (2013), 'Changes to the Ownership and Control of East Asian Corporations Between 1996 and 2008: The Primacy of Politics', *Journal of Financial Economics* 107, 494–513.

[9]Claessens, S., Djankov, S. and Lang, L.H.P. (2000), 'The Separation of Ownership and Control in East Asian Corporations', *Journal of Financial Economics* 58, 81–112.

[10]Table 2.4 is somewhat different from Table 2.3 from the ECGI study. While the ECGI study reports the total percentage of voting stakes of 5 per cent or more held by each type of shareholder, Table 2.4 reports the percentage of firms whose largest shareholder is of a particular type.

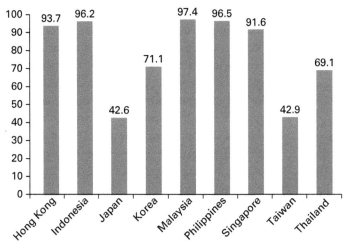

Figure 2.6
Percentage of listed East Asian firms with a 10% shareholder
Notes: Figure 2.6 is based on 1,386 publicly traded corporations in 2008, including both financial and non-financial institutions. Control rests with the institutional investors and the industrial corporations as these are widely held.
Source: Based on Carney, R.W. and Child, T.B. (2013), 'Changes to the Ownership and Control of East Asian Corporations between 1996 and 2008: The Primacy of Politics', *Journal of Financial Economics* 107, table 4.

Table 2.4 Distribution of control across types of large shareholders in East Asia

Country	Sample	Family	State	Institutional investors	Industrial corporations	Foreign state
10% cut-off						
Hong Kong	158	60.6	28.0	3.5	0.9	0.6
Indonesia	132	57.3	14.1	3.6	13.4	7.8
Japan	136	9.6	6.3	6.6	19.1	1.1
Korea	159	54.5	6.9	2.7	6.0	0.9
Malaysia	154	51.5	39.7	1.4	2.2	2.6
Philippines	114	78.5	5.2	3.3	6.1	3.4
Singapore	131	60.2	20.5	3.8	1.7	5.3
Taiwan	163	13.8	9.2	2.5	17.5	0.0
Thailand	149	37.8	12.8	3.4	6.7	8.5
East Asia nine	1,296	46.1	16.2	3.4	8.2	3.3
20% cut-off						
Hong Kong	167	55.1	27.2	3.3	2.4	0.0
Indonesia	137	50.0	13.5	2.2	13.3	7.8
Japan	176	6.0	4.5	2.3	14.5	0.6
Korea	172	35.8	5.5	0.0	10.2	0.3
Malaysia	159	44.7	33.5	0.6	4.3	3.7
Philippines	118	76.5	3.4	1.9	5.9	4.7
Singapore	135	51.9	19.6	1.7	3.9	4.3
Taiwan	169	4.7	6.5	1.2	12.4	0.0
Thailand	153	33.3	12.1	2.3	7.8	5.9
East Asia nine	1,386	37.7	14.0	1.7	8.5	2.8

Notes: Table 2.4 is based on 1,386 publicly traded corporations in 2008, including both financial and non-financial institutions. Control rests with the institutional investors and the industrial corporations as these are widely held.

Source: Adapted from Carney, R.W. and Child, T.B. (2013), 'Changes to the Ownership and Control of East Asian Corporations between 1996 and 2008: The Primacy of Politics', *Journal of Financial Economics* 107, table 3.

industrial corporation, respectively, with a stake of at least 10 per cent as their largest shareholder. In Indonesia, banks are not allowed to hold shares in other companies, which may explain the relatively low percentage of firms controlled by institutional investors in that country. The percentage of firms controlled by the government is highest in Malaysia and Singapore with roughly 40 per cent and 21 per cent of the votes, respectively.

When control is defined as a holding of at least 20 per cent, the differences between the countries become even more pronounced. The percentage of family controlled firms is now down to 6 per cent from about 10 per cent previously for Japan, to 36 per cent from 55 per cent in Korea, and to 5 per cent from 14 per cent in Taiwan. Apart from Hong Kong, the percentage of firms controlled by institutional investors has also dropped across all countries. In the case of Japan, it has dropped substantially from about 7 per cent to only 2 per cent. These decreases can in part be explained by regulation. For example, in Hong Kong, Japan, Korea and Singapore, there are limits to the percentage of ownership banks can hold in other companies.

From the above, Japan, Taiwan and to a lesser extent Korea stick out in terms of corporate control. Japan and Korea also differ from the other Asian countries in other ways. For example, in Japan some firms form part of so-called keiretsus. A keiretsu is a group of industrial companies with close ties to a single bank which acts as the principal lender to the group.[11] The bank, which is often widely held, also has ownership in the group's companies and there are typically cross-holdings between the group companies. A cross-holding consists of company A holding shares in company B and vice-versa. The keiretsus originated from the zaibatsus of the pre-Second World War period. The zaibatsus were groups of industrial companies or conglomerates controlled by families via a holding firm at the top of the group and with a bank as one of the group companies providing the financing. An example of a keiretsu that started as a zaibatsu is the Mitsubishi group of companies which consists of about 600 companies with a core of 29 companies. The group includes a bank, the Bank of Tokyo-Mitsubishi UFJ.[12] Nevertheless, Japan has been gradually experiencing marked changes in terms of corporate control starting with the aftermath of the 1997 Asian financial crisis and carrying over into the 2000s and 2010s. More specifically, a number of the cross-holdings between banks and firms and also among firms have now disappeared.[13]

Korea's industrial landscape is dominated by powerful chaebols. A chaebol is a group of industrial companies controlled by a family. Examples of famous conglomerates include Hyundai, LG and Samsung. Similar to Japan, Korea is dominated by cross-holdings. Importantly, in 2014 Korea's antitrust watchdog banned the creation of any new cross-holdings among the member firms of chaebols with the aim of improving the corporate governance of the latter.[14] While cross-holdings can shield firms from outside disciplinary actions, such as hostile takeovers, some studies have nevertheless highlighted an important benefit from such structures. For example, Heitor Almeida, Chang-Soo Kim and Brian Kim found that in the aftermath of the 1997 Asian financial crisis when outside funding was sparse, chaebols channelled funds from member firms with few investment opportunities to those with many such opportunities.[15] This suggests the existence of efficient internal capital markets within such business groups. Ronald Masulis, Peter Pham and Jason Zein confirmed the existence of efficient internal capital markets in their study of business groups from 45 different countries.[16]

[11]Prowse, S.D. (1992), 'The Structure of Corporate Ownership in Japan', *Journal of Finance* 47, 1121–40. See also Hoshi, T., Kashyap, A. and Scharfstein, D. (1991), 'Corporate Structure, Liquidity, and Investment: Evidence from Japanese Industrial Groups', *Quarterly Journal of Economics* 106, 33–60.

[12]www.mitsubishi.com/e/group/about.html, accessed on 2 February 2017.

[13]Miyajima, H., Ogawa, R. and Saito, T. (2016), 'Changes in the Corporate Governance System and Presidential Turnover', Working Paper – Waseda University, Japan.

[14]www.koreaherald.com/view.php?ud=20140725000716, accessed on 2 February 2017.

[15]Almeida, H., Kim, C.-S. and Kim, H.B. (2015), 'Internal Capital Markets in Business Groups: Evidence from the Asian Financial Crisis', *Journal of Finance* 70, 2539–86.

[16]Masulis, R.W., Pham, P.K. and Zein, J. (2011), 'Family Business Groups Around the World: Financing Advantages, Control Motivations, and Organizational Choices', *Review of Financial Studies* 24, 3556–600.

More specifically, they found that such markets work well for business groups that are in the form of owner-ship pyramids rather than horizontal structures. However, they also found that when ownership pyramids are combined with dual-class shares and cross-holdings, firm performance declines.

Ferdinand Gul, Jeong-Bon Kim and Annie Qiu studied the control of Chinese firms.[17] During the 1980s, China started a series of economic reforms that gave managers of state-owned enterprises (SOEs) more power and decision making moved from the government to the firm level (see also Chapter 9 on the role of the government and politicians in corporate affairs). In 1990 the Chinese government set up the Shenzen Stock Exchange and in 1991 the Shanghai Stock Exchange. From then on SOEs could issue shares to individual inves-tors, effectively starting their partial privatization. Chinese SOEs tend to have complex control and ownership structures. They tend to have some or all of five major types of shareholders: the central government, legal per-sons (i.e. institutions and the founder), employees, domestic investors who hold A shares and foreign investors who hold B and H shares.[18] H shares are issued on the Hong Kong Stock Exchange, which has more stringent regulation than the Shenzen and Shanghai Stock Exchanges. Gul et al.'s sample comprised 1,142 non-financial listed Chinese firms. They found that the largest shareholder on average held about 43 per cent of the shares and in 67 per cent of the firms the largest shareholder was the government or government related. The average stake of the government across their sample was 32 per cent whereas foreign investors held a mere 4 per cent.

Rajesh Chakrabarti, William Megginson and Pradeep Yadav studied the corporate control of the 500 largest Indian firms listed on the Bombay Stock Exchange.[19] In India, it is common practice to distinguish between so-called promoters and non-promoters. While these terms are not defined in Indian corporate law, promotion is normally interpreted as referring to the preliminary steps required to register the company and to float it on the stock market. Hence, the promoters tend to be the founders or insiders. Chakrabarti et al. reported that about 60 per cent of the 500 largest firms are part of conglomerates or so-called business groups. India's companies are characterized by concentrated ownership and control. Ownership structures tend to be complex and opaque with frequent use of ownership pyramids and cross-holdings. Control is often held indirectly via intermediate layers of unlisted firms and holding companies or trusts. While research on chaebols has suggested an advan-tage of such business groups – in the form of internal capital markets – research on Indian business groups highlights a disadvantage which is tunnelling, a form of minority shareholder expropriation.[20-21]

2.5 Corporate control in transitional economies

The former Communist countries of Eastern Europe started moving to market economies in the early 1990s by opening stock exchanges and starting ambitious programmes of privatization. Klaus Gugler, Natalia Ivanova and Josef Zechner reviewed control patterns in the Central and Eastern European economies of Bulgaria, Croatia, the Czech Republic, Estonia, Latvia, Lithuania, Poland, Romania, Slovakia and Slovenia as well as Russia.[22] They defined a firm as being widely held if it does not have an ultimate shareholder holding at least

[17]Gul, F.A., Kim, J.-B. and Qiu, A.A. (2010), 'Ownership Concentration, Foreign Shareholding, Audit Quality, and Stock Price Syncronicity: Evidence from China', *Journal of Financial Economics* 95, 425–42.
[18]Gul et al. (2010) discuss some of the recent policy changes which have led to a relaxation of the segmentation between A shares and B or H shares.
[19]Chakrabart, R., Megginson, W. and Yadav, P.K. (2008), 'Corporate Governance in India', *Journal of Applied Corporate Finance* 20, 59–72.
[20]Bertrand, M., Mehta, P. and Mullainathan, S. (2002), 'Ferreting out Tunneling: An Application to Indian Business Groups', *Quarterly Journal of Economics* 117, 121–48.
[21]See Section 1.6 of Chapter 1.
[22]Gugler, K., Ivanova, N. and Zechner, J. (2014), 'Ownership and Control in Central and Eastern Europe', *Journal of Corporate Finance* 26, 145–63.

10 per cent of the voting rights. They found that the most prevalent types of largest shareholder were individuals and the state. Similar to Western Europe, the percentage of firms that was widely held was low.

Table 2.5 focuses on those firms with an individual shareholder as their largest ultimate shareholder. The percentage of voting rights held by the largest individual shareholder is high, albeit a bit lower than that held by the largest ultimate shareholder in Western Europe (see also Table 2.6).

Table 2.5 Distribution of control across types of large shareholders in Eastern Europe and Russia

Country	Large individual shareholder	Industrial company	Institutional investor	State	Foreign	Widely held	Companies	Obs.
Bulgaria	42.4	25.5	3.6	16.4	0.0	12.1	28	165
Croatia	33.0	0.0	3.8	28.3	23.6	11.3	33	106
Czech Republic	25.0	0.0	0.0	35.0	40.0	0.0	13	60
Estonia	31.8	25.0	0.0	25.0	18.2	0.0	10	44
Latvia	38.2	27.3	1.8	1.8	30.9	0.0	20	55
Lithuania	21.2	12.4	4.7	30.6	13.5	17.6	29	170
Poland	41.5	11.6	1.7	8.7	27.4	9.1	48	241
Romania	23.3	8.3	0.0	29.4	8.3	30.6	29	180
Russia	32.6	8.2	0.0	56.8	2.5	0.0	142	562
Slovakia	0.0	0.0	0.0	0.0	100.0	0.0	31	79
Slovenia	0.0	32.0	13.2	37.2	15.1	2.5	51	325
Total firms	144	53	13	137	59	29	416	

Notes: Table 2.5 covers a pooled sample for the years 2000 to 2007.

Source: Adapted from Gugler, K., Ivanova, N. and Zechner, J. (2014), 'Ownership and Control in Central and Eastern Europe', *Journal of Corporate Finance* 26, table 2.

Table 2.6 Mean and median control held by the largest individual shareholder in Eastern Europe and Russia

Country	Mean	Median	Obs.
Bulgaria	47.7	44.6	65
Croatia	60.1	67.9	35
Czech Republic	44.5	58.0	15
Estonia	37.6	38.1	14
Latvia	42.2	45.3	21
Lithuania	34.9	29.1	32
Poland	40.4	42.3	95
Romania	53.2	60.2	34
Russia	48.8	48.1	152
Total firms	46.4	44.6	463

Notes: Table 2.6 covers the years 2000 to 2007.

Source: Adapted from Gugler, K., Ivanova, N. and Zechner, J. (2014), 'Ownership and Control in Central and Eastern Europe', *Journal of Corporate Finance* 26, table 3.

2.6 Conclusions

This chapter has reviewed the patterns of corporate control across the world. Contrary to Adolf Berle and Gardiner Means's thesis that ownership and control separate as companies grow, there is no such separation in most companies outside the UK and the USA. In fact, the average UK and US firm is the only firm for which the Berle-Means thesis is upheld. In the rest of the world, including Continental Western Europe, Asia and Eastern Europe, control is concentrated in the hands of one or more shareholders. Hence, the main type of conflicts of interests likely to emerge in most of the companies outside the UK and the USA is conflicts between the large shareholder and the minority shareholders.

The Berle-Means hypothesis is only upheld for the UK and the USA

The main types of shareholders in the UK and the USA are institutional investors – typically widely held and therefore subject to principal-agent problems – as well as the members of the board of directors. Conversely, in the rest of the world the main types of shareholders are families, industrial and holding companies as well as the government. While the countries of the former Communist Bloc as well as Communist China have undertaken ambitious programmes to privatize and/or decentralize their economies, corporate control remains heavily concentrated.

The main types of shareholders differ between the UK/USA and the rest of the world

2.7 Discussion questions

1   Compare corporate control in the UK and the USA to corporate control in the rest of the world. What can you say about the levels of control across the world? How do the different types of large shareholders vary across the world?

2   How does corporate control in Japan and Korea compare to the rest of Asia?

3   What are keiretsus and chaebols?

Reading list

Key reading

Barca, F. and Becht, M. (2001), *The Control of Corporate Europe*, Oxford, UK: Oxford University Press.

Carney, R.W. and Child, T.B. (2013), 'Changes to the Ownership and Control of East Asian Corporations between 1996 and 2008: The Primacy of Politics', *Journal of Financial Economics* 107, 494–513.

Chakrabart, R., Megginson, W. and Yadav, P.K. (2008), 'Corporate Governance in India', *Journal of Applied Corporate Finance* 20, 59–72.

Claessens, S., Djankov, S. and Lang, L.H.P. (2000), 'The Separation of Ownership and Control in East Asian Corporations', *Journal of Financial Economics* 58, 81–112.

Gugler, K., Ivanova, N. and Zechner, J. (2014), 'Ownership and Control in Central and Eastern Europe', *Journal of Corporate Finance* 26, 145–63.

Gul, F.A., Kim, J.-B. and Qiu, A.A. (2010), 'Ownership Concentration, Foreign Shareholding, Audit Quality, and Stock Price Syncronicity: Evidence from China', *Journal of Financial Economics* 95, 425–42.

Hoshi, T., Kashyap, A., and Scharfstein, D. (1991), 'Corporate Structure, Liquidity, and Investment: Evidence from Japanese Industrial Groups', *Quarterly Journal of Economics* 106, 33–60.

Prowse, S.D. (1992), 'The Structure of Corporate Ownership in Japan', *Journal of Finance* 47, 1121–40.

Further reading

Faccio, M. and Lang, L.H.P. (2002), 'The Ultimate Ownership of Western European Corporations', *Journal of Financial Economics* 65, 365–95.

Gilson, R.J. and Roe, M.J. (1993), 'Understanding the Japanese Keiretsu: Overlaps between Corporate Governance and Industrial Organization', *Yale Law Journal* 102, 871–906.

Holderness, C.G. (2009), 'The Myth of Diffuse Ownership in the United States', *Review of Financial Studies* 22, 1377–408.

La Porta, R., Lopez-de-Silanes, F., Shleifer, A. and Vishny, R. (1999), 'Corporate Ownership around the World', *Journal of Finance* 54, 471–517.

Masulis, R.W., Pham, P.K. and Zein, J. (2011), 'Family Business Groups around the World: Financing Advantages, Control Motivations, and Organizational Choices', *Review of Financial Studies* 24, 3556–600.

Pajuste, A. (2002), 'Corporate Governance and Stock Market Performance in Central and Eastern Europe: A Study of Nine Countries, 1994–2001', available at SSRN: ssrn.com/abstract=310419.

3 Control versus ownership rights

Chapter Aims

The aim of this chapter is to review the various devices that create a wedge between control and ownership. It is important to be aware of differences between control and ownership as they determine the types of conflicts of interests that a company and its stakeholders may be subject to.

Learning Outcomes

After reading this chapter, you should be able to:

1 Distinguish ownership from control

2 Explain how the various combinations of weak or strong control with dispersed or concentrated ownership can be obtained

3 Define security benefits of control and private benefits of control

4 Assess the importance of private benefits of control across countries

3.1 Introduction

The previous chapter highlighted marked differences in the control of large corporations across the world. While in the UK and the USA most listed corporations are widely held, in the rest of the world corporations tend to have large shareholders that have uncontested control or at least a substantial degree of control over the running of their firms. As these are all large corporations with substantial market values, the question arises as to how their large shareholders, frequently the company founders, manage to stay in control over a long time.

The simple answer to this question is that these large shareholders *leverage* control, i.e. they manage to hold a substantial percentage (and in some cases, all) of the voting rights while holding substantially fewer cash flow rights. In Chapter 1, we already saw one way of leveraging control which is ownership pyramids. However, there are other ways to achieve concentrated control at a reduced cost, i.e. at lower percentages of cash flow rights or ownership. We shall review the main such ways in this chapter.

More generally, we shall analyze each of the four combinations between ownership – which may be dispersed or concentrated – and control – which may be weak or strong. As we shall see, each of these combinations may give rise to different conflicts of interests.

3.2 Combinations of ownership and control

For simplicity's sake and as mentioned above we shall distinguish between two extremes for both control and ownership. They are strong control versus weak control and concentrated ownership versus dispersed ownership. The four possible combinations of control and ownership are summarized in Figure 3.1. Combinations A, B, C and D correspond to weak control and dispersed ownership, strong control and dispersed ownership, weak control and concentrated ownership, and strong control and concentrated ownership, respectively.

Figure 3.1 **Combinations of control and ownership**

		Control	
		Weak	**Strong**
Ownership	Dispersed	*Combination A:* weak control and dispersed ownership	*Combination B:* strong control and dispersed ownership
	Concentrated	*Combination C:* weak control and concentrated ownership	*Combination D:* strong control and concentrated ownership

Dispersed ownership has at least two major advantages. The first one is the increased liquidity of the shares. As more investors hold the shares, there is likely to be an active market in them. Hence, it is fairly easy for a seller to find another investor who wants to buy the shares and for an investor who wants to buy shares to find a seller. The higher liquidity of the shares ultimately results in a lower cost of capital, which is beneficial to the firm as a whole and increases its market value. A lower cost of capital implies that the hurdle rate that returns on potential investments need to achieve is lower and hence the company's pool of investment opportunities is bigger. The second advantage of dispersed ownership is that the company is vulnerable to hostile raiders that are on the lookout for badly performing management. Hence with dispersed ownership, the managers are under constant pressure to perform in order to avoid a fall in their company's stock price and the launch of a hostile takeover bid. Concentrated control and ownership also has a major advantage as there will be a shareholder with enough control (or power) and sufficient incentives (or ownership) to monitor the management and to ensure it runs the firm in the interests of the shareholders.

However, dispersed ownership as well as concentrated control and ownership also have major disadvantages. Dispersed ownership typically results in the free-rider problem formalized by Sanford Grossman and Oliver Hart.[1] If a firm has a large number of shareholders, then none of them may have sufficient incentives to monitor the firm's management. If one of them decides to spend the time, money and effort to monitor the management, the benefits from doing so will be shared across *all* the shareholders whereas the costs will be borne by the monitoring shareholder. Hence, the costs accruing to a single small shareholder from monitoring the management are likely to outweigh the pro rata benefits from doing so. As a result, there is likely to be little or no monitoring of the management in firms with dispersed ownership. We have already discussed the potential

[1]Grossman, S. and Hart, O. (1980), 'Takeover Bids, the Free-Rider Problem, and the Theory of the Corporation', *Bell Journal of Economics* 11, 42–64.

costs of concentrated control in Chapter 1. These costs stem from the potential expropriation of the minority shareholders by the large shareholder. Indeed, while the latter has enough power over the management to influence their decision making, he may abuse this power by forcing the management to make decisions that are clearly in his own interests, but cause harm to the other shareholders.

We shall now review each of the above four combinations of ownership and control by providing real-life examples of firms having these combinations in place and by discussing the corporate governance issues or conflicts of interests that are more likely to emerge under each combination. Before starting this discussion, it is important to point out that a priori one expects combination A to be the prevailing combination of ownership and control in UK and US corporations, and combination D to be the prevailing combination in corporations from the rest of the world. However, as we shall see it is combination B rather than combination D which prevails outside the UK and the USA.

3.3 Combination A: dispersed ownership and weak control

This combination is in place in most UK and US companies. It has the advantages of increased stock liquidity and the potential for hostile, value-increasing takeovers. The main disadvantage of this combination is the likely lack of monitoring by the dispersed shareholders. Hence, the main potential conflict of interests is between the management and the shareholders. In other words, firms with this combination of ownership and control may suffer from the classic principal-agent problem.

The example of Tesco Plc in Box 3.1 is a typical example of a firm with dispersed ownership and control. Tesco Plc's largest shareholder is Norges Bank Investment Management (NBIM), an institutional investor that

Box 3.1
The 10 largest shareholders in Tesco Plc in January 2016

Holder	Common Shares Held	% of CSO	Market Value (GBP in mm)
Norges Bank Investment Management	469,817,854	5.79	859.53
Schroder Investment Management	343,715,366	4.24	628.83
Artisan Partners	324,559,039	4.00	593.78
Silchester International Investors	308,552,449	3.80	564.50
GIC Private Ltd	267,840,626	3.30	490.01
Mondrain Investment Partners	266,297,983	3.28	487.19
Legal & General Investment Management	226,404,361	2.79	414.21
Magellan Asset Management Ltd	221,597,709	2.73	405.41
BlackRock Investment Management (UK)	217,018,938	2.67	397.04
Majedie Asset Management	199,182,712	2.45	364.40

Source: S&P Capital IQ

holds about 6 per cent of its shares. Tesco's other ten largest shareholders are also all institutional investors, from both the UK and overseas. Together the ten largest shareholders in Tesco hold just slightly more than 35 per cent of the votes.

Similarly, The Coca Cola Company (see Box 3.2), a US company, combines dispersed ownership with weak control as its largest shareholder, Berkshire Hathaway Inc.,[2] owns just above 9 per cent of the shares and together the ten largest shareholders hold slightly more than 37 per cent of the shares.

Box 3.2
The 10 largest shareholders in The Coca Cola Company Inc in January 2016

Holder	Common Stock Equivalent Held	% of CSO	Market Value (USD in mm)
Berkshire Hathaway Inc. (NY SEBRK.A)	400,000,000	9.27	16,380.0
The Vanguard Group, Inc.	280,640,593	6.51	11,492.2
Capital Research and Management Company	257,824,518	5.98	10,557.9
BlackRock, Inc. (NY SEBLK)	235,921,477	5.47	9,661.0
State Street Global Advisors, Inc.	167,756,110	3.89	6,869.6
Fidelity Investments	69,320,887	1.61	2,838.7
Wellington Management Group LLP	59,005,970	1.37	2,416.3
Northern Trust Global Investments	50,093,237	1.16	2,051.3
BNY Mellon Asset Management	42,284,070	0.98	1,731.5
Norges Bank Investment Management	33,608,453	0.78	1,376.3

Source: S&P Capital IQ

3.4 Combination B: dispersed ownership and strong control

Combining dispersed ownership with strong control creates two major advantages. First, there is an active market in the shares given the dispersion of ownership. Second, there is a controlling shareholder with enough power to prevent the managers from expropriating the shareholders. However, this combination also increases the risk of the minority shareholders being expropriated by the large shareholder. This combination prevails in most corporations outside the UK and the USA. Box 3.3 shows the control and ownership of Villeroy & Boch AG, the German producer of ceramics. Villeroy & Boch has two types of shares outstanding: voting stock, each of which carries one vote, and non-voting stock, which has preferential rights such as a guaranteed dividend but no voting rights. Both types of stock make up 50 per cent of the total equity capital. The founding families of Villeroy & Boch own 100 per cent of the voting stock. However, as the voting stock only makes up 50 per cent of the total equity, their ownership only amounts to 50 per cent. Hence, the founding families clearly hold uncontested control (i.e. 100% control) but at the cost of only 50 per cent of the ownership of the firm.

[2]The famous Warren E. Buffett is the chairman of Berkshire Hathaway Inc.

Box 3.3
Ownership and control of Villeroy & Boch AG

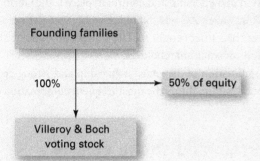

Voting stock 50%, non-voting stock 50%

Source: Author's own diagram based on information from Villeroy & Boch AG, www.villeroyboch-group.com/en/investor-relations/shares/preference-shares.html, accessed on 25 February 2017.

3.5 Combination C: concentrated ownership and weak control

This is a fairly rare combination. It applies to only a few firms across the world, including some Continental European firms and Indian banks with voting caps,[3] i.e. voting limits, in place. The Swiss food manufacturer Nestlé SA has a voting cap of 5 per cent in place (see Box 3.4).[4] The effect of such a voting cap is that it limits the maximum percentage of votes a single shareholder can vote for at the AGM. Hence, ownership may be concentrated but control is curtailed and weakened as a result. The advantage of such a combination of ownership and control is that minority shareholders are protected as no single shareholder is powerful enough to dominate the company's decision making. However, there are also clear disadvantages such as the lack of monitoring resulting from the concentration of ownership and the low liquidity and cost of capital.

Box 3.4
Voting cap in Nestlé SA

According to art. 5 par. 5 of the Articles of Association, no person or entity shall be registered with voting rights for more than 5% of the share capital as recorded in the commercial register. This limitation on registration also applies to persons who hold some or all their shares through nominees pursuant to that article. Legal entities that are linked to one another, through capital, voting rights, management or in any other manner, as well as all natural persons or legal entities achieving an understanding or forming a syndicate or otherwise acting in concert to circumvent the regulations concerning the limitation on registration or the nominees, shall be counted as one person or nominee (art. 5 par. 7 of the Articles of Association).

Source: Nestlé SA, 2015 corporate governance report, p.5

[3]Ghosh, C., Hilliard, J., Petrova, M. and Phani, B.V. (2016), 'Economic Consequences of Deregulation: Evidence from the Removal of Voting Cap in Indian Banks', *Journal of Banking and Finance* 72, S19–S38.
[4]The French food manufacturer Danone SA has a voting cap of 6 per cent. See Additional resources at the end of this chapter.

3.6 Combination D: concentrated ownership and strong control

This combination creates strong monitoring incentives given the large ownership stake held by the controlling shareholder. However, it also has the disadvantages of low liquidity and a reduced takeover probability. One of the most extreme examples of a firm that has this combination of ownership and control in place is the German car manufacturer AUDI AG. AUDI's main shareholder is Volkswagen AG which holds roughly 99.6 per cent of the votes making it a Volkswagen subsidiary. However, fewer than 1 per cent of AUDI's shares still trade on the stock exchange after the 1966 acquisition and are in the hands of small shareholders.

We shall now concentrate on combination B, i.e. the combination of dispersed ownership and strong control, and how this combination can be achieved. As mentioned before, this is the most frequent combination of ownership and control outside the UK and the USA.

3.7 How to achieve dispersed ownership and strong control

There are various ways of achieving combination B. They all consist of the main shareholder leveraging control, i.e. having control while holding a smaller ownership stake. The main ways of achieving this are pyramids of ownership, proxy votes, voting coalitions, dual-class shares and clauses in the articles of association that confer additional votes to long-term shareholders. Ownership pyramids have already been discussed in Section 1.6 of Chapter 1. Figure 3.2 shows a simple ownership pyramid consisting of a single firm at each tier of the pyramid, i.e. a control chain. Let us define control as ownership of a majority of (voting) shares. The focal point of the example in Figure 3.2 is firm A at the bottom of the pyramid. In line with the focus of this book, this firm must be a quoted firm. The main shareholder of firm A is firm B which may or may not be quoted. Firm B has a majority holding in firm A. While firm B is the largest, direct shareholder in firm A, control is unlikely to reside with firm B. Indeed, in turn firm B has a controlling shareholder, firm C. However, firm C does not have a majority or controlling shareholder and the pyramid ends with firm C. Hence, control over firm A lies with (the management of) firm C. Assuming that control transfers across the pyramid, i.e. firm C does effectively have control over firm A via the intermediary of firm B, firm C manages to have control over firm A by investing indirectly in only 26.01 per cent (51 per cent of 51 per cent) of its shares.

While the example in Figure 3.2 is fairly simple given that there is only one firm at each tier of the pyramid, pyramids of ownership in real life tend to be substantially more complex. Box 3.5 provides an example of

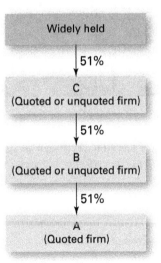

Figure 3.2 Simple ownership pyramid
Source: Correia da Silva, L., Goergen, M. and Renneboog, L. (2004), *Dividend Policy and Corporate Governance*, Oxford, UK: Oxford University Press.

a real-life pyramid. The example shows some of the holdings of the Agnelli family. All of their holdings can ultimately be traced back by their main holding company, Giovanni Agnelli & C. S.a.p.a.

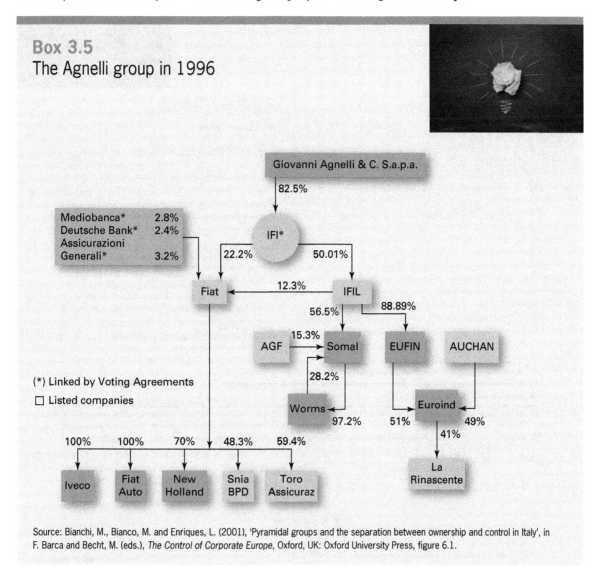

Box 3.5
The Agnelli group in 1996

Source: Bianchi, M., Bianco, M. and Enriques, L. (2001), 'Pyramidal groups and the separation between ownership and control in Italy', in F. Barca and Becht, M. (eds.), *The Control of Corporate Europe*, Oxford, UK: Oxford University Press, figure 6.1.

Another way of achieving this combination of ownership and control is via proxy votes. We have already discussed one type of proxy vote in Chapter 2, which is proxy votes held by banks in certain countries. These proxy votes originate from the shares the customers of the banks deposit with the latter and that the banks vote for. While banks are allowed to own shares in other companies, in some countries they also frequently increase their degree of control in their investee companies via the use of proxy votes. Another type of proxy votes is votes owned by the shareholders, but exercised by the company's management. Box 3.6 shows the example of US company Tesla Inc. Its management is soliciting proxy votes from its shareholders, recommending how shareholders vote for each proposal. Finally, in Section 8.7 of Chapter 8 we shall also discuss so-called proxy contests whereby one or several small shareholders seek the support of the other shareholders to obtain approval for a motion they have put forward for voting at the shareholders' meeting.

Box 3.6
Proxy votes solicited by the management

Admission Ticket

C123456789

000000000.000000 ext   000000000.000000 ext
000000000.000000 ext   000000000.000000 ext
000000000.000000 ext   000000000.000000 ext

Electronic Voting Instructions

Available 24 hours a day, 7 days a week!
Instead of mailing your proxy, you may choose one of the voting methods outlined below to vote your proxy.

VALIDATION DETAILS ARE LOCATED BELOW IN THE TITLE BAR.

Proxies submitted by the Internet or telephone must be received by 1:00 a.m., Central Time, on June 6, 2017.

Vote by Internet
• Go to www.envisionreports.com/TSLA
• Or scan the QR code with your smartphone
• Follow the steps outlined on the secure website

Vote by telephone
• Call toll free 1-800-652-VOTE (8683) within the USA, US territories & Canada on a touch tone telephone
• Follow the instructions provided by the recorded message

IMPORTANT ANNUAL MEETING INFORMATION   000004

ENDORSEMENT_LINE_____ SACKPACK_____
lllulllullllullllullulllllulllulllullllullllull

MR A SAMPLE
DESIGNATION (IF ANY)
ADD 1
ADD 2
ADD 3
ADD 4
ADD 5
ADD 6

Using a **black ink** pen, mark your votes with an **X** as shown in this example. Please do not write outside the designated areas.   **X**

Annual Meeting Proxy Card   1234 5678 9012 345

▼ IF YOU HAVE NOT VOTED VIA THE INTERNET **OR** TELEPHONE, FOLD ALONG THE PERFORATION, DETACH AND RETURN THE BOTTOM PORTION IN THE ENCLOSED ENVELOPE. ▼

A Proposals — The Board recommends a vote <u>FOR</u> all nominees, <u>FOR</u> Proposal 2, every <u>3 YRS</u> for Proposal 3, <u>FOR</u> Proposal 4, and <u>AGAINST</u> Proposal 5.

1. Election of three Class I Director Nominees:

	For	Against	Abstain		For	Against	Abstain		For	Against	Abstain
01 – Elon Musk	☐	☐	☐	02 – Robyn M. Denholm	☐	☐	☐	03 – Stephen T. Jurvetson	☐	☐	☐

	For	Against	Abstain		1 Yr	2 Yrs	3 Yrs	Abstain
2. A non-binding advisory vote on the approval of executive compensation.	☐	☐	☐	3. A non-binding advisory vote on the frequency of executive compensation votes.	☐	☐	☐	☐

	For	Against	Abstain		For	Against	Abstain
4. To ratify the appointment of PricewaterhouseCoopers LLP as Tesla's independent registered public accounting firm for the fiscal year ending December 31, 2017.	☐	☐	☐	5. A stockholder proposal regarding declassification of the Board of Directors.	☐	☐	☐

B Non-Voting Items

Change of Address – Please print your new address below.   **Comments** – Please print your comments below.   **Meeting Attendance**
Mark the box to the right ☐ if you plan to attend the Annual Meeting.

C Authorized Signatures — This section must be completed for your vote to be counted. — Date and Sign Below

Please sign exactly as name(s) appears hereon. Joint owners should each sign. When signing as attorney, executor, administrator, corporate officer, trustee, guardian, or custodian, please give full title.

Date (mm/dd/yyyy) — Please print date below.   Signature 1 — Please keep signature within the box.   Signature 2 — Please keep signature within the box.

/   /

C 1234567890   J N T   MR A SAMPLE (THIS AREA IS SET UP TO ACCOMMODATE 140 CHARACTERS) MR A SAMPLE AND MR A SAMPLE AND MR A SAMPLE AND MR A SAMPLE AND MR A SAMPLE AND MR A SAMPLE AND MR A SAMPLE AND MR A SAMPLE AND

1 U P X   3 2 7 7 5 2 1

02KZF8

2017 Annual Meeting Admission Ticket
2017 Annual Meeting of
Tesla, Inc. Stockholders
Tuesday, June 6, 2017 at 2:30 p.m. PDT
Computer History Museum
1401 N. Shoreline Blvd, Mountain View, CA 94043
Upon arrival, please present this admission ticket
and photo identification at the registration desk.

From San Jose via US-101 North

- **20 Minutes - 15 Miles**
- Take US-101 North toward San Francisco.
- Take Shoreline Blvd exit.
- Turn right onto Shoreline Blvd.
- Cross through intersection.
- Museum is on your right.

From San Francisco via US-101 South

- **40 Minutes - 35 Miles**
- Take US-101 South toward San Jose.
- Take Shoreline Blvd exit.
- Turn left onto Shoreline Blvd.
- Cross through intersection.
- Museum is on your right.

From East Bay via I-880 South

- **25 Minutes - 20 Miles**
- Take I-880 South toward San Jose.
- Merge onto CA-237 West toward Mountain View.
- Merge onto US-101 North toward San Francisco.
- Take Shoreline Blvd exit.
- Turn right onto Shoreline Blvd.
- Cross through intersection.
- Museum is on your right.

From Saratoga via CA-85 North

- **15 Minutes - 12 Miles**
- Take CA-85 North towards San Francisco.
- Take Shoreline Blvd exit.
- Turn right onto Shoreline Blvd.
- Cross through intersection.
- Museum is on your right.

▼ IF YOU HAVE NOT VOTED VIA THE INTERNET OR TELEPHONE, FOLD ALONG THE PERFORATION, DETACH AND RETURN THE BOTTOM PORTION IN THE ENCLOSED ENVELOPE. ▼

Proxy — Tesla, Inc.

Notice of 2017 Annual Meeting of Stockholders

Computer History Museum - 1401 N. Shoreline Blvd, Mountain View, CA 94043
This Proxy is Solicited on Behalf of the Board of Directors for Annual Meeting – June 6, 2017 at 2:30 p.m. PDT

Elon Musk, Deepak Ahuja and Todd Maron, or any of them, each with the power of substitution, are hereby authorized to represent as proxies and vote with respect to the proposals set forth on the reverse side and in the discretion of such proxies on all other matters that may be properly presented for action all shares of stock of Tesla, Inc. the undersigned is entitled to vote at the Annual Meeting of Stockholders to be held at 2:30 p.m. Pacific Time on Tuesday, June 6, 2017, or any postponement, adjournment or continuation thereof, and instructs said proxies to vote as specified on the reverse side.

Shares represented by this proxy will be voted as directed by the stockholder. If no such directions are indicate, the Proxies will have authority to vote <u>FOR</u> all nominees, <u>FOR</u> Proposal 2, every <u>3 YRS</u> for Proposal 3, <u>FOR</u> Proposal 4, and <u>AGAINST</u> Proposal 5.

In their discretion, the Proxies are authorized to vote upon such other business as may properly come before the annual meeting.

(Items to be voted appear on reverse side.)

Source: Tesla Inc. 2017 DEF 14A

A third way of leveraging control is via voting coalitions. A voting coalition or voting pool consists of several shareholders joining forces and agreeing to vote in the same way. Within Box 3.5 of the Agnelli family holdings there is an example of such a voting agreement between the German bank Deutsche Bank, the Italian Bank Mediobanca and the Italian assurance company Assicurazioni Generali. While each of them holds a fairly small stake in Fiat, together – via the voting agreement – they manage to increase their votes to a total of 8.4 per cent. Voting coalitions are fairly rare, especially those that persist in the long term. One of the reasons for the infrequency of voting coalitions may be the costs of such coalitions created by regulation. For example, the UK City Code on Takeovers and Mergers requires that shareholders that have acquired a stake of at least 30 per cent in a company make a tender offer to the remaining shareholders.[5] The same requirement applies to voting coalitions once their stake has reached the 30 per cent threshold. This requirement may also explain why some shareholders in the UK keep their stake just below the 30 per cent mark, as evidenced by Figure 3.3. However, there seems to be evidence from UK research that such coalitions are still formed on an ad hoc basis to intervene in poorly performing companies.[6]

Figure 3.3 Distribution of the size of the largest voting block in UK listed companies
Source: Goergen, M. and Renneboog, L. (2001), 'Strong Managers and Passive Institutional Investors in the UK', in F. Barca and Becht, M. (eds.), *The Control of Corporate Europe*, Oxford, UK: Oxford University Press, figure 10.3.

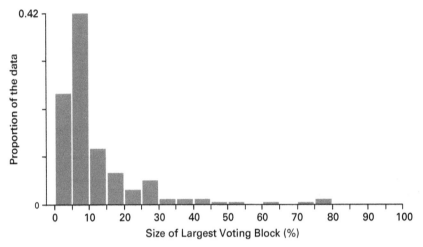

In Section 3.4, we have already discussed another way of combining strong control with dispersed owner-ship, i.e. so-called dual-class shares. Companies with dual-class shares have two classes of shares outstanding: a class with voting rights or superior voting rights and a second class with no voting rights or fewer voting rights. For firms that have voting shares and non-voting shares outstanding, the former class is typically called ordinary shares or common stock and the latter is called non-voting shares or non-voting stock. While non-voting shares disadvantage their holders in terms of the lack of voting rights, in some countries they come with other, preferential rights. These preferential rights typically confer preferential dividend rights, such as a guaranteed dividend, and a higher seniority relative to ordinary shareholders. For example, in Germany non-voting shares are so-called preference shares or preferred stock. These preference shares earn a guaranteed or fixed dividend, normally a percentage of the shares' face value. If the firm's net earnings are sufficient to cover the guaranteed dividend, then the holders of the preference shares receive their guaranteed dividend *first*. If after the distribution of the guaranteed dividend the firm still has some net earnings left, it then distributes a variable dividend to the ordinary shareholders. If not all of the net earnings have been distributed by now, the preference shareholders will receive the equivalent dividend the ordinary shareholders receive. In the case

[5]See www.thetakeoverpanel.org.uk/the-code/download-code. See also Section 6.6 of Chapter 6
[6]Crespi, R. and Renneboog, L. (2010), 'Is (Institutional) Shareholder Activism New? Evidence from UK Shareholder Coalitions in the Pre-Cadbury Era', *Corporate Governance: An International Review* 18, 274–95.

where the firm cannot afford the fixed dividend, the fixed dividend will be carried over to the next year. After a number of years (which can vary according to the articles of association but cannot exceed three years) of non-payment of the guaranteed dividend, the preference shares receive a temporary voting right each until the arrears have been paid. Preference shareholders also have preferential access to the firm's assets if the firm is in financial distress or is simply in liquidation. The existence of the fixed dividend and the higher seniority relative to ordinary shares explains why in some countries, such as the UK, preference shares are considered to be debt rather than equity. Finally, in some countries preference shares have a limited life-time or maturity making them even more comparable to debt.

Dual-class shares are issued by some Continental European firms, but also some American firms. In Box 3.3 of Section 3.4, we already discussed the example of German firm Villeroy & Boch AG which has voting shares and non-voting shares outstanding, enabling its founding families to hold 100 per cent of the votes with only 50 per cent of the cash flow rights. Box 3.7 illustrates the use of dual-class shares in Ford Motor Company.

There are marked differences across countries in terms of the characteristics of dual-class shares and the legal restrictions applying to them. For example, in Sweden, class B shares carry ten votes each whereas class A shares carry only one vote each. As we have already seen, in Germany class A shares have no votes, but preferential dividend and liquidation rights. There are also differences in terms of the legal restrictions. These relate to the minimum proportion of votes that have to be attributed to the lower class and the maximum proportion of non-voting shares in a firm's equity capital. In Germany and Norway, non-voting shares cannot represent more than 50 per cent of the total equity book value.

Box 3.7
Ford Motor Company dual-class shares

FORD MOTOR COMPANY AND SUBSIDIARIES
CONSOLIDATED BALANCE SHEET
(in millions)

	December 31, 2015	December 31, 2014
ASSETS		
Cash and cash equivalents	$ 14,272	$ 10,757
Marietable securities	20,904	20,393
Finance receivables, net (Note 5)	90,691	81,111
Other receivables, net	11,284	11,708
Net investment in operating leases (Note 6)	27,093	23,217
Inventories (Note 8)	8,319	7,870
Equity in net assets or affilited compnies (Note 9)	3,224	3,357

(Continued)

Note property (Note 10)		30,163		30,126
Defered income taxes (Note 21)		11,509		14,024
Other assets		7,446		6,052
Total assets	$	224,925	$	208,615
LIABILITIES				
Payables	$	20,272	$	20,035
Other liabilities and deferred revenue (Note 11)		42,546		44,032
Automotive debt (Note 13)		12,839		13,824
Financial Services debt (Note 13)		120,015		105,347
Deferred income taxes (Note 21)		502		570
Total liabilities		196,174		183,808
Redeemable non-controlling interest (Note 14)		94		342
EQUITY				
Capital stock (Note 23)				
Common Stock par value $0.1 per share (3,960 million shares issued of 6 billion authorized)		40		39
Class B Stock, par value $.01 per share (71 million shares issued of 530 million authorized)		1		1
Capital in excess of par value of stock		21,421		21,089
Retained earnings		14,414		9,422
Accumulated other comprehensive income (loss) (Note 17)		(6,257)		(5,266)
Treasury stock		(977)		(848)
Total equity attributable to Ford Motor Company		28,642		24,438
Equity attributable to non-controlling interests		15		27
Total equity		28,657		24,465
Total liabilities and equity	$	224,925	$	208,616

NOTE 23. CAPITAL STOCK AND EARNINGS PER SHARE

All general voting power is vested in the holders of Common Stock and Class B Stock. Holders of our Common Stock have 60% of the general voting power and holders of our Class B Stock are entitled to such number of votes per share as will give them the remaining 40%. Shares of Common Stock and Class B Stock share equally in dividends when and as paid, with stock dividends payable in shares of stock of the class held.

If liquidated, each share of Common Stock is entitled to the first $0.50 available for distribution to holders of Common Stock and Class B Stock, each share of Class B Stock is entitled to the next $1.00 so available, each share of Common Stock is entitled to the next $0.50 so available, and each share of Common and Class B Stock is entitled to an equal amount thereafter.

Ford Motor Company has dual-class shares outstanding. The common stock represents roughly 98 per cent of the equity (40 / (40 + 1)) and the class B stock 2 per cent in 2015. However, the common stock has only 60 per cent of the votes compared to 40 per cent for class B.

Source: Ford Motor Company – 2016 annual report FS-4 & FS-58

The Ford family owns all of the company's Class B Stock as well as some of the company's common shares. The family benefits from a special right, conferred at the time of Ford's IPO, which gives it 40 per cent of the votes as long as it owns at least 60.7 million of the Class B Stock.

Source: Keith Brasher (2000), 'Ford Motor to Pay $10 Billion Dividend and Ensure Family Control', New York Times, 14 April, Section C, p.1

Finally, an alternative way of achieving strong control with widely held ownership is to confer additional voting rights to the company's long-term shareholders. Until 2004, many French companies did this via a clause in their articles of association. Such a clause was normally put in place at the time of the IPO and was frequently retrospective, i.e. it was applied to existing shares or stakes in the firm.[7] The example in Box 3.8 shows the attribution of double voting rights to shareholders who have held their shares for at least three years in French luxury conglomerate LVMH SA.

A new law, 'Loi Florange', came into effect on 29 March 2014. While French corporate law already allowed companies to confer double voting rights to their long-term shareholders, again companies had to do so via a clause in their articles of association. The new law moved France from an opt-in system to an opt-out system. As a result, unless French companies explicitly opt out, shareholders having held their shares for at least two years are automatically granted double voting rights.

Box 3.8
Double voting rights conferred to long-term shareholders of LVMH SA

The voting right attached to a share is proportional to the share of the capital it represents. When having the same nominal value, each share, either in capital or redeemed ("*de jouissance*"), gives right to one vote.

However a voting right equal to twice the voting right attached to other shares, with respect to the portion of the capital that they represent, is granted:

- to all fully paid up registered shares for which evidence of registration under the name of the same shareholder during at least three years will be brought
- to registered shares allocated to a shareholder in case of increase of the capital by capitalization of reserves, or of profits carried forward or of issue premiums due to existing shares for which it was entitled to benefit from this right

BREAKDOWN OF SHARE CAPITAL AND VOTING RIGHTS
(at December 31, 2015)

	Number of shares	Number of voting rights[1]	% of the share capital	% of voting rights
Arnault family group	236,512,738	460,819,281	46.64	62.90
Other	270,626,322	271,760,361	53.36	37.10
TOTAL	**507,139,110**	**732,579,642**	**100.00**	**100.00**

(1) Total number of voting rights that may be exercised at Shareholders' Meetings.

Source: LVMH Reference document 2014, Bylaws, p.247; LVMH annual report 2015, p.47

3.8 The consequences of dispersed ownership and strong control

Sanford Grossman and Oliver Hart argue that large stakes create benefits of control.[8] There are two types of benefits of control: security benefits and private benefits of control. Security benefits of control are those benefits from large stakes that are shared by *all* the shareholders. These benefits originate from the increase in

---

[7]Goergen, M., Renneboog, L. and Khurshed, A. (2006), 'Explaining the Diversity in Shareholder Lockup Agreements', *Journal of Financial Intermediation* 15, 254–80.

[8]Grossman, S.J and Hart, O.D. (1988), 'One Share-One Vote and the Market for Corporate Control', *Journal of Financial Economics* 20, 175–202.

firm value due to the monitoring of the management carried out by the large shareholder. Given the existence of a large shareholder, the management is less likely to expropriate the shareholders by pursuing their own interests rather than maximizing the firm value. The increase in firm value from the reduction in the agency costs benefits all the shareholders. We shall discuss the monitoring role of large shareholders in more detail in Section 8.10 of Chapter 8.

Conversely, private benefits of control often come at the expense of the minority shareholders. These are the benefits that the large shareholder extracts from the firm and only accrue to him. In Section 1.6 of Chapter 1 we already discussed some of these benefits. They include related-party transactions, i.e. tunnelling and transfer pricing, as well as nepotism and infighting. Private benefits of control are normally non-transferable, i.e. specific to the incumbent controlling shareholder. They are also difficult to observe and measure by outsiders compared to security benefits.

In the previous section, we have seen five ways of creating a wedge between the control held by the large shareholder and his ownership. In other words, these are all ways of creating a difference between control and ownership – or of violating the rule of one-share one-vote. The main consequence of the violation of this rule is the increase in private benefits of control for the large shareholder and the increased probability of minority shareholder expropriation.

While private benefits of control are thought to be difficult to quantify, there are nevertheless several empirical studies that have tried to do just that. One of the first such studies was the study by Michael Barclay and Clifford Holderness.[9] They measured the value of private benefits by the premium above the market price that the buyer of a block of shares pays to the seller. Jeffrey Zwiebel later on criticized this approach as being too simplistic.[10] He argued that one also needs to take into account the size of the block changing hands as this size will determine the size of the private benefits of control the holder can extract from the firm. Alexander Dyck and Luigi Zingales did precisely that in their study of premiums paid for blocks of shares across 39 countries.[11] They defined the block premium as the difference between the price per share paid for the block and the stock price two days after the announcement of the transfer of the block divided by the latter price and multiplied by the proportion of cash flow rights that the block represents.

Table 3.1 summarizes the results from their study. They found that the average block premium ranges from −4 per cent in Japan to a staggering 65 per cent in Brazil. Some of the countries with relatively low premiums, i.e. premiums of less than 3 per cent, include the UK and the USA, as well as the other Commonwealth countries of Australia, Canada, New Zealand, Singapore and South Africa. They also include Hong Kong and Taiwan as well as some of the Continental European countries, i.e. Finland, France, the Netherlands and Norway. Finally, there are two Continental European countries with relatively high block premiums: Austria and Italy.

Dyck and Zingales also investigated the factors that may drive the differences in the size of the block premium across countries. They found that in countries where block premiums are larger, ownership and control is more concentrated, stock markets are less developed and privatizations are less likely to occur. They also found that the size of the block premium depends negatively on institutional factors such as the levels of shareholder protection, law enforcement, accounting standards, product market competition and tax compliance (we shall return to this issue in Chapter 4).

[9]Barclay, M.J. and Holderness, C.G. (1989), 'Private Benefits from Control of Public Corporations', *Journal of Financial Economics* 25, 371–95.

[10]Zwiebel, J. (1995), 'Block Investment and Partial Benefits of Corporate Control', *Review of Economic Studies* 62, 161–85.

[11]Dyck, A. and Zingales, L. (2004), 'Private Benefits of Control: An International Comparison', *Journal of Finance* 59, 537–600.

Table 3.1 **Block premiums per country**

Country	Mean	Median	Minimum	Maximum	Number of Observations
Argentina	0.27	0.12	0.05	0.66	5
Australia	0.02	0.01	−0.03	0.11	12
Austria	0.38	0.38	0.25	0.52	2
Brazil	0.65	0.49	0.06	2.99	11
Canada	0.01	0.01	−0.02	0.06	4
Chile	0.18	0.15	−0.08	0.51	7
Colombia	0.27	0.15	0.06	0.87	5
Czech Republic	0.58	0.35	0.01	2.17	6
Denmark	0.08	0.04	−0.01	0.26	5
Egypt	0.04	0.04	0.01	0.07	2
Finland	0.02	0.01	−0.07	0.13	14
France	0.02	0.01	−0.10	0.17	4
Germany	0.10	0.11	−0.24	0.32	17
Hong Kong	0.00	0.02	−0.12	0.05	8
Indonesia	0.07	0.07	0.05	0.09	2
Israel	0.27	0.21	−0.01	0.89	9
Italy	0.37	0.16	−0.09	1.64	8
Japan	−0.04	−0.01	−0.34	0.09	21
Malaysia	0.07	0.05	−0.08	0.39	40
Mexico	0.34	0.47	−0.04	0.77	5
Netherlands	0.02	0.03	−0.07	0.06	5
New Zealand	0.03	0.04	−0.17	0.18	16
Norway	0.01	0.01	−0.05	0.13	12
Peru	0.14	0.17	0.03	0.23	3
Philippines	0.13	0.08	−0.40	0.82	15
Poland	0.13	0.12	0.02	0.28	4
Portugal	0.20	0.20	0.11	0.30	2
Singapore	0.03	0.03	−0.01	0.06	4
South Africa	0.02	0.00	0.00	0.07	4
South Korea	0.16	0.17	0.04	0.22	6
Spain	0.04	0.02	−0.03	0.13	5
Sweden	0.07	0.03	−0.01	0.22	11
Switzerland	0.06	0.07	0.01	0.15	8
Taiwan	0.00	0.00	−0.01	0.00	3
Thailand	0.12	0.07	−0.08	0.64	12
Turkey	0.37	0.11	0.05	1.41	5
United Kingdom	0.01	0.00	−0.06	0.17	41
United States	0.01	0.02	−0.20	0.25	46
Venezuela	0.27	0.28	0.04	0.47	4
Average/Number	0.14	0.11	−0.04	0.48	393

Notes: The block premium is the difference between the price per share paid for the block and the stock price two days after the announcement of the transfer of the block divided by the latter price and multiplied by the proportion of cash flow rights presented by the block.

Source: Adapted from Dyck, A. and Zingales, L. (2004), 'Private Benefits of Control: An International Comparison', *Journal of Finance* 59, table 2.

3.9 Conclusions

This chapter has reviewed the various combinations of ownership and control. The focus has been on the following four combinations: dispersed ownership and weak control (combination A), dispersed ownership and strong control (combination B), concentrated ownership and weak control (combination C), and concentrated ownership and strong control (combination D). It is important to identify the combination of ownership and control applying to a particular company as the type of combination determines the conflicts of interests that the company may suffer from, i.e. the classic principal-agent problem or the expropriation of minority shareholders.

The combination of ownership and control determines the main potential conflict of interests

A priori combination A is likely to apply in the UK and the USA whereas elsewhere combination D is likely to dominate. However, in practice in most companies from the rest of the world a range of mechanisms create a wedge between ownership and control. Hence, in most companies from the rest of the world it is combination B rather than combination D that prevails. While firms that have combination A or C in place are more likely to suffer from the principal-agent problem, i.e. conflicts of interests between the shareholders and the management, firms with combination B or D are more likely to suffer from conflicts of interests between the large shareholder and the minority shareholders.

Combination A prevails in the UK and the USA whereas combination B prevails elsewhere

Combination B can be obtained via a range of mechanisms including ownership pyramids, proxy votes, voting coalitions, dual-class shares and conferring additional votes to long-term shareholders. However, what all of these mechanisms have in common is that they confer more control rights to the large shareholder than cash flow rights. All mechanisms create a difference between ownership and control and therefore violate the rule of one-share one-vote. The violation of this rule has important consequences as it determines the size of private benefits of control the large shareholder may extract from the firm at the expense of the minority shareholders.

How to achieve combination B and its main consequence

3.10 Discussion questions

1 Adolf Berle and Gardiner Means argued that as companies become large, they experience a separation of ownership and control. For each of the four combinations of ownership and control reviewed in this chapter determine whether there is a separation of ownership and control and identify those that are in control and those that own the corporation.

2 'Most stock-market listed companies in Continental Europe are characterized by strong control and concentrated ownership'. (Anonymous)

Discuss the validity of the above statement.

3 Discuss the devices that make control different from ownership. What impact do differences between ownership and control have on the conflicts of interests that are likely to prevail in a corporation?

3.11 Exercises

1   Base yourself on the example in Box 3.5.

  (a) Determine the ownership the Agnelli family has in La Rinascente, a chain of Italian department stores.

  (b) Spot the incidences of cross-holdings or interlocks. These were defined in Chapter 2. As a reminder, they consist of two companies holding shares in each other. What are the possible corporate governance implications of these cross-holdings?

2   There is something interesting going on in terms of the relative importance of common stock over 2014 and 2015 in Ford Motor Company (see Box 3.7). Have you spotted it? What are the implications?

Reading list

Key reading

Becht, M. and Mayer, C. (2001), 'Introduction', in Barca, F. and M. Becht (eds.), *The Control of Corporate Europe*, Oxford, UK: Oxford University Press.

Grossman, S.J and Hart, O.D. (1988), 'One Share-One Vote and the Market for Corporate Control', *Journal of Financial Economics* 20, 175–202.

Further reading

Barclay, M.J. and Holderness, C.G. (1989), 'Private Benefits from Control of Public Corporations', *Journal of Financial Economics* 25, 371–95.

Dyck, A. and Zingales, L. (2004), 'Private Benefits of Control: An International Comparison', *Journal of Finance* 59, 537–600.

Grossman, S. and Hart, O. (1980), 'Takeover Bids, the Free-rider Problem, and the Theory of the Corporation', *Bell Journal of Economics* 11, 42–64.

Zwiebel, J. (1995), 'Block Investment and Partial Benefits of Corporate Control', *Review of Economic Studies* 62, 161–85.

Additional resources

See the author's blog post at www.profmarcgoergen.com/2014/10/danone-sa.html about the voting cap in Danone SA.

Macro corporate governance

PART II

4 Taxonomies of corporate governance systems

Chapter Aims

This chapter reviews the main taxonomies of corporate governance systems. Before proceeding with this review, the chapter discusses the economic and political context in which global capitalism has risen. In line with the book's philosophy of multidisciplinarity, this chapter reviews both the classifications based on the law and finance literature (La Porta et al. on the quality of law and investor protection; Pagano and Volpin on electoral systems; and Roe on political orientation of governments in power) and the varieties of capitalism (VOC) literature. An important distinction between the two is that the former prescribes a hierarchy of systems whereas the latter argues that very different institutional arrangements may generate similar economic performance.

Learning Outcomes

After reading this chapter, you should be able to:

1 Understand the economic and political context which has enabled global capital to rise

2 Critically review the assumptions underlying the taxonomies from the law and finance literature and those from the VOC literature

3 Assess the possible limitations of the various taxonomies as well as the validity of their predictions

4 Explain path dependence and distinguish between the two types of path dependence

4.1 Introduction

Chapter 2 pointed out the main differences in corporate control that exist across countries. Chapter 3 then jointly considered control and ownership, as the two can be combined in various ways. Identifying the specific combination of control and ownership that applies to a particular company – or even prevails in an entire country – is important as it determines the types of likely conflicts of interests between corporate stakeholders. The same chapter also highlighted the dangers of combining dispersed ownership with strong control. Indeed, this combination generates so-called private benefits of control, i.e. benefits which accrue to the controlling shareholder but at the expense of the other shareholders. Importantly, studies that have tried to quantify private benefits of control suggest that there is a link between the concentration of control on the one side and the size of private benefits of control, shareholder protection and the degree of development of capital markets on the other. The aim of this chapter, as well as the following chapters in this part of the book, is to explore this issue further. More generally, this chapter will review the various classifications or taxonomies of corporate governance systems and investigate how well they fit with the observed patterns of control and ownership across the world.

What is important to realize is that these various taxonomies have very different premises. For example, the taxonomies from the law and finance literature are based on rational individuals who maximize their utilities in the presence of institutions, such as law and the government, acting as constrainers on individual behaviour. The focus of most of this literature is on property rights, more specifically investor rights. Improving the rights of other stakeholders, such as workers, is seen to reduce property rights. In contrast, the varieties of capitalism literature does not assume that investor rights and worker rights are a zero-sum game as it is based on the concept of complementarities.

4.2 The economic and political context giving rise to global capitalism

Adolf Berle and Gardiner Means, in their widely cited book published in 1932 and entitled *The Modern Corporation and Private Property*, spelled out a new, important social phenomenon and a major step in the development of capitalism, which was the emergence of professional managers who run large corporations on behalf of their owners or shareholders.[1] The first major challenge faced by this new class of professional managers was the stock market crash of 1929 which caused the Great Depression of the 1930s. The Great Depression started major, government-run programmes worldwide to revive the economy. The most famous one was US President Franklin Delano Roosevelt's New Deal. In the USA, and as a direct response to the recent failures of its commercial banks, the Glass-Steagall Act of 1933 introduced a clear segmentation between commercial banks, which were to specialize in payment and financial intermediation, and investment banks which were to focus on the securities side. The Great Depression was followed by the Second World War.

In summer 1944, before the end of the Second World War, the Allied Nations gathered in Bretton Woods in the United States to design the post-war global economic system. The Bretton Woods agreement established a system of rules as well as new global institutions, including the International Monetary Fund (IMF) and the International Bank for Reconstruction and Development (IBRD), also referred to as the World Bank. The main feature of the Bretton Woods agreement was to put in place a system of fixed currency exchange rates pegged to the US dollar, which in turn was pegged to the price of gold. At the end of the Second World War, the USA as well as the Soviet Union emerged as the two main pillars of political power in the world.

The post-war period saw substantial improvements in workers' rights and the emergence of the welfare state. The social class of professional managers now faced the social class of blue-collar and white-collar workers who were represented by powerful trade unions. While Nazi Germany had had powerful industrial organizations (i.e. employer organizations) and conglomerates supporting the Hitler government in its war efforts, the Allies put in place a system of Co-determination, i.e. strong employee voice reflected by workers' councils and worker representation on the boards of directors of German corporations (see also Section 15.5 of Chapter 15). It is no surprise that Co-determination first started in the strategically important industries of coal and steel that had been fuelling the German war effort.

During the 1960s, Western economies experienced unprecedented economic growth (see Figure 4.1). However, the Bretton Woods system was already in a state of crisis at the beginning of the 1970s. The USA was experiencing a massive trade deficit due to its war with Vietnam. The USA financed her trade deficit by printing more and more US dollar notes which fuelled an increase in inflation. In 1971, US president Nixon decided to put an end to the convertibility of the dollar into gold. Inflationary pressures were further fuelled

[1]Berle, A. and Means, G. (1932), *The Modern Corporation and Private Property*, New York: Macmillan.

by the 1973–4 oil crisis. By 1976, the Bretton Woods agreement had completely broken down and all the major international currencies were now floating. Developed countries were experiencing the new economic phenomenon stagflation, i.e. stagnation combined with high inflation and unemployment. Rising oil prices and central banks' efforts to counteract these price increases fed an inflationary spiral of wage and price adjustments (see Figure 4.2). The combination of an economic recession with high inflation shattered the belief that Keynesian economic policies (Keynesianism), which consisted of strong government intervention during periods of recession to counteract the lack of demand from households and corporations, would be a way out of the economic crisis of the 1970s.

Figure 4.1 **GDP growth**
Notes: GDP growth is based on the annual growth rate of gross domestic product in constant year 2010 US dollars.
Source: World Development Indicators (edition February 2017)

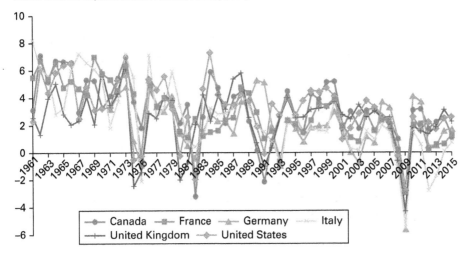

Figure 4.2 **Inflation rates**
Notes: Inflation rates are measured by the annual growth rate of the GDP implicit deflator which shows the rate of price change in the economy as a whole. The GDP implicit deflator is the ratio of GDP in current local currency to GDP in constant local currency.
Source: World Development Indicators (edition February 2017)

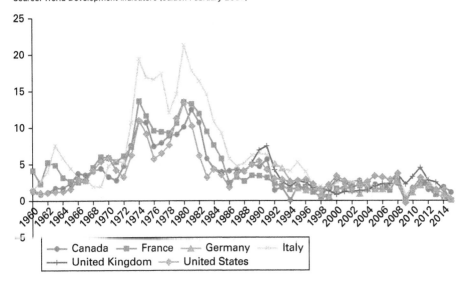

The 1970s provided an excellent breeding ground for neoliberalism or marketism to emerge as the new and increasingly dominant political ideology. Neoliberalism (called neo-conservatism in the USA) is the doctrine that, compared to governments, markets are better at allocating resources and ensuring economic efficiency and that individuals are better at making economic choices.[2] The next decades were to be dominated by what some call financialization and others call globalization or neoliberalism.[3] Financialization refers to two different, but related phenomena. First, it refers to the increasingly important role of capital markets and the financial services industry at a global level, taking over the key economic role that was previously assumed by the manufacturing industry. Second, financialization also refers to the process of turning any asset which generates cash flows into a financial security or a derivative of a financial security. Some argue that the latter meaning of financialization was the direct cause of the recent financial crisis. While it is impossible to give a complete account of the process of globalization and financialization in the short amount of space that is available here, this section will nevertheless try to outline the political and technological processes that fuelled this phenomenon.

In May 1979, the Conservative Party won the parliamentary elections in the UK and Margaret Thatcher became the Prime Minister. In 1980, Ronald Reagan, a Republican, became the President of the USA. Both Thatcher and Reagan engaged in ambitious programmes of market liberalization and deregulation. One of the major manifesto points of the Conservative Party in the UK was to 'roll back the frontiers of the state'.[4] Margaret Thatcher curbed trade union power with a succession of laws during the 1980s which put an end to closed trade union shops. As a result, trade union membership fell from roughly 50 per cent of the working population in 1979 to 33 per cent in 1990 when Margaret Thatcher resigned as Prime Minister (see Figure 4.3).

Figure 4.3 Trade union density in the UK
Notes: Union density is the number of trade union members as a percentage of the total working population eligible for trade union membership.
Source: Price and Bain, 1983 (for 1950–81); Department of Trade and Industry, 2006 (for 1982–88); *Labour Force Survey*, Office of National Statistics, 2015 (for 1989–2015)

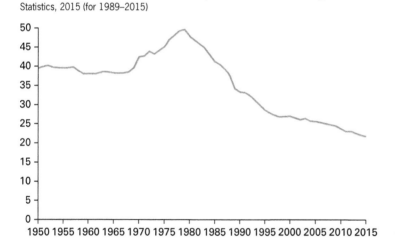

[2]For a critique of neoliberalism see Palma, J.G. (2009), 'The Revenge of the Market on the Rentiers. Why Neo-Liberal Reports of the End of History Turned Out to Be Premature', *Cambridge Journal of Economics* 33, 829–69.
[3]Dore, R. (2000), *Stock Market Capitalism: Welfare Capitalism. Japan and German versus the Anglo-Saxons*, Oxford, UK: Oxford University Press.
[4]Vickers, J. and Yarrow, G. (1988), *Privatization. An Economic Analysis*, Cambridge, MA: The MIT Press. See also Useem, M. (1990), 'Business and Politics in the United States and United Kingdom', in S. Zukin and P. DiMaggio, *Structures of Capitalism*, Cambridge, UK: Cambridge University Press.

Union membership has been falling ever since and in 2015 it dropped to slightly below 22 per cent. In the USA, union density fell from about 23.5 per cent in 1970 to 15.5 per cent in 1990.[5]

While the value of state-owned enterprises (SOEs) that were privatized during Margaret Thatcher's first term in office (1979–1983) was relatively negligible and did not exceed £500 million per year, annual privatization proceeds reached £5 billion during 1987–1990.[6] In fact, the UK was the first country in Europe to start an ambitious programme of privatizations, including well-known company names such as British Aerospace (privatized in 1981), British Telecom (1984), British Airways (1987) and Rolls Royce (1987). British Rail was privatized under John Major's Conservative government in 1993. Two of the major aims of the British privatization programme were to widen share ownership and to encourage employee share ownership. However, as Table 4.1 suggests, these aims were not achieved. Other European countries were to follow with their own privatization programmes as the percentage of shares owned by individuals dropped from a high of 54 per cent in 1963 to less than 12 per cent in 2015.

In the USA, Ronald Reagan was a fervent follower of a school of economic thought in direct contrast with Keynesianism. This school, called supply-side economics, argues that a necessary and sufficient condition to achieve economic growth is to reduce barriers to the supply side of the economy rather than stimulating the demand side. Such barriers include tax rates and regulation. Reagan's economic policies, nicknamed Reagonomics, consisted of keeping inflation low by controlling the supply of money, as well as reducing tax rates and government spending.

The 1970s and 1980s saw a wave of deregulation in the major financial markets. On 1 May 1975 (May Day), US stock exchanges moved from a system of fixed commissions to negotiated commissions. While shares of foreign companies could not be directly traded on an American stock exchange, American Depositary Receipts (ADRs) enabled foreign corporations to list indirectly, via an intermediary, in the USA (see also Section 10.4 of Chapter 10). The intermediary, typically a large American bank, would buy a block of shares in the foreign corporation and then issue ADRs, which would then trade on an American exchange. As a result of the reduction in trading costs induced by May Day, many large foreign companies issued ADRs and a major chunk of the trading in their shares moved to the USA.

In 1986, in reaction to the gradual loss of its business to the USA, the London Stock Exchange (LSE) underwent major changes, the so-called Big Bang. The most important change concerned removing the minimum commissions on trades of shares. These minimum commissions had applied to trades, irrespective of their size. This change enabled brokers to charge lower commissions on larger trades. Another important change in the UK concerned mutual building societies. During the 1980s and 1990s, a number of UK building societies changed their legal status to stock corporations, enabling them to apply for a stock-exchange listing. The main reason for doing so was the growing criticism that mutual forms of organization were inefficient and inferior to stock corporations (see also Section 1.7 of Chapter 1).

In 1985, Mikhail Gorbachev succeeded Leonid Brezhnev as the head of state of the Union of Soviet Socialist Republics (USSR). He is famous for his glasnost (opening of the Soviet Union) and perestroika (economic and political reform) policies. During the late 1980s, revolutions swept across the Communist Bloc, eventually resulting in its dismantling, the reunification of West and East Germany and the breakdown of the USSR into independent states with the remaining states forming the Russian Federation. The fall of the Communist Bloc was seen as proof that communism and socialism, until now serious alternatives to capitalism, do not work and are not sustainable.

---

[5]Visser, J. (2006), 'Union Membership Statistics in 24 Countries', *Monthly Labor Review* 1, 38–49.
[6]Op. cit. footnote 3.

Table 4.1 Beneficial ownership of UK quoted shares, 1963–2014

	1963	1969	1975	1981	1989	1990	1991	1992	1993	1994	1997	1998	1999	2000	2001	2002	2003	2004	2006	2008	2010	2012	2014
Rest of the world	7.0	6.6	5.6	3.6	12.8	11.8	12.8	13.1	16.3	16.3	28.0	30.7	33.0	35.7	35.7	35.9	36.1	36.3	40.0	41.5	43.4	53.2	53.8
Insurance companies	10.0	12.2	15.9	20.5	18.6	20.4	20.8	19.5	20.0	21.9	23.6	21.6	21.6	21.0	20.0	19.9	17.3	17.2	14.7	13.4	8.8	6.2	5.9
Pension funds	6.4	9.0	16.8	26.7	30.6	31.7	31.3	32.4	31.7	27.8	22.1	21.7	19.6	17.7	16.1	15.6	16.0	15.7	12.7	12.8	5.6	4.7	3.0
Individuals	54.0	47.4	37.5	28.2	20.6	20.3	19.9	20.4	17.7	20.3	16.5	16.7	15.3	16.0	14.8	14.3	14.9	14.1	12.8	10.2	10.2	10.7	11.9
Unit trusts	1.3	2.9	4.1	3.6	5.9	6.1	5.7	6.2	6.6	6.8	4.2	2.0	1.6	1.1	1.3	1.2	1.5	1.4	1.6	1.8	8.8	9.6	9.0
Investment trusts	11.3	10.1	10.5	6.8	1.6	1.6	1.5	2.1	2.5	2.0	1.2	1.3	1.2	1.3	1.6	1.3	1.7	2.5	2.4	1.9	2.1	1.7	1.8
Other financial institutions					1.1	0.7	0.8	0.4	0.6	1.3	1.3	2.7	3.1	2.8	7.2	7.7	8.3	8.2	9.6	10.0	12.3	6.6	7.1
Charities	2.1	2.1	2.3	2.2	2.3	1.9	2.4	1.8	1.6	1.3	1.9	1.4	1.3	1.4	1.0	1.1	1.2	1.1	0.9	0.8	0.8	0.6	1.2
Private non-financial companies	5.1	5.4	3.0	5.1	3.8	2.8	3.3	1.8	1.5	1.1	1.2	1.4	2.2	1.5	1.0	0.8	0.7	0.6	1.8	3.0	2.3	2.3	2.0
Public sector	1.5	2.6	3.6	3.0	2.0	2.0	1.3	1.8	1.3	0.8	0.1	0.1	0.1	–	–	0.1	0.1	0.1	0.1	1.1	3.1	2.5	2.9
Banks	1.3	1.7	0.7	0.3	0.7	0.7	0.2	0.5	0.6	0.4	0.1	0.6	1.0	1.4	1.3	2.1	2.2	2.7	3.4	3.5	2.5	1.9	1.4
Total	100.0	100.0	100.0	100.0	100.0	100.0	100.0	100.0	100.0	100.0	100.0	100.0	100.0	100.0	100.0	100.0	100.0	100.0	100.0	100.0	100.0	100.0	100.0

Source: Office of National Statistics

During this period of upheaval, another Communist country, China started a programme of ambitious economic reforms that gave managers of SOEs more discretion and transferred some of the corporate decision making from the government to the firm. The Chinese government set up the Shenzhen Stock Exchange in 1990 and the Shanghai Stock Exchange in 1991. By 2002, their combined market capitalization already amounted to 45 per cent of China's GDP. At its 14th National Congress held in 1992, the Communist Party of China, under the leadership of Deng Xiaoping, endorsed the move to a socialist market economy. While a dual pricing system for goods and services had been in operation between 1985 and 1991, with prices being fixed by the state and by the market, there was a gradual move towards pricing by the market and a phasing out of the dual system. Steps to introduce private ownership go back to the mid-1980s, when Chinese-foreign joint-ventures and the first stock corporations as well as township and village enterprises emerged. However, during the 1990s, political and academic discourse in China further shifted towards advocating private property as a means towards prosperity and that share ownership could be used both by socialist and capitalist systems. While previously it had been argued that the main difference between a socialist and capitalist system was the existence of private property in the latter and its absence from the former, the main difference between the two was now seen to be the greater fairness of the former.[7]

In 1992, the Single European Act came into effect in the European Union (EU). It removed barriers to capital flows and the movement of citizens between the member states of the EU. It brought about a liberalization of financial as well as labour markets. In the USA, the Gramm-Leach-Bliley Act of 1999 practically repealed the 1933 Glass-Steagall Act enabling banks to engage in both commercial banking and securities business and to have their subsidiaries conduct financial activities that the banks themselves were not allowed to carry out (see also Section 16.5 of Chapter 16 about the effects of this deregulation). Some argue that this deregulation ultimately caused the 2008 financial crisis. Others argue that it was brought about by low interest rates and hence the availability of cheap credit. Still, Germany and Japan since their industrialization have only ever known the system of universal banks, i.e. banks that conduct both commercial lending and engage in securities business.

There were also major technological changes during the 1980s and 1990s which increased the pace of globalization and the integration of national capital markets. These include advances in information technology with the advent of the personal computer, breakthroughs in communication technology such as mobile telephony and, last but not least, the invention of the internet. All of these have improved the access to information as well as reduced its cost. In particular, the internet is likely to remove the costs of voting for small shareholders and there is early indication that social media, such as Twitter, have increased levels of shareholder activism.

While the role of the state in the economy has been reduced over the last decades, we shall see in Chapter 6 that since the 1990s, there has been a steady increase in codes of best practice and regulation trying to constrain opportunistic behaviour by managers. Finally, the years following the 2008 financial crisis have been marked by major cuts in government spending, i.e. austerity programmes, across the world, further reducing the role of the public sector in the economy.

However, despite all these political and technological changes, we shall see in this chapter that national systems of corporate governance still have major idiosyncrasies which set them apart and which are likely to persist over the next decades. There is little evidence of *rapid* convergence towards the Anglo-American system of corporate governance. Brexit is likely to put a damper on convergence between the UK and the rest of the EU.

---

[7]Ezzamel, M., Xiao, J.Z. and Pan, A. (2007), 'Political Ideology and Accounting Regulation in China', *Accounting, Organizations and Society* 32, 669–700.

4.3 First attempts to classify corporate governance systems

The British economist Sir John Hicks and the American business historian Alfred Chandler Jr. were the first to attempt to categorize the different systems of capitalism.[8] Hicks distinguished between market-based economies and bank-based economies. The former relied on well developed capital markets and the issue of publicly traded securities to finance investments by corporations. Colin Mayer found empirical evidence in support of the Hicks classification as bank loans in France, Germany and Japan are significantly more important sources of corporate financing than in the UK and the USA.[9] Chandler studied the differences between American, British, German and Japanese capitalism from a historical perspective.

Mark Roe also highlighted the importance of history and past regulation in order to understand differences across countries in terms of the organization of their industrial production and corporate governance.[10] In particular, regulation pertaining to the banking industry has had a major impact on whether national corporate governance systems developed into market-based or bank-based systems. In the USA, the Glass-Steagall Act of 1933 and the Bank Holding Company Act of 1956 prevented banks from holding direct equity stakes in commercial and industrial companies. While other financial institutions, such as mutual funds, pension funds and insurance companies, could hold stakes in such companies they were restricted to a maximum stake in order to prevent them from having control over their investee firms. Similarly, in the UK there is a limit as to the stake an insurance company can hold in an industrial company. Conversely, there are no restrictions as to bank ownership of industrial corporations in France and Germany. In Chapter 3, we also saw the importance of proxy votes, which increase the influence of banks beyond the direct stakes they hold.

In line with Douglas Diamond's model of delegated monitoring, a strong role of banks as providers of finance to corporations potentially creates value, as banks benefit from synergies when monitoring other companies and hence provide monitoring at a lower cost than if debt were in the form of traded securities that are widely held.[11] However, powerful banks may also limit the development of capital markets and the availability of publicly traded equity and debt securities. Powerful banks will not only have an impact on the ways companies finance their investment but they will also determine the types of investments available to households: in market-based systems households will invest a significant proportion of their wealth in equity whereas in bank-based systems they will mostly hold cash and bonds.[12]

Julian Franks and Colin Mayer developed a more nuanced classification which does not focus on the sources of financing available to corporations.[13] They distinguished between the insider system and the outsider system. The insider system is characterized by concentrated control and complex ownership structures, including ownership pyramids and cross-holdings. Managers are monitored by the large shareholder, frequently the founding family. The large shareholder is typically represented on the board of directors and is also frequently directly involved in the management of the company. Given the concentration of control, the takeover market is underdeveloped and hostile takeovers are virtually unheard of. Stock markets are also relatively underdeveloped. This system is referred to as the insider system, as the monitoring of the management is mainly done by

[8]Hicks, J. (1969), *A Theory of Economic History*, Oxford, UK: Clarendon Press. Chandler, A.D., Jr. (1977), *The Visible Hand: The Managerial Revolution in American Business*, Cambridge, MA: The Belknap Press of Harvard University Press. Chandler, A.D., Jr. (1984), 'The Emergence of Managerial Capitalism', *Business History Review* 58, 473–503.

[9]Mayer, C. (1988), 'New Issues in Corporate Finance', *European Economic Review* 32, 1167–89.

[10]Roe, M.J. (1994), *Strong Managers. Weak Owners. The Political Roots of American Corporate Finance*. Princeton, NJ: Princeton University Press.

[11]Diamond, D.W. (1984), 'Financial Intermediation and Delegated Monitoring', *Review of Economic Studies* 51, 393–414.

[12]Allen, F. and Gale, D. (2000), *Comparing Financial Systems*, Cambridge, MA: MIT Press.

[13]Franks, J. and Mayer, C. (2001), 'Ownership and Control of German Corporations', *Review of Financial Studies* 14, 943–77.

the large shareholder, i.e. one of the company's insiders. Continental European countries are representatives of the insider system. Conversely, the outsider system is characterized by dispersed ownership and control, well developed stock markets – including a large number of listed firms – and an active takeover market. This system is called the outsider system given that badly performing managers are disciplined by outsiders, in particular hostile raiders that are on the lookout for firms whose stock price has suffered a major decline because of bad management. The mere threat of a hostile takeover puts pressure on the managers to act in the interests of their shareholders. The UK and the USA are representatives of the outsider system.

Lucian Bebchuk and Mark Roe provided a more general and formalized account of how the past shapes a country's current corporate governance.[14] They argued that there are two forms of path dependence. There is structure-driven path dependence as current corporate governance arrangements and current corporate control structures depend on the structures that were initially in place. There is also rule-driven path dependence. Current regulation is influenced by the corporate structures that were initially in place in the country. In particular, powerful economic actors are likely to resist changes in regulation which will harm their own interests even though these changes would have brought about more efficient regulation and better corporate governance. The characteristics of each national corporate governance system will tend to persist over time given that there is both structure-driven and rule-driven dependence.

4.4 Legal families

Rafel La Porta, Florencio Lopez-de-Silanes, Andrei Shleifer and Robert Vishny started the so-called law and finance literature by developing a new, path-breaking theory which explains differences in corporate governance and the development of stock markets.[15] Their theory is based on the importance of property rights, in particular investor protection. They argued that in countries where investor protection is high, capital markets will be highly developed, as investors are willing to invest in equity and debt securities. Conversely, countries with weak investor protection have underdeveloped capital markets, as investors are concerned about parting with their funds. Ultimately, the degree of protection that investors enjoy has consequences not only for the development of stock markets, but also for economic growth. Indeed, if investors are well protected, funding for corporate investments is easily available as well as relatively cheap.

If investors are well protected, then conflicts of interests between them and the managers can be kept at bay. At the worst, investors may need to take the managers to court to enforce their rights. In turn, better investor protection guarantees that a greater part of the firm's cash flows is paid out to the investors in the form of dividends and stock repurchases. In contrast, if the legal protection of investor rights is low, then a considerable part of the firm's cash flows may be wasted by the managers and may be used by them to entrench themselves. In other words, La Porta et al. argued that good law reduces the principal-agent problem. They distinguished between two main legal families, i.e. common law and civil law. Common law is case-based law. In the common law system, the judges are the lawmakers as they pronounce judgements based on the cases that are presented to them and these judgements then create precedents for other, similar future cases. In contrast, civil law, which originates from Roman law, is based on extensive codes of law such as the Napoleonic code of law. The role of

---

[14]Bebchuk, L. and Roe, M. (1999), 'A Theory of Path Dependence in Corporate Governance and Ownership', *Stanford Law Review* 53, 127–70.

[15]See e.g. La Porta, R., Lopez-de-Silanes, F., Shleifer, A. and Vishny, R. (1997), 'Legal Determinants of External Finance', *Journal of Finance* 52, 1131–50. La Porta, R., Lopez-de-Silanes, F., Shleifer, A. and Vishny, R. (1998), 'Law and Finance', *Journal of Political Economy* 106, 1113–55.

the judges is limited to the interpretation of the law texts in a court of law and the judges are merely the mouth of the law. According to La Porta et al., the fact that common law is case-based makes it more flexible than civil law. While the former can easily adapt to new forms of managerial misuse of shareholder funds, the latter will always lag behind managers' ingenuity as it relies on rewriting and supplementing existing codes of law to adapt to new forms of shareholder abuse by the managers.

Common law is the law of the UK, the USA, as well as most of the former colonies of the UK. In terms of civil law, La Porta et al. further distinguished between French (or Latin) civil law, German civil law and Scandinavian civil law. In their 1998 study, La Porta et al. measured the protection of shareholders from managerial abuses as well as the protection of creditors for a total of 49 countries.[16] Table 4.2 shows the values per country for their measure of investor protection – the antidirector rights index – and their measure of creditor protection. The antidirector rights index measures how well shareholders are protected against the management or the large shareholder. It ranges from 0 to 6. It increases by 1 for each of the following criteria that is met: shareholders can mail their proxy votes, shareholders are not required to deposit their shares before the AGM, cumulative voting is allowed, minority shareholders are protected, shareholders have a pre-emptive right to buy newly issued shares, and the percentage of shares required to call an extraordinary shareholders meeting is 10 per cent or less. As an additional measure, one-share one-vote is set to 1 if the one-share one-vote rule is upheld and 0 otherwise. The creditor rights index measures how well creditor rights are protected. It ranges from 0 to 4. It increases by 1 for each of the following criteria that is met: secured creditors can withdraw their collateral before the completion of the reorganization, secured creditors have the right to collateral in the reorganization, creditors' approval is needed before managers can file for reorganization, and managers are replaced by a third party appointed by the creditors or the court while the reorganization is pending. Shareholder protection and creditor protection are highest in common law countries and lowest in French civil law countries. Countries with German law and Scandinavian law are somewhere in between.

La Porta et al. also studied the link between investor and creditor protection on the one side and the size of capital markets on the other. They found that stock markets, as measured by the number of domestic listed firms, are largest in common law countries and smallest in French law countries. Countries of German and Scandinavian law are somewhere in between. This suggests that the greater the investor protection the larger the stock market. However, when the size of the stock market is measured by the value of IPO shares over GDP, the relationship between shareholder protection and stock market size is somewhat less clear. The relationship between the La Porta et al. creditor protection index and the size of the debt market (as measured by the ratio of the sum of bank debt of the private sector and bonds issued by non-financial firms over GNP) is also somewhat ambiguous as German law countries have larger debt markets than common law countries. However, French law countries still rank at the bottom of the league in terms of the size of debt markets. Finally, La Porta et al. investigated the link between investor protection and ownership concentration. In line with their expectations, they found that ownership concentration is highest in French law countries. They interpreted this as evidence that ownership stays concentrated and does not disperse in countries with weak legal systems in order to avoid expropriation by managers. In other words, ownership concentration seems to act as a substitute for low investor protection. To summarize, there is evidence that the size of capital markets and ownership dispersion increase with investor protection.

---

[16]There is also an updated version of the La Porta et al. study which covers 72 countries (Djankov, S., La Porta, R., Lopez-de-Silanes, F. and Shleifer, A. 'The Law and Economics of Self-Dealing', *Journal of Financial Economics* 88, 430–65). However, this study no longer includes the measure for creditor protection.

Table 4.2 La Porta et al.'s indices of investor protection and creditor protection and size of capital markets

Country	Antidirector rights index	One-share one-vote rule	Creditor rights index	No. of domestic listed firms/ population	IPO value/ GDP	Debt/ GNP	Ownership held by three largest shareholders
Australia	4	0	1	64.61	8.71	0.76	0.28
Canada	5	0	1	77.34	8.57	0.72	0.40
Hong Kong	5	0	4	103.99	9.12		0.54
India	5	0	4	6.03	0.60	0.29	0.40
Ireland	4	1	1	21.54	6.09	0.68	0.39
Israel	3	0	4	108.67	0.39	0.66	0.51
Kenya	3	1	4	2.00	0.71		
Malaysia	4	0	4	32.55	6.18	0.84	0.54
New Zealand	4	0	3	36.46	0.06	0.90	0.48
Nigeria	3	0	4	1.59	0.00		0.40
Pakistan	5	0	4	5.88	0.40	0.27	0.37
Singapore	4	0	4	83.28	5.94	0.60	0.49
South Africa	5	0	3	15.51	0.65	0.93	0.52
Sri Lanka	3	0	3	12.61	0.50	0.25	0.60
Thailand	2	1	3	6.91	0.82	0.93	0.47
UK	5	0	4	34.65	11.27	1.13	0.19
US	5	0	1	29.83	5.47	0.81	0.20
Zimbabwe	3	0	4	5.71	1.29		0.55
English law average	*4.00*	*0.17*	*3.11*	*36.06*	*3.71*	*0.70*	*0.43*
Austria	2	0	3	12.29	1.16	0.79	0.58
Germany	1	0	3	9.93	2.78	1.12	0.48
Japan	4	0	2	19.27	2.39	1.22	0.18
South Korea	2	1	3	20.49	5.32	0.74	0.23
Switzerland	2	1	1	32.34	7.11		0.41
Taiwan	3	0	2	20.20	10.07		0.18
German law average	*2.33*	*0.33*	*2.33*	*19.09*	*4.81*	*0.97*	*0.34*
Argentina	4	1	1	3.71	0.56	0.19	0.53
Belgium	0	0	2	15.58	2.35	0.38	0.54
Brazil	3	0	1	3.08	0.05	0.39	0.57
Chile	5	0	2	19.02	0.51	0.63	0.45
Colombia	3	0	0	4.00	0.01	0.19	0.63
Ecuador	2	0	4	2.94	0.00		
Egypt	2	1	4	13.82	2.22		0.62

Country	Antidirector rights index	One-share one-vote rule	Creditor rights index	No. of domestic listed firms/ population	IPO value/ GDP	Debt/ GNP	Ownership held by three largest shareholders
France	3	1	0	13.17	2.31	0.96	0.34
Greece	2	0	1	24.87	8.78	0.23	0.67
Indonesia	2	0	4	1.36	1.67	0.42	0.58
Italy	1	1	2	4.47	5.94	0.55	0.58
Jordan	1	0		28.60	0.00	0.70	
Mexico	1	1	0	2.00	0.22	0.47	0.64
Netherlands	2	0	2	13.70	2.63	1.08	0.39
Peru	3	0	0	9.75	0.04	0.27	0.56
Philippines	3	0	0	3.02	2.22	0.10	0.57
Portugal	3	0	1	13.55	2.27	0.64	0.52
Spain	4	0	2	15.00	2.41	0.75	0.51
Turkey	2	0	2	4.29	1.48	0.15	0.59
Uruguay	2	0	2	5.29	0.00	0.26	
Venezuela	1	0		3.83	0.68	0.10	0.51
French law average	*2.33*	*0.22*	*1.63*	*9.76*	*1.73*	*0.45*	*0.54*
Denmark	2	0	3	44.30	1.20	0.34	0.45
Finland	3	1	1	24.23	3.78	0.75	0.37
Norway	4	0	2	43.00	2.20	0.64	0.36
Sweden	3	0	2	29.39	6.33	0.55	0.28
Scandinavian law average	*3.00*	*0.25*	*2.00*	*35.23*	*3.38*	*0.57*	*0.37*

Notes: The antidirector rights index ranges from 0 to 6. It increases by 1 for each of the following criteria that are met: shareholders can mail their proxy votes, shareholders are not required to deposit their shares before the AGM, cumulative voting is allowed, minority shareholders are protected, shareholders have a pre-emptive right to buy newly issued shares, and the percentages of shares required to call an extraordinary shareholders meeting is 10 per cent or less. One-share one-vote is set to 1 if the one-share one-vote rule is upheld and 0 otherwise. The creditor rights index ranges from 0 to 4. It increases by 1 for each of the following criteria that are met: secured creditors can withdraw their collateral before the completion of the reorganization, secured creditors have the right to collateral in the reorganization, creditors' approval is needed before managers can file for reorganization, and managers are replaced by a third party appointed by the creditors or the court while the reorganization is pending. The number of domestic listed firms over the population (in millions) and the value of IPO shares over GDP (in thousands) are average numbers over 1996–2000. Debt over GNP is the ratio of the sum of bank debt by the private sector and bonds issued by non-financial firms over GNP for 1994. Ownership held by the three largest shareholders is the proportion of ownership of common stock held by the three largest shareholders in the ten largest non-financial and non-government owned companies in 1994.

Source: Based on table II, p.1138 from La Porta, R., Lopez-de-Silanes, F., Shleifer, A. and Vishny, R. (1997), 'Legal Determinants of External Finance', *Journal of Finance* 52, 1131–50. Table 7, p.1147, from La Porta, R., Lopez-de-Silanes, F., Shleifer, A. and Vishny, R. (1998), 'Law and Finance', *Journal of Political Economy* 106, 1113–55. Additional material and updates from www.economics.harvard.edu/faculty/shleifer/dataset (accessed on 21 April 2011)

4.5 Political determinants of corporate governance

Mark Roe proposed politics and political ideology as the main driver behind corporate governance.[17] In fact, political ideology determines how different countries achieve social peace. Roe argued that differences in political ideology explain the marked differences between the corporate governance systems of Continental Europe and the USA. The Continental European social democracies have achieved social peace by favouring employees over investors. Layoffs will be relatively hard even though they may increase economic efficiency; unemployment benefits will be high as will unemployment rates. Managers will less likely focus exclusively on the maximization of shareholder value. High incentive packages for managers will also be less common, given the resulting envy from other social classes. There will be less takeover activity as takeovers may generate layoffs. In summary, social democracies will seek social equality at the cost of economic efficiency. As a result of the focus of social democracies on employees rather than investors, control and ownership will remain concentrated as this is the only way to keep managers and employees at bay. In contrast, in countries with more Conservative governments, the focus will be on improving the rights of investors rather than those of workers. Given the strong legal protection of investor rights, ownership and control will separate and large corporations will be characterized by diffuse ownership and control. Mark Roe tested the validity of his prediction for OECD countries and found support for it: corporate ownership and control are more concentrated in countries with more left-wing governments.

Marco Pagano and Paolo Volpin proposed an alternative theory based on electoral systems.[18] They argued that the outcome of the trade-off between strong investor protection and strong employee rights will depend on the type of electoral system. They distinguished between majoritarian electoral systems and proportional electoral systems. Their theoretical model is based on three different types of economic actors: managers, employees and so-called *rentiers*. Managers run the firms on behalf of the rentiers, but do not themselves own shares. Rentiers live off the revenues of their investments. Managers and employees have relatively similar preferences as they both prefer weaker investor rights. Weaker investor rights give more power to the managers and make it easier for them to extract private benefits of control from their firms. Weaker investor rights also provide better job security for employees, in particular less productive employees that would otherwise face dismissal. In contrast, the rentiers have much less homogenous preferences. Under a majoritarian system, in order to win the elections a political party will need to win a majority of electoral districts. Pagano and Volpin assumed that the pivotal district is the district of the rentiers. Hence, in a majoritarian system political parties will focus on rentiers and cater for their preferences, i.e. improvements in investor protection. In a proportional system, the political party that obtains a majority of votes will win the elections. Hence, political parties will concentrate on winning the votes of the homogenous social groups of the managers and the employees. In turn, the focus will be on employee rights at the expense of weaker investor protection.

Pagano and Volpin tested their theory on 21 OECD countries (see Table 4.3). In line with their predictions, they found that countries with more proportional voting systems tend to have stronger employment protection and weaker investor rights. They also ran two separate linear regressions: one to explain the level of investor protection and another one to explain the level of worker rights. They found that both are driven by the proportionality of the electoral system. However, the legal family the country belongs to only has an influence on the level of worker rights, but *not* on the level of investor protection. Hence, Pagano and Volpin concluded that the proportionality of the electoral system is better at explaining the level of investor rights than the type of legal family.

---

[17] Roe, M.J. (2003), *The Political Determinants of Corporate Governance*, Oxford, UK: Oxford University Press.
[18] Pagano, M. and Volpin, P. (2005), 'The Political Economy of Corporate Governance', *American Economic Review* 95, 1005–30.

Table 4.3 Antidirector index, employment protection, proportionality rule and legal family

Country	Antidirector index	Employment protection	Proportionality
Australia	4	1.06	1
Canada	5	0.63	0
Ireland	4	1.00	3
New Zealand	4	1.01	0
UK	5	0.51	0
USA	5	0.22	0
English law average	*4.50*	*0.74*	*0.67*
Austria	2	2.39	3
Germany	1	3.55	2
Japan	4	2.64	0
Switzerland	2	1.27	2
German law average	*2.25*	*2.46*	*1.75*
Belgium	0	3.02	3
France	3	2.73	1
Greece	2	3.61	2
Italy	1	4.15	3
Netherlands	2	3.06	3
Portugal	3	4.20	3
Spain	4	3.66	2
French law average	*2.14*	*3.49*	*2.43*
Denmark	2	2.43	3
Finland	3	2.22	3
Norway	4	3.09	3
Sweden	3	3.45	3
Scandinavian law average	*3.00*	*2.80*	*3.00*

Notes: The antidirector index is taken from table 5, pp. 1142–3, from La Porta, R., Lopez-de-Silanes, F., Shleifer, A. and Vishny, R. (1998), 'Law and Finance', *Journal of Political Economy* 106, 1113–55. Employment protection is the 1990 average of the OECD Employment Protection Legislation (EPL) indicators for regular contracts (procedural inconveniences, notice and severance pay for no-fault individual dismissals, difficulty of dismissal) and for short-term (fixed-term and temporary) contracts. Proportionality measures the proportional nature of the electoral system. It equals 0 if none of the seats is allocated via proportional rule, 1 if a minority of seats are allocated via this rule, 2 if the majority of seats are allocated proportionally and 3 if all of the seats are allocated proportionally.

Source: Based on table 2 of Pagano, M. and Volpin, P. (2005), 'The Political Economy of Corporate Governance', *American Economic Review* 95, table 2.

4.6 The varieties of capitalism literature

So far, the focus of this chapter has been on the so-called law and finance literature which argues that the main role of institutions is to constrain the behaviour of economic actors such as managers and employees. While Mark Roe's theory on politics did not pronounce any judgement as to which system – the social democracies of Continental Europe or the market-oriented economies of the UK and the USA – is superior, his theory nevertheless made the same assumption as the other two law and finance theories – that strong investor rights *cannot* coexist with strong employment protection. More specifically, Roe argued that the focus of social democracies on employee welfare rather than on shareholder value maximization explains why ownership and control in

Continental Europe is so concentrated: shareholders need to be strong to face managers and employees who have strong legal rights in order to mitigate agency problems. While Roe did not advocate for the superiority of a particular system, La Porta et al. as well as Pagano and Volpin clearly stated that systems with stronger investor rights are superior to those with stronger employment protection.

In contrast, the so-called varieties of capitalism (VOC) literature does not necessarily favour a particular system. For example, Peter Hall and David Soskice studied a wide range of questions relating to the distribution of wealth and the resolution of coordination problems in economies.[19] [20] Hall and Soskice argued that economic systems are not just about investments in assets and technologies, but also about investments in human capital such as the development of workers' skills and competencies. The way economic coordination problems are resolved depends on whether an economy is a liberal market economy (LME) or a coordinated market economy (CME) (see Figure 4.4).

Figure 4.4 Complementarities in the VOC literature
Source: Hall, P.A. and Soskice, D. (2001), *Varieties of Capitalism: The Institutional Foundations of Comparative Advantage*, Oxford, UK: Oxford University Press, figure 1.

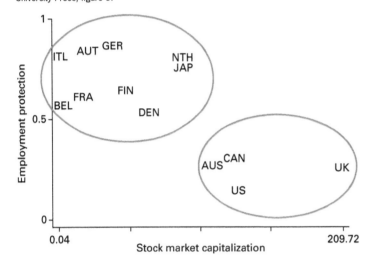

In LMEs, the coordination mechanism is the markets. Labour markets and markets for assets are both highly flexible and well developed. Given the emphasis on markets, firms tend to invest in highly marketable and liquid assets that can easily be sold or transferred should the need arise. There is an emphasis on assets that have relatively short payback periods and generate fairly quick cash flows. Firms tend to keep the training of their employees to a minimum as there is the danger that competitors may free-ride on a particular firm's training efforts by poaching its employees once they have been fully trained. Innovation in LMEs is mainly of the blue

[19]Hall, P.A. and Soskice, D. (2001), *Varieties of Capitalism: The Institutional Foundations of Comparative Advantage*, Oxford, UK: Oxford University Press.
[20]Strictly speaking, Hall and Soskice's work is the culmination of a tradition of work by Dore and by Lincoln and Kalleberg advocating a more stakeholder-oriented approach to corporate governance. In contrast to Hall and Soskice, Dore et al. argued that more stakeholder-oriented varieties of capitalism are superior to other varieties. In part, their view as to the superiority of stakeholder-based systems is based on the better economic performance of Germany and Japan relative to the UK and the USA in the 1980s. See e.g. Dore, R. (2000), *Stock Market Capitalism: Welfare Capitalism*, Cambridge, UK: Cambridge University Press; and Lincoln, J. and Kalleberg, A. (1990), *Culture, Control and Commitment: A Study of Work Organization in the United States and Japan*, Cambridge, UK: Cambridge University Press.

skies nature. LMEs tend to excel in highly competitive, innovative industries as well as low value-added services industries. The UK, the USA and Australia are examples of LMEs.

In contrast, CMEs are based on complex networks used to coordinate economic decision making. Markets such as the labour market and the capital market are fairly illiquid and inflexible. Hence, there is less focus on highly liquid and generic assets and the emphasis tends to be on more specific, less marketable assets. Firms provide in-house, industry-specific training for their workers and powerful employers' associations police firms to ensure that none free-ride on their competitors' training efforts by poaching their employees. Strong employment protection and inflexible labour markets provide workers with the right incentives to invest over the long term in their human capital by acquiring highly firm-specific skills and competencies. CMEs tend to do relatively well in industries associated with incremental innovation such as high value-added manufacturing. Examples of CMEs are France, Germany and Italy.

At the base of the VOC literature lies the concept of complementarities. Two institutions have **complementarities** if their joint existence increases the efficiency of one or both. This implies that substantially different sets of institutions may still generate very similar levels of economic output and wealth creation.

4.7 How do the various taxonomies perform?

While the first attempts to arrive at taxonomies of corporate governance systems consisted of finding commonalities as well as differences across countries, later attempts had a theoretical foundation, generating predictions as to how various institutional arrangements may have come about and/or how existing institutional arrangements may explain differences in corporate governance and corporate or economic performance.

One of the basic criticisms that can be made about the La Porta et al. thesis on the importance of legal families is that it is entirely static.[21] Taken to an extreme, today's characteristics of the Italian corporate governance system are mainly due to what happened in the distant past, starting with the 12 Tables which laid down the foundations of Roman law in the fifth century BC. Hence, La Porta et al. assumed that once a country has adopted a certain legal system, it will be stuck with it and this system will determine economic development and the set-up of institutions for centuries or even millennia to come. In other words, their thesis relies heavily on path dependence. La Porta et al. justified the static nature of their theory by stating that law only changes slowly over time and that it is very difficult for a country to carry out significant reforms of its legal system within a short amount of time. However, if one studies recent developments, Japan springs to mind, as it has reformed its takeover regulation by adopting a US Delaware case-based approach even though it is part of the German civil law family which would assume a code-driven rather than a case-based approach to law and regulation. Finally, Aldo Musacchio and John Turner investigated whether the law and finance literature stands the test of history. They found that economic and political crises, conflict and inflation are much better at explaining differences in corporate governance and financial development than legal origin.[22]

Apart from this fairly general criticism, more specific critiques of La Porta et al. have also been made. The main four critiques concern the way La Porta et al. measured investor protection; encoding errors in their antidirector rights index; the possibility that law and legal families are merely proxies for other factors, such as culture, that are the true drivers behind the differences in corporate governance across countries; and that ownership dispersion in the UK could be observed before investor protection was in place. The first critique

[21]Pagano, M. and Volpin, P. (2001), 'The Political Economy of Finance', *Oxford Review of Economic Policy* 17, 502–19.
[22]Musacchio, A. and Turner, J.D. (2013), 'Does the Law and Finance Hypothesis Pass the Test of History?', *Business History* 55, 524–42.

was formulated by Michael Graff.[23] He argued that La Porta et al. included criteria in their antidirector rights index that are irrelevant whereas other, clearly relevant criteria have been omitted. Two criteria that should not have been included are whether shareholders can mail their proxy votes and whether shareholders are not required to deposit their shares before the AGM. Two criteria that should have been included, according to Graff, are the existence of mandatory dividends and whether the rule of one-share one-vote is upheld. When La Porta et al.'s antidirector rights index is adjusted as proposed by Graff, then the link between investor protection and legal origin disappears. Holger Spamann's critique was based on errors of encoding. Spamann revisited the encoding of the antidirector rights index and found errors for 33 out of the 46 countries covered by La Porta et al.[24] After the errors had been corrected, there was no longer a link between legal origin and the level of investor protection. In other words, La Porta et al.'s main result that legal families differ in terms of the rights they confer to investors is no longer upheld. Spamann argued that the encoding errors were caused by La Porta et al.'s use of secondary sources rather than the law texts themselves. According to the third critique, legal families are a proxy, i.e. an indirect measure for the true drivers of the differences in corporate governance across countries. For example, Amir Licht, Chanan Goldschmidt and Shalom Schwartz argued that culture is the true driver behind these differences.[25] Based on survey data on cultural attitudes, they found that countries that were under British rule are much more willing to deal with conflicts of interests in the courts of law and are much more litigious countries than the rest of the world. They found a strong correlation between cultural attitudes on the one side and investor and creditor protection on the other. Importantly, as cultural attitudes tend to persist over time, they may prevent law reforms from succeeding and bringing about true change. Licht et al. argued that this may be the reason why most of the countries from the former Communist Bloc have failed to improve investor protection in practice, despite wide ranging changes to their legal codes. Finally, Julian Franks, Colin Mayer and Stefano Rossi performed a historical study of ownership dispersion in the UK covering the period from 1900 to 2000.[26] They found that ownership dispersion was already high before 1930 despite the absence of investor protection. They argued that the separation between ownership and control occurred in the absence of strong shareholder rights and was made possible by the existence of local stock exchanges which were close to the shareholder base of the firms that were listed on these markets. In other words, the proximity of the firm to its shareholders created trust between its managers and shareholders, substituting for the lack of legal investor protection.[27]

René Stulz and Rohan Williamson also investigated the role of culture behind the differences across countries in terms of corporate governance.[28] They measured differences in culture by religion and language. They found that generally, differences in investor rights cannot be explained by differences in culture. However, within a given legal family, differences in culture explain differences in investor protection across the countries of that legal family. This relationship is particularly strong for creditor rights. For example, Catholic countries provide much weaker creditor protection than Protestant countries. Interestingly, La Porta et al. in a much less frequently cited paper than their papers on investor protection, found a strong link between trust

[23]Graff, M. (2008), 'Law and Finance: Common Law and Civil Law Countries Compared – An Empirical Critique', *Economica* 75, 60–83.
[24]Spamann, H. (2010), 'The "Antidirector Rights Index" Revisited', *Review of Financial Studies* 23, 467–86.
[25]Licht, A., Goldschmidt, C. and Schwartz, S. (2005), 'Culture, Law, and Corporate Governance', *International Review of Law and Economics* 25, 229–55.
[26]Franks, J., Mayer, C. and Rossi, S. (2009), 'Ownership: Evolution and Regulation', *Review of Financial Studies* 22, 4009–56.
[27]Graeme Acheson and colleagues argue that the separation of ownership and control emerged even earlier as it can be traced back to at least the mid-1800s. See Acheson, G.G., Campbell, G., Turner, J.D. and Vanteeva, N. (2015), 'Corporate Ownership and Control in Victorian Britain', *Economic History Review* 68, 911–36.
[28]Stulz, R. and Williamson, R. (2003), 'Culture, Openness, and Finance', *Journal of Financial Economics* 70, 313–49.

within a society, i.e. how much citizens of a society trust complete strangers, and economic outcomes (see also Chapter 5).[29]

Similar to legal origin, culture is also fairly static across time. However, Marco Pagano and Paolo Volpin argued that politicians can change laws and can also improve the enforcement of existing laws if enforcement in the past has been weak.[30] Hence, changes in governments as well as more general changes in the political system can explain changes over time across countries.

Steve Bank, Brian Cheffins and Marc Goergen tested Roe's proposition that corporate governance characteristics can be explained by the political orientation of a country's government.[31] They used the dividend payouts of UK-listed firms as a measure of corporate governance. Their period of study was 1949 to 2002, a period characterized by successive changes in the political orientation of the government. Bank et al. argued that if Roe's theory is correct, dividends should have been higher during Conservative governments and lower during Labour governments. However, they did not find any such evidence.

There has also been criticism of the simple version of the VOC literature which is based on only two types of capitalist systems, i.e. liberal market economies or LMEs and coordinated market economies or CMEs. For example, Bruno Amable[32] as well as Mark Harcourt and Geoffrey Wood[33] argued that this bipolar taxonomy fails to account for the distinct character of the Rhineland economies of Continental Europe, the Nordic social democracies and the economies of Southern Europe (see also Section 15.3 of Chapter 15). Hence, Bruno Amable proposed, in addition to the fairly homogenous group of LMEs, three distinct types of CMEs. These are the social democratic economies of Denmark, Finland, Norway and Sweden; the Southern European economies of Greece, Italy, Portugal and Spain; and Continental European capitalism found in Austria, Belgium, France and Germany.

4.8 Conclusions

While the last few decades have seen major political, economic and technological upheavals on a global level, giving rise to global capitalism, national systems of corporate governance and capitalism nevertheless are still characterized by a series of idiosyncrasies. This chapter has reviewed the various taxonomies of national systems that have been proposed by business historians, as well as financial, legal and management scholars.

The rise of global capitalism

The first attempts at categorizing national corporate governance systems were grounded in historical analysis and were made by John Hicks and Alfred Chandler Jr. Hicks distinguished between market-based capitalism and bank-based capitalism. A more recent attempt by Julian Franks and Colin Mayer distinguished between insider and outsider systems of corporate governance. In the insider system, stock markets are relatively underdeveloped, corporate control is highly concentrated and badly performing managers are disciplined by the

First attempts at categorizing corporate governance systems

[29] La Porta, R., Lopez-de-Silanes, F., Shleifer, A. and Vishny, R. (1997), 'Trust in Large Organizations', *American Economic Review* 87, 333–8.
[30] See op. cit. footnote 18.
[31] Bank, S., Cheffins, B. and Goergen, M. (2009), 'Dividends and Politics', *European Journal of Political Economy* 25, 208–24.
[32] Amable, B. (2003), *The Diversity of Modern Capitalism*, Oxford, UK: Oxford University Press.
[33] Harcourt, M. and Wood, G. (2003), 'Under What Circumstances do Social Accords Work?', *Journal of Economic Issues* 37, 747–67.

large shareholder. In the outsider system, organized capital markets are highly developed, most companies are listed on the stock market and have dispersed ownership and control and managerial disciplining is done via the market for corporate control.

Lucian Bebchuk and Mark Roe formalized the way history shapes current corporate governance via their concept of path dependence. They distinguished between structure-driven path dependence and rule-driven path dependence. Structure-driven path dependence refers to how the original structures of a country have influenced its current structures. Rule-driven path dependence refers to how current regulation was influenced by the structures or economic actors that initially dominated the country's economy.

Path dependence

An important strand of the academic literature is the so-called law and finance literature. This literature proposes taxonomies based on legal families (La Porta et al.) and political determinants, i.e. a country's way of achieving social peace and the government's political orientation (Mark Roe) as well as the type of electoral system (Marco Pagano and Paolo Volpin). At the core of the taxonomies originating from the law and finance literature is the premise that highly flexible and liquid markets, such as capital markets and labour markets, are better at allocating resources than other mechanisms, such as informal networks and governments. According to this school of thought, corporate governance systems, which put in place regulation that facilitates rather than constrains the operation of markets, are superior to those that do not.

The law and finance literature and the hierarchy of corporate governance systems

In contrast, the varieties of capitalism (VOC) literature is based on the notion of complementarities. This notion implies that very different sets of institutional arrangements may still generate similar levels of economic growth and output. Importantly, the VOC literature does not assume that well developed capital markets and weak employment rights are the only way of achieving strong economic growth.

The VOC literature and the concept of complementarities

4.9 Discussion questions

1   Compare the assumptions and the predictions of the varieties of capitalism (VOC) literature with those of the law and finance literature.

2   Critically review the La Porta et al. (1997, 1998) taxonomy of corporate governance systems in the light of recent corporate scandals and academic research.

Reading list

Key reading

Andres, C., Betzer, A., Goergen, M. and Metzger, D. (2010), 'Corporate Governance Systems', in H. Kent Baker and Ronald Anderson (ed.), *Corporate Governance, Companions to Finance Series, Kolb Series in Finance*, New York: John Wiley, chapter 3.

Franks, J., Mayer, C. and Rossi, S. (2009), 'Ownership: Evolution and Regulation', *Review of Financial Studies* 22, 4009–56.

Graff, M. (2008), 'Law and Finance: Common Law and Civil Law Countries Compared: An Empirical Critique', *Economica* 75, 60–83.

La Porta, R., Lopez-de-Silanes, F., Shleifer, A. and Vishny, R. (1997), 'Legal Determinants of External Finance', *Journal of Finance* 52, 1131–50.

La Porta, R., Lopez-de-Silanes, F., Shleifer, A. and Vishny, R. (1998), 'Law and Finance', *Journal of Political Economy* 106, 1113–55.

Licht, A., Goldschmidt, C. and Schwartz, S. (2005), 'Culture, Law, and Corporate Governance', *International Review of Law and Economics* 25, 229–55.

Pagano, M. and Volpin, P. (2005), 'The Political Economy of Corporate Governance', *American Economic Review* 95, 1005–30.

Spamann, H. (2010), 'The "Antidirector Rights Index" Revisited', *Review of Financial Studies* 23, 467–86.

Further reading

Acheson, G.G., Campbell, G., Turner, J.D. and Vanteeva, N. (2015), 'Corporate Ownership and Control in Victorian Britain', *Economic History Review* 68, 911–36.

Chandler, Alfred D., Jr. (1977), *The Visible Hand: The Managerial Revolution in American Business*, Cambridge, MA: The Belknap Press of Harvard University Press.

Chandler, Alfred D., Jr. (1984), 'The Emergence of Managerial Capitalism', *Business History Review* 58, 473–503.

Dore, R. (2000), *Stock Market Capitalism: Welfare Capitalism. Japan and German versus the Anglo-Saxons*, Oxford, UK: Oxford University Press.

Ezzamel, M. Xiao, J.Z. and Pan, A. (2007), 'Political Ideology and Accounting Regulation in China', *Accounting, Organizations and Society* 32, 669–700.

Goergen, M. (2007), 'What Do We Know about Different Systems of Corporate Governance?', *Journal of Corporate Law Studies* 8, 1–15.

Hall, P.A. and Soskice, D. (2001), *Varieties of Capitalism: The Institutional Foundations of Comparative Advantage*, Oxford, UK: Oxford University Press.

Musacchio, A. and Turner, J.D. (2013), 'Does the Law and Finance Hypothesis Pass the Test of History?', *Business History* 55, 524–42.

Palma, J.G. (2009), 'The Revenge of the Market on the Rentiers. Why Neo-Liberal Reports of the End of History Turned Out to Be Premature', *Cambridge Journal of Economics* 33, 829–69.

Roe, M.J. (2003), *The Political Determinants of Corporate Governance*, Oxford, UK: Oxford University Press.

Additional resources

Andrei Shleifer's website at Harvard Business School contains most of the data, including data on the antidirector rights index, used in the La Porta et al. studies. The data on offer also include indices on politics and electoral systems. scholar.harvard.edu/shleifer/publications.

5 Corporate governance, types of financial systems and economic growth

Chapter Aims

This chapter aims to review the link between capital market development, corporate governance and economic growth. The chapter contrasts the two main financial systems, the bank-based system and the stock-market-based system. It assesses the advantages and disadvantages of each system and draws conclusions as to the types of industries that are likely to flourish in each. Finally, the chapter discusses the link between trust and economic growth.

Learning Outcomes

After reading this chapter, you should be able to:

1 Explain the link between capital market development and economic growth

2 Understand why and under which circumstances particular types of industries are more likely to thrive in an economy

3 Contrast bank financing with stock-market financing of corporations

4 Assess the importance of strong and efficient institutions in promoting economic growth

5 Comprehend the impact of religion and trust on economic growth

5.1 Introduction

In Chapter 4, we saw that one of the taxonomies of corporate governance systems distinguishes between bank-based and market-based systems. This chapter focuses on the link between these two types of financial systems and economic growth. Both types of systems perform particularly well in specific situations, but may fail or at least be deficient in others. As a result, they influence the types of industries that are likely to prosper in a country and those that are likely to do less well. The chapter also looks at other important determinants of economic growth, mainly trust, but also government efficiency as well as the efficiency of social institutions and religion.

An extensive body of the literature investigates the issue of the direction of causality between the development of financial markets and economic growth. While it is now generally accepted that the former drives the latter, there are still some sceptics that argue that financial markets grow in anticipation of future growth rather than drive economic growth. This chapter assumes that the causality flows from financial market development to economic growth. There is also a large body of literature on financial development more generally defined and economic performance. However, the focus in this chapter is on institutional arrangements relating to financial markets and corporate governance rather than on broad financial development. The paper by Ross Levine provides an excellent overview of the literature on both issues.[1] Finally, Chapter 14 will study the role of banks and other debtholders in corporate governance, while Chapter 9 will discuss the role of the financial system, in particular stock markets, in emerging economies.

5.2 The functions of financial markets and institutions

Financial markets and institutions are typically set up to deal with market imperfections, in particular problems of asymmetry of information and transaction costs. There are five principal functions of financial markets and institutions. These are:

- collecting small amounts of savings from households and turning them into larger loans.
- risk sharing.
- facilitating the exchange of goods and services by offering various means of payment.
- the monitoring and disciplining of corporate managers.
- the allocation of economic resources.

In what follows, we shall focus on the latter two functions as they relate directly to corporate governance.

5.3 Bank-based versus market-based systems

Both banks and stock markets may reduce the monitoring efforts which individual investors would have to expend in the absence of these institutions. Starting with the former, banks tend to have better monitoring skills than small investors and they also benefit from economies of scale in terms of monitoring due to the many corporations they lend to. As banks hold highly diversified portfolios of loans, this reduces the amount of monitoring that savers have to provide.[2] They also frequently have long-term relations with their borrowers which further reduces information problems. Hence, the bank-based system is also sometimes referred to as the relationship-based system. The relationship-based system is thought to overcome weak law as it is based on agreements between parties. If one of the parties fails to honour the agreement, it risks losing its reputation and risks being excluded from future business relationships. In other words, powerful banks may be better at forcing companies to repay their loans than small investors, especially in countries with weak investor protection and/or weak law enforcement.

Similar to banks, stock markets reduce the need for, or at least facilitate, monitoring by investors for at least two reasons. First, owners of firms that are listed on a stock market can use the stock price to monitor the performance of the management. They can also use stock prices to incentivize the management via performance related pay (see Sections 8.8–8.9 of Chapter 8). Second, stock markets also provide a mechanism to discipline managers via the market for corporate control, in particular via hostile takeovers. The mere threat of a hostile takeover may be enough to prevent managers from shirking. However, doubts have been raised about the monitoring role of stock markets. First, the empirical evidence suggests that the pre-acquisition performance

[1]Levine, R. (1997), 'Financial Development and Economic Growth', *Journal of Economic Literature* 35, 688–726.
[2]See Diamond, D.W. (1984), 'Financial Intermediation and Delegated Monitoring', *Review of Economic Studies* 51, 393–414.

of targets of hostile takeovers is no different from that of targets of friendly takeovers (see Section 8.4 of Chapter 8). Hence, the reasons behind hostile takeovers do not seem to be badly performing managers. Second, stock markets may promote takeovers that result in so-called breaches of trust. According to Andrei Shleifer and Lawrence Summers, the change in management brought about by a takeover may result in the violation of implicit contracts the incumbent management had with its employees, suppliers and other stakeholders (see also Section 15.6 of Chapter 15).[3] For example, such implicit contracts may relate to firm-specific training. Employees are asked to spend time and effort on firm-specific training with the promise of more rapid career progression in the future. However, ex-post it makes sense for the *new* management to renege on these contracts. As a result of this risk, employees may be reluctant to invest in firm-specific training in the first place. Hence, takeovers may hinder rather than facilitate the efficient use of resources. Third, stock markets may also promote exit rather than voice by reducing transaction costs.[4] In other words, it may be cheaper for a small investor to sell her holdings in an underperforming company rather than spend time and effort to call for major changes in the way the company is managed. This is particularly true for firms with highly dispersed ownership and control given that the benefits from monitoring performed by a single shareholder are shared across all the shareholders whereas the costs from doing so accrue to the single active shareholder only. Finally, stock markets have also been accused of being myopic or short-termist, i.e. focusing on short-term increases in firm value rather than on the long-term survival of companies. In line with this argument, one of the motives for going-private transactions is operational and strategic changes to the company which take time before they generate value and which may not be possible to make if the company remains on the stock exchange.

Whereas the relationship-based system thrives on opacity as the latter protects a relationship from competitors, the market-based system relies on transparency such as high accounting standards. However, the lack of transparency may reduce the efficiency of the relationship-based system, as the company which is seeking funding from its bank has no means of assessing whether the cost of borrowing charged by the bank is justified or not. The fact that the company is unable to obtain an independent assessment, via the stock market, of whether its project is worth pursuing may also cause it to make the wrong investment decisions. In contrast, companies operating in market-based economies can obtain the stock market's view on whether their investment opportunity is worthwhile undertaking or not. Further, as we shall see in Chapter 14, banks that provide both equity and debt capital to a company may suffer from specific conflicts of interests.

As a result of the differences between relationship-based and market-based systems, companies are likely to specialize in those assets that are favoured by their particular system. These tend to be tangible assets in the bank-based system given their ability to serve as collateral. However, due to the absence of liquid markets, these assets also tend to be firm-specific and highly illiquid. In contrast, in the market-based system, the focus is on highly liquid, fairly generic assets and/or intangible assets that have little value as collateral.[5]

Finally, it is important to note that while the sources of financing in bank-based and market-based systems may differ (e.g. in the bank-based system debt tends to be in the form of bank loans rather than tradable bonds), the empirical evidence does not suggest that there are significant differences in leverage between the two systems.[6] In other words, while German firms may have historically been more reliant

[3]Shleifer, A. and Summers, L. (1990), 'Breach of Trust in Hostile Takeovers', in A.J. Auerbach (ed.), *Corporate Takeovers: Causes and Consequences*, Chicago, IL: University of Chicago Press, 33–56.

[4]Dhide, A. (1993), 'The Hidden Costs of Stock Market Liquidity', *Journal of Financial Economics* 34, 31–51.

[5]See e.g. Brown, J.R., Martinsson G. and Petersen, B.C. (2013), 'Law, Stock Markets, and Innovation', *Journal of Finance* 68, 1517–49.

[6]Rajan, R.G. and Zingales, L. (1995), 'What Do We Know about Capital Structure? Some Evidence from International Data', *Journal of Finance* 50, 1421–60.

on bank debt, they are nevertheless no more indebted than UK firms that have relied more on bond and debenture issues.[7]

5.4 The link between types of financial systems and economic growth

Classic economic theory predicts that a country's economic growth depends on its initial allocation of resources. Hence, all that matters are the resources an economy starts off with. Economies endowed with significant resources will do well whereas those with few resources will stagnate and fail to develop. However, there are also three theories that link financial systems to economic growth and competitive advantages in particular industries. In other words, these theories are less fatalistic than classic economic theory as they suggest that there is a role for countries in the design of their institutions. These theories are:

* the information collection theory.
* the renegotiation theory.
* the corporate governance theory.

The information collection theory predicts that stock markets are better at valuing assets whose value is highly uncertain and difficult to assess.[8] Such assets include intangible assets and new technologies as well as other assets for which individual investors are likely to come up with highly divergent valuations. In other words, stock markets are better at valuing assets that generate diverging views about their value. In contrast, banks are better at valuing more traditional assets, as they benefit from economies of scale from doing so.

The second theory is the renegotiation theory.[9] Financial systems with many small banks impose tighter budget constraints than those with few large banks. Hence, the former tend to promote short-term investment projects whereas the latter favour long-term projects. As a result, young and high-tech industries will thrive in systems with many small banks whereas more mature industries, characterized by incremental innovation, will prosper in systems with only a few, large banks.

The third theory is based on corporate governance. To overcome the free-rider problem and to ensure active monitoring of the management, there needs to be a large shareholder.[10] However, the large shareholder may interfere too much in tasks that are best carried out by the management. In other words, the large shareholder may leave too little discretion to the management and prevent the latter from running the firm efficiently. The large shareholder may also expropriate the minority shareholders. Conversely, dispersed ownership can more credibly commit not to interfere with the management of the firm and it will fare better with activities requiring investments from management and other stakeholders such as employees. In contrast, concentrated ownership is suited for activities requiring active monitoring.[11]

[7]See Fan, J.P.H., Titman, S. and Twite, G. (2012), 'An International Comparison of Capital Structure and Debt Maturity Choices', *Journal of Financial and Quantitative Analysis* 47, 23–56, for a more recent and more detailed analysis of the impact of the institutional setting – including the size of the government bond market and the importance and nature of the pension fund industry – on the level of leverage and debt maturity for 39 developed and less developed countries.

[8]Allen F. (1993), 'Stock Markets and Resource Allocation', in Mayer, C. and Vives, X. (eds.), *Capital Markets and Financial Intermediation*, Cambridge, UK: Cambridge University Press. Allen, F. and Gale, D. (1999), 'Diversity of Opinion and the Financing of New Technologies', *Journal of Financial Intermediation* 8, 68–89.

[9]Dewatripont, M. and Maskin, E. (1995), 'Credit Efficiency in Centralized and Decentralized Economies', *Review of Economic Studies* 62, 541–55.

[10]Shleifer, A. and Vishny, R. (1986), 'Large Shareholders and Corporate Control', *Journal of Political Economy* 94, 461–88.

[11]Burkart, M., Gromb, D. and Panunzi, F. (1997), 'Large Shareholders, Monitoring, and the Value of the Firm', *Quarterly Journal of Economics* 112, 693–728.

Based on a univariate analysis of their data, Wendy Carlin and Colin Mayer tested the validity of the above three theories as well as the classic theory on a sample of 27 different manufacturing industries across 14 developed OECD countries and four less developed OECD countries (Greece, Korea, Mexico and Portugal) for the period of 1970–95.[12] In their regression analysis, they explained GDP growth, fixed investment as well as research and development (R&D) by two sets of variables: country characteristics and industry characteristics. The country characteristics consist of three measures, one for each of the above three theories on the link between type of financial system and growth. The first variable measures the quality of accounting standards, i.e. disclosure. It tests the information collection theory. The second variable measures the concentration of the banking industry to test the validity of the renegotiation theory. The third variable is ownership concentration and is used to test the corporate governance theory. The three industry characteristics are each industry's dependence on equity finance, the dependence on bank finance and the dependence on other stakeholders as measured by workers' skills. The equity dependence of each industry was measured by the share of equity finance in the capital structure of the industry in the USA. The USA was chosen as the benchmark country as it is normally considered to have the most developed stock market. In other words, Carlin and Mayer assumed that companies in the USA are able to raise their *optimal* amount of equity financing whereas they may not be able to do so in other countries. Similarly, bank financing was measured by taking Japan as the benchmark given that this country has been traditionally seen as good at providing bank financing. Finally, dependence on other stakeholders was measured by the percentage of skilled workers employed by each industry in Germany, a country thought to excel in providing workers' skills (see also Box 5.1).

Box 5.1
The comparative advantages of individual nations

'**I**n heaven, the policemen are English, the cooks are French, the mechanics are German, the lovers are Italian and it is all organized by the Swiss. In hell, the cooks are English, the policemen are German, the mechanics are French, the lovers are Swiss and it is all organized by the Italians'.

Source: Mayer, C. (1999), 'Firm Control', Inaugural Lecture, Saïd Business School, Oxford University, available at: users.ox.ac .uk/~ofrcinfo/file_links/finecon_papers/1999fe07.pdf.

Carlin and Mayer decomposed deviations of country growth rates from world averages into three distinct effects, which are:

- the share effect.
- the growth effect.
- the interactive effect.

The share effect measured the contribution to economic growth via the deviation of a country's initial share of an industry from the world average at the start of the period, i.e. 1970. Hence, the share effect measured the validity of the classical theory that states that differences in economic growth over time are due to differences in the initial allocation of economic resources across countries. The growth effect was the contribution to growth of the deviation of the growth rate of a country from the world average assuming initial shares are at

[12]Carlin, W. and Mayer, C. (2003), 'Finance, Investment, and Growth', *Journal of Financial Economics* 69, 191–226.

world averages. This effect measured the contribution to growth of the institutional setting rather than that of the share of the initial allocation of resources. The interactive effect accounted for the possibility that economic growth in a country may have been higher given that its initial allocation was greater.

Carlin and Mayer found that the differences in country growth are almost entirely due to the growth effect. This suggests that classical theory has only limited explanatory power and that one or several of the above theories on institutions are likely to have more explanatory power.

Carlin and Mayer reported that the country rankings according to fixed investment and R&D – both expressed as a proportion of value added – are very different. For example, while Spain has the lowest ratio for both, the UK and the USA have some of the highest R&D ratios but the lowest fixed investment ratios. Growth is also more strongly correlated with R&D than with fixed investment. Accounting standards are highest in the UK. Despite being a more heavily regulated country, US accounting standards are lower than in the UK. Accounting standards in Germany are much lower. This is to some extent due to the fact that in Germany accounting income is dictated by taxable income. In Germany, contrary to the UK, there is virtually no difference between accounts drawn up for tax purposes and those published in the financial report. Bank concentration is highest in Finland and Sweden. Finally, ownership concentration is lowest in the UK and USA and is highest in Continental Europe.

Carlin and Mayer found the following. Better accounting disclosure is associated with higher growth of equity- and skills-dependent industries. A larger share of R&D is devoted to these industries in countries with better disclosure. There is a more pronounced relation of growth and R&D with disclosure than with the size of financial markets as measured by stock markets or the banking sector. This suggests the importance of the information theory. Further, concentration of the banking industry is associated with slower growth and a lower share of R&D in equity-dependent industries. Finally, ownership concentration is associated with higher growth and R&D in equity-dependent industries and faster growth in skill-dependent industries. Contrary to what corporate governance theory predicts, ownership concentration rather than ownership dispersion is associated with faster growth of equity- and skill-dependent industries. These results suggest that it is concentrated rather than dispersed owners who credibly signal their commitment to external investors and stakeholders, inducing the latter to invest in the firm.

For developing countries, the role of institutions appears to be different for bank-dependent industries. In these countries, bank concentration and disclosure are positively related to growth in bank-dependent industries.

To sum up, Carlin and Mayer found support for both the information collection and renegotiation theories as the growth of equity-dependent industries is particularly strong in advanced countries with good accounting standards, i.e. good information disclosure, as well as a dispersed banking industry. In addition, the link between institutional structure and cross-industry growth for advanced countries was more strongly associated with investment in R&D than fixed capital. However, these relations were quite different for developing countries. Further, the theory on corporate governance was rejected, as industries that are dependent on external financing and other stakeholders grow more rapidly in countries with concentrated rather than dispersed ownership. Hence, concentrated rather than dispersed owners seemed to offer what outside investors and stakeholders were after.

5.5 How trust and other factors influence economic growth

Section 4.4 of Chapter 4 reviewed the link between legal families and economic growth. As a reminder, the theoretical and empirical work of La Porta et al. suggested that the main driver for economic growth is strong investor protection which guarantees the development of capital markets. Hence, La Porta et al.'s theory is in direct contrast to the varieties of capitalism literature, which argue that more than one type of institutional setting generates the same level of economic outcome.

Indeed, other drivers of economic growth, with a link to the institutional setting, have been proposed. These are cultural factors such as trust and religion, both of which seem to be linked to each other. More precisely, trust may be a means of overcoming situations dominated by asymmetric information where the actions of an agent cannot be directly observed. In a much less frequently cited paper than their papers on legal families, La Porta et al. defined trust as the 'propensity of people in a society to cooperate to produce socially efficient outcomes and to avoid inefficient non-cooperative traps such as that in the prisoner's dilemma'.[13] Examples of such situations are the provision of goods and services on credit, tasks carried out by an employee which are difficult to monitor by a manager and investments that may be expropriated by the investee or the government. In other words, in higher-trust environments, economic agents tend to spend less time protecting themselves from getting expropriated.

Game theory, such as the prisoner's dilemma, suggests that trusting strangers, i.e. cooperating with strangers, is not an optimal strategy whereas mistrust is. This then leads to economic outcomes that are not socially optimal. However, experimental research suggests that in practice people tend to trust even complete strangers and in turn expect a certain degree of cooperation from them. Further, trust tends to be required in interactions with complete strangers as well as those that are only dealt with rarely. This makes sense as persons who deal with each other on a regular basis establish a reputation vis-à-vis each other. They can also punish any party failing to stick to an agreement by refusing to deal with them in the future. George Akerlof proposed another reason why individuals are cooperative rather than purely selfish.[14] While honesty may reduce an individual's welfare in the short run, it will maximize the individual's economic returns in the long run. Akerlof called this loyalty. He also argued that being dishonest or faking honesty is much harder than being honest. His theoretical model also explained why people may be loyal to institutions, such as elite universities or military academies, as well as their social class. He cited the example of the British cabinet office under Margaret Thatcher which had 18 public school graduates out of a total of 22 members with only two of the members not being Oxbridge graduates.

In 1970, as a result of a constitutional reform, Italy created regional governments.[15] Robert Putnam argued that the reason why the governments of the Northern regions have been relatively efficient while those from the Southern regions have failed is that the North of Italy has a long tradition of what he calls civic engagement, i.e. involvement of citizens in public affairs. Members of a civic community are not just active, but they also trust each other even when they do not share the same opinions on key issues. Putnam claimed that horizontal associations, i.e. non-hierarchical associations such as tennis clubs, encourage trust. Conversely, strong vertical associations, such as the hierarchical religions, discourage trust. In contrast to Putnam, Mancur Olson argued that horizontal associations are often self-serving associations, such as lobbying groups – which divert economic resources into their own pockets to the detriment of the rest of society.[16] Hence according to Olson, associational activity is likely to reduce rather than increase economic growth.

Francis Fukuyama looked into the possible reasons for the decline of sociability in the USA, i.e. the increasing mistrust among American citizens.[17] Compared to other developed countries, the USA's expenditure on police protection and the proportion of its population locked up in prisons are substantially higher. The USA

[13]La Porta, R., Lopez-de-Silanes, F., Shleifer, A. and Vishny, R.W. (1997), 'Trust in Large Organizations', *American Economic Review* 87, 333–8.

[14]Akerlof, G.A. (1983), 'Loyalty Filters', *American Economic Review* 73, 54–63. See also Kuran, T. (1995), *Private Truths, Public Lies: The Social Consequences of Preference Falsification*, Cambridge, MA: Harvard University Press.

[15]Putnam, R.D. (1993), *Making Democracy Work. Civic Traditions in Modern Italy*, Princeton, NJ: Princeton University Press.

[16]Olson, M. (1982), *The Rise and Decline of Nations: Economic Growth, Stagflation, and Social Rigidities*, New Haven, CT: Yale University Press.

[17]Fukuyama, F. (1995), *Trust. The Social Virtues and the Creation of Prosperity*, London: Hamish Hamilton.

is also a much more litigious society, as evidenced by the significantly higher spend on lawyer fees than e.g. Europe and Japan. However, Fukuyama did not propose that a return to family values would improve sociability and ultimately trust among citizens. He cited the examples of China and Italy where family ties are important. While strong family or blood ties – Fukuyama referred to these as familism – may not be directly dampening economic growth, they nevertheless restrict the type of firms, the size of firms as well as the industry sectors that will develop within a country. Hence, a return to family values is unlikely to improve economic growth.

Paul Zak and Stephen Knack studied the link between trust and economic performance.[18] They developed a theoretical model which was based on the trade-off that economic actors face between monitoring their agents and spending more time on production. Zak and Knack based their model on the relationship that investors have with their investment brokers. In the model, trust is defined as the aggregate time the investors in a society spend on economic production rather than on monitoring. The amount of monitoring each investor expends depends on the wealth he has invested and the revenue he obtains from production. The higher an investor's salary the less time he spends on monitoring given the higher opportunity cost of the lost salary. However, the larger the amount invested the more time the investor tends to spend on monitoring his broker. Wage inequality will increase the aggregate amount of monitoring spent by the society. In other words, wage inequality will decrease trust. Conversely, the existence of strong formal and informal institutions reduces the need for monitoring. To summarize, the model makes the following assertions:

- Trust has a positive effect on investment and economic growth.
- Homogeneous societies invest more and have stronger economic growth.
- Improving income equality increases trust. In turn, higher trust increases investment and economic growth.
- Some societies may get stuck in a low-trust poverty trap.

Zak and Knack tested their model on 44 countries. They accounted for two types of trust. The first type is trust in fellow citizens. We call this trust in what follows. This is measured by the percentage of respondents in each country replying that 'most people can be trusted'. They used the data from the World Values Survey which is conducted every few years across a large number of countries (see Table 5.1). The second type of trust is trust in the government. This is measured via the strength of property rights. This measure is similar to the La Porta et al. measure of investor protection. Zak and Knack found the following results:

- Investment in a country increases with trust and the level of incomes, but decreases with the price of investment goods.
- Trust increases economic growth.
- While growth is positively related to the trust in the government, i.e. the strength of property rights in a country, trust towards fellow citizens remains significant. This implies that the quality of a country's law matters, but that trust has additional explanatory power.

They identified the following determinants of trust:

- Trust follows a U-shaped relationship with ethnic homogeneity, i.e. trust is lowest in countries with several small, but similarly sized ethnic groups as well as in countries where one very large ethnic group dominates several small groups.
- Trust increases with property rights.
- Trust decreases with income inequality and land property inequality.

---

[18]Zak, P.J. and Knack, S. (2001), 'Trust and Growth', *Economic Journal* 111, 295–321.

Table 5.1 Trust across countries

	No. of respondents	Most people can be trusted	Can't be too careful
Andorra	995	20.10%	79.90%
Argentina	989	17.60%	82.40%
Australia	1,404	46.10%	53.90%
Brazil	1,477	9.40%	90.60%
Bulgaria	883	22.20%	77.80%
Burkina Faso	1,443	14.70%	85.30%
Canada	2,113	42.80%	57.20%
Chile	985	12.60%	87.40%
China	1,873	52.30%	47.70%
Colombia	2,993	14.50%	85.50%
Cyprus	1,031	9.90%	90.10%
Egypt	3,045	18.50%	81.50%
Ethiopia	1,314	24.40%	75.60%
Finland	999	58.90%	41.10%
France	996	18.80%	81.20%
Georgia	1,455	18.10%	81.90%
Germany	1,893	36.80%	63.20%
Ghana	1,527	8.50%	91.50%
Great Britain	1,023	30.50%	69.50%
Guatemala	995	15.70%	84.30%
Hong Kong	1,230	41.10%	58.90%
India	1,778	23.30%	76.70%
Indonesia	1,775	42.50%	57.50%
Iran	2,647	10.60%	89.40%
Iraq	2,555	40.80%	59.20%
Italy	953	29.20%	70.80%
Japan	1,026	39.10%	60.90%
Jordan	1,192	30.90%	69.10%
Malaysia	1,201	8.80%	91.20%
Mali	1,303	17.50%	82.50%
Mexico	1,548	15.60%	84.40%
Moldova	1,030	17.90%	82.10%
Morocco	1,177	13.00%	87.00%
Netherlands	993	45.00%	55.00%
New Zealand	905	51.20%	48.80%
Norway	1,018	74.20%	25.80%
Peru	1,479	6.30%	93.70%

	No. of respondents	Most people can be trusted	Can't be too careful
Poland	954	19.00%	81.00%
Romania	1,685	20.30%	79.70%
Russian Federation	1,905	26.20%	73.80%
Rwanda	1,499	4.90%	95.10%
Serbia	1,086	15.30%	84.70%
Slovenia	999	18.10%	81.90%
South Africa	2,966	18.80%	81.20%
South Korea	1,190	28.20%	71.80%
Spain	1,184	20.00%	80.00%
Sweden	962	68.00%	32.00%
Switzerland	1,178	53.90%	46.10%
Taiwan	1,225	24.20%	75.80%
Thailand	1,525	41.50%	58.50%
Trinidad and Tobago	999	3.80%	96.20%
Turkey	1,339	4.90%	95.10%
Ukraine	889	27.50%	72.50%
United States	1,242	39.30%	60.70%
Uruguay	865	28.40%	71.60%
Vietnam	1,460	52.10%	47.90%
Zambia	1,403	11.50%	88.50%
Total	79,801	26.10%	73.90%

Source: *2005–2008 World Values Survey*, www.worldvaluessurvey.org/WVSContents.jsp, accessed on 3 April 2011.

Worryingly, there is relatively little variation of trust across time compared to the cross-country differences in trust which are substantial. While countries may be able to improve their property rights and the enforcement of these rights, the Zak and Knack study suggests that it is much more challenging to improve trust among citizens. There are two reasons for this. First, as stated trust varies little across time. Second, some of the drivers of trust are a given – such as the distribution of ethnic groups within a country – whereas others – such as income and land property inequality are difficult to change.

While Zak and Knack considered that the two types of trust are essentially trust in different types of economic actors (fellow citizens and the government), in another study with Philip Keefer, Stephen Knack allowed for the possibility that trust in fellow citizens may substitute for a lack of trust in the government.[19] In other words, trust in other citizens may act as a substitute for weak institutions such as weak property rights and weak law enforcement. High-trust societies have norms of civic cooperation in place that limit opportunistic behaviour by ordinary citizens as well as politicians. They also have sanctions that punish trespassers. The sanctions are of two types. The first type is internal, such as guilt. The second type is external, such as ostracism

[19]Knack, S. and Keefer, P. (1997), 'Does Social Capital Have an Economic Payoff? A Cross-Country Investigation', *Quarterly Journal of Economics* 112, 1251–88.

and shame. As in a high-trust society, the norms and sanctions are powerful enough to prevent opportunistic behaviour, its citizens have more time to spend on production and there is less need for costly monitoring of other people's actions.

Knack and Keefer found that:

- Trust as well as the strength of civic norms has a positive impact on both economic growth and investment.
- The positive impact of trust on growth and investment is greater in poorer countries where formal institutions and the quality of law are likely to be weaker, suggesting that trust does indeed act as a substitute for the latter two.
- While income inequality is highly correlated with trust and civic norms, the latter two still explain differences in growth and investment when the former is adjusted for.
- Horizontal associational activity does not have any impact on economic growth and investment. Knack and Keefer interpreted this absence of an effect as evidence that horizontal associational activity has both a positive effect – as hypothesized by Robert Putnam – and a negative effect – as argued by Mancur Olson – on growth and that both effects effectively cancel each other out.

Rafel La Porta, Florencio Lopez-de-Silanes, Robert Vishny and Andrei Shleifer found that trust has a positive impact on the efficiency of government,[20] the participation in civic organizations, the performance of large companies and social efficiency.[21] [22] They also tested Fukuyama's thesis of the negative effect of familism on large firms and found support for it. Indeed, the contribution of the top 20 firms to the gross national product (GNP) decreases with the trust people place in their family. Hence, strong family ties seem to limit the development of large firms. Finally, they also tested the validity of Putnam's hypothesis on the negative effect of strong hierarchical religions on economic performance. They considered the Catholic, Eastern Orthodox and Muslim religions to be such hierarchical religions. They found that countries where these religions dominate have a less efficient judiciary, more corruption, inferior bureaucracies, lower tax compliance, lower rates of civic participation, a lower share of GNP generated by the largest 20 firms, lower-quality infrastructures and higher inflation. While La Porta et al. found evidence that strong hierarchical religions nurture distrust, they did not find that ethnic heterogeneity as measured by ethnolinguistic heterogeneity[23] reduces trust.

To summarize, there is consistent evidence that trust has a positive effect on economic growth, investment and institutional performance. In turn, trust is determined by factors such as income inequality, ethnolinguistic or ethnic diversity and hierarchical religions.

---

[20]Their measures of government efficiency are the efficiency of the judiciary, the level of corruption, the quality of the bureaucracy and tax compliance.
[21]Social efficiency is measured by the rate of infant mortality, the percentage of the population with a high school education, the adequacy of the educational system, inflation and growth.
[22]Op. cit. footnote 13.
[23]This is the probability that any two randomly chosen inhabitants of a given country will have different mother tongues.

5.6 Conclusions

Both bank-based and market-based financial systems have certain advantages as well as disadvantages. Given the different comparative advantages of each financial system, economic actors, including companies, are likely to specialize in those assets that are favoured by their system. These tend to be tangible assets in the bank-based system given the ability of these assets to serve as collateral. However, due to the absence of liquid markets, these assets also tend to be firm-specific and highly illiquid. In contrast, the market-based system favours highly liquid, generic assets and/or intangible assets that have little value as collateral.

Bank-based versus market-based systems

There is also a link between the type of financial system and the emergence and success of specific industries. Stock markets tend to favour the growth of industries that are highly reliable on equity finance. Such industries have substantial intangible assets, but few tangible assets that can serve as debt collateral. They are also characterized by blue sky innovation. The growth of equity-dependent industries is particularly strong in developed countries with good disclosure or accounting standards and lots of small banks. In contrast, countries with a concentrated banking industry are more likely to excel in industries with incremental innovation and with sizeable tangible assets. These patterns provide support for the so-called information and renegotiation theories. Conversely, the theory on corporate governance is rejected as industries that depend on external financing and other stakeholders grow faster in countries with larger shareholders rather than those with dispersed ownership.

The link between industrial activities and type of financial system

Finally, there is also consistent evidence that high-trust countries grow faster, invest more and have better institutions than low-trust countries. Trust itself is lower in the presence of income inequality, ethnolinguistic or ethnic diversity, and hierarchical religions. Importantly, trust has explanatory power above and beyond the quality of a country's legal system as measured by its government's protection of property rights.

The impact of trust on economic growth

5.7 Discussion questions

1　What institutional factors have been shown to drive investment and economic growth?

2　If you were to be the economic advisor to a developing country, how would you advise that country to design its institutions in

order to promote economic growth and investment?

3　How do you reconcile what you have learnt from this chapter with the various taxonomies reviewed in Chapter 4?

Reading list

Key reading

Allen F. (1993), 'Stock Markets and Resource Allocation', in Mayer, C. and Vives, X. (eds.), *Capital Markets and Financial Intermediation*, Cambridge, UK: Cambridge University Press.

Allen, F. and Gale, D. (1999), 'Diversity of Opinion and the Financing of New Technologies', *Journal of Financial Intermediation* 8, 68–89.

Brown, J.R., Martinsson G. and Petersen, B.C. (2013), 'Law, Stock Markets, and Innovation', *Journal of Finance* 68, 1517–49.

Burkart, M., Gromb, D. and Panunzi, F. (1997), 'Large Shareholders, Monitoring, and the Value of the Firm', *Quarterly Journal of Economics* 112, 693–728.

Carlin, W. and Mayer, C. (2003), 'Finance, Investment, and Growth', *Journal of Financial Economics* 69, 191–226.

Dewatripont, M. and Maskin, E. (1995), 'Credit Efficiency in Centralized and Decentralized Economies', *Review of Economic Studies* 62, 541–55.

Knack, S. and Keefer, P. (1997), 'Does Social Capital Have an Economic Payoff? A Cross-Country Investigation', *Quarterly Journal of Economics* 112, 1251–88.

La Porta, R., Lopez-de-Silanes, F., Shleifer, A. and Vishny, R.W. (1997), 'Trust in Large Organizations', *American Economic Review* 87, 333–8.

Mayer, C. (1999), 'Firm Control', Inaugural Lecture, Saïd Business School, Oxford University, available at: users.ox.ac.uk/~ofrcinfo/file_links/finecon _papers/1999fe07.pdf.

Zak, P.J. and Knack, S. (2001), 'Trust and Growth', *Economic Journal* 111, 295–321.

Further reading

Akerlof, G.A. (1983), 'Loyalty Filters', *American Economic Review* 73, 54–63.

Bhide, A. (1993), 'The Hidden Costs of Stock Market Liquidity', *Journal of Financial Economics* 34, 31–51.

Fan, J.P.H, Titman, S. and Twite, G. (2012), 'An International Comparison of Capital Structure and Debt Maturity Choices', *Journal of Financial and Quantitative Analysis* 47, 23–56.

Fukuyama, F. (1995), *Trust. The Social Virtues and the Creation of Prosperity*, London: Hamish Hamilton.

Goergen, M., Chahine, S., Brewster, C. and Wood, G. (2013), 'Trust, Owner Rights, Employees and Firm Performance', *Journal of Business Finance & Accounting* 40, 589–619.

Levine, R. (1997), 'Financial Development and Economic Growth', *Journal of Economic Literature* 35, 688–726.

Olson, M. (1982), *The Rise and Decline of Nations: Economic Growth, Stagflation, and Social Rigidities*, New Haven, CT: Yale University Press.

Putnam, R.D. (1993), *Making Democracy Work. Civic Traditions in Modern Italy*, Princeton, NJ: Princeton University Press.

6 Corporate governance regulation in an international context

Chapter Aims

The aim of this chapter is to introduce you to various national and cross-national initiatives (including EU regulation and the G20/OECD Principles of Corporate Governance) about improving corporate governance and to contrast the different approaches to regulation on corporate governance. Rather than providing an exhaustive, but mostly descriptive review of national and international regulation, the chapter focuses on the philosophy behind the various regulatory approaches, the effectiveness of these approaches within their original context as well as in other contexts and the question as to whether regulation will cause national systems to converge.

Learning Outcomes

After reading this chapter, you should be able to:

1 Understand the rationale behind various national and international codes of corporate governance

2 Contrast the different national approaches to improving corporate governance

3 Critically review the effectiveness of corporate governance codes

4 Assess whether cross-country regulatory changes will bring about convergence of national systems

6.1 Introduction

As the UK is frequently seen to be at the forefront of regulation on corporate governance, this chapter starts with an overview of the development of UK regulation. However, it is important to put this development in the context of UK corporate control and ownership. While UK codes of corporate governance have guided the efforts of many other countries, such as Australia, Canada, China, France, Greece, Hong Kong, Ireland, the Netherlands and South Africa, in developing their own regulation, the main conflicts of interests that UK corporations are likely to suffer from could not be more different from those in most corporations from the rest of the world (see Chapters 2 and 3).

It is also important to bear in mind the evidence on the effectiveness of the various corporate governance devices (see Chapters 7 and 8). Indeed, this is likely to identify areas the regulators should concentrate on in order to improve corporate governance. However, as we shall see, regulators frequently ignore that evidence, tend to make rash decisions due to political and public pressure and/or are captured by those they are supposed to regulate. More recently, existing regulation has been accused of promoting box ticking rather than encouraging companies to follow the spirit of the regulation.

6.2 UK codes of corporate governance

The 1992 Cadbury Report, the 1995 Greenbury Report and the 1998 Hampel Report were published in reaction to a wave of corporate scandals that hit the UK in the late 1980s to early 1990s. Since, then the Cadbury Report has served as a model and starting point for other countries intent on developing their own corporate governance regulation. The three codes were combined in the first Combined Code in 1998.

In May 1991, the Financial Reporting Council (FRC), the London Stock Exchange (LSE) and the accountancy profession set up the Committee on the Financial Aspects of Corporate Governance. The Committee was chaired by Sir Adrian Cadbury, who had been chairman of Cadbury Schweppes until his retirement in 1989 and was a director of the Bank of England from 1970 to 1994. At first, the Committee's remit was limited to financial fraud as a reaction to financial scandals such as Polly Peck and Coloroll. However, its remit was extended beyond the financial aspects after the Bank of Credit and Commerce International (BCCI) and Robert Maxwell scandals. A common feature of most of these scandals was a strong, domineering CEO and a weak board of directors dominated by executives.

In line with this pattern, Jay Dahya, John McConnell and Nickolaos Travlos report that in 1988 only 21 of the *Financial Times* (FT) 500 firms had boards consisting of a majority of non-executive directors, whereas 387 of the US Fortune 500 companies had a majority of non-executive directors.[1] However, the percentages of UK FT 500 firms and US Fortune 500 firms with CEO-chairman duality were very similar in 1988 with 66 per cent and 70 per cent, respectively. Another concern was the mostly passive nature of institutional investors, such as pension funds, that typically abstained from exercising their voting rights at AGMs.

The Cadbury Committee's Code of Best Practice was published in December 1992. It is commonly known as the 'Cadbury Report'. It is a code of best practice aimed at companies listed on the LSE. Since June 1993, listed companies have been required to 'comply or explain', i.e. to provide a statement which states whether they comply with the recommendations of the Code or to provide an explanation why they have decided not to follow a specific recommendation.

Its main recommendations include:

- The roles of chairman and CEO of the board should be separated, i.e. there should be no duality.
- There should be a sufficient number of non-executives on the board, who should be of a sufficient calibre and be independent of the company.
- There should be a remuneration committee making recommendations on executive pay and the committee should be composed of mostly non-executives.
- There should be an audit committee consisting of at least three non-executives.
- There should also be a nomination committee in charge of making recommendations as to the nomination of both executives and non-executives to the board. The committee should be composed of a majority of non-executives and should be chaired by a non-executive.
- Institutional investors should be aware of the importance of their votes and disclose their voting policy.

Although a voluntary, self-regulatory code, the evidence suggests that compliance with the Cadbury Code gradually increased after 1992. Also, the number of firms separating the roles of chairman and CEO increased substantially over the years following Cadbury, as did the proportion of non-executives on the boards and the number of firms having audit, nomination and remuneration committees in place.

---

[1] Dahya, J., McConnell, J. and Travlos, N.G. (2002), 'The Cadbury Committee, Corporate Governance, and Top Management Turnover', *Journal of Finance* 57, 461–83.

In addition, Dahya et al. found that there was a significant increase in management turnover after Cadbury came into effect as well as a higher sensitivity of management turnover to financial performance. However, Dahya et al. failed to find support for the claim that changes to board composition and the increase in management turnover also resulted in better financial performance.

In January 1995, the Confederation of British Industry (CBI) set up the Study Group on Directors' Remuneration. Its remit was to look into executive remuneration following a public outcry about what were thought to be excessive levels of managerial pay in listed companies, including recently privatized utilities such as British Gas whose CEO Cedric Brown saw his salary rise by 75 per cent and became synonymous with the corporate 'fat cat' in Britain (see Box 6.1).

Box 6.1
Fat Cats?

Cedric Brown, fat cat in the dog house; So why all the fuss about Cedric Brown and his massive salary? Maybe it's what he spends it on – a neo-Georgian home with crew-cut lawns – says Jonathan Glancey. And, as Vicky Ward discovers below, people don't much like his suburban lifestyle either.

In a contest to decide the Least Popular Man in Britain, there would be politicians and peers jostling for position with villains and the odd soap character, but Cedric Brown would be running as the short-priced favourite. Few people have the power to excite the combined outrage of tabloid headline writers, broadsheet columnists, Home Counties matrons and the Prime Minister, but the chief executive of British Gas – the man with the 900 per cent salary increase – has managed, albeit unwittingly, to unite the nation.

What is curious about the flak flying in Mr Brown's direction is how much of it is aimed not at him – his talents, his achievements, his suits – but at his house. The Sun took one look at his neo-Georgian home in Beaconsfield, Buckinghamshire, and said 'That's the Booty of Gas'; together, the tabloids have exhausted their cliché dictionaries finding words to describe 'fat cat' Cedric's domestic lifestyle. The Browns, Cedric and Joan, live, variously, in a 'luxury home', a 'mansion', 'seven-bedroomed neo-Georgian luxury', or in an 'antiques-laden home' surrounded with 'three acres of manicured garden' in a 'leafy, private road' with a 'chauffeur-driven, silver M-reg Mercedes' (though actually, it's a Jaguar) parked outside.

The image of Cedric Brown's awkwardly proportioned and all too unlived-in neo-Georgian house is one that appears to have gripped the public imagination. It seems to sum up all the many reasons why Mr Brown has become Private Enterprise Enemy Number One over the past few weeks.

The tabloids are out to get him because he is prospering at a time when the economic certainties of the Eighties have long been flushed down the avocado toilet suite. The middle classes dislike him for earning too much money and then squandering it on a decidedly non-U home and lifestyle. The Establishment wants the fellow blackballed: aside from not having the right address, he is the man most likely to lose the Tories the next election. The Labour party like the idea of Mr Brown only in so far as he will help do for Mr Major. And Mr Major himself is painfully aware that Cedric Brown, a man earning five times his own salary, has all the timing and sense of occasion of the gas man who comes to investigate a leak with a fag smouldering between his lips.

Most of all, the tabloids have got it in for Mr Brown for living the very lifestyle that the majority of their readers aspire to. Mr Brown is the boy next door made too good ('fat' in tabloid talk), the Yorkshire lad who has grafted 44 years with British Gas and its predecessors to reach the top, and, having got there, is reaping what he considers to be his reward (or 'market value' as he would say). That reward comprises a salary of pounds 475,000 (47 times that

(Continued)

of your average Joe at British Gas), a pounds 600,000 incentive deal, pounds 1m worth of share options, a pounds 180,000 annual pension on his retirement in five years' time and, of course, that 'mansion' in suburban Bucks.

At a time when the professional middle class are no longer sure of the kind of job security that once guaranteed a seven-bedroomed home with three acres and a Jaguar, and when market values mean wage-cutting for counter staff at British Gas, no wonder Mr Brown's secure and cushy suburban home life is the envy of Express and Sun readers alike. 'As long as these swines have freedom to bury their toffee-noses in the trough', the People thundered, 'they will swallow as much silver as their bloated bellies can carry'.

The middle-class sophisticates' view of Mr Brown is equally damning. They see in his house the vulgar symbol of a man who obviously earns far more money than he knows what to do with. Imagine the house we would buy if we earned half a million! A real Georgian rectory. A Jacobean farmhouse. Maybe even a city-centre flat converted from a warehouse and done up in chic minimalist style. We'd sooner live in the dog house than a house like Cedric Brown's. The criticism is all the more stinging because to belittle an Englishman's home is to cut the man to the quick.

Curiously, while Cedric Brown and Brown Towers have been the target of flak from all sides, Richard Giordano, Mr Brown's chairman, has sailed quite comfortably through this unseemly squabble over money. Mr Giordano, an American as self-made as Cedric Brown, earns pounds 450,000 a year from British Gas working a three-day week (the other two days, he notches up a further pounds 550,000 in director's fees). But, unlike his chief executive, Mr Giordano understands the value of a good address, or three. A chap, even a bloody Yank, must be all right if, like Mr Giordano, he has a flat in Cadogan Square, an apartment in Manhattan and a weekend house in Martha's Vineyard (where he stows his 63ft yacht). He even wears hand-made shoes.

Immediately before privatization in 1986, the chief executive of British Gas (Brown's current position) earned pounds 50,000; that salary has risen 900 per cent since then, vastly above the rate of inflation and little to do with British Gas, a monopoly in private hands, having become 900 per cent more efficient. This was the magic of Thatcherism working for Cedric Brown and his ilk.

As it happens, Mr Brown's spick-and-span 'antiques-filled home' is almost identical to the one Mrs Thatcher bought in an executive cul-de-sac in Dulwich, a south-east London suburb, as a retirement home for her and Denis. Barrett's designed and built his house: it might even be called 'Thatchers'. Cedric Brown's domestic style is the apotheosis of the Thatcher dream, an England neatly creased, nicely polished and never less than profitable. It has nothing to do with old money or the World of Interiors, and even less with the international glitz of Hello!. It has much to do with the houses shown in women's magazines such as She and Homes and Gardens, where none is featured unless it is brand new or else modernised to the point where it might as well be, an interior world where sofas are free from dog hairs, carpets are never threadbare, beds are always made and you could eat your TV supper from the floor of the centrally heated double garage.

Mr Brown is not toffee-nosed; he does not live in a world where one's friends are all 'marvellous people' or where one 'nurtures mammoth hangovers' after weekend drinks parties. He is simply doing what the majority of Sun, Express and People readers would do if they could afford to turn up the gas.

Nor is the silver from Mr Brown's trough – a crew-cut lawn, a bastardised Palladian façade set a hundred yards back from the road (a public road, by the way) – any different in weight from that earned by the great public- spirited captains of industry of, say, 60 years ago. Mr Brown has been criticised by politicians of both sides of the House for earning 47 times as much as British Gas showroom staff; yet, Frank Pick, chief executive of the London Passenger Transport Board from 1933–40 (when he shaped what was the world's finest integrated urban public transport system) earned pounds 10,000 a year, 43 times as much as a bus driver, and in 1935 London bus drivers were among the best-paid workers in Britain.

We warm to Frank Pick not simply for his professional achievements but for the fact that he chose to live in a particularly civilised, architect-designed Arts and Crafts house in an orchard on the edge of Hampstead Garden Suburb, was the greatest patron of the arts in Britain this century, was a member of the Reform Club (when the name meant what it said) and, when not travelling by Underground, was chauffeured in a hand-some black Daimler. Prime ministers found him as admirable and as daunting as they find Cedric Brown insensitive and suburban.

Cedric Harold Brown: the very name, his values, way of life, aspirations and luxury home are as monumentally English as Nigel Mansell or a 'jumbo G & T, ice'n'slice' sunk at the Mock Tudor bar of a Surrey golf club. Mr Brown's sumptuous pay rise is badly timed, but perhaps the one sure lesson to be drawn from this porcine tale of greed, envy and hot air is that we get the leaders, the business executives and the luxury, antiques-laden neo-Georgian homes we want and deserve.

Source: Ward, V. (1995), 'Cedric Brown, Fat Cat in the Dog House', *The Independent*, 13 March, p.17.

The Group was chaired by Sir Richard Greenbury, chairman and CEO of Marks & Spencer plc from 1988 to 1999, and its set of recommendations – which were published in July 1995 – is commonly referred to as the 'Greenbury Report'.

The Greenbury Report's main recommendations are:

- There should be a remuneration committee which is made up of non-executives. The committee should report to the shareholders on an annual basis about the company's executive pay policy.
- Executive pay should be disclosed on an individual basis. Until then it had been common practice to disclose only the total amount of executive pay and the executive pay of the 'highest paid director' without revealing the identity of the latter.
- Executive pay should be linked to company performance and the performance of individual directors.

In November 1995, the FRC set up the Committee on Corporate Governance which was chaired by Sir Ronald Hampel, chairman of ICI plc from 1995 to 1999. It was sponsored by the CBI, the LSE, the Consultative Committee of Accountancy Bodies (CCAB), the National Association of Pension Funds (NAPF), the Association of British Insurers (ABI) and the Institute of Directors (IOD). Its remit was to review the existing codes, to propose new recommendations and to merge the various recommendations into a single combined code.

The Committee published its final report in January 1998 and the Combined Code was published in June 1998. The Hampel Report stated that institutional shareholders 'have a responsibility to make considered use of their votes'. This was in reaction to research and consultancy reports which suggested that despite the Cadbury and Greenbury Reports highlighting the important role of institutional investors in corporate governance, the votes cast at the AGMs of FTSE100 companies were roughly 41 per cent in spring 1998, down from more than 43 per cent, also a lacklustre figure, in the previous year.[2]

The Code adopted the 'comply or explain' approach of the previous two codes, acknowledging that one size might not fit all and that flexibility was required to take account of different corporate realities. Companies now also had to provide a narrative on how they complied with the Code.

The Code also recommended that:

- A system of internal control be put in place to ensure that the company is run in the interests of the shareholders.
- The directors review the system's effectiveness at least once a year and report back to the shareholders.

The Turnbull Committee was set up by the Institute of Chartered Accountants in England and Wales (ICAEW) and chaired by Sir Nigel Turnbull, director of the Rank Group from 1987 to 1999. Its aim was to provide guidance on the internal control and its review as recommended by the first Combined Code. In

[2]manifest.co.uk/news/1998/1998062b.htm, accessed on 25 October 2010.

September 1999, it published its report entitled *Internal Control. Guidance for Directors on the Combined Code.* It confirmed that it was the directors' responsibility to make sure that a sound system of internal control was in place and that this system was effective. Further, the directors' review of this system should be published in the annual report.

While all previous codes, including the Combined Code, already referred to the important role of institutional investors, the Myners Report was to emphasize this role. The report was commissioned by the government and the review was led by Paul Myners, later Lord Myners and Financial Services Secretary to the Treasury under the Gordon Brown government. The report, which is entitled *Institutional Investment in the UK: A Review* was published in March 2001. It focused on the duties trustees of investment trusts and pension funds have towards their shareholders. These duties include intervening in the wake of poor performance in their portfolio firms.

Sir Derek Higgs conducted a review of the effectiveness of boards of directors and in particular non-executive directors, which was published in January 2003. This review supported the Combined Code, but also made a set of recommendations including:

- The roles of CEO and chairman of the board should be separated.
- The annual report should state the number of board meetings and committee meetings as well as the attendance of individual directors at these meetings.
- At least half of the board (excluding the chairman) should be composed of independent non-executive directors.
- The non-executives should meet at least once a year without the executives being present.
- There should be a senior independent director the shareholders should have access to in the case where their concerns could not be addressed by the chairman or CEO.
- There should be a nomination committee, consisting of a majority of non-executives, which would make recommendations to the board about board appointments.
- No one non-executive director should sit on all three company committees (audit, remuneration and nomination).
- The remuneration committee should set the policy for the remuneration of the executives, the chairman as well as the company secretary.

However, even as late as 2008 some larger firms chose not to follow some of the key recommendations of the Combined Code, such as the recommendation about separating the roles of chairman and CEO. Further, there were examples of companies, such as Marks & Spencer plc (see Box 6.2), which moved from a separation of the two roles back to combining the two roles.

The Combined Code was revised along the recommendations of the Higgs Report (2003) and Smith Report (2003) on the role of the audit committee. However, it replaced the Higgs recommendation that no one non-executive should sit on all three committees by the phrasing that there should be no 'undue reliance' on a single independent director. There was a second revision of the Combined Code in 2006. The three main changes were:

- The chairman, if considered to be independent, is allowed to sit on (but not to chair) the remuneration committee.
- Proxy forms should offer an option of abstention to vote.
- The proxy forms lodged at the annual general meeting (AGM) should be published on the company's website.

The 2008 credit crunch and the failures of large UK banks led to the Walker Review[3] which focused on the governance of banks and other financial institutions (published in November 2009) as well as yet another review of the Combined Code started in March 2009. The latter review, which was conducted by the FRC, was published in December 2009. While there had been consultation whether a move towards a more prescriptive code would be welcome, the general opinion was that the 'comply or explain' approach was still valid. The Code, which was approved in May 2010, was named 'The UK Corporate Governance Code' and replaced the Combined Code of 2006. The main changes were:

- The board should ensure that appropriate systems exist to identify, evaluate and manage the significant risks the company is exposed to.
- The annual report should include an explanatory statement about the company's business model and financial strategy.
- All directors of FTSE 350 companies should be re-elected annually.
- Performance-related pay should be aligned to the long-term interests of the company as well as its risk policies and systems.

Box 6.2
Duality at Marks & Spencer plc

NEW BOARD STRUCTURE

On 10 March 2008 we announced Board and senior management changes. We stated that Lord Burns would stand down as Chairman from 1 June 2008, when Sir Stuart Rose would be appointed Executive Chairman.

On 3 April 2008 Lord Burns wrote to shareholders setting out the detailed reasons behind the Board decisions. A copy of this letter is available on our website. The Board has taken this decision, cognisant of its prime objects to ensure the Company's ongoing commercial success, and has put in place balancing controls to mitigate the governance concerns:

- limited period of appointment of combined Chairman and Chief Executive until July 2011;
- appointment of Sir David Michels as Deputy Chairman;
- clear specification of duties of Executive Chairman and Deputy Chairman to ensure proper division of responsibilities and balance of power;
- appointment of two new executive directors and increased responsibility for the Group Finance and Operations Director;
- recruitment of an additional non-executive director to ensure a majority of independent directors on the Board. Following that appointment, the Boards will consider the appointment of a further non-executive; and
- annual voting by shareholders for Sir Stuart Rose's reappointment as a director starting at the 2008 AGM.

The Board unanimously believes that the overall arrangements represent a sensible way forward and provide a sound transitional governance structure leading to the appointment of a new Chairman and separate Chief Executive by summer 2011. The new structure will ensure continuity of leadership, strengthen the Board and streamline the

(Continued)

---

[3]The review was chaired by Sir David Walker, chairman of Morgan Stanley International from 1995 to 2001. This appointment was met with criticism from institutional investors (see e.g. *The Times*, 10 February 2009).

organisation. This will focus everyone on business performance during a period of significant trading uncertainty and it addresses investor concerns over succession.

CONSULTATION WITH SHAREHOLDERS

The Code states that: "if exceptionally a Board decides that a Chief Executive should become Chairman, the Board should consult major shareholders in advance and should set out its reasons to shareholders at the time of the appointment and in the next annual report".

In the period leading up to the announcement on 10 March 2008 of the Board and senior management changes, the Board considered how best to communicate with shareholders. The changes proposed as part of the new governance and management structure were wide-ranging and not only included the appointment of the Executive Chairman and Deputy Chairman but two new Board appointments, the extension of the Finance Director's role and a large number of senior management appointments, as well as news of the departures of several member of the senior management team.

In light of these proposed changes and their sensitivities the Board was concerned about the risk of leaks and did not consult major shareholders in advance. The Board was unanimous and clear that the proposed changes, taken as a whole, were in the interests of shareholders, customers and employees. The Board was also clear that whatever consultation was undertaken in advance of an announcement, its deliberations would nonetheless be subject to comment and scrutiny. The Board also knew that it would, rightly, be obliged under the Code to explain why it was proposing to combine the Chairman and Chief Executive roles and to answer questions from any shareholders with concerns.

Since the announcement, Lord Burns has consulted with a number of principal investors and shareholder representative bodies and he and Sir David Michels have met with those who have requested a meeting. A letter was also sent to all shareholders on 3 April 2008 setting out the detailed reasons behind the Board's decisions.

Source: Marks & Spencer plc, *2008 Annual Report*, pp.39–40.

The UK Corporate Governance Code was first revised in 2012 and then again in 2014 and 2016. The 2012 changes were as follows:

- FTSE 350 companies should put out to tender their external auditing contract at least every ten years.
- The audit committee should inform the shareholders on how it has carried out its responsibilities, including its assessment of the effectiveness of the external audit process.
- The board should confirm that the annual report and accounts are fair, balanced and understandable, and that the narrative sections of the report are consistent with the financial statements and that they are an accurate reflection of the company's performance.
- Companies should explain, and report on their progress with, their policies on board diversity.
- Companies should provide more extensive explanations about why they choose not to comply with a recommendation of the Code.

The 2014 revision focused on the disclosure of the risks which affect the company's longer-term viability. Companies should provide information to give a clearer and broader view of solvency, liquidity, risk management and viability. Investors should assess these statements thoroughly and engage accordingly. In addition, executive remuneration should be aligned to the long-term success of the company and this should be demonstrated more clearly to the shareholders. The main change made by the 2016 revision was to scrap the recommendation that FTSE 350 companies should put out to tender their external auditing contract at least every ten years.

The FRC issued the first UK Stewardship Code in 2010. The aim of the Code is to improve the quality of engagement between institutional investors and their investee firms to increase long-term returns to shareholders and to improve corporate governance. The Code was revised in 2012.

To summarize, successive UK codes of best practice have been based on the 'comply or explain' approach, the rationale being that there is a need for flexibility (e.g. for smaller firms which may find it too costly to comply with all the recommendations) which would not be provided if a more prescriptive approach were to be adopted. The various codes have consistently emphasized the role of non-executive directors as well as institutional investors in corporate governance. However, it is as yet uncertain whether these actors are ever going to meet the expectations put on them by the regulators (see Chapters 7 and 8).

6.3 The UK approach versus the US approach

The UK approach to corporate governance regulation has been self-regulation rather than prescriptive, statutory requirements. The 'comply or explain' approach has given listed companies, especially smaller companies, the possibility to opt out of certain provisions as one size may not fit all. Further, there has been a lot of emphasis on the role of boards starting with the first code, the Cadbury Report, and to a lesser extent on the role of institutional shareholders. This emphasis largely reflects the UK corporate governance landscape where the dominant type of shareholder is institutional investors (see Chapter 2) and the main conflict of interests is between the management and the shareholders (see Chapter 3).

Other countries have based themselves on the Cadbury Report and its successors to design their own corporate governance codes. However, it is debatable whether the emphasis on strong boards is the way forward given the different conflicts of interests and different types of scandals that are likely to affect firms outside the UK and the USA.[4] Hence, how does one ensure the independence of directors in a system which is dominated by large shareholders, and is this desirable in the first place given the potential monitoring benefits from having a large shareholder? Hence, an emphasis on regulating related-party transactions may be more appropriate than the focus on independent boards. In addition, Iram Ansari, Marc Goergen and Svetlana Mira found that for UK-listed firms that are family controlled and whose incumbent CEO is a family member, reported board independence drops by 21 per cent when they adjust for ties so-called independent directors have with the controlling family.[5] In contrast, for the equivalent French and German family controlled firms the drop is much greater with 43 per cent and 27 per cent, respectively.

The 'comply or explain' approach has not always worked well in other parts of the world. For example, Christian Andres and Erik Theissen report that the recommendation of the German Corporate Governance Code (the 'Cromme Code') to disclose executive remuneration on an individual basis was followed by only 10 out of the 146 firms they studied in 2002 and just 22 of these firms in 2003.[6] As a result, this provision was turned into a statutory requirement effective from the 2006 financial year.

Similarly, the 'Dutch Answer to the Cadbury Report', the 1997 Peters Report, which made 40 recommendations about corporate governance, only had limited success. This was mainly because companies could choose

---

[4]John Coffee argues that managers in corporate governance systems with dispersed ownership and control are more likely to manipulate earnings, whereas in corporate governance systems with concentrated control there is a greater risk of minority shareholder expropriation. See Section 16.3 of Chapter 16.

[5]Ansari, I.F., Goergen, M. and Mira, S. (2014), 'The Determinants of the CEO Successor Choice in Family Firms', *Journal of Corporate Finance* 28, 6–25.

[6]Andres, C. and Theissen, E. (2008), 'Setting a Fox to Keep the Geese: Does the Comply-or-Explain Principle Work?', *Journal of Corporate Finance* 14, 289–301.

whether or not to comply with the recommendations, but did not have to explain if they chose not to comply. Hence, in 2003 the Peters Report was replaced by the Dutch Corporate Governance Code which contains compulsory rules as well as a set of recommendations that companies have to comply with or explain non-compliance. In contrast, the 'comply or explain' approach has worked well with successive French codes of corporate governance which include the Viénot I Report, the Viénot II Report and the Bouton Report. All three reports were combined in the Corporate Governance of Listed Companies (*Le Gouvernement d'Entreprise des Sociétés Cotées*) in 2003.

While La Porta et al.'s categorization of legal families (see Chapter 4) suggests that there should be little difference between the UK and USA, the US approach is substantially different. The 2,300-page long 2010 Dodd-Frank Wall Street Reform and Consumer Protection Act is a good illustration of the prescriptive nature of US regulation. In particular, US regulation is much more prescriptive than the UK principles-based approach. In addition, the 50 federal states in the USA also compete in terms of corporate law and regulation. In practice, the competition is between Delaware and the other 49 states: firms decide either to stay in their own state or to (re)incorporate in Delaware (see also Section 10.3 of Chapter 10). Indeed, 95 per cent of the firms that incorporate outside their state choose Delaware. The question that arises is whether this regulatory competition will result in a race to the top (i.e. firms move to the place with the best regulation) or a race to the bottom (i.e. firms move to the place with the weakest regulation). The main argument in favour of a race to the top is that directors will choose the law and regulation that maximizes firm value. The main argument in favour of a race to the bottom is that the above argument only applies to those rules that do not affect private benefits of control. If rules affecting private benefits are taken into account, states may cater for managers rather than shareholders. One way of catering for managers is to offer anti-takeover devices, enabling managers to entrench themselves.

These anti-takeover devices protect managers from hostile raiders. Takeover defences or anti-takeover devices include voting caps, dual-class shares (see Sections 3.4 and 3.5 of Chapter 3 for a discussion of both as well as Box 6.3 for an example of the latter), and staggered boards of directors. In 2014/15, according to Institutional Shareholder Services 16.8 per cent of Standard & Poor's (S&P) 500 companies had a staggered board.[7] A staggered board, also sometimes called a classified board, consists of a board segmented into classes, typically three, with only one class of directors coming up for election in a given year (see Box 6.4). Hence, in the case of a board with three classes of directors it will take the shareholders two elections to replace the majority of directors.[8]

Setting up such takeover defences may not be in the interest of shareholders as it may prevent value-increasing takeovers. In line with this argument, a large body of empirical studies finds that the stock price reacts negatively to the adoption of takeover defences.[9] Further, firms frequently reincorporate to set up takeover defences. However, a number of practitioners and academics argue that anti-takeover devices, including staggered boards, can be in the interests of the shareholders. They base their argument on the following two reasons.[10] First, such devices may enable managers to extract a higher premium in the case of a takeover. Nevertheless, the above-mentioned negative market reaction to the adoption of anti-takeover devices fails to provide empirical support for this reason. Second, such devices may protect valuable firm projects and assets

[7] corpgov.law.harvard.edu/2016/06/01/iss-2016-board-practices-study/, accessed on 7 February 2017.
[8] Bebchuk, L.A., Coates, J. IV and Subramanian, G. (2002), 'The Powerful Antitakeover Force of Staggered Boards: Theory, Evidence & Policy', *Stanford Law Review* 54, 887–951.
[9] See e.g. Gompers, P., Ishii, J. and Metrick, A. (2003), 'Corporate Governance and Equity Prices', *Quarterly Journal of Economics* 118, 107–36; Bebchuk, L., Cohen, A. and Ferrell, A. (2009), 'What Matters In Corporate Governance?' *Review of Financial Studies* 22, 738–827.
[10] Johnson, W.C., Karpoff, J.M. and Yi, S. (2015), 'The Bonding Hypothesis of Takeover Defenses: Evidence from IPO Firms', *Journal of Financial Economics* 117, 307–32. See also Section 11.7 of Chapter 11.

that create shareholder value in the long term, but that myopic or short-term investors in the stock market may undervalue. Mark Humphery-Jenner found evidence in support of the latter as firms that are hard to value make acquisitions that generate more shareholder value and more innovation.[11]

Box 6.3
Dual-class shares

COMMON STOCK

As of December 31, 2015, Revlon, Inc.'s authorized common stock consisted of 900 millions shares of Class A Common Stock, with a par value of $0.01 per share (the "Class A Common Stock"), and 200 million shares of Class B Common stock, par value $0.01 per share ("Class B Common Stock" and together with the Class A Common Stock, the "Common Stock"). In October 2009, Revlon, Inc., amended its certificate of incorporation to (1) clarify that the provision requiring that holders of its Class A Common Stock and holders of its Class B Common Stock receive the same consideration in certain business combinations shall only apply in connection with transactions involving third parties; and (2) increase the number of Revlon, Inc.'s authorized shares of preferred stock from 20 million to 50 million and, accordingly, to increase the number of Revlon, Inc.'s authorized shares of capital stock from 1,120 million to 1,150 million. The holders of Class A Common Stock and Class B Common Stock vote as a single class on all matters, except as otherwise required by law, with each share of Class A Common Stock entitling its holder to one vote and each share of the Class B Common Stock entitling its holder to ten votes. The holders of the Company 's two classes of authorized Common Stock are entitled to share equally in the earnings of the Company from dividends, when and if declared by Revlon, Inc's Board of Directors. Each share of Class B Common Stock is convertible into one share of Class A Common Stock.

Source: Revlon, Inc., Form 10-K, 2015, pp. F-53–F-54.

Box 6.4
Fitbit Inc.'s staggered board

Section 2.2: Election; Resignation; Removal; Vacancies. Election of directors need not be by written ballot. Unless otherwise provided by the Certificate of Incorporation and subject to the special rights of holders of any series of Preferred Stock to elect directors, immediately following the Voting Threshold Date (as defined in the Certificate of Incorporation), the Board shall be divided into three classes, designated: Class I, Class II and Class III. Each class shall consist, as nearly as may be possible, of one-third of the Whole Board. Each director shall hold office until the annual meeting at which such director's term expires and until such director's successor is elected and qualified or until such director's earlier death, resignation, disqualification or removal …

Source: Fitbit Inc., Exhibit 3.2, 'Restated Bylaws', as adopted 27 May 2015 and as effective 23 June 2015.

---

[11]Humphery-Jenner, M. (2014), 'Takeover Defenses, Innovation, and Value Creation: Evidence from Acquisition Decisions', *Strategic Management Journal* 35, 668–90. See also Section 11.7 of Chapter 11.

While anti-takeover devices are commonplace in US corporations, the UK City Code on Takeovers and Mergers[12] prohibits the use of such devices unless they are put in place *after* the company has received a take-over offer and *only* with the approval of the shareholders. In other words, while in the USA it is acceptable for companies to have *anticipatory* anti-takeover devices in place, these are not allowed in the UK.

The Employee Retirement Income Security Act (ERISA) of 1974 (as well as the Department of Labor Bulletin 29 CFR 2509.94-2 which provided a clarification as to proxy voting) is a federal law that sets out minimum requirements for private health and retirement funds. It has effectively been interpreted as requiring compulsory voting by private pension funds. Again, this is in direct contrast with UK regulation which only recommends that institutional investors make considerate use of their votes. This interpretation of ERISA in principle also affects equity holdings in foreign corporations. Hence, pension funds are encouraged to conduct a cost-and-benefit analysis before investing in foreign equity markets. The 'statement on investment policy' in the annual report may include general guidelines on voting (rather than specific voting instructions).

The Sarbanes-Oxley Act (SOX) of 2002 was a direct reaction to the Enron scandal and the failure of their auditors, Arthur Andersen, to prevent the fraud (see also Section 16.2 of Chapter 16). SOX reinforces the need for independent auditors and exposes auditors to increased penalties in the event of audit failures. Section 404 requires the management and the auditors to prepare an internal control report and to comment on the soundness of the company's internal control over financial reporting (ICFR). Some have argued that this is the costliest provision of SOX. SOX has also been accused of being a knee-jerk reaction to Enron and other corporate scandals, and it may have caused up to 300 voluntary delistings of US companies in the years following its introduction. There is also evidence that some foreign companies cross-listed on a US stock exchange may have delisted in response to SOX (see Box 6.5 for the example of a UK firm delisting from Nasdaq).

Box 6.5
Delisting from Nasdaq

'**D**uring the year [2005] it was decided to terminate the Group's ADR programme in the USA and to de-list from NASDAQ thus reducing compliance costs significantly, freeing management time and avoiding unnecessary and onerous commitments'.

Source: 2005 annual report of Provalis plc, p. 2.

The Dodd-Frank Act was signed on 21 July 2010 by US President Barack Obama. It gradually came into effect over 2010/11 as the government agencies concerned issued the rules to implement the various sections of the Act. The Act is 2,300 pages long and its aim is to reform Wall Street, improve the protection of consumers of financial products and services, and to provide new tools to deal with financial crises and waves of bankruptcies. Importantly, the Act includes a set of new requirements relating to executive remuneration, advisory (i.e. non-binding) votes on the latter and pay disclosure that the SEC has to impose on listed companies. These requirements include the following:

---

[12]See www.thetakeoverpanel.org.uk/the-code/download-code.

- Bank holding companies must appoint a risk committee.
- Companies must hold advisory votes on their managerial compensation policy in 2011. Thereafter, it is up to individual companies to ask their shareholders for triannual, biannual or annual advisory votes.
- Companies are required to hold a non-binding vote on golden parachutes, i.e. managerial severance pay, when shareholders vote on mergers, acquisitions and substantial asset sell-offs.
- Institutional investors that manage more than US$100 million have to disclose annually how they vote on advisory resolutions and golden parachutes.
- Companies must disclose their policy on how they address the link between managerial compensation and financial performance, including stock prices and dividends.
- Companies must provide pay equity disclosure by comparing the CEO's total annual compensation with the median compensation of all the other employees.
- All listed companies must have an independent remuneration committee.
- Companies also must disclose the reasons for having CEO-chairman duality or for separating the two roles. However, a similar disclosure rule had already been put in place in December 2009 by the SEC for listed firms.

Still, the SEC is allowed to exempt smaller firms from the requirements of the Dodd-Frank Act as to advisory votes and golden parachutes.

6.4 The G20/OECD Principles of Corporate Governance

The Principles, originally named 'OECD Principles on Corporate Governance', were first issued in 1999, revised in 2004 and revised again in 2014/15. The latter revision was undertaken to reflect the lessons learnt from the 2008 financial crisis in the Principles. The 2004 review was undertaken by the OECD Steering Group on Corporate Governance, which comprises representatives from all 30 member governments; observers from the World Bank, the International Monetary Fund, the Bank for International Settlements, the Financial Stability Forum, the International Organization of Securities Commissions (IOSCO) and the Basel Committee. The Business and Trade Union consultative committees to the OECD (BIAC and TUAC) also took part in the Steering Group's meetings. For the 2014/15 revision, the non-OECD G20 countries were also invited to participate in the review of the Principles alongside relevant international organizations such as the Basel Committee on Banking Supervision, the Financial Stability Board and World Bank Group. This revision resulted in the 'G20/OECD Principles of Corporate Governance'.

The Principles are intended to serve as guidance to OECD as well as non-OECD countries that aim at improving their national legal and institutional framework for corporate governance. They are mainly aimed at stock-market listed companies, but may also be valuable for improving corporate governance in privately held companies. It is explicitly stated in the Principles that there is no '*single* model of good corporate governance' and that the Principles are general enough to be applicable and relevant across the whole range of corporate governance systems. The Principles have been adopted by the World Bank in its work. They have also guided various countries, such as China and Greece, in drafting their corporate governance codes.

The Principles are as follows:

| *Ensuring the basis for an effective corporate governance framework.* This is about transparent, fair, efficient and well-regulated markets with effective institutions that supervise the markets and enforce existing regulation.

A   The corporate governance framework should be developed taking into account its impact on economic performance, the integrity of markets, the incentives it provides to market participants and the promotion of well-functioning and transparent markets.

B   The law and regulations pertaining to corporate governance practice should be transparent, consistent with the rule of law and be enforceable.

C   The division of responsibilities among authorities should be clearly stated and be in the public interest.

D   Stock market regulation should promote good corporate governance.

E   Supervisory, regulatory and enforcement authorities should be able to carry out their duties in an objective and professional way. Their rulings should be timely, fully justified and transparent.

F   Cooperation across borders should be enhanced, including bilateral and multilateral exchange of information.

II *The rights and equitable treatment of shareholders and key ownership functions.*

A   Shareholders should have basic rights which include ownership rights (i.e. the right to register their ownership and to transfer their ownership). They should be able to obtain material information on the company and to be provided with such information on a regular and timely basis. They should be able to participate and vote at the AGMs. They should be able to elect and dismiss members of the board. Shareholders should be able to share in the company's earnings.

B   Shareholders should be consulted on substantial changes to the nature of the firm (e.g. changes to the articles of association) and be provided with all the relevant information.

C   Shareholders should be able to attend the shareholders' meetings, vote at the meetings and be adequately informed about the meetings' procedures, including the voting process.

D   Shareholders, including institutional investors, should be able to consult each other on their basic shareholder rights as defined in the Principles.

E   All shareholders of the same class should be treated in the same way. Arrangements that give certain shareholders disproportionate control relative to their ownership should be disclosed.

F   Related-party transactions should be made and approved in such a manner that conflicts of interests are properly managed and that the interests of the company and its shareholders are protected.

G   Minority shareholders should be protected from harmful action by the controlling shareholders and should have effective means of redress. Abusive self-dealing should not be allowed.

H   Markets for corporate control should be permitted to work efficiently and transparently.

III *Institutional investors, stock markets and other intermediaries.* The corporate governance framework should provide sound incentives throughout the investment chain and enable stock markets to work in a way that promotes good corporate governance.

A   Institutional investors acting in a fiduciary capacity should disclose their policies on corporate governance and voting as well as their procedures for deciding whether to vote.

B   Custodians and nominees should cast votes as instructed by the beneficiary owners of the shares.

C   Institutional investors acting in a fiduciary capacity should disclose how they deal with material conflicts of interests that may affect the exercise of the key ownership rights of their investments.

D   Proxy advisers, analysts, brokers, rating agencies and others that provide advice and research to guide investors' decisions should disclose conflicts of interests that might compromise their advice and research and minimise such conflicts.

E   Market manipulation and insider trading should not be allowed and the relevant rules should be enforced.

F   The corporate governance laws and regulation applicable to companies that are listed in a jurisdiction other than their jurisdiction of incorporation should be clearly disclosed. For cross-listings, the criteria and procedures in place for recognizing the listing requirements of the primary listing should be disclosed and be transparent.

G Stock markets should provide efficient and fair price discovery to promote good corporate governance.

IV *The role of stakeholders in corporate governance.* The corporate governance framework should respect the rights of stakeholders as specified by the law or mutual agreements. It should also encourage cooperation between companies and stakeholders to create wealth, jobs and the sustainability of financially sound companies.

A The rights of stakeholders as specified by law or mutual agreements must be respected.

B Stakeholders should be able to ask for effective redress if their legal rights are violated.

C Mechanisms for employee participation should be allowed to develop.

D Where stakeholders participate in corporate governance processes, they should be provided with relevant, sufficient and reliable information in a regular and timely fashion.

E Stakeholders, including employees and their representatives, should be able to raise concerns about unethical and illegal practices with the board or the relevant public authorities. Their rights should not be compromised for doing so.

F The corporate governance framework should ensure the effective enforcement of creditor rights and provide an efficient and effective framework for insolvency.

V *Disclosure and transparency.* All shareholders should have access to timely and accurate information on all matters regarding the company, including the company's financial performance and situation, its governance and ownership.

A Disclosure should include material information, but not be limited to:

- The financial and operating results of the company.
- The company's objectives and non-financial information.
- Major share ownership, including beneficial owners and voting rights.
- The compensation of the board and key executives.
- Information on the board members, including the selection process, as well as the board members' qualifications, their other directorships and whether they are regarded to be independent by the board.
- Related-party transactions.
- Foreseeable risk factors.
- Issues relating to employees and other stakeholders.
- Governance structures and policies.

B Information should be prepared and disclosed following high-quality standards of accounting, financial and non-financial reporting.

C There should be an annual audit by an independent, qualified and competent auditor following high-quality auditing standards.

D The auditor should be accountable to the shareholders and have a duty to the company to exercise due professional care.

E Information should be disseminated via channels that provide equal, timely and cost-effective access for users to relevant information.

VI *The responsibilities of the board.* The board should ensure that it fulfils its roles of strategic guidance and monitoring and that it is accountable to the company and the shareholders.

A The board should act on a fully informed basis, in good faith, with due diligence and care, and in the best interest of the company and its shareholders.

B   The board should treat all shareholders fairly.

C   The board should follow high ethical standards and take into account the interests of stakeholders.

D   The board should fulfil certain key functions, including:

- The review of and guidance on strategy, major plans of actions, managerial policies and procedures, annual business plans and budgets; the setting of performance targets; the monitoring of implementation and corporate performance; and monitoring major capital expenditures, acquisitions and divestitures.
- Monitoring the effectiveness of the company's governance practices and making changes where required.
- The selection, compensation, monitoring and, if necessary, the replacement of key executives and overseeing succession planning.
- Aligning the compensation of the board and key executives with the longer-term objectives of the company and its shareholders.
- Ensuring that nominations and elections to the board are transparent and formal.
- Monitoring and managing conflicts of interests of managers, board members and shareholders, including abuse in related-party transactions and misuse of company assets.
- Ensuring the integrity of the company's accounting and financial reporting systems and that appropriate control systems exist.
- Overseeing disclosure and communications.

E   The board should be able to exercise objective judgement on company affairs.

F   The board members should be able to access accurate, relevant and timely information to fulfil their responsibilities.

G   Where employee board representation is mandatory, the access to information and training for employee representatives should be facilitated so that employee board representation is effective and best contributes to enhancing board skills, information and independence.

6.5 Corporate governance regulation in the rest of the world

This section provides a brief overview of corporate governance regulation in the major economies in the world. Rather than providing exhaustive reviews of the regulation, the focus is on the broad approach and the key aspects of the regulation.

6.5.1 CHINA

China launched a number of major economic reforms during the late 1980s/early 1990s to move its economy towards a socialist market economy (see Section 4.2 of Chapter 4). These reforms included the creation of the Shenzen Stock Exchange in 1990 and the Shanghai Stock Exchange a year later, the platforms for the part privatization of China's state-owned enterprises (SOEs). A number of corporate scandals during the first ten years of the two stock exchanges led to China's first code of corporate governance in 2001. The code, which was issued by the China Securities Regulatory Commission (CSRC), is called the 'Code of Corporate Governance for Listed Companies in China'. The Code was modelled on the 1999 OECD Principles on Corporate Governance. It is a mandatory code applying to all companies listed in China. It lays down shareholder rights as well as the duties and moral standards for directors, supervisors and managers.

The following rules apply to independent or non-executive directors[13]:

- Independent directors and their immediate family members cannot work for the company or own a significant stake in the company.
- Independent directors cannot own a significant stake in any of the controlling shareholders' other companies.
- Independent directors are not allowed to provide consulting services to the company.
- At least one of the independent directors must have an accounting qualification.

Since 2003, Chinese firms have to have at least one-third of their directors that are independent. The term of an independent director is three years and a director can serve a maximum of two consecutive terms. An independent director cannot hold more than five directorships at any given time.

6.5.2 JAPAN

In September 1997, as a reaction to a series of corporate scandals the *Keidanren*, the Japanese Business Federation, issued a document entitled 'Urgent Recommendations Concerning Corporate Governance'. This document urged Japanese corporations to ensure that their governance is effective in maintaining ethical standards and good management. Among other issues, the document called for the strengthening of the auditors' function. This was followed a month later by the 'Corporate Governance Principles'. The Principles spell out the idiosyncrasies of the Japanese corporate governance system, including the key role of the *shacho*, the Japanese equivalent of the CEO, who typically also happens to be the chair of the board of directors, the stakeholder approach – such as the implicit guarantee of long-term employment with the company given to workers – and the governance structure. The latter includes the board of directors, typically dominated by executive directors, and the board of auditors. The board of auditors does not have any decision-making power and performs ex-post internal auditing. There are two types of principles: principles A which should be adopted in approximately five years and principles B which should be adopted by the twenty-first century. The Principles focus on accountability and disclosure as well as the governance structure (directors and the board of directors, auditors and the board of auditors, shareholder meetings). The Principles were revised in 2001.

The year 2004 then saw the first publication of the 'Principles of Corporate Governance for Listed Companies', which was broadly modelled on the OECD Principles. Interestingly, the preface states that the Principles should not be seen as minimum standards and that companies not following the Principles should not be forced to explain why:

> The purpose of these Principles is to provide a necessary common base for recognition, thereby enhancing corporate governance through the integration of voluntary activities by listed companies and demands by shareholders and investors.[14]

Importantly, the 2004 Principles offered companies a choice of two governance systems:

- A 'corporate auditors' system' consisting of general meetings of the shareholders, the board of directors and the board of corporate auditors; and

---

[13]Zhu, J., Ye, K., Wu Tucker, J. and Chan, K.J.C. (2016), 'Board Hierarchy, Independent Directors, and Firm Value: Evidence from China', *Journal of Corporate Finance* 41, 262–79.
[14]See Tokyo Stock Exchange (2004), *Principles of Corporate Governance for Listed Companies*, Tokyo: Tokyo Stock Exchange, Inc., p. 3.

- A 'committees' system' consisting of general meetings of the shareholders and the board of directors (encompassing the nomination committee, audit committee and compensation committee).

The 2004 Principles were revised in 2009. While the 2004 Principles offered companies a choice of two governance structures, the 2009 Principles introduced a third choice, i.e. a system centred around outside or non-executive directors which was similar to the corporate auditors' system but with the board of directors having at least one-third to one-half of non-executive directors. In 2015, the 2009 Principles were replaced by 'Japan's Corporate Governance Code Seeking Sustainable Corporate Growth and Increased Corporate Value over the Mid- to Long-Term'.

6.5.3 INDIA

In 1998, the Confederation of Indian Industry (CII) issued 'Desirable Corporate Governance in India – A Code'. This was superseded by the 'Report of the Kumar Mangalam Birla Committee on Corporate Governance' which was published in 2000 by the Securities and Exchange Board of India (SEBI). The Code applies to both listed companies and public sector companies. It contains two types of 'recommendations': mandatory recommendations and non-mandatory recommendations. The Code recommends a minimum of one-third of non-executives on the board of directors. However, in the case where the chairman is an executive, there is a mandatory minimum of 50 per cent of non-executives. In contrast to consecutive UK codes, the Indian Code does not recommend that CEO-chair duality should be avoided.

Partly as a reaction to the 2008 financial crisis but also in reaction to India's very own corporate scandal around Satyam Computers, the Ministry of Corporate Affairs issued the 'Corporate Governance – Voluntary Guidelines' in 2009. The Guidelines take into account the recommendations of the 2000 SEBI Code and work on an incremental, but voluntary basis. It is important to note that India's response has been more in line with the UK approach of developing broad principles of corporate governance rather than adopting the much more prescriptive US approach.[15]

6.5.4 GERMANY

As highlighted in Section 6.3, the 'comply or explain approach' did not work well in Germany. An early example of the limited success of transposing this approach into the German corporate governance system is the 1995 Takeover Code (*Übernahmekodex der Börsensachverständigenkommission beim Bundesministerium der Finanzen*). The Code was a voluntary code, similar to the UK City Code on Takeovers and Mergers. It called for a mandatory takeover bid for the remaining equity once a party had acquired control (50 per cent of the votes or 75 per cent of the votes represented at the latest AGM). However, the Code had few followers and even the signatories to the Code tended to ignore its recommendations.[16]

The German Corporate Governance Code, or 'Cromme Code' named after Dr Gerhard Cromme who chaired the commission which developed the Code, was published in 2002. This Code also adopted the 'comply or explain' approach. The Code includes a summary of the regulatory changes in terms of disclosure and transparency. Its main focus, however, is on the duties of the management board and supervisory board, which

[15]Varottil, U. (2010), 'India's Corporate Governance Voluntary Guidelines 2009: Rhetoric or Reality?', *National Law School of India Review* 22, 1–22. Available at SSRN: ssrn.com/abstract=1634821.
[16]Goergen, M., Manjon, M. and Renneboog, L. (2008), 'Recent Developments in German Corporate Governance', *International Review of Law and Economics* 28, 175–93; Goergen, M., Manjon, M. and Renneboog, L. (2008), 'Is the German System of Corporate Governance Converging Towards the Anglo-American Model?', *Journal of Management and Governance* 12, 37–71.

form the German two-tier board system. Importantly, the issue of CEO-chairman duality does not arise under the German system as German company law prohibits individuals from sitting on both the management board and the supervisory board. This results in a clear delineation between executive and non-executive directors.[17] Nevertheless, Germany faces its own corporate governance challenges. These include the practice that members of the management board (including the CEO), once retired, join the supervisory board. Hence, the Code recommends that the supervisory board should not have more than two former members from the management board.

The Code has been revised virtually every year since 2002. An important revision occurred in 2005 when the following definition of independence for the supervisory board members was included:

[t]he Supervisory Board shall include what it considers an adequate number of independent members. A Supervisory Board member is considered independent if he/she has no business or personal relations with the company or its Management Board which cause a conflict of interests.[18]

6.6 The harmonization of corporate governance regulation across the European Union

Marc Goergen, Marina Martynova and Luc Renneboog studied the likely long-term effects of the 2004 European Union (EU) Takeover Directive on the corporate governance systems of the EU member states.[19] The Directive was eventually adopted in April 2004 after much opposition from a number of countries that argued that the Directive would damage their national corporate governance systems.

Will this EU Directive eventually cause the various systems to converge with each other? As the EU Directive was largely modelled on the UK City Code on Takeovers and Mergers, will the rest of Europe move closer to the UK in terms of corporate governance? Goergen et al. argued that a given rule, such as the mandatory bid rule, may have very different effects depending on the corporate governance system that is in place. They argued that some of the rules may further strengthen some of the characteristics of the insider system while others will weaken them.

Their argument is as follows. Takeover regulation influences a country's corporate governance system in two ways. First, it either facilitates or hinders changes in ownership and control. Second, it also affects the level of investor protection. The level of investor protection can be affected by:

- curbing private benefits of control of large shareholders and
- reducing managerial discretion or power by improving external monitoring of the management via the market for corporate governance (e.g. via the prohibition of anti-takeover devices).

Hence, any reform of takeover regulation is likely to have a major impact on a country's corporate governance system. However, the impact the reform will have on ownership and control depends on the initial characteristics of the country's corporate governance system. If a country's system has initially high levels of managerial discretion, then it is unlikely that a decrease in private benefits of control reduces ownership and

[17]Goergen, M., Limbach, P. and Scholz, M. (2015), 'Mind the Gap. The Age Difference between the CEO and the Chair', *Journal of Corporate Finance* 35, 136–58.

[18]Government Commission on the German Corporate Governance Code (2005), *German Corporate Governance Code*, Frankfurt am Main, Germany: Government Commission on the German Corporate Governance Code, p. 10.

[19]Goergen, M., Martynova, M. and Renneboog, L. (2005), 'Corporate Governance Convergence: Evidence from Takeover Regulation Reforms in Europe', *Oxford Review of Economic Policy* 21, 243–68.

control concentration, as the only way for shareholders to curb managerial excesses is to stay in control. In contrast, if managerial discretion is already low via, e.g. effective external monitoring, then a reduction in the private benefits of control accruing to large shareholders is likely to result in even higher dispersion of ownership and control. Likewise, if private benefits of control accruing to large shareholders are already low, then reducing managerial power or discretion will further disperse ownership and control. Finally, if private benefits of control are high, then reducing managerial power is unlikely to increase the dispersion of ownership and control as the incumbent will prefer to keep control and carry on enjoying the private benefits of control. Ownership and control may only change hands if there exists a new large shareholder who values the company as much as the incumbent does. This will only be the case if the new large shareholder expects to derive private benefits of control from the company which are at least as great as those enjoyed by the incumbent. Hence given the low likelihood of this occurring, ownership and control are unlikely to experience changes and are even less likely to end up being dispersed. Table 6.1 summarizes the likely impact of a reform of takeover regulation on ownership and control based on the initial characteristics of the country's system of corporate governance.

Table 6.1 Initial characteristics of a country's corporate governance system and likely impact of a reform of takeover regulation

Initial characteristics of the system	Takeover regulation reform	Likely impact on ownership and control
High managerial discretion	Decrease in private benefits of control	Remains concentrated
Low managerial discretion		Increase in dispersion
Low private benefits of control	Reduction in managerial discretion	Increase in dispersion
High private benefits of control		Remains concentrated

Source: adapted from Goergen et al. (2005)

The mandatory bid rule is one of the provisions of the EU Takeover Directive which is likely to have a different impact across the various national corporate governance systems. The mandatory bid aims at providing an exit from the firm on fair terms to all shareholders in the case of a takeover bid. An investor who acquires a stake exceeding a certain threshold has to make a tender offer for the remaining shares of the firm. The minimum price that can be offered in the tender is also prescribed. For example, the price may have to be equal to or higher than the highest price the bidder paid for the shares she has already acquired over the last 12 months or it may have to be equal to or higher than a given percentage (e.g. 75 per cent) of the average share price over the previous 12 months.

The mandatory bid rule may reduce the risk of expropriation of minority shareholders by the large shareholder. However, as it makes changes in control more expensive it may also discourage some bids from being made. The impact of this rule on systems with concentrated ownership and control is likely to be major for at least three reasons. First, it reduces the trade in controlling stakes which is the dominant way of transferring control in the insider system. Second, it restricts the size of the stake an investor can acquire without triggering a compulsory tender offer. Third, the higher the price that a potential bidder will have to pay in a mandatory tender offer the more unlikely he will make a bid in the first place. The price at which the incumbent large shareholder is willing to sell the firm is likely to reflect her private benefits of control. In other words, an incumbent large shareholder with large private benefits of control is unlikely ever to find a buyer that puts an adequate value on her private benefits of control as the latter are typically not transferable. Hence, the mandatory bid rule is unlikely to increase the dispersion of ownership and control in the insider system. Even worse, it is likely to prevent changes in controlling blocks of shares which did occur before the reform. In contrast, ownership and control in the outsider system is unlikely to be affected by this rule. To conclude, the same rule causes existing control patterns in the insider system to prevail while it has little impact on the outsider system.

6.7 Conclusions

This chapter started with a review of successive UK codes of corporate governance given that the UK has been at the forefront of corporate governance regulation in the world. The emphasis of the UK codes has been on the corporate governance roles of the board of directors and institutional investors. Successive codes have focused on improving the independence of the board and encouraging institutional investors to make considerate use of their votes at the AGMs of their investee firms.

The UK at the forefront of corporate governance regulation

While the UK has been successful in exporting its regulation, it is important to bear in mind that the UK system of corporate governance is very different from other systems in terms of the likely conflicts of interests that corporations may suffer from. In particular, there is mixed evidence as to the success of transplanting the 'comply or explain' approach into other cultures, such as France, Germany and the Netherlands. Regulators are frequently far too obsessed about the principal-agent problem, i.e. they give too much attention to protecting shareholders from being expropriated by the management while the prevailing corporate governance problems may be caused by the presence of a large shareholder.

The limited success of the 'comply or explain' approach outside the UK

While La Porta et al.'s theory on legal families suggested that the UK and US approaches to corporate governance regulation should be very similar, in practice they are very different. Indeed, the UK approach is based on self-regulation and voluntary codes of conduct whereas the US approach is based on prescriptive law. To a great extent, the US approach – in particular the use of mandatory law rather than codes of best practice with broad principles – fits much better with what one would expect from a civil law country than a common law country.

The very different UK and US approaches to corporate governance regulation

The G20/OECD Principles of Corporate Governance are a cross-national initiative to provide minimum standards of good corporate governance. While the Principles aim to establish minimum standards, they also try to take account of different national approaches to doing things. The Principles have guided not only the OECD member states, but also non-OECD and G20 states such as China.

The G20/OECD Principles of Corporate Governance

Finally, the EU has also made efforts to harmonize corporate governance regulation across its member states. However, it is as yet unclear whether over the long run these steps will reduce the existing differences in terms of corporate control and ownership across the EU or whether they will reinforce them. Indeed, the effects on ownership concentration of provisions aimed at reducing private benefits of control may be very different depending on whether a country's managers enjoy high or low discretion.

Convergence across the EU

6.8 Discussion questions

1 'According to La Porta et al. (1998), both the UK and USA are common law countries using case law. However, the two countries' approaches to corporate governance regulation could not be more different'. (Anonymous)

Critically discuss the above statement.

2 'The main problem with corporate governance regulation and codes of best practice is that they are reactive. Each new wave of corporate scandals causes yet another regulatory reform and frequently politicians, as a result of public pressure, resort to knee-jerk reactions, producing new regulation that does not address the real causes of corporate failures. Hence, corporate governance will never improve and corporate scandals will never cease'. (Anonymous)

Discuss the above statement in the light of recent regulatory developments in the UK and/or the USA.

Reading list

Key reading

Andres, C. and Theissen, E. (2008), 'Setting a Fox to Keep the Geese – Does the Comply-or-Explain Principle work?', *Journal of Corporate Finance* 14, 289–301.

Cheffins, B. (2000), 'Corporate Governance Reform: Britain as an Exporter', *Hume Papers on Public Policy* 8, 10–28.

Dahya, J., McConnell, J. and Travlos, N.G. (2002), 'The Cadbury Committee, Corporate Governance, and Top Management Turnover', *Journal of Finance* 57, 461–83.

Goergen, M., Martynova, M. and Renneboog, L. (2005), 'Corporate Governance Convergence: Evidence from Takeover Regulation Reforms in Europe', *Oxford Review of Economic Policy* 21, 243–68.

Further reading

Shrives, P.J and Brennan, N.M. (2015), 'A Typology for Explaining the Quality of Explanations for Non-compliance with UK Corporate Governance Regulations', *British Accounting Review* 47, 85–99.

Additional resources

Consult the website of the European Corporate Governance Institute (ECGI) for links to the electronic versions of the various current as well as historical national and cross-national corporate governance codes and regulations:
http://www.ecgi.global/content/codes

Improving corporate governance

PART III

7 Boards of directors

Chapter Aims

This chapter focuses on the board of directors. The board of directors is an important corporate governance mechanism – in addition to those reviewed in Chapter 8 – to ensure that managers run the firm in the interests of the shareholders as well as possibly other stakeholders. Boards of directors exist across corporate governance systems, i.e. the insider and outsider systems. However, boards differ across countries as some countries have single-tier boards whereas other countries have two-tier boards. Another important characteristic of boards is duality, whereby the CEO also acts as the chairman of the board of directors. The chapter also reviews the factors that explain board turnover as well as discussing board gender balance and board diversity.

Learning Outcomes

After reading this chapter, you should be able to:

1 Compare the single-tier to the two-tier board system

2 Discuss the advantages and disadvantages of CEO-chairman duality

3 Assess the evidence on the link between board independence and firm performance

4 Explain the factors that drive board turnover

5 Describe the role of the market for directors

6 Evaluate the effectiveness of mandatory board gender quotas

7 Synthesize the literature on the effects of board gender balance and board diversity on risk taking and monitoring intensity

7.1 Introduction

This chapter reviews an important corporate governance mechanism, the board of directors, which applies to both the insider system and the outsider system. Given the importance various codes of best practice, starting with the UK Cadbury Report, as well as academic research have attached to the board of directors, in particular its independence, this mechanism deserves its own chapter.

The board of directors is the ultimate governing body within the corporation. Its duty, and in particular the duty of the non-executive directors, is to look after the interests of all the shareholders as well as sometimes those of other stakeholders such as the corporation's employees or banks. The non-executives have two main roles. First, to monitor the firm's top management, including the executive directors which are the other type of directors sitting on the firm's board. Second, to provide advice, such as strategic direction.

A number of debates relating to boards of directors are still ongoing. The first debate relates to which of the two board systems, the single-tier board or the two-tier board, is superior. While under the single-tier board system, the non-executives are likely to be better informed, the independence of the latter is likely to be stronger under the two-tier system. Another debate concerns CEO-chairman duality. While duality may create certain advantages, especially during periods of corporate restructuring and major strategic change, it can also result in an over-powerful and entrenched CEO. This chapter also looks at board turnover, including its determinants, and the role of the market for directors.[1]

Finally, there is also a debate on whether and how board gender balance, as well as board diversity more generally, should be achieved. Norway was the first country to introduce a mandatory board gender quota. While the Norwegian approach has not been spared from criticism, other countries have followed suit. Still, the Swedish parliament has recently rejected a proposal to establish a mandatory board gender quota.

7.2 Single-tier versus two-tier boards

UK and US firms as well as firms from lots of other countries, such as Italy and Spain, have single-tier boards, i.e. unitary or one-tier boards, where both the executive and non-executive directors sit. According to US terminology, executive directors sitting on the board are officers and the other members of the board are the directors. In what follows, we shall stick to the international terminology, which uses the terms executive and non-executive directors (see also Section 1.1 of Chapter 1).

Conversely, a few countries – such as Germany, China and Norway[2] – have two separate boards, also sometimes called the two-tier board. The two boards are the supervisory board (in German, *Aufsichtsrat*) and the management board (*Vorstand*). The supervisory board consists of the non-executive directors, i.e. the shareholder representatives, and also frequently the representatives of other stakeholders, such as trade union and employee representatives. The management board consists of the top management of the company and is normally chaired by the chief executive officer (CEO).

In France, companies have a choice between the Anglo-American one-tier board (*conseil d'administration*) and the two-tier German board (*conseil de surveillance* (the supervisory board)) and the management board (*directoire*)). However, in practice, most French firms have opted for the single-tier board. In the UK, non-executives are to represent *all* the shareholders and not specific or individual shareholders (such as the large shareholder(s)). They are to adopt a so-called arm's length approach and remain independent of particular shareholders or interest groups. Conversely, in the rest of the world large shareholders, suppliers, customers and employees are frequently represented on the board of directors and frequently openly pursue the interests of the party or parties they represent (see Box 7.1).

There is an ongoing debate about the advantages and disadvantages of both single-tier and two-tier boards of directors. Some argue that having two separate boards ensures the independence of the non-executive directors from the executive directors and guarantees the ethical conduct of the corporation.[3] In practice, however, frequently the non-executive directors happen to be former executives of the company. Others argue that supervisory boards are frequently to blame for the problems of their companies (see Box 7.2) and/or do not have the necessary information to be effective monitors of the executive directors.[4]

---

[1]Readers interested in the board representation of banks, employees and politicians should refer to Section 8.10 of Chapter 8, Section 15.5 of Chapter 15 and Section 9.4 of Chapter 9, respectively.
[2]In Norway, only firms above a certain size have a two-tier board.
[3]See e.g. Tieman, R. (2003), 'German Two-Tier Structure Seen as Role Model', *Financial Times*, 24 February, p. 2.
[4]Milne, R. (2007), 'Misdirected? Germany's Two-Tier Governance System Comes Under Fire', *Financial Times*, 9 May, Analysis Section, p. 13.

Box 7.1
Board representation of L'Oréal S.A.'s large shareholders

A t December 31st, 2015, the Board of Directors comprises 15 members:

- the Chairman and Chief Executive Officer, Mr Jean-Paul Agon;
- five Directors appointed by the majority shareholders, three of whom are from the Bettencourt Meyers family, Mrs Françoise Bettencourt Meyers, Mr Jean-Pierre Meyers, Mr Jean-Victor Meyers and two appointed by Nestlé, Mr Peter Brabeck-Letmathe and Mrs Christiane Kuehne, (the two Vice-Chairmen of the Board being chosen from among these members);
- seven independent Directors: Mrs Sophie Bellon (since April 22nd, 2015), Mrs Belén Garijo, Mrs Virginie Morgon, Mr Charles-Henri Filippi, Mr Xavier Fontanet, Mr Bernard Kasriel and Mr Louis Schweitzer;
- two Directors representing the employees, Mrs Ana Sofia Amaral and Mr Georges Liarokapis, since July 2014.

Shareholder Structure at December 31st, 2015

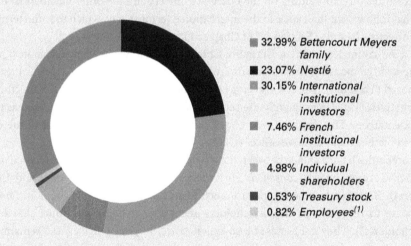

- 32.99% *Bettencourt Meyers family*
- 23.07% *Nestlé*
- 30.15% *International institutional investors*
- 7.46% *French institutional investors*
- 4.98% *Individual shareholders*
- 0.53% *Treasury stock*
- 0.82% *Employees[(1)]*

(1) Of which 0.74% is in the L'Oréal Company savings plan (PEE) as defined by Article L. 225–102 of the French Commercial Code.

6.3.1. LEGAL ENTITIES OR INDIVIDUALS ACTING IN CONCERT OVER THE COMPANY TO THE COMPANY'S KNOWLEDGE

The Bettencourt Meyers family, on the one hand, and Nestlé S.A., on the other hand, are shareholders of the Company and have declared that they are acting in concert (see the sections below pp. 292–294 on *Changes in allocation of the share capital and voting rights* and *Shareholders' agreements relating to shares in the Company's share capital*).

Source: L'Oréal S.A. registration document 2015 annual financial report, pp. 52–3 and p. 291

Box 7.2
Is the German two-tier system really superior or is it to blame for a lot of corporate mishaps?

Siemens and Volkswagen have several things in common – not only are they Germany's two most emblematic companies but both have recently been embroiled in two of the country's biggest corporate corruption scandals.

On top of the recent controversies, there is another shared issue: opaque goings-on in their supervisory boards. Chief executives at both companies have been ousted in efforts led by their chairmen despite being respected by investors and not implicated in the scandals. 'Many of the problems in corporate Germany are the fault of supervisory boards', says the chief executive of one of Germany's largest industrial companies.

Germany's supervisory boards, normally made up of 20 non-executive directors, are meant to oversee a management board as part of a two-tier system that historically was envied across the world because of the stability and long-term perspective it brought to companies. Even critics of how the current system works underline the benefits of the two levels in delineating responsibilities more clearly than the unitary boards common in Anglo-Saxon countries.

But Siemens, VW and other examples show that the supervisory board increasingly represents the last unreformed part of German capitalism. 'Management boards have changed quite a bit. But supervisory boards are an unreformed area', says Hans Hirt, head of European corporate governance at Hermes, the UK activist investor.

Years after the infamous Deutschland AG system of cross-shareholdings – designed to protect companies postwar from the full blast of capitalism – was dismantled as finance groups sold their stakes, in the most part to foreign investors, its spirit lives on in the boardroom.

A lack of outsiders leaves an elite group of German non-executive directors, often sitting on each other's boards, to run most of Germany's top companies. 'Change is still slow in coming. The recent events highlight the remnants of Deutschland AG in supervisory boards', says a member of Germany's corporate governance commission. The fact that the supervisory boards contain workers' representatives in addition to directors chosen by shareholders further dilutes investors' influence.

The new chairman of Siemens' supervisory board, Gerhard Cromme, holds the distinction of being the German director with the most board mandates, holding six in Germany and three in France (he will soon give up four of them) as well as being head of the corporate governance commission. Alongside him sit officials from the country's biggest bank and insurer – Josef Ackermann, chief executive of Deutsche Bank, and Henning Schulte-Noelle, chairman of Allianz.

Together, the three led an effort that ended last month in the ousting of Heinrich von Pierer, the then-chairman of Europe's largest engineering group, and Klaus Kleinfeld, the well-regarded chief executive, within days of each other. For the trio, this was necessary to provide a 'new start' for a company embroiled in corporate Germany's biggest bribery scandal; but for many inside and outside Siemens it was little more than a boardroom coup.

Investors were particularly dismayed because Mr Kleinfeld, the chief executive, had not just lifted Siemens' profitability and share price but also promised a full investigation into the corruption. Whichever view of his departure was correct, it has led some investors to say the board was not acting in their interests. A top-five shareholder says: 'The entire supervisory board at Siemens should be replaced'.

Mr Cromme has in private rejected any suggestion that he acted against the interests of shareholders. 'It is total codswallop. The board only behaved in the interests of investors', people close to the board report him as saying.

At VW, likewise, investors have been harshly critical of the ousting of a similarly respected chief executive, Bernd Pischetsrieder, who was forced out by a controversial and domineering chairman. That put a sharp end to Mr Pischetsrieder's attempts to use a bribery and sex scandal to force traditionalists from both the carmaker's boards.

Nobody wants to comment directly or officially on the two cases, but chief executives at German companies, from Porsche and MAN to Linde and Hochtief, argue in general terms that supervisory boards need to be reformed. 'The

(Continued)

whole thing is still a bit of Deutschland AG. It is certainly not good: we should have as a target more internationalisation and more independence of directors', says Hakan Samuelsson, the Swedish head of truckmaker MAN.

Hans-Peter Keitel, the former chief executive of builder Hochtief, says: 'Supervisory boards today are made up of people either from industry who have no time or 67-year-old pensioners'.

The fifth annual report into European corporate governance by Heidrick & Struggles, a leading headhunter, confirms the gloom. German supervisory boards score the worst of 10 leading European countries in terms of their set-up and composition. They have the fewest number of foreigners on them – just seven per cent compared with Switzerland's 45 per cent – they have the fewest meetings a year and are paid the third-most.

The report highlights several problems with German supervisory boards, led by the three-decade-old system of co-determination, or Mitbestimmung, that gives workers half the board seats and a key role in strategic decisions.

VW is a case in point. Sales outside Germany account for 81 per cent of the carmaker's total and yet there is not one foreigner among the 20 non-executive directors (excluding Ferdinand Piech, VW's chairman, who was born in Austria but who has worked in German industry all his life).

Wolfgang Reitzle, the chief executive of Linde, highlights a similar situation at his industrial gas company. 'Why should a country with nine per cent of the sales get all the seats on the board? The internationalisation of the board will not happen from one day to another. But when you are a global company operating in countries with different habits and cultures then you should have people who know these countries'.

VW's board also underlines the problem of potential conflicts of interest. Porsche, a competitor, is also its largest shareholder and controls the VW board, holding the chairmanship and two other seats. 'Only we are allowed conflicts of interest now', jokes Wendelin Wiedeking, head of Porsche. Indeed, there is a special board committee designed to monitor these conflicts.

Most controversial at VW, however, is the role of Mr Piech, a controlling shareholder at Porsche, who is also due to take over as MAN's chairman later this week. Mr Piech has often sided with labour representatives on the board rather than shareholder ones, installing a union official as a management board member as well as ousting Mr Pischetsrieder as chief executive. 'VW is a company run by Piech and the unions, and that is not healthy', says one non-executive director.

A chairman of an industrial group in the DAX-30 is more scathing, arguing that weakness, not strength, causes directors to side with workers against investors: 'It is an unholy alliance of the losers'. He also points to DaimlerChrysler where Jurgen Schrempp, its former chief executive, used union support to help him stay in office.

The role of workers through Mitbestimmung is widely credited as helping minimize labour tensions. Reform of the politically-sensitive system is also unlikely. But corporate governance experts publicly and executives privately are clear that the system holds back companies.

One issue is the very size of boards – having 20 members, of whom 10 are labour representatives, does not always make for efficient discussions. In fact, as the Heidrick and Struggles report suggests, the very presence of workers on boards mean the main issues are all discussed and agreed on beforehand, reducing the effectiveness of meetings hugely.

The key question is whether any of the problems with supervisory boards will be addressed. Here the signs are mixed, in part because investors appear to accept or at least be resigned to many of the issues.

Siemens highlights one of the specificities of German law in that senior executives are appointed by the supervisory board. That means shareholders have no direct control over managers but have to content themselves with voting for supervisory board members. This made it possible for non-executive directors voted on to the board by shareholders to help oust Mr Kleinfeld.

Taken together with VW and RWE, the utility, where another chief executive respected by the markets was ousted, Siemens shows that investors should pay more attention to the appointment of supervisory board members, says Mr Hirt of Hermes. He recommends a simple majority of 50 per cent instead of the normal 75 per cent should be necessary to oust a non-executive director at annual meetings. But the reluctance of shareholders at Siemens,

VW or MAN to speak out publicly – particularly at annual meetings – suggests investors are themselves at least partly to blame for the situation.

More often, change will come from inside the company. Mr Samuelsson urges more controversial decisions to be taken, where the shareholder side votes against labour representatives: 'There are too many 20-0 decisions in Germany. We need some 11-9 ones too'. Mr Wiedeking at Porsche argues that non-executives need to challenge management more. He himself spends one and a half days each week focusing solely on VW matters. He says: 'I think that many mandates are not taken seriously'.

Mr Cromme himself wants more managers to do what he did and step down early from an executive role to become a professional non-executive director. Karlheinz Hornung, MAN's chief executive, agrees but adds: 'We need to pay our directors more if we want more professionals'.

Several companies are turning towards the European Company (SE) set-up that allows them to shrink their supervisory board to 12 members and invite foreign workers on to the labour side. Allianz, Porsche and chemicals group BASF have taken this path and more are likely to join them. The smaller board makes discussions more efficient and the presence of foreign workers weakens co-determination, although half the board remain labour representatives.

But for all the talk of change, few want to abandon the supervisory board system altogether. Paul Achleitner, Allianz's head of investment, highlights the greater flexibility and increased internationalisation an SE represents. But he adds: 'We very clearly chose a two-tier structure. I am convinced that a well-run two-tier board structure is more effective than a one-tier board'.

Source: Richard Milne (2007), 'Misdirected? Germany's Two-Tier Governance System Comes Under Fire', *Financial Times*, 9 May, Analysis Section, p. 13.

7.3 CEO-chairman duality

There has been a long debate about whether the roles of the chairman of the board and the CEO should be separated or whether duality (i.e. the same person assuming both roles) makes more sense. Proponents of duality argue that there are three advantages from combining the two roles. First, duality ensures that there is strong leadership. This may be particularly important when the firm requires restructuring or a major strategic change. Second, splitting the two roles may create tensions and rivalry between the chairman and the CEO. Third, having a separate chairman and CEO may make it difficult to designate a single spokesperson for the firm.

Those opposed to duality argue that combining the two roles reduces board independence as there may be no one powerful enough on the board to challenge the CEO and this increases CEO entrenchment. Finally, from an agency perspective duality makes little sense as it combines the task of monitoring the executive directors (including the CEO) and the task of leading the top management team of the company in a single person.

In the USA minds are split as to whether duality is good or bad. Similarly, empirical evidence on US firms is inconsistent as to whether duality is good or bad.[5] Conversely, in the UK successive codes of best practice in corporate governance, starting with the 1992 Cadbury Report, have recommended the separation of the

[5]See Brickley, J.A., Coles, J.L. and Jarrell, G. (1997), 'Leadership Structure: Separating the CEO and Chairman of the Board', *Journal of Corporate Finance* 3, 189–220, who found that separating the two roles destroys values. In contrast, Rechner, I.F. and Dalton, D.R. (1991), 'CEO Duality and Organizational Performance: A Longitudinal Analysis', *Strategic Management Journal* 12, 155–60, found evidence that separating the roles creates value.

two roles (see also Section 6.2 of Chapter 6). However, in contrast to the US evidence, which is inconclusive, evidence from UK firms seems to suggest that duality has *no* impact on firm value and performance.[6]

7.4 Board independence and board turnover

Apart from duality, the following questions about boards of directors arise:

- Is there a link between board independence and financial performance?
- Do boards fire executive directors in the wake of poor performance?
- What factors determine board turnover?

We shall now answer each of these questions in turn. As most of the existing research on boards of directors is on US firms, the discussion that follows is based on single-tier, US-style boards unless otherwise specified.

7.4.1 IS THERE A LINK BETWEEN BOARD INDEPENDENCE AND FINANCIAL PERFORMANCE?

The number or percentage of non-executive directors is normally seen as a measure of board independence. Boards that are dominated by non-executive directors are likely to be more independent from the management and better monitors than those that are dominated by executive directors. However, there is very little empirical evidence in support of a positive link between firm performance and board independence.[7] Nevertheless, a possible issue these studies may suffer from is that board structure and composition are not exogenous, i.e. are endogenous. Indeed, it may be the case that, among other factors, current board composition is the result of past performance. If poor performance causes an increase in the number of non-executives, e.g. via shareholder pressure to appoint additional non-executives, then this may explain why studies on the relationship between performance and board independence have not found an effect between the two. In line with this argument, there is some evidence that suggests firms with historically poor performance have more non-executives.[8] Another issue affecting these studies is that frequently the so-called independent directors are only independent by name.[9]

Another reason for the lack of evidence between board independence and firm performance may be that one size does not fit all and that greater board independence may not suit all types of company. Renée Adams

[6]See Dedman, E. and Lin, S. (2002), 'Shareholder Wealth Effects of CEO departures: Evidence from the UK', *Journal of Corporate Finance* 8, 81–104; Dahya J. and McConnell, J.J. (2007), 'Board Composition, Corporate Performance, and the Cadbury Committee Recommendation', *Journal of Financial and Quantitative Analysis* 42, 535–64.

[7]For the US evidence, see e.g. MacAvoy, P., Cantor, S., Dana J. and Peck, S. (1983), 'ALI Proposals for Increased Control of the Corporation by the Board of Directors: An Economic Analysis', in Statement of the Business Roundtable on the American Law Institute's Proposed Principles of Corporate Governance and Structure: Restatement and Recommendation, New York: Business Roundtable; Hermalin, B. and Weisbach, M. (1991), 'The Effects of Board Composition and Direct Incentives on Firm Performance', *Financial Management* 20, 101–12; Mehran, H. (1995), 'Executive Compensation Structure, Ownership, and Firm Performance', *Journal of Financial Economics* 38, 163–84; and Bhagat, S. and Black, B. (2002), 'The Non-Correlation Between Board Independence and Long-Term Firm Performance', *Journal of Corporation Law* 27, 231–73. For the UK evidence, see e.g. Lasfer, M. and Faccio, M. (1999), 'Managerial Ownership, Board Structure and Firm Value: The UK Evidence', available at SSRN: ssrn.com/abstract=179008; and Weir, C., Laing D. and McKnight, P. (2002), 'Internal and External Governance Mechanisms: Their Impact on the Performance of Large UK Public Companies', *Journal of Business Finance and Accounting* 29, 579–611.

[8]Hermalin, B. and Weisbach, M. (1998), 'Endogenously Chosen Boards of Directors and their Monitoring of the CEO', *American Economic Review* 88, 96–118. Börsch-Supan, A. and Köke, J. (2000), 'An Applied Econometricians' View of Empirical Corporate Finance Studies', working paper, Center for European Economic Research (ZEW), University of Mannheim, Germany.

[9]See e.g. Ansari, I.F., Goergen, M. and Mira, S. (2014), 'The Determinants of the CEO Successor Choice in Family Firms', *Journal of Corporate Finance* 28, 6–25.

and Daniel Ferreira's model focuses on the optimal level of board independence.[10] Their model emphasizes the two main roles of boards, i.e. monitoring and the provision of advice. The CEO will have to share information with the board if he wants to receive advice from the latter. However, this information will also make it easier for the board to monitor the CEO. Hence, the CEO may be reluctant to share information with the board. This suggests that for firms that are more likely to require advice rather than monitoring from their board, a friendly, i.e. less independent board may be optimal.[11]

Given the lack of evidence in favour of a link between corporate performance and board independence, it might be somewhat surprising that corporate governance codes of best practice, such as the UK ones, have consistently argued for the increased importance of non-executives in the governance of corporations (see also Chapter 6).[12]

However, there is some indirect evidence of the effectiveness of non-executive directors as monitors of the executive directors. Indeed, board turnover is higher in firms with more independent boards when stock or accounting performance is down. Still, as will be argued in what follows dismissals of directors do not necessarily equate with good corporate governance. They are rather a measure of last resort when all other measures have failed. There is also evidence for the UK by Noel O'Sullivan and Pauline Wong[13] and for the USA by James Brickley et al. and James Cotter et al.[14] that boards dominated by non-executive directors resist takeover bids in ways that force the bidder to revise her price for the firm, thereby creating greater value for the target firm's shareholders.

While there is no conclusive evidence about a direct link between financial performance and board independence, the academic literature is fairly conclusive that large boards are bad for firm performance. Martin Lipton and Jay Lorsch argued that large boards are less effective and more bureaucratic.[15] David Yermack found support for this.[16] In addition, Robert Gertner and Steven Kaplan found that when the targets of LBOs go back to the stock market, their board size has decreased.[17] LBOs are a particular type of acquisition, financed mostly by debt and very little equity. They are thought to bring about improvements in the targets' operations, strategy and governance. The fact that studies report that the board size of LBO targets has decreased once they return to the stock exchange provides further, albeit indirect evidence, that smaller boards are more effective. In a similar vein, board busyness has been associated with weaker corporate governance.[18] Board busyness is typically defined as a board with a majority of non-executive directors sitting on three or more boards.

Further, boards may also be used as anti-takeover devices by reducing the number of board members that can be replaced in a single year. This can be achieved by setting up so-called staggered boards (see Section 6.3 of Chapter 6 for further details). In other words, the structure of the board may reflect weak corporate governance and may be a means for the managers to entrench themselves.[19]

[10]Adams, R. and Ferreira, D. (2007), 'A Theory of Friendly Boards', *Journal of Finance* 62, 217–50.

[11]See also Section 11.7 of Chapter 11.

[12]In their seminal paper, A. Alchian and Demsetz, H. ask the important question: 'who monitors the monitor?'. See Alchian, A.A. and Demsetz, H. (1972), 'Production, Information Costs, and Economic Organization', *American Economic Review* 62, 777–95.

[13]O'Sullivan, N. and Wong, P. (1998), 'Internal versus External Control: An Analysis of Board Composition and Ownership in UK Takeovers', *Journal of Management and Governance* 2, 17–35.

[14]Brickley, J.A., Coles J.L. and Terry, R. (1994), 'Outside Directors and the Adoption of Poison Pills', *Journal of Financial Economics* 35, 371–90; and Cotter, J.F., Shivdasani A. and Zenner, M. (1997), 'Do Independent Directors Enhance Target Shareholder Wealth During Tender Offers?', *Journal of Financial Economics* 43, 195–218.

[15]Lipton, M. and Lorsch, J.W. (1992), 'Modest Proposal for Improved Corporate Governance', *Business Lawyer* 48, 59–78.

[16]Yermack, D. (1996), 'Higher Valuation of Companies with a Small Board of Directors', *Journal of Financial Economics* 40, 185–212.

[17]Gertner, R. and Kaplan, S. (1996), 'The Value-Maximizing Board', Working Paper, University of Chicago, IL.

[18]Fich, E.M. and Shivdasani, A. (2006), 'Are Busy Boards Effective Monitors?', *Journal of Finance* 61, 689–724.

[19]See e.g. Gompers, P., Ishii, J. and Metrick, A. (2003), 'Corporate Governance and Equity Prices', *Quarterly Journal of Economics* 118, 107–56; Bebchuk, L., Cohen, A. and Ferrell, A. (2009), 'What Matters in Corporate Governance?' *Review of Financial Studies* 22, 738–827.

Finally, there is evidence that so-called interlocked directorships cause collusion. Interlocked directorships consist of one or several directors of one firm sitting on the board of another firm while some of the directors of the latter firm also sit on the board of the former firm. Indeed, Kevin Hallock found that interlocked CEOs are more highly paid than other CEOs.[20]

7.4.2 DO BOARDS FIRE EXECUTIVE DIRECTORS IN THE WAKE OF POOR PERFORMANCE?

There is consistent evidence of an increase in CEO turnover, as well as board turnover more generally, in the wake of poor performance. This evidence exists across corporate governance systems. There is such evidence for the UK[21] and the USA,[22] two representatives of the outsider system, as well as for Germany[23] and Japan,[24] two representatives of the insider system.

However, it is important to bear in mind that board dismissals are not necessarily a sign of good corporate governance. Rather they are the ultimate means to address poor managerial performance when all other means have failed to do so. In line with this argument, managerial dismissals only seem to occur in cases of extremely poor performance.[25]

7.4.3 WHAT FACTORS DETERMINE BOARD TURNOVER?

Benjamin Hermalin and Michael Weisbach found that for the case of the USA[26]:

- Inside directors are more likely to be replaced by outside directors in poorly performing companies. When the CEO is fired, he is normally replaced by an outsider. This suggests that the inside directors are blamed for the past poor performance.
- Inside directors normally replace retiring CEOs.
- When the CEO is replaced by an outsider, some inside directors – possibly the losers in the contest to the succession – leave the firm.
- Firms leaving their product market to enter new markets normally replace their inside directors with outside directors. One explanation for this pattern is that often firms leave their product markets because of their poor performance.

[20]Hallock, K. (1997), 'Reciprocally Interlocking Boards of Directors and Executive Compensation', *Journal of Financial and Quantitative Analysis* 32, 331–4. Hallock, K. (1999), 'Dual Agency: Corporate Boards with Reciprocally Interlocking Relationships', in Carpenter, J. and Yermack, D. (eds.), *Executive Compensation and Shareholder Value*, Amsterdam: Kluwer Academic Publishers, 55–75.

[21]Franks, J., Mayer, C. and Renneboog, L. (2001), 'Who Disciplines Management of Poorly Performing Companies?' *Journal of Financial Intermediation* 10, 209–48.

[22]Weisbach, M. (1988), 'Outside Directors and CEO Turnover', *Journal of Financial Economics* 20, 431–60. Huson, M., Parrino, R. and Starks, L. (2000), 'Internal Monitoring and CEO Turnover: A Long-Term Perspective', Working Paper, University of Texas, TX.

[23]Franks, J. and Mayer, C. (2001), 'Ownership and Control of German Corporations', *Review of Financial Studies* 14, 943–77. Kaplan, S. (1994), 'Top Executives, Turnover and Firm Performance in Germany', *Journal of Law, Economics and Organization* 10, 142–59. Köke, J. (2003), 'The Market for Corporate Control in a Bank-Based Economy: A Governance Device?' *Journal of Corporate Finance* 10, 53–80.

[24]Kaplan, S. (1994), 'Top Executive Rewards and Firm Performance: A Comparison of Japan and the U.S.', *Journal of Political Economy* 102, 510–46. Kaplan, S.N. and Minton, B.A. (1994), 'Appointments of Outsiders to Japanese Boards: Determinants and Implications for Managers', *Journal of Financial Economics* 36, 225–58.

[25]See e.g. Franks, J., Mayer, C. and Renneboog, L. (2001), 'Who Disciplines Management of Poorly Performing Companies?' *Journal of Financial Intermediation* 10, 209–48.

[26]Hermalin, B.E. and Weisbach, M.S. (1988), 'The Determinants of Board Composition', *RAND Journal of Economics* 19, 589–606.

In addition, Steven Kaplan and Bernadette Minton reported that banks appoint representatives to the board in poorly performing Japanese firms that are part of a keiretsu (see Section 2.4 of Chapter 2).[27]

In a later paper, Hermalin and Weisbach formulated a theoretical model about the selection of members for the board of directors. At the base of the model is a negotiation process between the CEO and the board of directors.[28] This negotiation process affects not only the selection of new directors, but also the determination of the CEO's compensation. The CEO's bargaining power stems from her ability relative to alternative CEOs in the labour market. The bargaining between the CEO and the board ultimately determines the board's independence as a powerful CEO is unlikely to choose directors who will monitor her extensively. In contrast, a highly independent board will monitor the CEO more extensively. In turn, the monitoring generates information about the CEO's ability and whether she should be replaced by a better CEO or retained. Ultimately, Hermalin and Weisbach's model suggests that board independence is not necessarily exogenous, but that it might be influenced by the CEO's power.

7.5 The market for directors

The previous section discussed how boards may discipline badly performing directors by firing them from the firm. The threat of being fired if they underperform may pressure managers to perform well and to run the firm in the interests of the shareholders. However, there is another related threat, albeit an external one. This threat relates to the managerial labour market or market for directors.[29] Eugene Fama was the first to discuss the role of the labour market for directors as a corporate governance device.[30] The market for directors not only offers outside job opportunities to directors, but it also acts as a disciplinary device as the number and quality of these outside opportunities will depend on the director's reputation, which among other factors will depend on his past performance.

A number of studies find evidence that well performing CEOs are rewarded with more outside directorships whereas badly performing CEOs are penalized with fewer such appointments.[31] Steven Kaplan and David Reishus looked at executives more broadly. They found that executives of firms that reduce their dividend hold fewer outside directorships three years after the dividend cut.[32]

Another body of studies focuses on non-executive directors. These studies found that non-executive directors of firms that perform well[33] as well as non-executives who fire badly performing CEOs[34] are rewarded with additional directorships. There is also evidence that non-executives are punished with fewer additional

[27]Kaplan, S.N. and Minton, B.A. (1994), 'Appointments of Outsiders to Japanese Boards: Determinants and Implications for Managers', *Journal of Financial Economics* 36, 225–58.

[28]Hermalin, B. and Weisbach, M. (1998), 'Endogenously Chosen Boards of Directors and their Monitoring of the CEO', *American Economic Review* 88, 96–118.

[29]Studies on the labour market for directors do not always clearly distinguish between executive and non-executive directors. Hence, in what follows we use the term (labour) market for directors rather than managerial labour market.

[30]Fama, E.F. (1980), 'Agency Problems and the Theory of the Firm', *Journal of Political Economy* 88, 288–307.

[31]See e.g. Brickley, J., Linck, J. and Coles, J. (1999), 'What Happens to CEOs after they Retire? New Evidence on Career Concerns, Horizon Problems, and CEO Incentives', *Journal of Financial Economics* 52, 341–77; Ferris, S.P., Jagannathan, M. and Pritchard, A.C. (2003), 'Too Busy to Mind the Business? Monitoring by Directors with Multiple Board Appointments', *Journal of Finance* 68, 1087–111; Fich, E.M. (2005) 'Are Some Outside Directors Better than Others? Evidence from Director Appointments by Fortune 1000 Firms', *Journal of Business* 78, 1943–71.

[32]Kaplan, S. and Reishus, D. (1990), 'Outside Directorships and Corporate Performance', *Journal of Financial Economics* 27, 389–410.

[33]Yermack, D. (2004), 'Remuneration, Retention and Reputation Incentives for Outside Directors', *Journal of Finance* 59, 2281–308.

[34]Farrell, K.A. and Whidbee, D.A. (2000), 'The Consequences of Forced CEO Succession for Outside Directors', *Journal of Business* 73, 597–627.

directorships if their firms restate their earnings[35] or are subject to financial fraud lawsuits.[36] To sum up, there is consistent evidence of a market for directors which rewards well performing directors and penalizes badly performing directors.

7.6 Board gender balance and board diversity

Marianne Bertrand and Kevin Hallock reported that females occupy only about 2.5 per cent of top management jobs in listed US firms.[37] In addition to this *glass ceiling*, female top executives also earn 45 per cent less. Similarly, for listed UK firms, Clara Kulich and colleagues found that only three per cent of executives are female and that female executives on average earn 19 per cent less than their male counterparts.[38] Their compensation contracts are also less performance sensitive and have less upward potential when corporate performance is good, but also have less downward potential when performance is poor.

Siri Terjesen and Val Singh studied the determinants of female board representation in 43 countries.[39] They found that women are more likely to sit on corporate boards in those countries with more women in top management positions, a smaller pay gap between genders and, somewhat surprisingly, a shorter history of female politicians.

Given the under-representation of women in top management positions as well as the disparity in managerial salaries between genders, there may be a need for positive action to reduce gender discrimination and get rid of the glass ceiling. The aim of such action would be to improve individual rights, i.e. promote equality of opportunities, rather than to promote the rights of a collective, such as the workforce via, e.g. worker representation on the board of directors (see also Chapter 15). In turn, companies may practice positive action for one or several of the following reasons:

- to comply with the law.
- because this is seen as ethical or morally desirable and/or.
- it may help in the case of litigation (i.e. it may be presented as evidence that the organization does not systematically discriminate).

Norway was the first country in Europe to impose a quota, i.e. a minimum percentage of women on the boards of directors of companies. This minimum percentage is 40 per cent and it has been in place since 2004 for state-owned enterprises (SOEs) and since 2006 for a limited group of privately owned companies. Privately owned companies had to comply with the requirement by 2008 or face their dissolution. As a result, the percentage of women on the boards increased from 36 per cent in 2004 to 42 per cent in 2009, making Norway the European country with the highest percentage of female board members. Among the 28 EU member states, France has the highest percentage of women on boards with 37.1 per cent and Malta the lowest with 5.0 per cent (see Figure 7.1).

The 2000 European Union (EU) Equal Status Act and the 2002 Gender Equality Act require that companies that are majority owned by the government have a gender balance across the organization, including

[35]Srinivasan, S. (2005), 'Consequences of Financial Reporting Failure for Outside Directors: Evidence from Accounting Restatements and Audit Committee Members', *Journal of Accounting Research* 43, 291–334.

[36]Fich, E.M. and Shivdasani, A. (2007), 'Financial Fraud, Director Reputation and Shareholder Wealth', *Journal of Financial Economics* 86, 306–36.

[37]Bertrand M. and Hallock, K. (2001), 'The Gender Gap in Top Corporate Jobs', *Industrial and Labor Relations Review* 55, 3–21.

[38]Kulich, C., Trojanowski G., Ryan M.K., Haslam S.A. and Renneboog, L. (2010), 'Who Gets the Carrot and Who Gets the Stick? Evidence of Gender Disparities in Executive Remuneration', *Strategic Management Journal* 32, 301–21.

[39]Terjesen, S. and Singh, V. (2008), 'Female Presence on Corporate Boards: A Multi-Country Study of Environmental Context', *Journal of Business Ethics* 83, 55–63.

their boards.[40] A number of EU countries have introduced mandatory gender quotas in recent years, including Austria, Belgium, France, Germany, Greece, Italy and Spain (see Table 7.1). However, these mandatory quotas only apply to the largest firms and/or state-owned firms. These quotas are typically supplemented by self-regulation. Self-regulation also exists in a number of countries that do not have any mandatory quotas in place. Interestingly, the Swedish parliament rejected a mandatory board gender quota in 2017.[41]

Figure 7.1 Gender distribution on the boards of directors of the large listed EU firms in 2016
Source: European Commission (2016), *Gender Balance on Corporate Boards. Europe is Cracking the Glass Ceiling*, European Commission, Directorate-General for Justice and Consumers, p. 1.

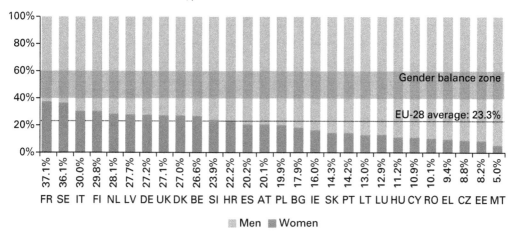

There have been criticisms of the Norwegian approach of imposing a quota on the participation of women in boardrooms. The main criticism is that the policy has been too ambitious and, due to the lack of suitable candidates, too few women (the so-called 'golden skirts') are spread too thinly across too many boards. More generally, the question that arises is whether more women on the board of directors is good or bad for firm value and financial performance. There are two divergent views on this in the academic literature. According to the diversity view, having more females on boards of directors creates value as women have different types of experience, knowledge and skills which complement those of the male board members. In contrast, according to the equality view, the gender of a director does not matter as females and males have intrinsically similar skills and competencies.

Some studies suggest that the introduction of the Norwegian board gender quota has had negative economic implications. For example, Kenneth Ahern and Amy Dittmar found that the announcement of the new law caused a significant drop in stock price and firm value (Tobin's q) of the firms subject to the law.[42] In addition, Øvind Bøhren and Siv Staubo reported that about half of the Norwegian firms subject to the new law converted to an organizational form that is not subject to the new law to avoid the imposition of the quota.[43] Again, this would suggest that firms perceived the new law to be costly. Clearly, this does not necessarily mean that board gender balance is undesirable from a societal point of view. However, the evidence suggests that there may initially be significant costs attached to boosting board gender diversity via mandatory quotas, possibly reflecting the dearth of suitable candidates, overly busy female directors and suboptimal board independence.

[40]Norway is not part of the European Union.
[41]*The Guardian* (2017), 'Sweden Rejects Quotas for Women on Boards of Listed Companies', *The Guardian*, 12 January, www.theguardian.com/world/2017/jan/12/sweden-rejects-quotas-women-boardroom-listed-companies?CMP=twt_gu, accessed on 7 February 2017.
[42]Ahern, K.R and Dittmar, A.K. (2012), 'The Changing of the Boards: The Impact on Firm Valuation of Mandated Female Board Representation', *Quarterly Journal of Economics* 127, 137–97.
[43]Bøhren, Ø. and Staubo, S. (2014), 'Does Mandatory Gender Balance Work? Changing Organizational Form to Avoid Board Upheaval', *Journal of Corporate Finance* 28, 152–68.

Table 7.1 Board gender quotas and other national measures

Member state	Quotas in place	Other national measures in place
Austria	Yes: only state-owned companies (35% for supervisory boards by 2018).	Self-regulation: The Corporate Governance Code of 2009 recommends representation of both genders in appointments to supervisory boards.
Belgium	Yes: 33% for executives and non-executives in state-owned and listed companies-by 2017 and in listed SMEs-by 2019.	Self-regulation: The Corporate Governance Code of 2009 recommends that the composition of a board is determined on the basis of gender diversity.
Bulgaria	No	No
Croatia	No	No
Cyprus	No	No
Czech Republic	No	No
Denmark	No	Boards in state-owned companies should 'as far as possible' have an equal gender balance; a man and a woman nominated for every vacancy (executives and non-executives). From 2013, obligation to all companies (listed and non-listed) to self-regulate and set their own targets. A company can be fined if it has not set any target figures or has not submitted any reporting.
Estonia	No	No
Finland	No	State-owned companies are required to have an 'equitable proportion of women and men'. The Corporate Governance Code for listed companies contains recommendation that 'boards shall consist of both sexes'.
France	Yes: from 2011; 40% by 2017. Applicable to non-executive directors in large listed and non-listed companies.	The AFEP-MEDEF Corporate Code: recommendation containing same quotas as in the Law of 2011, applicable to all board members.
Germany	Yes: from 2016, 30% for supervisory boards of the listed companies that are submitted to parity co-determination (the roughly 110 biggest listed companies).	Other companies that are either listed or fall under parity co-determination have to set individual quantitative objectives of women on boards with regard to non-executive and executive board members and senior managers below board level and deadlines to achieve them.
Greece	Yes, 33%; only companies fully or partially owned by the State. Applicable to all board positions (executives and non-executives).	Soft positive action measures in public sector.
Hungary	No	Soft positive action measures in public sector.
Ireland	No	A policy target of 40% female participation on all state boards and committees. Soft positive action measures in public sector employment.

Table 7.1 (*Continued*)

Member state	Quotas in place	Other national measures in place
Italy	Yes: 33% by 2015 for listed companies and state-owned companies. Applicable to management boards and supervisory boards (i.e. executives and non-executives).	Yes
Latvia	No	Soft positive action measures in the public sector.
Lithuania	No	No
Luxembourg	No	Soft positive action measures. The Corporate Code of 2009 recommends the board to have an appropriate representation of both genders. The rule is applicable to all board members.
Malta	No	No
Netherlands	Target of 30% in the executive boards and supervisory boards of large companies – 'comply or explain' mechanism, no sanctions. Measure to expire in 2016.	Self-regulation: diversity clauses in the Dutch Corporate Governance Code of 2009, applicable to both executives and non-executives. Voluntary Charter with targets for more women in management.
Poland	No	The executive ordinance of Minister of State Treasury obliges state-owned companies to 'choose adequately prepared members of supervisory boards, taking into account the balanced participation of women and men'. The Code of good practices attached to that ordinance establishes a target of 30% for 2015 and a priority rule for equally qualified women. No sanctions are envisaged.
Portugal	No	A government resolution of 2015 encourages listed companies to attain 30% of the under-represented sex at their administrative bodies by 2018.
Romania	No	Soft positive action measures in public sector employment.
Slovakia	No	No
Slovenia	No	Regulation on state-owned companies: A principle of 40% representation of each sex applies to the nomination or appointment of government representatives to management and supervisory boards of SOEs (executives and non-executives). No sanctions apply if the principle is not respected.
Spain	Yes: 40% (both executives and non-executives) by 2015 (but no sanctions, thus rather a recommendation by nature) in state-owned companies with 250 or more employees. New possible models under discussion.	Soft positive action measures in public sector employment.

(*Continued*)

Table 7.1 (Continued)

Member state	Quotas in place	Other national measures in place
Sweden	No	Self-regulation: The Corporate Governance Code of 2004 has a voluntary goal of parity for listed companies; 'comply or explain' mechanism.
United Kingdom	No	Self-regulation – from 2012 on the basis of principles of UK Corporate Governance Code (following the Lord Davies recommendation). The recommended target for listed companies in FTSE 100: 25%, by 2015 is applicable to all board members. FTSE 350 companies recommended setting their own aspirational targets to be achieved by 2013 and 2015.

Source: Adapted from European Commission (2016), *Gender Balance on Corporate Boards. Europe is Cracking the Glass Ceiling*, European Commission, Directorate-General for Justice and Consumers, pp. 6–7.

More generally, the empirical literature on the impact of female board representation on financial performance does not provide consistent results as to the effect of board membership by women on corporate performance. Some studies suggest that while female CEOs have a positive effect, other female directors reduce performance.[44] These studies tend to justify their results as follows. First, female CEOs have a positive effect on performance as they had to work particularly hard to break through the glass ceiling and succeed in a male dominated world. Second, female directors other than the CEO seem to be appointed as a token of gender equality rather than for their skills and competencies. However, there are also studies that find an overall positive effect of female board membership and of diversity more generally on firm performance.[45] Finally, the study on UK firms by Stephen Brammer, Andrew Millington and Stephen Pavelin suggested that the effect of female board representation depends on the industry.[46] They focus on corporate reputation and measure this by basing themselves on the 'Britain's most admired companies' survey from *Management Today*, which was based on methodology similar to that employed by Fortune in the USA. Their study found that corporate reputation increases with female board representation in industries which are close to their final customers, e.g. consumer manufacturing and consumer services, whereas there is no such effect for, e.g. producer services.

The debate on gender equality on corporate boards has been further fuelled by the 2008 subprime mortgage crisis and the resulting bank failures which some have blamed on excessive risk taking by white, middle-aged, testosterone-fuelled males. There is evidence by John Coates and Joe Herbert that human biology, in particular gender differences in terms of hormones, drive risk-taking behaviour (see Section 12.7 of Chapter 12 for further details).[47] This research suggested that board diversity may be good in terms of avoiding unnecessary and excessive risk taking, i.e. risk taking that increases the firm's risk, but does not increase its expected return.

[44]See e.g. Shrader, C.B., Blackburn, V.B. and Iles, P. (1997), 'Women in Management and Firm Financial Performance: An Exploratory Study', *Journal of Managerial Issues* 9, 355–72; Smith, N., Smith, V. and Verner, M. (2006), 'Do Women in Top Management Affect Firm Performance? A Panel Study of 2,300 Danish Firms', *International Journal of Productivity and Performance Management* 15, 569–93; Adams, R.B. and Ferreira, D. (2009), Women in the Boardroom and their Impact on Governance and Performance', *Journal of Financial Economics* 94, 291–309.
[45]See e.g. Carter, D.A., Simkins, B.J. and Simpson, W.G. (2003), 'Corporate Governance, Board Diversity, and Firm Value', *Financial Review* 38, 33–53; Campbell, K. and Minguez-Vera, A. (2008), 'Gender Diversity in the Boardroom and Firm Financial Performance', *Journal of Business Ethics* 83, 435–51.
[46]Brammer, S., Millington, A. and Pavelin, S. (2009), 'Corporate Reputation and Women on the Board', *British Journal of Management* 20, 17–29.
[47]Coates J.M. and Herbert, J. (2008), 'Endogenous Steroids and Financial Risk Taking on a London Trading Floor', *Proceedings of the National Academy of Sciences of the United States of America* 105, 6167–72.

In relation to corporate governance, Renée Adams and Daniel Ferreira found that female directors are more likely to attend board meetings.[48] Attendance at board meetings by male directors of firms with female directors is also improved. Female directors are also more likely to sit on the board committees engaged in monitoring, i.e. the auditing, nomination and corporate governance committees. This suggests that female directors put more emphasis on monitoring than their male counterparts. Finally, while many countries now have policies on gender equality in place, positive policies targeting ethnic minorities as well as other minorities are less developed.

In contrast to board gender balance, there is as yet little research on board diversity more generally, including cultural, social, ethnic, religious and age diversity. Some of the literature that is emerging suggests that similar to board gender diversity, diversity more generally seems to affect firm decision making. For example, Marc Goergen, Peter Limbach and Meik Scholz found that for German firms a generational age difference (a difference of 20 years or more) between the chair of the supervisory board and the CEO increases the intensity of monitoring as measured by the number of board meetings.[49] This evidence suggests that greater differences in demographic traits, including age, result in more cognitive dissonance and ultimately more monitoring of the executives by the non-executives.

7.7 Conclusions

While most countries in the world have adopted the single-tier board, some countries have gone down the route of the two-tier board, which consists of a separate supervisory board where the non-executives sit and a management board where the executives sit. The main advantage of the two-tier board system is that it clearly delineates the role of the executives from that of the non-executives. However, it may also reduce the information that the non-executives have about how the company is managed.

Single-tier vs two-tier boards

Although regulators have typically taken a stance against duality, the debate about whether duality creates or destroys value has not yet been settled.

CEO-chairman duality

The literature is as yet inconclusive as to whether board independence improves firm performance and firm value. In contrast, there is consistent empirical evidence from a number of countries which suggests that CEO and board turnover is sensitive to firm performance.

Board turnover

Firms experiencing bad financial performance may be under pressure from their shareholders to appoint more independent directors. This may explain why studies investigating the link between firm performance and board independence have found little evidence of such a link. Another reason for the absence of such a link may be that for some firms the advisory role is more important than the monitoring role. Hence, less rather than more board independence may be optimal for these firms.

The likely endogeneity of board independence

There is conclusive evidence of the existence of a market for directors as well as of its disciplinary role whereby well-performing directors are rewarded with more outside board seats and badly performing directors are penalized with less outside board seats.

The market for directors

---

[48] Op. cit. footnote 44.
[49] Goergen, M., Limbach, P. and Scholz, M. (2015), 'Mind the Gap. The Age Difference between the CEO and the Chair', *Journal of Corporate Finance* 35, 136–58.

Finally, the literature on the effects of female directors on firm performance is as yet inconclusive. Nevertheless, the literature suggests that female CEOs improve firm performance whereas other female directors may destroy value. However, this does not imply that board gender balance may not be desirable from a social point of view. Female board representation has also been shown to affect corporate risk-taking behaviour and monitoring intensity. More generally, while progress has been made to improve the gender balance within large corporations, in particular at the level of the boardroom, much still needs to be done. Indeed, it is still a long way until gender balance will be achieved. There is also a need to increase the supply of highly qualified female managers. Failure to do so will worsen rather than improve corporate governance as a few top female directors are likely to be spread too thinly across corporate boards. In addition, positive policies targeting other minorities such as ethnic minorities are even less developed.

Board gender balance and board diversity

7.8 Discussion questions

1 'One way of achieving good corporate governance is to ensure the independence of non-executives sitting on the board of directors'. (Anonymous)

  Discuss the above statement in the light of the empirical evidence on the impact of independent directors on firm performance.

2 Compare and contrast single-tier boards with two-tier boards.

3 Discuss the arguments in favour of and against mandatory board gender quotas.

Reading list

Key reading

Adams, R. and Ferreira, D. (2007), 'A Theory of Friendly Boards', *Journal of Finance* 62, 217–50.

Ahern, K.R and Dittmar, A.K. (2012), 'The Changing of the Boards: The Impact on Firm Valuation of Mandated Female Board Representation', *Quarterly Journal of Economics* 127, 137–97.

Bøhren, Ø. and Staubo, S. (2014), 'Does Mandatory Gender Balance Work? Changing Organizational Form to Avoid Board Upheaval', *Journal of Corporate Finance* 28, 152–68.

Campbell, K. and Minguez-Vera, A. (2008), 'Gender Diversity in the Boardroom and Firm Financial Performance', *Journal of Business Ethics* 83, 435–51.

Dahya J. and McConnell, J.J. (2007), 'Board Composition, Corporate Performance, and the Cadbury Committee Recommendation', *Journal of Financial and Quantitative Analysis* 42, 535–64.

Dedman, E. and Lin, S. (2002), 'Shareholder Wealth Effects of CEO Departures: Evidence from the UK', *Journal of Corporate Finance* 8, 81–104.

Denis, D.K. and McConnell, J.J. (2003), 'International Corporate Governance', *Journal of Financial and Quantitative Analysis* 38, 1–36.

Fama, E.F. (1980), 'Agency Problems and the Theory of the Firm', *Journal of Political Economy* 88, 288–307.

Goergen, M. (2007), 'What Do We Know about Different Systems of Corporate Governance?', *Journal of Corporate Law Studies* 8, 1–15.

Goergen, M., Limbach, P. and Scholz, M. (2015), 'Mind the Gap. The Age Difference between the CEO and the Chair', *Journal of Corporate Finance* 35, 136–58.

Hermalin, B.E. and Weisbach, M.S. (1988), 'The Determinants of Board Composition', *RAND Journal of Economics* 19, 589–606.

Hermalin, B.E. and Weisbach, M.S. (1998), 'Endogenously Chosen Boards of Directors and their Monitoring of the CEO', *American Economic Review* 88, 96–118.

Further reading

Alchian, A.A. and Demsetz, H. (1972), 'Production, Information Costs, and Economic Organization', *American Economic Review* 62, 777–95.

Brickley, J.A., Coles J.L. and Terry, R. (1994), 'Outside Directors and the Adoption of Poison Pills', *Journal of Financial Economics* 35, 371–90.

Coates, J.M. and Herbert, J. (2008), 'Endogenous Steroids and Financial Risk Taking on a London Trading Floor', *Proceedings of the National Academy of Sciences of the United States of America* 105, 6167–72.

Cotter, J.F., Shivdasani A. and Zenner, M. (1997), 'Do Independent Directors Enhance Target Shareholder Wealth During Tender Offers?', *Journal of Financial Economics* 43, 195–218.

Fich, E.M. and Shivdasani, A. (2006), 'Are Busy Boards Effective Monitors?', *Journal of Finance* 61, 689–724.

Rechner, I.F. and Dalton, D.R. (1991), 'CEO Duality and Organizational Performance: A Longitudinal Analysis', *Strategic Management Journal* 12, 155–60.

Terjesen, S. and Singh, V. (2008), 'Female Presence on Corporate Boards: A Multi-Country Study of Environmental Context', *Journal of Business Ethics* 83, 55–63.

8 Incentivizing managers and disciplining of badly performing managers

Chapter Aims

This chapter reviews the main devices or mechanisms that are believed to ensure that managers run the firm in the interests of the shareholders and punish badly performing managers. The chapter assesses the effectiveness and importance of these mechanisms across the insider system and outsider system of corporate governance. It covers among others the following mechanisms: the market for corporate control and hostile takeovers, dividend policy, institutional shareholders, shareholder activism, managerial compensation, managerial ownership, monitoring by large shareholders and creditors or banks.

Learning Outcomes

After reading this chapter, you should be able to:

1 Assess the importance of various corporate governance devices across the insider and outsider systems of corporate governance

2 Judge the efficiency of the various devices in terms of preventing bad performance by the management and/or disciplining bad managers

3 Critically evaluate the empirical research on the importance and effectiveness of corporate governance devices

4 Identify the gaps in the existing literature

8.1 Introduction

In line with the definition of corporate governance adopted in this book (see Chapter 1), we define corporate governance devices or mechanisms as those arrangements that mitigate conflicts of interests that corporations may face. These conflicts of interests are those that may arise between

- the shareholders and the managers.
- the shareholders and the debtholders.
- the shareholders and the non-financial stakeholders.
- different types of shareholders (mainly the large shareholder and the minority shareholders).

Chapter 7 focused on boards of directors which play an important role across corporate governance systems. Still, specific corporate governance devices or mechanisms are more likely to prevail in one corporate governance system than in others given that the prevalence of the above conflicts of interests also varies across systems (see Chapters 2 and 3). Hence, in order to study the effectiveness of the various corporate governance devices, one needs to adopt one of the taxonomies of national corporate governance systems that were reviewed in Chapter 4. The taxonomy we adopt here is the taxonomy by Julian Franks and Colin Mayer, i.e. the one that distinguishes between insider and outsider systems of corporate governance.[1] We adopt this taxonomy for two reasons. First, it does not advocate the superiority of one system and is therefore more neutral than most of the other taxonomies. Second, it provides a broad, yet convenient framework to analyze the various corporate governance devices, taking into account the control and ownership patterns that prevail in various national systems and the likely conflicts of interests that they may generate.

However, while specific corporate governance mechanisms are more likely to prevail in one of the two systems, we may also review the empirical evidence on the efficiency of those mechanisms in the other system. This is due to two reasons. First, most of the existing theoretical and empirical research is based on the USA and the UK. Second, there is a dearth of empirical research on the effectiveness of some mechanisms.

8.2 Product market competition

It may be the case that competition in product and service markets reduces managerial slack across corporate governance systems. For example, a French manufacturer of household appliances operates in the same global market as an American, German, Italian and UK manufacturer. If the French manufacturer suffers from weak corporate governance and badly performing management, then it will ultimately be driven out of the market. Hence, global competition within industries may ensure that managers use their resources as well as possible to avoid being pushed out of their market and losing their jobs and livelihoods.

Benjamin Hermalin developed a theoretical model about the effects of competition on managerial performance and effort.[2] He argued that competition has four distinct effects on managerial performance. These are:

- the income effect.
- the risk-adjustment effect.
- the change-in-information effect.
- the effect on the value of managerial actions.

The income effect consists of the following. Expected income decreases with increases in competition, but competition may also put pressure on the managers to perform better, e.g. via reducing their on-the-job consumption as well as other costs. The risk-adjustment effect refers to the fact that competition changes the riskiness attached to the various actions the managers can take and ultimately the extraction of private benefits of control by the latter. The change-in-information effect consists of the following. Competition makes it easier for the principal to make inferences about her agent's actions. For example, competition makes it easier to factor out common shocks to stock prices which would otherwise cloud the principal's judgement about the agent's actual effort. In other words, if there are only a handful of firms operating in an industry, the principal may have difficulties assessing the performance of the management of her firm given that the peer group to which she can compare her firm's performance is small. Hence, meaningful comparisons of performance may be difficult. In contrast, if there is a lot of competition within an industry the peer group will be large and the principal will have a relatively easier job to evaluate the performance of the managers of her firm. However, the information effect may also influence managerial actions. Indeed, an increase in information also affects the riskiness of managerial actions. Remember that the principal-agent problem is about managers shirking, i.e. choosing an easy life rather than working hard to look after the interests of the principal. Hence more generally, managers have a choice

[1]Franks, J. and Mayer, C. (2001), 'Ownership and Control of German Corporations', *Review of Financial Studies* 14, 943–77.
[2]Hermalin, B.E. (1992), 'The Effects of Competition on Executive Behavior', *RAND Journal of Economics* 23, 350–65.

between easy actions, i.e. those that cost little or no effort, and hard actions, i.e. those that cost a lot of effort.[3] An increase in information reduces the riskiness of both easy and hard actions. However, this reduction is not necessarily uniform across both types of actions. Hence as a result of an increase in information, managers who used to take easy actions may now have the incentives to take hard actions. However, an increase in information may also compel managers who used to take hard actions to switch over to taking easier actions given that the increase in information has caused a higher reduction in the risk of easy actions than hard actions. Hence, the effect of competition on managerial actions via the information effect is also ambiguous. Finally, increased competition also changes the relative value of managerial actions. Increased competition tightens the price cap, i.e. reduces the price that managers can charge for their product in the market. Hence, increased competition reduces the agent's expected income thereby reducing the incentives to work hard. However, it also increases the value attached to cost-saving actions, improving the incentives to work harder.

A priori, all four of the above effects have ambiguous signs. However, Hermalin showed that under certain conditions the overall effect of an increase in competition on managers' performance is positive. Under these conditions, the positive income effect from competition will dominate the other three effects, making the overall effect of an increase in competition positive by improving managerial performance and reducing agency costs. Still, *generally* it is not clear whether an increase in competition will increase or decrease managerial performance.

While theory does not provide a straight answer to the question as to whether competition increases managerial effort as well as firm performance and productivity, the existing empirical literature on the impact of competition tends to suggest that high levels of competition force managers to work harder and may even be a substitute for good corporate governance. For example, Xavier Giroud and Holger Mueller[4] found that US firms in non-competitive industries benefit more from good corporate governance than those in competitive industries.[5] This suggests that competition acts as a substitute for corporate governance. Interestingly, they also find evidence in another study that a lack of competition makes managers more likely to enjoy a 'quiet life' rather than engage in empire building.[6]

8.3 Incentivizing and disciplining managers in the insider system and the outsider system

As the names of the two systems of corporate governance suggest, the mechanisms that ensure that managers perform well are mainly (but not exclusively) *external* to the corporation in the *outsider* system and *internal* to the corporation in the *insider* system. More precisely, the main mechanisms that are thought to keep managers in check in the outsider system of corporate governance are:

- the market for corporate control.
- dividend policy.

---

[3]Hard actions may also consist of those actions that result in fewer perquisites and/or less empire building.

[4]Giroud, X. and Mueller, H.M. (2011), 'Corporate Governance, Product Market Competition, and Equity Prices', *Journal of Finance* 66, 563–600.

[5]See Nickell, S., Nicolitsas, D. and Dryden, N. (1997), 'What Makes Firms Perform Well?', *European Economic Review* 41, 783–96, for the case of the UK. See Januszewski, S.I., Köke, J and Winter, J.K. (2002), 'Product Market Competition, Corporate Governance and Firm Performance: An Empirical Analysis for Germany', *Research in Economics* 56, 299–332, for the case of Germany. See Köke, J. and Renneboog, L. (2005), 'Does Strong Corporate Control and Intense Product Market Competition Lead to Stronger Productivity Growth? Evidence from Market-Oriented and Blockholder-Based Governance Regimes', *Journal of Law and Economics* 48, 475–516, for the case of both Germany and the UK.

[6]Giroud, X. and Mueller, H.M. (2010), 'Does Corporate Governance Matter in Competitive Industries?' *Journal of Financial Economics* 95, 312–31.

- institutional shareholders.
- shareholder activism.
- managerial remuneration.
- managerial ownership.

In the insider system, they are:

- monitoring by large shareholders.
- monitoring by banks and other large creditors.

As stated in the introduction to this chapter, an effort is being made in this chapter to assess the effectiveness of each of the above mechanisms within the specific system where they prevail. However, as most of the existing empirical research is based on the UK and the USA this is not always possible. Further, for some mechanisms where fortunately there is empirical evidence for both systems, we shall make reference to this.

8.4 The market for corporate control

The disciplinary role of the market for corporate control or the market for takeovers was first proposed by Henry Manne.[7] He argued that badly performing firms see their share price drop and they then become easy targets for hostile raiders. After taking control over the failing firm, the hostile[8] raider kicks out the badly performing management, puts in place better management and then turns around the firm. Eventually, the hostile raider will take the firm back to the stock market and then sell it off, benefiting from the increase in the firm's value generated by his disciplinary action. The argument here is simple. Managers of failing firms are disciplined and wastage of economic resources is corrected by the market for control. Manne even argued against anti-trust legislation which prevents takeovers from happening and thereby increases bankruptcies of failing firms as their financial performance cannot be improved via a takeover by a better management team.

However, the empirical evidence does not support Manne's argument. William Schwert for the case of the USA[9] and Julian Franks and Colin Mayer[10] for the case of the UK investigated whether there are any differences in pre-acquisition accounting and stock performance between targets of hostile takeovers and targets of friendly takeovers. Hostility is defined as the target management's attitude towards the proposed takeover bid of their firm. Neither the study by Schwert nor that by Franks and Mayer found any difference in pre-acquisition performance between the targets of friendly and hostile bids. There was also no evidence that non-acquired firms outperform targets of hostile takeovers.

However, the mere threat of a hostile takeover may be enough to ensure that managers do not shirk and run their firm in the interests of the shareholders. Nevertheless, even if Manne is correct, hostile takeovers are an extreme and expensive mechanism to correct managerial failure. Further, while hostile takeovers occur regularly in the UK and the USA (Franks and Mayer reported 80 hostile takeovers in the UK for 1985–86 and 40 in the USA for 1986), they are virtually unheard of in other countries. For example, since the Second World War, Germany has only seen four hostile takeovers, the latest being the largest hostile takeover in history,

[7]Manne, H.G. (1965), 'Mergers and the Market for Corporate Control Mergers and the Market for Corporate Control', *Journal of Political Economy* 73, 110–20.
[8]Hostility is in the eyes of the management and not the shareholders. If shareholders are 'hostile' to a takeover offer, they will simply vote against it. In contrast, managers may be hostile to a takeover bid as they fear losing their jobs should the offer be successful.
[9]Schwert, W.G. (2000), 'Hostility in Takeovers: In the Eyes of the Beholder?', *Journal of Finance* 55, 2599–640.
[10]Franks, J. and Mayer, C. 'Hostile Takeovers and the Correction of Managerial Failure', *Journal of Financial Economics* 40, 163–81.

involving the British firm Vodafone Plc taking over the engineering and telecommunications conglomerate Mannesmann AG (see Box 8.1).

Finally, it is important to bear in mind that the number of hostile takeovers in the UK and USA reached its peak during the 1980s (the so-called '4th Merger Wave') and has been in decline since then. In contrast, other corporate governance mechanisms have become increasingly important. These mechanisms include shareholder activism (see Section 8.7).

Box 8.1
The hostile takeover of Mannesmann AG by Vodafone AirTouch Plc

21 October 1999: Mannesmann agrees to a £19.8 billion bid for Orange, the UK mobile operator, thereby challenging Vodafone's market position in the European mobile telecommunications market.

19 November: Vodafone reacts by making an all-share offer of £79 billion for Mannesmann, the biggest hostile takeover bid in history.

20 November: German media come out against the move. Leading tabloid paper *Bild-Zeitung* headlines front-page with: 'The Englanders are coming, with a knockout offer ... will greed triumph today?'

28 November: Mannesmann's supervisory board advises the shareholders to reject the Vodafone offer formally.

20 December: Vodafone sets 7 February 2000 as the closing date for its bid, now worth £85 billion.

20 January 2000: Vodafone indicates it is prepared to raise its 'final' offer but Mannesmann rejects the offer.

3 February: After being locked in on-off talks with the German group's board for nearly two whole days and nights, Vodafone chief executive Chris Gent seals the deal. Mannesmann directors agree to recommend the revised deal, now worth £112 billion to their shareholders. Mannesmann CEO Klaus Esser received a payment of €16 million. A total of €57 million was paid to current and former directors of Mannesmann. A lengthy lawsuit questioning the legality of these payments was to follow. Deutsche Bank AG executive director Josef Ackermann and the German trade-union official Klaus Zwickel, who both sat on the Mannesmann supervisory board at the time of the bid, were also part of the investigation.

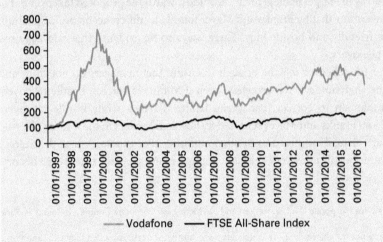

Source for share prices: Thomson Reuters Datastream

8.5 Dividends and dividend policy

Frank Easterbrook[11] and Michael Rozeff[12] were the first to formalize the potential corporate governance role played by dividends. In Rozeff's model, dividends decrease the free cash flow available to the firm and hence reduce the agency costs. However, they also increase transaction costs as higher dividends make the firm more reliant on costly external financing. Hence, there is an optimal level of dividend payout, consisting of the dividend payout that minimizes the sum of both costs. Similarly, Easterbrook argued that by committing themselves to paying out large dividends, managers reduce the free cash flow within the firm and expose themselves to regular scrutiny by outside investors. The latter occurs as the firm has to regularly raise outside financing; each time it does so it subjects itself to the scrutiny of the media, financial analysts and large institutional investors that will review the firm's recent financial performance. If the firm's managers have been performing badly, then outside financing is unlikely to be made available. Hence, by committing themselves to paying out high dividends managers set up a device which reduces Jensen's free cash flow problem and ultimately reduces agency costs.

For dividends to be able to fulfil their disciplinary role, managers will need to stick to paying out high dividends even if profits are temporarily down. Put differently, outside investors will expect managers to carry on paying high dividends in the wake of temporarily weak performance. Indeed, if dividends are allowed to vary substantially over the short term, reflecting temporary changes in profits, the disciplinary role of dividends is likely to be much reduced. Further, the role of dividends as a disciplinary mechanism is likely to be more important in the outsider system, which lacks large shareholders intent on monitoring the management than in the insider system (see Box 8.2).

Box 8.2
The need for dividends

I n October 2002, Michael McLintock, the chief executive of M&G which is part of Prudential, one of the most important institutional investors in the UK, wrote a letter to the major UK companies about the importance of maintaining dividends despite shrinking profits. The letter said that 'the investment case for dividends in the majority of circumstances is a strong and well-supported one, has stood the test of time, and is likely to be increasingly appreciated in the economic and stock market conditions which we seem likely to face for the foreseeable future'.

Source: Martin Dickson (2002), 'M&G Stresses Need to Maintain Dividends', *Financial Times*, 8 October, Front page – First section, p.1.

Marc Goergen, Luc Renneboog and Luis Correia da Silva studied the flexibility of German dividends compared to that of UK and US dividends.[13] They found that German firms are much more willing to cut or even omit their dividends when their profits are only temporarily down compared to UK and US firms. Further, German firms controlled by banks are even more likely to cut or omit their dividends than other German firms. They interpreted this as evidence that large shareholder monitoring acts as a substitute for high dividends.

[11]Easterbrook, F. (1984), 'Two Agency-Cost Explanations of Dividends', *American Economic Review* 74, 650–9.
[12]Rozeff, M.S. (1982), 'Growth, Beta and Agency Costs as Determinants of Dividend Payout Ratios', *Journal of Financial Research* 3, 249–59.
[13]Goergen, M., Renneboog, L. and Correia da Silva, L. (2005), 'When Do German Firms Change Their Dividends?' *Journal of Corporate Finance* 11, 375–99.

Rafel La Porta, Florencio Lopez-De-Silanes, Andrei Shleifer and Robert Vishny tested the validity of two models of dividends: the outcome model and the substitute model. According to the outcome model, minority shareholders pressurize insiders (managers and large shareholders) to pay out high dividends. According to the substitute model, insiders pay out high dividends to build up a reputation that they treat their minority shareholders well, as this reputation is needed when the firm needs more external financing. La Porta et al. tested the validity of the two theories by studying the link between their antidirector rights index (see Chapter 4) and dividend payout for more than 4,000 companies from 33 countries.[14] They found that dividends are higher in countries where investor rights are stronger. They argued that this is evidence in favour of the outcome model: outside investors force managers to pay out cash in countries with strong shareholder protection, whereas in countries with weak shareholder protection managers are able to keep the cash within the company. However, a close analysis of their data shows that this pattern is not as clear-cut as the authors claim. They use three different measures of dividend payout: the ratio of dividends over cash flows, the ratio of dividends over earnings and that of dividends over sales. Although, the medians of these three measures are significantly lower for the civil law countries, there are some countries that do not conform to this simple pattern. For example, Germany and Japan, both civil law countries, have dividend payouts – as measured by dividends over earnings – that are higher than the median payout of the common law countries. Taiwan, another civil law country, has a dividend payout which – depending on the measure used – is between 2.5 and six times the level of the median dividend payout of the common law countries. Conversely, Canada, a common law country, has a dividend payout which is lower than the median dividend payout of the civil law countries. The critique of the La Porta et al. antidirector rights index by Michael Graff also specifically questioned the exclusion of rules on mandatory dividends from the index (Chapter 4). Finally, as the La Porta et al. study was a cross-sectional study, it missed out year-to-year variations in dividends as well as differences in the flexibility of dividends across corporate governance systems.

8.6 Institutional investors

Institutional investors are the most important type of shareholder in the UK and the USA, as well as a few other countries such as the Netherlands. However, the jury is still out as to whether institutional investors monitor the management of their investee companies and whether they create shareholder value by doing so. Some studies found that institutional investors have a positive effect on firm value,[15] increase the sensitivity of managerial pay to performance and reduce the levels of managerial pay.[16] Other studies found that institutional investors have short-term horizons, often reducing expenditure necessary for sustaining the competitive position of the firm in the long term, that they increase the likelihood and severity of financial misreporting and that they have a negative effect on firm value.[17]

[14]La Porta, R., Lopez-de-Silanes, F., Shleifer, A. and Vishny, R. (2000), 'Agency Problems and Dividend Policies around the World', *Journal of Finance* 55, 1–33.

[15]Lee, D. and Park, K. (2009), 'Does Institutional Activism Increase Shareholder Wealth? Evidence from Spillovers on Non-Target Companies', *Journal of Corporate Finance* 15, 488–504. Gugler, K., Mueller, D. and Yurtoglu, B. (2008), 'Insider Ownership, Ownership Concentration and Investment Performance: An International Comparison', *Journal of Corporate Finance* 14, 688–705.

[16]Hartzell, J., and Starks, L. (2003), 'Institutional Investors and Executive Compensation', *Journal of Finance* 58, 2351–74.

[17]Bhide, A. (1993), 'The Hidden Costs of Stock Market Liquidity', *Journal of Financial Economics*. 34, 31–51. Coffee, J. (1991), 'Liquidity versus Control: The Institutional Investor as Corporate Monitor', *Columbia Law Review* 91, 1277–368. Bushee, B. (1998), 'The Influence of Institutional Investors on Myopic R&D Investment Behaviour', *Accounting Review* 73, 305–33. Bushee, B. (2001), 'Do Institutional Investors Prefer Near-Term Earnings Over Long-Run Value?', *Contemporary Accounting Research* 18, 207–46. Burns, N., Kedia S. and Lipson, M. (2010), 'Institutional Ownership and Monitoring: Evidence from Financial Misreporting', *Journal of Corporate Finance* 16, 443–55.

In the UK, successive codes of best practice in corporate governance (see Chapter 6) have urged institutional investors to take on a more active role in the corporate governance of their investee firms. For example, the 2001 Myners Report states that institutional investors 'remain unnecessarily reluctant to take an activist stance in relation to corporate underperformance, even where this would be in their clients' financial interests'. In line with this observation, a number of studies in the UK find that institutional investors are mostly passive and prefer exit over voice.[18] For example, Jana Fidrmuc, Marc Goergen and Luc Renneboog tested the impact of a firm's ownership and control on the market reaction to insider trades.[19] They argued that shareholders that monitor the management should reduce the asymmetry of information between the managers and the shareholders as monitoring requires the collection of information and the release of at least some of the information. Hence, firms with active shareholders should experience less substantial market reactions to insider trades than firms with passive shareholders. Fidrmuc et al. found that institutional shareholders *amplify* rather than reduce the market reaction to insider transactions, implying that institutions do not monitor the management of their investee firms. Further, evidence from interviews suggests that institutional investors frequently follow directors' trades, thereby amplifying the market reaction to these trades. Conversely, families and corporations seem to monitor the management of their investee firms as the market reaction to insider trades in their firms is significantly lower.

April Klein and Emanuel Zur studied the effects of hedge funds buying stakes in firms. While hedge funds generate large gains for the shareholders of the targeted firms, they also reduce bondholder wealth as bond prices drop on average by almost four per cent on the filing date of the purchase of the stake by the hedge fund and by another 4.5 per cent on average over the remaining year after the filing date.[20] Further, the losses to the bondholders are negatively correlated with the short-term and long-term returns earned by the shareholders, suggesting a transfer of wealth from the former to the latter (see also Section 14.4 of Chapter 14). The losses are amplified if the hedge fund obtains a board seat within the year following the filing date. All this suggests that hedge funds do not create value via monitoring.

However, there is evidence from case study research of active and positive involvement by *some* institutional investors. For example, Marco Becht, Julian Franks, Colin Mayer and Stefano Rossi found evidence of shareholder activism by the Hermes U.K. Focus Fund, the fund manager for the British Telecom Pension Fund.[21] Becht et al. were given access to letters, minutes, memos, presentations, transcripts and recordings of telephone conversations and client reports documenting the interactions of Hermes with its investee companies over 1998–2004. When the interventions led to actual outcomes, the economic effects tended to be large. However, as the interventions by institutional investors are frequently behind the scenes, they cannot normally be observed by outsiders. Still, from a theoretical, principal-agent perspective, it is not clear why institutional investors should be the panacea to all corporate governance problems. Why should they mitigate problems of agency between the managers and the shareholders as, in turn, they are agents who act on behalf of their own members or shareholders?

[18]Stapledon, G. (1996), *Institutional Shareholders and Corporate Governance*, Oxford, UK: Clarendon Press. Goergen, M. and Renneboog, L. (2001), 'Investment Policy, Internal Financing and Ownership Concentration in the UK', *Journal of Corporate Finance* 7, 257–84. Faccio M. and Lasfer, M. (2000), 'Do Occupational Pension Funds Monitor Companies in Which They Hold Large Stakes?' *Journal of Corporate Finance* 6, 71–110.

[19]Fidrmuc, J., Goergen M. and Renneboog, L. (2006), 'Insider Trading, News Releases and Ownership Concentration', *Journal of Finance* 61, 2931–73.

[20]Klein, A. and Zur, E. (2010), 'The Impact of Hedge Fund Activism on the Target Firm's Existing Bondholders', *Review of Financial Studies* 24, 1735–71.

[21]Becht, M., Franks, J.R., Mayer, C. and Rossi, S. (2009), 'Returns to Shareholder Activism: Evidence from a Clinical Study of the Hermes UK Focus Fund', *Review of Financial Studies* 22, 3093–129.

8.7 Shareholder activism

Shareholders such as institutional investors may prefer operating behind the scenes to address poor managerial performance as well as other issues of concern in their investee firms in order to avoid too much negative media attention and a further fall in the stock price. They may nevertheless launch so-called proxy contests or proxy fights as a means of last resort if the management remains unresponsive. Proxy contests consist of soliciting the support – via their votes at the AGM – of the other shareholders to bring about change. While shareholder-initiated proxy voting is frequent in the USA and on the increase in the UK, Peter Cziraki, Luc Renneboog and Peter Szilagyi reported that it remains relatively rare in Continental Europe.[22] In addition, shareholder proposals enjoy a relatively high success rate in the USA compared to the UK and Continental Europe. Nevertheless, in the USA managers are not bound to implement shareholder proposals whereas they are required to do so in the UK and most of Continental Europe. Hence in the USA, some shareholder proposals fail to get implemented by highly entrenched managers.

Cziraki et al. also found that for UK and Continental Europe on average there is a negative stock price reaction to the submission of shareholder proposals to the annual general meeting. This suggests that the stock market interprets shareholder proposals as a negative signal, reflecting substantial shareholder concerns about the firm's corporate governance, rather than a positive signal about likely future improvements in the way the firm is run. Hence, Cziraki et al. qualified shareholder proposals as serving as 'an emergency brake rather than a steering wheel: they signal dissent to the market but come short of providing a reassuring solution'. In contrast, in the USA the stock market reaction to shareholder proposals is normally positive. As expected, this positive price reaction is mainly observed for those proposals that aim at addressing poor firm performance and weak corporate governance.[23]

Apart from proxy contests, there are two other types of shareholder activism in the USA. They are shareholder proposals and direct negotiations with managers. **Shareholder proposals** are normally lodged under Securities and Exchange Commission (SEC) Rule 14a-8. This rule allows a shareholder to include a proposal and a 500-word supporting statement in the proxy statement that is distributed to the firm's shareholders in advance of the AGM. Hence, in contrast to proxy contests a shareholder proposal under Rule 14a-8 does not normally generate costs to the shareholder(s) behind the proposal, which constitutes a big advantage. However, shareholder proposals have to be submitted at least six months in advance of the AGM and the subjects they can cover are also limited. Importantly, such proposals cannot nominate candidates for the board of directors. Examples of shareholder proposals include the removal of duality and specific anti-takeover devices. Shareholder proposals are non-binding and managers often ignore them even when a proposal has received a majority of votes. The other type of shareholder activism consists of putting pressure ('jawboning') on the managers or the board of directors to achieve changes in management and/or strategy.[24] For both types of shareholder activism, the effect on the stock price is typically low.[25]

[22]Cziraki, P., Renneboog, L. and Szilagyi, P.G. (2010), 'Shareholder Activism through Proposals: The European Perspective', *European Financial Management* 16, 738–77.

[23]Renneboog, L. and Szilagyi, P.G. (2011), 'The Role of Shareholder Proposals in Corporate Governance', *Journal of Corporate Finance* 17, 167–88.

[24]Black, B.S. (1998), 'Shareholder Activism and Corporate Governance in the United States', in P. Newman (ed.), *The New Palgrave Dictionary of Economics and the Law*, 459–65.

[25]Denes, M.R., Karpoff, J.M. and McWilliams, V.B. (2017), 'Thirty Years of Shareholder Activism: A Survey of Empirical Research', *Journal of Corporate Finance* 44, 405–24.

8.8 Managerial compensation

One possible way of aligning the interests of the managers with those of the shareholders is managerial compensation packages. By designing managerial compensation in such a way that it is sensitive to firm performance, managers should have the right incentives to run the firm in the interest of the shareholders. Managerial compensation may consist of various components including:

- the basic or cash compensation.
- long-term incentive plans (LTIPs) such as stock options and restricted stock grants.
- benefits.
- perquisites.

Figure 8.1 shows the level and composition of CEO pay for 25 countries. It shows that the average level of CEO pay ranges from as little as US$169,300 in Taiwan to more than fourteen fold that amount, i.e. more than US$2.4 million in the USA. The composition of CEO pay also varies quite substantially across these countries with American CEOs receiving a relatively low proportion of their compensation in the form of a (fixed)

Figure 8.1 Level and composition of CEO pay for 2013

Notes: Figure 8.1 reports the estimated level and composition of 2013 pay for CEOs. The units are thousands of US$ converted at the 1 April 2013 exchange rate. Salary includes the base salary, other regular payments (e.g. vacation allowance and 13th month salary) and non-performance related bonuses. Bonus represents target performance-based cash awards. Options/LTIPs includes the expected value of option grants at the grant date and annualized targets from long-term incentive plans (LTIPs). Stocks and other includes stock grants/restricted stock awards plus other compensation.

Source: Based on data from Capital IQ.

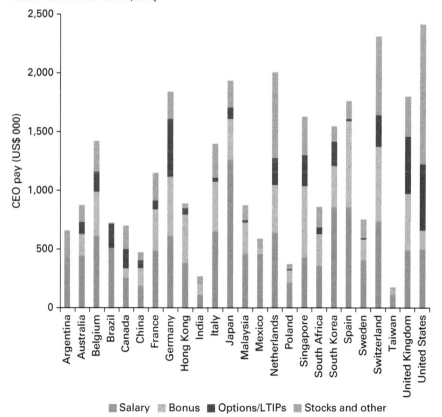

salary and relatively high proportions in the form of stocks and stock options or LTIPs. UK CEOs receive roughly the same amount of cash pay as US CEOs, but because their variable pay is lower their total compensation is still lower. Further, while UK CEOs earn similar amounts of total compensation to their counterparts in Germany, the Netherlands and Spain their fixed salary is much lower.

Three questions about managerial compensation arise. The first question is whether managerial compensation is sensitive to firm performance and, if yes, to what extent. Pay sensitivity to performance has been documented for a range of countries including the USA, the UK and Germany.[26] However, other factors have also been shown to determine the level of pay as well as its sensitivity to performance. These factors include firm size as well as ownership and control.

An important factor is firm size. This is a concern as it suggests that executive directors benefit from value-destroying growth strategies, such as empire building, via increases in their salary. The first paper to study explicitly the link between changes in firm size and managerial remuneration was Ajay Khorana and Marc Zenner.[27] They analyzed changes in managerial remuneration around mergers and acquisitions. By comparing their sample of executives making large acquisitions to a control sample of executives from firms not making large acquisitions, they found that in the pre-acquisition period changes in remuneration are linked to changes in firm size in the former, but not the latter. They interpreted this result as evidence that the design of managerial compensation packages determines the likelihood of firms making large acquisitions. They also investigated changes to executive compensation after the large acquisition. They found that over the two years following the acquisition cash and total remuneration increased by 10.5 per cent and 4.9 per cent, respectively. While stock returns and sales on average decrease after the acquisition and consequently have a negative impact on compensation, the net increase in cash and total compensation is still positive. Hence, overall there is evidence from this study that managers gain from increasing their firm's size via acquisitions. Jarrad Harford and Kai Li investigated the link between merger gains and CEO compensation.[28] They found that CEOs obtain substantial rewards from acquisitions. In line with Khorana and Zenner, they also reported that the negative effect of poor post-merger performance on managerial compensation is largely offset by the post-merger increase in compensation. They concluded that, except for bidders with strong boards, CEO compensation reacts asymmetrically to post-merger performance. While it increases in line with good performance, it is completely insensitive to bad performance. Further, they reported that 78 per cent of CEOs of underperforming firms are better off after the acquisition. Conversely, changes in CEO compensation after large capital expenditures are much smaller and are also more sensitive to bad performance. This suggests that executives successfully use the higher asymmetry surrounding acquisitions compared to capital investments to boost their compensation.

Another factor that has been shown to influence managerial pay is ownership and control. For example, Julie Ann Elston and Lawrence Goldberg found that executives of widely held German firms have higher cash pay than those of firms with large shareholders.[29] Likewise, Rafel Crespí-Cladera and Carles Gispert found a negative link between managerial compensation and ownership concentration for Spanish firms, suggesting that managerial compensation contracts are substitutes for large shareholder monitoring in widely held firms.[30]

[26]For the USA, see e.g. Coughlan, A. and Schmidt, R. (1985), 'Executive Compensation, Managerial Turnover, and Firm Performance: An Empirical Investigation', *Journal of Accounting and Economics* 7, 43–66; and Jensen, M. and Murphy, K. (1990), 'Performance Pay and Top-Management Incentives', *Journal of Political Economy* 98, 225–64. For Germany and the UK, see e.g. Conyon, M.J. and Schwalbach, J. 'Executive Compensation: Evidence from the UK and Germany', *Long Range Planning* 33, 504–26. For Germany, see also Elston, J.A. and Goldberg, L.G. (2003), 'Executive Compensation and Agency Costs in Germany', *Journal of Banking and Finance* 27, 1391–410.

[27]Khorana, A. and Zenner, M. (1998), 'Executive Compensation of Large Acquirors in the 1980s', *Journal of Corporate Finance* 4, 209–40.

[28]Harford, J. and Li, K. (2007), 'Decoupling CEO Wealth and Firm Performance: The Case of Acquiring CEOs', *Journal of Finance* 62, 917–49.

[29]Op. cit. footnote 26.

[30]Crespi-Cladera, R. and Gispert, C. (2003), 'Total Board Compensation, Governance and Performance of Spanish Listed Companies', *Labour* 17, 10–126.

The second question that arises is whether managerial compensation can address corporate governance issues. Some argue that rather than being the solution, managerial compensation is a corporate governance issue in itself as directors are often able to set their own excessive pay in firms with poor corporate governance. This may be especially true for widely held corporations as Lucian Bebchuk and Jesse Fried argued.[31] Also, frequently, managerial remuneration contracts do not include benchmarks that can distinguish between value creation from good management and value increases due to luck. In line with this argument, Gerald Garvey and Todd Milbourn found that benchmarking for managerial compensation is asymmetric as pay is sensitive to good luck, but not to bad luck.[32] Lucian Bebchuk and Jesse Fried went a step further in their 2004 book by arguing that executives are entirely self-serving as they maximize their compensation subject to a public outrage constraint, i.e. they increase their compensation up to a point where it just about prevents public outrage about excessive pay.[33] As a reaction to what are perceived to be excessive levels of managerial compensation, a number of countries have recently introduced advisory or mandatory 'say on pay' consultation with shareholders.[34]

The third question that arises about managerial compensation is how to design the compensation package and what components to include. There is an extensive theoretical as well as empirical literature on the design of managerial compensation. In a few words, the evidence seems to suggest that both stock ownership and stock options have their advantages and drawbacks. Stock ownership tends to make managers even more risk averse than they already are. Even in the absence of stock ownership, managers tend to be too risk averse and may shy away from risky, but shareholder-value-increasing projects given that all of their human capital is invested in a single firm. Stock ownership tends to make managers even more risk averse given the stock's downside and it may also cause managerial entrenchment (see Section 8.9 as to the impact of managerial ownership on firm performance and managerial entrenchment). Stock options may address this issue as they tend to have a limited downside and still have an unlimited upside. However, given the limited downside, they may exacerbate conflicts of interests between the managers and the shareholders (see also Section 11.6 of Chapter 11).

8.9 Managerial ownership

The principal-agent problem stems from the separation of ownership and control. On the one side, the managers are in control of the firm as they make the day-to-day decisions, but own few or no shares in the firm. On the other, the shareholders own the firm, but as ownership tends to be dispersed in firms in the outsider system they have little control over how the firm is run. Hence, one way of aligning the interests of the managers with those of the shareholders may be managerial ownership.[35] However, managerial ownership – especially in widely held firms – may also have a downside. Indeed, managerial ownership may shield managers from disciplinary actions by the other shareholders. For example, in the UK Sections 376–8 of the Companies Act 1985 give shareholders (including managers) owning more than five per cent the right to introduce ordinary and special resolutions to the AGM agenda. These include the dismissal of directors. However, directors owning more than

---

[31]Bebchuk, L.A. and Fried, J.M. (2003), 'Executive Compensation as an Agency Problem', *Journal of Economic Perspectives* 17, 71–92.

[32]Garvey, G.T. and Milbourn, T.T. (2006), 'Asymmetric Benchmarking in Compensation: Executives Are Rewarded for Good Luck But Not Penalized for Bad', *Journal of Financial Economics* 82, 197–225.

[33]Bebchuk, L. and Fried, J. (2004), *Pay Without Performance. The Unfulfilled Promise of Executive Compensation*, Harvard, MA: Harvard University Press.

[34]See Correa, R. and Lel, U. (2016), 'Say on Pay Laws, Executive Compensation, Pay Slice, and Firm Valuation Around the World', *Journal of Financial Economics* 122, 500–20.

[35]Jensen, M.C. and Meckling, W.H. (1976), 'Theory of the Firm: Managerial Behaviour, Agency Costs, and Ownership Structure', *Journal of Financial Economics* 3, 305–60.

five per cent can create a blocking minority to prevent an extraordinary AGM (an EGM) being held in less than the statutory notice period, as Section 307 of the Companies Act 2006 requires a majority of at least 95 per cent to hold an EGM in a shorter period of time than the statutory notice period. Further, directors with more than five per cent ownership may also create counter-resolutions. Hence, high levels of managerial ownership may cause managers to become entrenched. Finally, in the UK unless a resolution is controversial voting is done by show of hands, conferring further power to the directors as they must attend the AGM whereas minority shareholders are less likely to attend.

There is a vast body of empirical literature on the impact of managerial ownership on firm value. This body can largely be organized into two strands. The first strand of studies covers the earlier studies on the link between firm value and managerial ownership. These studies assume that managerial ownership is exogenous, i.e. it is randomly determined and does not depend on other factors such as the firm's characteristics, including its past performance. The second strand of studies allows for ownership to be endogenous, i.e. for it to depend on firm characteristics such as past performance.

One of the most cited studies belonging to the first strand is the study by Randall Morck, Andrei Shleifer and Robert Vishny on large US corporations.[36] Morck et al. measured firm value by Tobin's q, which is the ratio of the market value of equity and debt over its book value. In a nutshell, a Tobin's q in excess of 1 means that the firm creates value as its market value exceeds its book or accounting value or roughly the resale value of its assets. Conversely, a Tobin's q of less than 1 implies that the firm's shareholders would be better off liquidating the firm. Morck et al. found a non-linear, stepwise relationship between Tobin's q and managerial ownership. Firm value increases at first in line with managerial ownership when the latter amounts to less than five per cent of the equity. It then decreases as managerial ownership enters the region of five per cent to 25 per cent. Above 25 per cent of managerial ownership, firm value increases again, but at a lower rate than in the 0 per cent to five per cent region.

Morck et al. interpreted their results as follows. In the region of 0 per cent to five per cent, managerial ownership aligns the interests of the directors with those of the shareholders; hence the increase in firm value. However, in the region of five per cent to 25 per cent managers become entrenched and destroy shareholder value. Finally, if managerial ownership exceeds 25 per cent, the managers' interests are again aligned with those of the shareholders. Apart from ignoring the possibility that managerial ownership may depend on other factors, the Morck et al. study also suffered from at least three other shortcomings. First, the cross-sectional variation in managerial ownership explained only about two per cent of the cross-sectional variation in firm value.[37] Second, given that this study focused on large, Fortune 500 US corporations, there were very few observations with relatively high levels of managerial ownership. Third, the study ignored other types of shareholders. In particular, while it may indeed be the case that managers holding 10 per cent of the shares in a widely held firm are entrenched, they are less likely to be entrenched in the presence of another, larger shareholder.

Karen Wruck focused on 128 firms with large changes in ownership.[38] Contrary to Morck et al., she also considered non-managerial ownership. She replicated the Morck et al. stepwise linear model between firm value as measured by Tobin's q and managerial ownership. She found the same positive effect and the same negative effect in the 0–5 per cent range and the 5–25 per cent range, but no effect if managerial ownership exceeds 25 per cent. In fact, she only found a positive effect in the 25–100 per cent range when *total* ownership rather than just managerial ownership is considered.

[36]Morck, R., Shleifer, A. and Vishny, R. (1988), 'Managerial Ownership and Market Valuation: An Empirical Analysis', *Journal of Financial Economics* 20, 293–315.
[37]In other words, the Morck et al. regressions have an R^2 of only 0.02.
[38]Wruck, K. (1989), 'Equity Ownership Concentration and Firm Value', *Journal of Finance* 23, 567–92.

Finally, John McConnell and Henri Servaes distinguished clearly between managerial and non-managerial ownership.[39] Contrary to the two previous studies, they found a concave link between Tobin's q and managerial ownership with the maximum for firm value being achieved in the 40–50 per cent range of managerial ownership. They also found a positive, but linear link between firm value and institutional ownership.

Figure 8.2 summarizes the results from the above three studies. As Figure 8.2 suggests, the form and the nature of the link between firm value and managerial ownership change quite substantially across the studies.

Figure 8.2 The relationship between firm value and managerial ownership
Notes: MSV stands for Morck, R., Shleifer, A. and Vishny, R. (1988), 'Managerial Ownership and Market Valuation: An Empirical Analysis', *Journal of Financial Economics* 20, 293–315; McC&S stands for McConnell, J. and Servaes, H. (1990), 'Additional Evidence on Equity Ownership and Corporate Value', *Journal of Financial Economics* 27, 595–612; and Wruck stands for Wruck, K. (1989), 'Equity Ownership Concentration and Firm Value', *Journal of Finance* 23, 567–92.

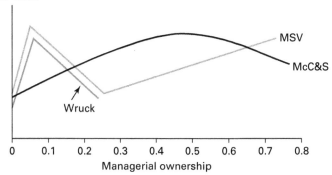

A more recent study by Ulf von Lilienfeld-Toal and Stefan Ruenzi found that firms with high CEO ownership earn excess (abnormal) stock returns.[40] Importantly, these excess stock returns are greater in firms with high managerial discretion, i.e. firms that otherwise have weak corporate governance (such as low institutional ownership). Von Lilienfeld-Toal and Ruenzi concluded that firms that would typically qualify as having weak governance can still do well if the CEO is incentivized via stock ownership.

Contrary to the above studies, studies that adjust for the possible endogeneity of managerial ownership do not typically find a link between firm value and managerial ownership. For example, Stacey Kole argued that if (managerial) ownership influences firm value, there should be corrective transfers as these transfers would be an easy way to create value.[41] While she used the same sample as Morck et al., she found the same effects only for the 0–5 per cent range and the 5–25 per cent range, but no effect above 25 per cent of managerial ownership. She then regressed performance for each of the years 1977–85 on ownership for 1980. She reported a link between performance and managerial ownership for the years 1977–80, but no such link for the years 1981–85. She argued that this calls for a reversal of causality between firm value and managerial ownership. In other words, her study suggests that past performance has an effect on current managerial ownership, but that past managerial ownership does not have an effect on current performance.

[39]McConnell, J. and Servaes, H. (1990), 'Additional Evidence on Equity Ownership and Corporate Value', *Journal of Financial Economics* 27, 595–612.
[40]Von Liliendfeld-Toal, U. and Ruenzi, S. (2014), 'CEO Ownership, Stock Market Performance and Managerial Discretion', *Journal of Finance* 69, 1013–50.
[41]Kole, S. (1996), 'Managerial Ownership and Firm Performance: Incentives or Rewards?' in *Advances in Financial Economics 2*, London: JAI Press, 119–49.

Apart from managerial ownership, Anup Agrawal and Charles Knoeber looked at six other corporate governance mechanisms that may have an impact on firm value.[42] The latter include institutional ownership, large shareholders, non-executive directors, the managerial labour market, the market for corporate control and monitoring by debtholders. They employed a whole battery of different econometric techniques. The only persistent effect they found was for non-executive directors who have a negative impact on firm value. They concluded that this negative effect may be due to the fact that frequently non-executive directors represent interest groups other than the shareholders with objectives other than shareholder value maximization. These interest groups include environmental groups and consumer groups.

Finally, a study by Charles Himmelberg, Glenn Hubbard and Darius Palia allowed for both ownership and financial performance to be endogenous. In line with Kole as well as Agrawal and Knoeber, their study did not find that current financial performance depends on past ownership.[43]

To summarize, studies that allow for the possible endogeneity of managerial ownership do not normally find that the latter affects firm value and performance. This is in direct contrast to the earlier studies which argue that there is such a link.

8.10 Large shareholder monitoring

As Chapter 2 suggested, firms from most of the world – except for the UK and the USA and a few other countries – have a large shareholder. The key question that arises is whether large shareholders enhance firm value. Some theoretical papers suggest that they create value via their monitoring of the management, which overcomes the free-rider problem that exists in widely held corporations.[44] However, there is little empirical evidence that large shareholders create value, i.e. create so-called security benefits (see also Chapter 3). For example, Julian Franks, Colin Mayer and Luc Renneboog did not find any evidence of increased board turnover in badly performing UK firms with large shareholders.[45] Saugata Banerjee, Bernard Leleux and Theo Vermaelen did not find that the main type of large shareholder in France, i.e. holding companies, creates value.[46] On the contrary, they found a negative effect of this type of shareholder on firm value and performance. Similarly, Luc Renneboog failed to uncover evidence of generalized monitoring by large shareholders in Belgian corporations.[47] However, he found evidence that firms controlled by other industrial and commercial firms experience board restructuring when accounting and share price performance declines.

There is some evidence from US firms and German firms that family control and ownership creates value. For example, Ronald Anderson and David Reeb found that US family firms in the Fortune 500 list perform

[42]Agrawal, A. and Knoeber, C. (1996), 'Firm Performance and Mechanisms to Control Agency Problems between Managers and Shareholders', *Journal of Financial and Quantitative Analysis* 31, 377–97.

[43]Himmelberg, C.P., Hubbard, R.G. and Palia, D. (1999), 'Understanding the Determinants of Managerial Ownership and the Link between Ownership and Performance', *Journal of Financial Economics* 53, 353–84.

[44]See e.g. Admati, R.A., Pfleiderer, P. and Zechner, J. (1994), 'Large Shareholder Activism, Risk Sharing, and Financial Markets Equilibrium', *Journal of Political Economy* 102, 1097–130; and Kahn, C. and Winton, A. (1998), 'Ownership Structure, Speculation, and Shareholder Intervention', *Journal of Finance* 53, 99–129.

[45]Franks, J., Mayer, C. and Renneboog, L. (2001), 'Who Disciplines Management of Poorly Performing Companies?' *Journal of Financial Intermediation* 10, 209–48.

[46]Banerjee, S., Leleux, B. and Vermaelen, T. (1997), 'Large Shareholders and Corporate Control: An Analysis of Stake Purchases by French Holding Companies', *European Financial Management* 3, 23–43.

[47]Renneboog, L. (2000), 'Ownership, Managerial Control and the Governance of Poorly Performing Companies Listed on the Brussels Stock Exchange', *Journal of Banking and Finance* 24, 1959–95.

better than non-family firms.[48] However, they also found that the superior performance of family firms is mainly driven by those firms whose CEO is a family member. Further, the relation between performance and family control is non-linear as the latter is only beneficial up to a certain threshold, but beyond the threshold reduces firm value. Belen Villalonga and Raphael Amit confirmed that the generation of the family is important.[49] They found that Fortune 500 family firms whose founder acts as the CEO or as the chairman and has a hired CEO have superior performance whereas those where a descendant of the founder acts as the CEO suffer from inferior performance. In line with this evidence from the USA, Christian Andres found that German family firms only have superior performance if the founder family is on the management or supervisory board as firms that are controlled by a family that is not on either board perform no differently from other firms.[50] Conversely, Mara Faccio, Larry Lang and Leslie Young found that family controlled firms in East Asia expropriate their minority shareholders by paying out dividends that are too low.[51] Returning to the observed generational effect whereby the first generation of the family creates shareholder value whereas subsequent generations destroy shareholder value, Vikas Mehrotra and colleagues argued that Japanese family shareholders use an exceptional way of avoiding this effect. Japanese families not only arrange marriages to inject new talent into the family, but they also adopt promising adult males as their main heirs.[52] Mehrotra et al. found that the practice works, as family firms run by non-consanguineous heirs outperform those run by consanguineous heirs. Nevertheless, consanguineous heirs outperform professional managers running family firms. This suggests that non-consanguineous heirs displace the least talented consanguineous heirs and this practice puts pressure on the remaining consanguineous heirs to perform well for fear of being displaced.

Finally, some theoretical papers argue that large shareholders may overmonitor the management, i.e. leave the latter too little discretion to run the firm efficiently (see also Section 5.4 of Chapter 5), and may also engage in self-dealing (see Section 3.8 of Chapter 3).[53] The fact that empirical studies do not find a consistently positive or negative effect of large shareholders on firm value suggests that large shareholders may have both negative and positive effects that on average may cancel each other out.

8.11 Bank and creditor monitoring[54]

Debt on its own may represent a powerful disciplinary mechanism mitigating Jensen's free cash flow problem (see Chapter 1) and preventing managers from wasting shareholder funds. As debt forces managers to commit a certain part of the firm's cash flows to its servicing, i.e. the interest payments and the repayment of the principal, it reduces managerial discretion and wastage, thereby mitigating agency problems.

---

[48]Anderson, R.C. and Reeb, D.M. (2003), 'Founding-Family Ownership and Firm Performance: Evidence from the S&P 500', *Journal of Finance* 58, 1301–28.

[49]Villalonga, B. and Amit, R. (2006), 'How Do Family Ownership, Control and Management Affect Firm Value?' *Journal of Financial Economics* 80, 385–417.

[50]Andres, C. (2008), 'Large Shareholders and Firm Performance: An Empirical Examination of Founding-family Ownership', *Journal of Corporate Finance* 14, 431–45.

[51]Faccio, M., Lang, L.H.P. and Young, L. (2001), 'Dividends and Expropriation', *American Economic Review* 91, 54–78.

[52]Mehrotra, V., Morck, R., Shim, J. and Wiwattanakantang, Y. (2013), 'Adoptive Expectations: Rising Sons in Japanese Family Firms', *Journal of Financial Economics* 108, 840–54.

[53]See e.g. Aghion, P. and Bolton, P. (1992), 'An Incomplete Contracts Approach to Financial Contracting', *Review of Economic Studies* 59, 473–94; Burkart, M., Gromb, D. and Panunzi, F. (1997), 'Large Shareholders, Monitoring, and the Value of the Firm', *Quarterly Journal of Economics* 112, 693–728; and Pagano, M. and Röell, A. (1998), 'The Choice of Stock Ownership Structure: Agency Costs, Monitoring and the Decision to Go Public', *Quarterly Journal of Economics* 113, 187–225.

[54]See Chapter 14 for a more extensive review of monitoring by debtholders as well as a discussion of other issues relating to debtholders.

Further, firms whose debt financing stems from a single creditor or small number of creditors may benefit from a further advantage. Indeed, Andrei Shleifer and Robert Vishny argued that large creditors have similar incentives to large shareholders to monitor the management of their investee firms.[55] As the German corporate governance system has been traditionally qualified as being bank-based or centred, there is a body of the empirical literature which studies the effects of German banks on firm performance. For example, John Cable studied the impact of the proportion of bank lending to total corporate lending in the 100 largest German companies.[56] He also adjusted for the voting power as well as the board representation of the banks. He found that all three matter and have a positive effect on firm performance. Similarly, Gary Gorton and Frank Schmid found that bank voting power stemming from equity ownership has a positive impact on the performance of German firms.[57] In contrast, Bob Chirinko and Julie Ann Elston did not find such a link.[58] Finally, Ingolf Dittmann, Ernst Maug and Christoph Schneider found a negative effect on firm performance of bank representation on the board of directors.[59]

8.12 Conclusions

As ownership and control vary across corporate governance systems, conflicts of interests are also likely to be different. In turn, the importance and effectiveness of various corporate governance mechanisms are also likely to vary across corporate governance systems. For example, in the outsider system of the UK and the USA the market for corporate control, dividend policy, institutional shareholders, managerial remuneration and managerial ownership are thought to be the main mechanisms used to ensure that managers operate the firm in the interests of the shareholders. In contrast, in the insider system, the main mechanisms are monitoring by large shareholders as well as monitoring by banks and other large creditors.

The relative importance of corporate governance mechanisms varies across the insider and outsider systems

In terms of the main mechanisms used in the outsider system, there is little evidence that the market for corporate control disciplines badly performing firms as targets of hostile takeovers have been shown to perform no worse than targets of friendly takeovers as well as non-acquired firms. However, the mere threat of a hostile takeover may ensure that managers act in the interests of their shareholders. There is some evidence that dividends are less flexible in the UK and the USA, given the lack of shareholder monitoring, but more flexible in Germany, a representative of the insider system where control is concentrated and the need for costly dividends as a disciplinary mechanism is likely to be less pronounced.

The effectiveness of the various corporate governance mechanisms

[55]Shleifer, A. and Vishny, R. (1997), 'A Survey of Corporate Governance', *Journal of Finance* 52, 737–84.
[56]Cable, J. (1985), 'Capital Market Information and Industrial Performance: The Role of West German Banks', *Economic Journal* 95, 118–32.
[57]Gorton, G. and Schmid, F. (2000), 'Universal Banking and the Performance of German Firms', *Journal of Financial Economics* 58, 29–80.
[58]Chirinko, R. and Elston, J.A. (1996), 'Banking Relationships in Germany; What Should Regulators Do?' in Federal Reserve Bank of Chicago (ed.), *Rethinking Bank Regulation: What Should Regulators Do?*, Chicago, IL: Federal Reserve Bank of Chicago, 239–55; Chirinko, R.S. and Elston, J.A. (2006), 'Finance, Control and Profitability: The Influence of German Banks', *Journal of Economic Behavior & Organization* 59, 69–88. See also Agarwal, R. and Elston, J.A. (2001), 'Bank-Firm Relationships, Financing and Firm Performance in Germany', *Economics Letters* 72, 225–32.
[59]Dittmann, I., Maug, E. and Schneider, C. (2010), 'Bankers on the Boards of German Firms: What They Do, What They Are Worth, and Why They Are (Still) There', *Review of Finance* 14, 35–71. See also Elsas, R. (2005), 'Empirical Determinants of Relationship Lending', *Journal of Financial Intermediation* 14, 32–57.

Further, while there is some evidence from case studies that individual institutional investors are active and intervene in their investee firms, generally this type of shareholder seems to be passive and refrains from intervening. While shareholder activism is relatively strong in the USA as well as the UK, it has only recently emerged in Continental Europe. In addition, in the USA stock markets typically react positively to shareholder proposals put to the AGM whereas in the UK and Continental Europe the reaction is mainly negative. The jury is still out as to the effectiveness of managerial remuneration as an incentivizing mechanism. While there is evidence of performance-sensitivity of managerial pay across both corporate governance systems, pay also increases with firm size and tends to be excessive in firms with poor corporate governance. Finally, studies that take into account the possible effect of past financial performance on managerial ownership find no consistent evidence of an effect of managerial ownership on current firm value. Moving onto the corporate governance mechanisms prevailing in the insider system, the evidence is inconclusive as to the effect of bank monitoring on financial performance. In addition, there is little evidence suggesting that large shareholders in general increase firm value. Nevertheless, studies on listed family firms suggest that families create value, but only when they are actively involved in the management of the firm. This positive effect is also typically limited to the founder himself whereas his descendants tend to destroy firm value. Hence, generally there is little support for the argument that large shareholders and creditors improve corporate performance.

While the body of the theoretical and empirical literature on corporate governance mechanisms has been growing steadily over the last decades, there is still need for further research. First, earlier studies typically did not adjust for the possible endogeneity of corporate governance mechanisms. In addition to board independence (see Chapter 7), managerial ownership is another example of a corporate governance mechanism that may depend on firm characteristics, including its past performance.

The likely endogeneity of corporate governance mechanisms

Second, as corporate governance mechanisms are substitutes for each other and/or are more efficient when acting in conjunction with other mechanisms, it is important that studies investigating the effectiveness of a particular mechanism take this into account. Finally, while there is now a sizeable body of the literature on the UK and the USA, research on other corporate systems and countries is still sparse.

The interdependence of corporate governance mechanisms

8.13 Discussion questions

1 Critically review the academic literature on the impact of managerial ownership on firm value.

2 'Hostile takeovers are an effective means of turning around failing companies'. Discuss the above statement with reference to relevant empirical literature.

3 What do we know about the effects of institutional and family shareholders on firm performance and value?

Reading list

Key reading

Bebchuk, L.A. and Fried, J.M. (2003), 'Executive Compensation as an Agency Problem', *Journal of Economic Perspectives* 17, 71–92.

Denis, D.K. and McConnell, J.J. (2003), 'International Corporate Governance', *Journal of Financial and Quantitative Analysis* 38, 1–36.

Goergen, M. (2007), 'What Do We Know about Different Systems of Corporate Governance?', *Journal of Corporate Law Studies* 8, 1–15.

Goergen, M. and Renneboog, L. (2009), 'Dividend Policy in a Global Perspective', in H. Kent Baker (ed.), *Dividends and Dividend Policy, Companions to Finance Series, Kolb Series in Finance*, New York: John Wiley, chapter 27, 481–98.

Goergen, M. and Renneboog, L. (2011), 'Managerial Compensation', *Journal of Corporate Finance* 17, 1068–77.

Hermalin, B. and Weisbach, M. (1998), 'Endogenously Chosen Boards of Directors and Their Monitoring of the CEO', *American Economic Review* 88, 96–118.

Himmelberg, C.P., Hubbard, R.G. and Palia, D. (1999), 'Understanding the Determinants of Managerial Ownership and the Link between Ownership and Performance', *Journal of Financial Economics* 53, 353–84.

Jensen, M. and Murphy, K. (1990), 'Performance Pay and Top-Management Incentives', *Journal of Political Economy* 98, 225–64.

Mehrotra, V., Morck, R., Shim, J. and Wiwattanakantang, Y. (2013), 'Adoptive Expectations: Rising Sons in Japanese Family Firms', *Journal of Financial Economics* 108, 840–54.

Schwert, W.G. (2000), 'Hostility in Takeovers: In the Eyes of the Beholder?', *Journal of Finance* 55, 2599–640.

Shleifer, A. and Vishny, R. (1997), 'A Survey of Corporate Governance', *Journal of Finance* 52, 737–84.

Von Liliendfeld-Toal, U. and Ruenzi, S. (2014), 'CEO Ownership, Stock Market Performance and Managerial Discretion', *Journal of Finance* 69, 1013–50.

Further reading

Admati, R.A., Pfleiderer, P. and Zechner, J. (1994), 'Large Shareholder Activism, Risk Sharing, and Financial Markets Equilibrium', *Journal of Political Economy* 102, 1097–130.

Anderson, R.C. and Reeb, D.M. (2003), 'Founding-Family Ownership and Firm Performance: Evidence from the S&P 500', *Journal of Finance* 58, 1301–28.

Andres, C. (2008), 'Large Shareholders and Firm Performance: An Empirical Examination of Founding-Family Ownership', *Journal of Corporate Finance* 14, 431–45.

Becht, M., Franks, J., Mayer, C. and Rossi, S. (2009), 'Returns to Shareholder Activism: Evidence from a Clinical Study of the Hermes UK Focus Fund', *Review of Financial Studies* 22, 3093–129.

Brickley, J.A., Coles J.L. and Terry, R. (1994), 'Outside Directors and the Adoption of Poison Pills', *Journal of Financial Economics* 35, 371–390.

Burkart, M., Gromb, D. and Panunzi, F. (1997), 'Large Shareholders, Monitoring, and the Value of the Firm', *Quarterly Journal of Economics* 112, 693–728

Cotter, J.F., Shivdasani A. and Zenner, M. (1997), 'Do Independent Directors Enhance Target Shareholder Wealth During Tender Offers?', *Journal of Financial Economics* 43, 195–218.

Faccio, M., Lang, L.H.P. and Young, L. (2001), 'Dividends and Expropriation', *American Economic Review* 91, 54–78.

Ferri, F. and Maber, D.A. (2013), 'Say on Pay Votes and CEO Compensation: Evidence from the UK', *Review of Finance* 17, 527–63.

Franks, J., Mayer, C. and Renneboog, L. (2001), 'Who Disciplines Management of Poorly Performing Companies?', *Journal of Financial Intermediation* 10, 209–48.

Gorton, G. and Schmid, F. (2000), 'Universal Banking and the Performance of German Firms', *Journal of Financial Economics* 58, 29–80.

Jameson, M., Prevost, A. and Puthenpurackal, J. (2014), 'Controlling Shareholders, Board Structure, and Firm Performance: Evidence from India', *Journal of Corporate Finance* 27, 1–20.

O'Sullivan, N. and Wong, P. (1998), 'Internal versus External Control: An Analysis of Board Composition and Ownership in UK Takeovers', *Journal of Management and Governance* 2, 17–35.

Villalonga, B. and Amit, R. (2006), 'How Do Family Ownership, Control and Management Affect Firm Value?', *Journal of Financial Economics* 80, 385–417

9 Corporate governance in emerging markets[1]

Chapter Aims

The focus of this chapter is on the challenges that emerging markets face in terms of stepping up their economic development and enhancing the governance of their corporations. Such challenges include the institutional design, in particular the role accorded to the stock market, the privatization of state-owned enterprises (SOEs) as well as social and political barriers to economic development such as crony capitalism.

Learning Outcomes

After reading this chapter, you should be able to:

1 Critically review whether well-developed equity markets combined with strong investor rights are a necessary and sufficient condition for economic development

2 Comprehend the challenges that emerging markets face in their attempt to improve corporate governance

3 Evaluate corporate governance issues that may arise in privatized or part-privatized SOEs

4 Assess the potential benefits and costs of political connections

9.1 Introduction

Chapters 4 and 5 suggest that there is a link between a country's institutional setting, including its political, legal and financial systems, and the access of its corporations to external capital via well-developed stock markets. It is argued that a well-developed stock market is a necessary and sufficient driver of economic growth. While this view is held by a substantial body of the academic literature and also by international organizations, such as the World Bank and the International Monetary Fund (IMF),[2] there are some dissenting voices in academia that argue that some emerging as well as developed economies have done rather well despite weak legal institutions and that there are substitutes that may overcome weak investor protection and law. This chapter will start with

---

[1]This chapter is dedicated to Prof. Ajit Singh of Cambridge University, who passed away in 2015. Prof. Singh was a great scholar as well as a true gentleman. I am thankful to him for his encouragement when I was an early career researcher.
[2]See e.g. Iskander, M.R. and Chamlou, N. (2000), *Corporate Governance: A Framework for Implementation*, Washington, DC: The World Bank.

a discussion of the opposing views as to whether a large stock market combined with good quality law is a *necessary and sufficient* condition for strong economic growth.

This chapter will also look at two manifestations of crony capitalism that tend to prevail in developing countries. These are inherited billionaire wealth as well as political connections and government interference in corporate affairs. One of the dangers of old money is that it becomes entrenched via the control it exerts over the political system and other national institutions. One of the consequences of this control may be the reduction in capital mobility and preventing the opening of the country's economy to foreign firms and investors. There are extreme examples of countries where major capitalists and political elites have been inextricably linked. One such example is the Philippines under the Ferdinand Marcos regime (see Box 9.1). Finally, the chapter will make some recommendations about how to design corporate governance in former SOEs. Interested readers may also want to consult the 'OECD Guidelines on Corporate Governance of State-Owned Enterprises' (see Additional resources at the end of this chapter).

Box 9.1
Politics and capitalism

'We practically own everything in the Philippines from electricity, telecommunications, airlines, banking, beer and tobacco, newspaper publishing, television stations, shipping, oil and mining, hotels and beach resorts, down to coconut milling, small farms, real estate and insurance'. (Imelda Marcos, widow of Ferdinand Marcos)

Source: Tony Tassel (1998), 'Mrs Marcos in Legal Fight to Get $13bn', *Financial Times*, 8 December, Asia-Pacific Section, p. 5, as cited in Claessen, S., Djankov, S. and Lang, L.H.P. (2000), 'The Separation of Ownership and Control in East Asian Corporations', *Journal of Financial Economics* 58, 81–112.

9.2 Are large equity markets combined with strong property rights the only way to achieve economic growth?

The law and finance literature argues that legal and political institutions shape corporate governance and ultimately drive economic growth (see Chapter 4). According to La Porta et al., capital markets will only properly develop in countries with strong investor rights. The absence of liquid capital markets impedes the growth of corporations as outside capital is sparse and investment opportunities cannot be taken up. Mark Roe proposed the political orientation of the government in power as the main driver of corporate governance. He argued that under conservative governments, capital markets flourish whereas under social-democratic governments the emphasis is on improving workers' rights and stock markets remain underdeveloped. Finally, Pagano and Volpin suggested that electoral systems determine whether political parties cater for the rights of workers or the rights of investors, with proportional electoral systems catering for the former and majoritarian systems catering for the latter. Similar to La Porta et al. and Roe, they argued that capital markets will only develop and dispersed ownership will only emerge under strong property rights.

Franklin Allen argued that at the core of the law and finance literature is a rather narrow view of what the corporation is all about (see also Chapter 1).[3] This view states that the objective of the corporation is to

[3] Allen, F. (2005), 'Corporate Governance in Emerging Economies', *Oxford Review of Economic Policy* 21, 164–77.

maximize shareholder value. However, it is based on the assumptions that markets are perfect and complete. These assumptions are unlikely to hold, even for the case of highly developed economies. For example, markets are not perfect given the existence of negative externalities. A negative externality is a cost imposed on others by one's economic activity. For example, in its pursuit of creating shareholder value a firm may end up badly polluting the environment. While the benefits from polluting the environment, via the cost savings from failing to install pollution-reducing equipment, accrue to the firm's shareholders, the pollution caused by the firm affects the local community and may result in a substantial reduction in its quality of life. Allen argued that while the assumptions behind the law and finance literature are likely to be violated for the case of developed economies, this is even more likely to be the case for emerging economies.

Hence, Allen proposed a much broader view of corporate governance along the lines of how corporate governance is typically defined in countries such as Germany and Japan where the objective of the firm is to look after all its stakeholders, and not just after its shareholders.[4] Allen argued that this broader view is likely to overcome one of the shortcomings of the shareholder-centred view of corporate governance, which is the omission of the issue of equitable income distribution across society. This issue is likely to be of major concern in developing countries where the distributions of wealth and income are highly skewed.

Given that the assumptions behind the law and finance literature do not hold in practice, Allen argued that the quality of law is not a *necessary* condition for strong economic growth; neither is it a *sufficient* condition.[5] He cited two examples of countries that illustrate the irrelevance of the quality of the legal system in terms of economic growth. The first example is China. Despite weak legal institutions, weak law enforcement and past weak accounting standards, China has experienced an impressive rate of economic growth since it opened its economy in 1979. China is now the largest economic power in the world after the USA. The second example is the UK. The historical study by Julian Franks, Colin Mayer and Stefano Rossi suggested that ownership dispersion in the UK *predates* the existence of strong shareholder rights and cannot therefore be a consequence of the latter as argued by La Porta et al.[6]

The question then arises as to how economic growth could be sustained in each of these two countries in the absence of a strong legal system. Allen proposed the following four alternatives to good laws:

- competition.
- trust and reputation.
- family ownership.
- foreign ownership.

Competition is strong in China. There is fierce competition from domestic firms as well as foreign firms. China has also managed to overcome the weaknesses of its legal institutions by developing institutions similar to those that eleventh-century traders developed to overcome commitment problems and which consisted of linkages between social and economic institutions and between market and non-market institutions. In addition, as suggested by the Franks et al. historical study, owners of UK firms managed to disperse their ownership in the absence of strong investor protection by going public on *local* stock exchanges, thereby ensuring the geographic proximity of their firm and its directors to its outside shareholders and reducing asymmetry of information. In other words, while UK firms experienced a separation of ownership and control, outside ownership was

[4]See also O'Sullivan, M. (2000), *Contests for Corporate Control*, Oxford, UK: Oxford University Press.
[5]See also Section 5.3 of Chapter 5 for the advantages and shortcomings of bank-based systems and market-based systems.
[6]Franks, J., Mayer, C. and Rossi, S. (2009), 'Ownership: Evolution and Regulation', *Review of Financial Studies* 22, 4009–56. See also Section 4.7 of Chapter 4. See also Acheson, G.G., Campbell, G. Turner, J.D. and Vanteeva, N. (2015), 'Corporate Ownership and Control in Victorian Britain', *Economic History Review* 68, 911–36.

geographically concentrated to reduce informational problems and inspire trust (see Box 9.2). Finally, Graeme Acheson, Gareth Campbell and John Turner argued that during Victorian times investor protection provided by company law was virtually non-existent. UK firms then provided as much investor protection via their articles of association as is provided by modern company law.[7]

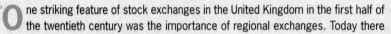

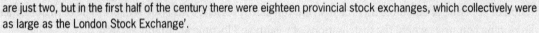

Box 9.2
The importance of local stock exchanges in the UK during the first half of the twentieth century

One striking feature of stock exchanges in the United Kingdom in the first half of the twentieth century was the importance of regional exchanges. Today there are just two, but in the first half of the century there were eighteen provincial stock exchanges, which collectively were as large as the London Stock Exchange'.

Source: Franks, J., Mayer, C. and Rossi, S. (2009), 'Ownership: Evolution and Regulation', *Review of Financial Studies* 22, p. 4017.

While Allen did not explicitly refer to the varieties of capitalism (VOC) literature and one of its key propositions that networks and relationships act as substitutes for markets (see Chapter 4), his argument is nevertheless very much in line with that literature. Moreover, family ownership has been important across Asia and many successful Chinese firms have a lot of ownership by their founders and executives. Finally, joint ventures between domestic investors and foreign investors are another way of overcoming institutional weaknesses and ensuring access to outside capital.

Conglomerates or business groups may be an additional way of bridging bad laws and institutions (see also Section 2.4 of Chapter 2). Conglomerates may operate internal capital markets whereby affiliated companies with excess funds channel these to those affiliated companies in need of funding. Tarun Khanna and Krishna Palepu found evidence in support of this argument.[8] They found that in India, companies affiliated to highly diversified business groups have better accounting as well as stock performance than independent companies.

Another critique by Franklin Allen concerns the motives behind financial innovation.[9] Allen argued that there is evidence that financial innovation is sometimes motivated by the desire to create complexity and to expropriate the purchaser. He called this the *dark side of financial innovation* and blamed this on financial deregulation.

Ajit Singh and colleagues also questioned the role of stock markets as drivers of economic growth (see also Sections 5.4 and 5.5 of Chapter 5).[10] Compared to Franklin Allen who stated that a large equity market is neither a necessary nor a sufficient condition for strong economic growth, Singh et al.'s view of the stock market was rather damning. Singh et al. disputed the argument that US economic growth, in particular the spectacular growth of its information technology (IT) industry during the late 1990s, has been mainly due to its large and

[7]Acheson, G.G., Campbell, G. and Turner, J.D. (2016), 'Common Law and the Origin of Shareholder Protection', Queen's University Centre for Economic History Working Paper Series, available at www.quceh.org.uk/uploads/1/0/5/5/10558478/wp16-04.pdf.
[8]Khanna, T. and Palepu, K. (2000), 'Is Group Affiliation Profitable in Emerging Markets? An Analysis of Diversified Indian Business Groups', *Journal of Finance* 55, 867–91.
[9]Allen, F. (2012), 'Trends in Financial Innovation and their Welfare Impact: An Overview', *European Financial Management* 18, 493–514.
[10]Singh, A., Glen, J., Zammit, A., De-Hoyos, R., Singh, A. and Weisse, B. (2005), 'Shareholder Value Maximisation, Stock Market and New Technology: Should the US Corporate Model be the Universal Standard?' *International Review of Applied Economics* 19, 419–37.

well-developed stock markets. They claimed the assertion that stock markets are better at allocating resources than, e.g. banks and governments is wrong for at least two reasons.

First, stock markets may suffer from mispricing and investor over-optimism. Singh et al. argued that the overvaluation of the New Economy stocks combined with the undervaluation of the Old Economy stocks during the late 1990s is an example where resources were allocated to firms that were chronically overvalued, a lot of which had not yet generated a profit and were also unlikely to do so in the future. In support of Singh et al.'s argument, the work by Robert Shiller, the behavioural economist who won the Nobel Prize in Economic Sciences in 2013, suggested that stock prices have been deviating significantly from their fundamental values, i.e. company earnings, since the 1990s.[11] Figure 9.1 compares the inflation-adjusted US S&P stock price index to the inflation-adjusted (or real) S&P earnings index. It shows that while stock prices were significantly higher than their fundamental values during the late 1920s, just before the stock market crash of 1929 and the subsequent Great Depression, there is no comparison to the last two decades to the mid 2010s when prices deviated so much more substantially from earnings. Singh et al. added that the widespread use of stock options by New Economy firms to incentivize their employees favoured over-reporting of earnings and fuelled the stock market bubble of the late 1990s. They also considered the growing use of stock options as one of the contributing factors of increasing income inequality in the USA over the 1990s.[12]

Figure 9.1 **Real S&P stock price index and real S&P composite earnings index – 1871–2017**
Source: Robert J. Shiller's online data website, www.econ.yale.edu/~shiller/data.htm, accessed on 9 February 2017 (data taken from www.econ.yale.edu/~shiller/data/ie_data.xls).

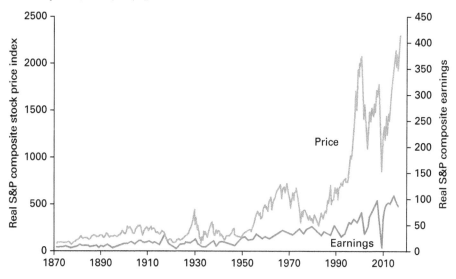

Second, one of the key mechanisms whereby stock markets reallocate resources to the most productive firms is the market for corporate control, i.e. takeovers. However, Singh et al. claimed that the market for corporate control is far from being efficient as it does not necessarily favour the survival of the fittest. On the contrary, large but relatively less profitable firms are much more likely to survive than small, profitable firms given that the latter are frequently targeted by the former via mergers and acquisitions (see also Section 8.4 of Chapter 8).

[11]Shiller, R.J. (2005), *Irrational Exuberance*, Princeton, NJ: Princeton University Press, 2nd edition.
[12]See also Isaacs, J.B., Sawhill, I.V. and Haskins, R. (2008), *Getting Ahead or Losing Ground: Economic Mobility in America*, Washington DC: Brookings Institution Press, available at: www.brookings.edu/reports/2008/02_economic_mobility_sawhill.aspx, about the increase in wealth and income inequality in the USA over the previous decades.

Singh et al. concluded that if stock markets are prone to bubbles and overvaluation in highly developed economies – such as the USA – that have stringent regulation, good information disclosure and high accounting standards, then stock markets in emerging economies are likely to fare even worse. The main consequence of policy makers in emerging economies focusing on developing local stock markets would then be an increase in the volatility of their economy rather than steady economic growth. Singh et al. cited the example of Indonesia, which despite having been commended by the IMF for the good management of its economy, experienced a drop in its stock market capitalization of 80 per cent during the height of the Asian crisis (September–December 1997). The stock market crash was followed by an equivalent drop in the value of its currency, which had a disastrous effect on the Indonesian economy. Further, Singh et al. claimed that venture capital, which tends to finance early business ventures, does not necessarily require the existence of a well-developed equity market as the case of Israel illustrates. Since 1991, the Israeli government has been engaged in a programme promoting technological development by providing entrepreneurs with funding, professional and administrative support as well as physical premises. Governments in other countries such as France, India and Singapore have also taken on the role of venture capitalists and been paramount in pushing technological advances.[13]

While Franklin Allen questioned the need for strong investor rights and large stock markets to achieve strong economic growth and Ajit Singh et al. considered stock markets to cause more harm than good in emerging economies, Dennis Mueller argued that the existence of a well-developed stock market can only constitute an advantage and not a disadvantage as it offers firms the option to finance their investments via equity, in addition to internal funds (i.e. retained profits), bank financing and bonds.[14] Hence, the best policy for emerging countries to develop their national economy would be legal reforms that improve corporate governance and encourage the development of a large equity market.

9.3 Inherited wealth

In an influential study covering 42 economies, Randall Morck, David Stangeland and Bernard Yeung found that countries, where the wealth of inherited (heir) billionaires is large relative to the gross domestic product (GDP), have slower economic growth and technological change than other countries at a similar stage of economic development.[15] Their study showed great variation in terms of inherited wealth (see Table 9.1). On average, inherited wealth is highest in East Asia, amounting to about 3.5 per cent of GDP, with Hong Kong being the country with the highest heir billionaire wealth as a percentage of GDP (16 per cent) across all 42 countries. In Latin America, inherited billionaire wealth is about 1.4 per cent of GDP with Venezuela having the highest percentage at 4.3 per cent. Industrialized countries where inherited billionaire wealth is higher than two per cent of GDP include Canada, Germany, Greece and Switzerland. Entrepreneur billionaire wealth, which is not inherited but the result of the entrepreneur's own efforts, is highest as a percentage of GDP in Hong Kong (19 per cent), Malaysia (seven per cent) and Taiwan (five per cent).

---

[13]See e.g. Bottazzi, L. and da Rin, M. (2002), 'Venture Capital in Europe and the Financing of Innovative Companies', *Economic Policy* 17, 229–69, and Mayer, C., Schoors, K. and Yafeh, Y. (2005), 'Sources of Funds and Investment Activities of Venture Capital Funds: Evidence from Germany, Israel, Japan and the United Kingdom', *Journal of Corporate Finance*, 11, 586–608, for the characteristics (including the different sources of funding) of various national venture capital industries.

[14]Mueller, D.C. (2006), 'The Anglo-Saxon Approach to Corporate Governance and its Applicability to Emerging Markets', *Corporate Governance: An International Review* 14, 207–19.

[15]Morck, R., Stangeland, D. and Yeung, B. (2000), 'Inherited Wealth, Corporate Control and Economic Growth: The Canadian Disease?' in R. Morck (ed.), *Concentrated Corporate Ownership*, National Bureau of Economic Research and University of Chicago Press, IL, pp. 319–69.

Table 9.1 **Inherited wealth**

Country	Billionaires per million people	Percentage of GDP					
		Total billionaire wealth	Entrepreneur billionaire wealth	Heir billionaire wealth	Probable heir billionaire wealth	Entrepreneur and heir control	Political family billionaire wealth
Argentina	0.118	2.64	0.00	2.64	0.00	0.00	0.00
Australia	0.056	0.77	0.77	0.00	0.00	0.00	0.00
Austria	0	0.00	0.00	0.00	0.00	0.00	0.00
Belgium	0	0.00	0.00	0.00	0.00	0.00	0.00
Brazil	0.038	2.29	1.24	0.49	0.00	0.55	0.00
Canada	0.173	4.02	0.00	2.49	1.53	0.00	0.00
Chile	0.218	10.22	3.70	3.48	0.00	3.04	0.00
Colombia	0.086	3.93	0.00	0.00	3.93	0.00	0.00
Denmark	0.193	1.73	0.00	0.00	0.00	1.73	0.00
Ecuador	0	0.00	0.00	0.00	0.00	0.00	0.00
Finland	0	0.00	0.00	0.00	0.00	0.00	0.00
France	0.191	1.68	0.21	1.19	0.29	0.00	0.00
Germany	0.504	5.46	0.65	3.99	0.83	0.00	0.00
Greece	0.48	13.33	0.00	6.67	6.67	0.00	0.00
Hong Kong	2.188	36.13	19.32	15.78	1.03	0.00	0.00
Iceland	0	0.00	0.00	0.00	0.00	0.00	0.00
India	0.002	1.20	0.00	0.82	0.37	0.00	0.00
Indonesia	0.02	16.06	3.59	1.18	1.76	0.00	9.52
Ireland	0	0.00	0.00	0.00	0.00	0.00	0.00
Israel	0.395	4.14	4.14	0.00	0.00	0.00	0.00
Italy	0.088	1.04	0.47	0.57	0.00	0.00	0.00
Japan	0.289	1.83	0.55	0.79	0.49	0.00	0.00
Korea	0.068	3.20	1.24	1.96	0.00	0.00	0.00
Malaysia	0.213	12.50	7.00	0.00	5.50	0.00	0.00
Mexico	0.267	12.82	1.60	0.23	6.05	3.14	0.00
Netherlands	0.196	3.67	0.00	1.87	0.00	0.38	1.42
Norway	0	0.00	0.00	0.00	0.00	0.00	0.00
Peru	0	0.00	0.00	0.00	0.00	0.00	0.00
Philippines	0.072	10.00	1.77	3.71	2.74	1.77	0.00
Portugal	0	0.00	0.00	0.00	0.00	0.00	0.00
Singapore	0.935	8.60	2.81	2.28	3.51	0.00	0.00
South Africa	0.025	1.32	1.32	0.00	0.00	0.00	0.00
Spain	0.077	0.89	0.00	0.57	0.33	0.00	0.00
Sweden	0.229	5.64	0.00	0.00	0.66	4.97	0.00

(Continued)

Table 9.1 (*Continued*)

Country	Billionaires per million people	Percentage of GDP					
		Total billionaire wealth	Entrepreneur billionaire wealth	Heir billionaire wealth	Probable heir billionaire wealth	Entrepreneur and heir control	Political family billionaire wealth
Switzerland	1.133	7.70	0.94	4.77	0.74	1.25	0.00
Taiwan	0.287	7.26	4.89	0.00	0.96	1.42	0.00
Thailand	0.105	12.28	1.25	2.66	4.14	2.97	1.27
Turkey	0.034	2.84	0.00	0.00	0.00	2.84	0.00
UK	0.086	1.12	0.11	0.74	0.00	0.23	0.03
USA	0.465	3.95	0.93	1.47	1.25	0.30	0.00
Venezuela	0.097	4.31	0.00	4.31	0.00	0.00	0.00

Source: Morck, R., Stangeland, D. and Yeung, B. (2000), 'Inherited Wealth, Corporate Control and Economic Growth: The Canadian Disease?', in R. Morck (ed.), *Concentrated Corporate Ownership*, National Bureau of Economic Research and University of Chicago Press, table 11.1.

Morck et al. found that inherited billionaire wealth is negatively correlated with economic growth whereas the correlation between entrepreneur billionaire wealth and economic growth is positive. They justified the negative effect of inherited wealth on GDP growth by the following four arguments. First, inherited wealth may keep bad and incompetent family managers in place, as family CEOs are frequently succeeded by other family members rather than the most qualified candidate for the job in the labour market (see Section 1.6 of Chapter 1). Second, highly unequal wealth distribution may create market power in capital markets, thereby reducing the efficiency of the latter in pricing securities and allocating economic resources. Third, inherited wealth tends to be conservative and opposed to technological change that may endanger its economic power. Finally, heir billionaires often have strong ties to politicians, further entrenching their position by reducing capital mobility and increasing other barriers to trade. Morck et al.'s condemnation of inherited wealth is somewhat similar to, albeit stronger than, that of Francis Fukuyama who argued that countries where family ties are strong (he called this familism) will suffer in terms of limitations to the maximum size of their firms as well as to the types of industry sectors that will prosper (see Section 5.5 of Chapter 5).[16]

Gomiluk Otokwala argued that the Nigerian government has been taking steps to stamp out family control and ownership of its banks since 2004.[17] In 2009, the Central Bank of Nigeria took control of five of its banks, dismissed their management and replaced it with outsiders, in a US$2.6 billion bailout of the banking system. The governor of the Central Bank announced that there would be a reform of the banking industry and that 'sole proprietorships', a euphemism for family-owned banks, would no longer be permissible. The following year the press reported that the Central Bank 'ha[d] affirmed its preparedness to reduce the influence of individuals with large stakes in banks in the country, as it announced … that it was set to ensure that no individual or group owned more than five per cent equity stake in the banks … This is the practice in other countries'.[18]

[16]Fukuyama, F. (1995), *Trust. The Social Virtues and the Creation of Prosperity*, London: Hamish Hamilton.
[17]Otokwala, G. (2010), 'Whither Family Firms in Developing Countries?', Harvard Law School, available at ssrn.com/abstract=1714526, p. 8.
[18]Op. cit. footnote 17, p. 9. Later on, this statement was retracted in a press release by the Central Bank.

9.4 The role of the government

Government ownership of large corporations can be substantial in some emerging markets. The most extreme example of the importance of government ownership is China. China started an ambitious programme of economic reforms during the 1980s which resulted in increased power for the managers of SOEs and reduced government interference (see also Section 2.4 of Chapter 2). In the early 1990s, the Chinese government set up the Shenzhen and Shanghai Stock Exchanges which acted as the platform for the part-privatization of Chinese SOEs. However, as Ferdinand Gul, Jeong-Bon Kim and Annie Qiu reported, the control of most Chinese firms is still firmly in the hands of public authorities.[19] The largest shareholder on average holds about 43 per cent of the shares and in 67 per cent of the firms the largest shareholder is the government or government-related. The average stake of the government across their sample is 32 per cent whereas foreign investors hold just four per cent.

Overall, the empirical evidence suggests that the performance of privatized firms improves after their privatization. Narjess Boubakria, Jean-Claude Cosset, Omrane Guedhami investigated the post-privatization performance of 230 companies from 32 developing countries.[20] They found that profitability, efficiency (as measured by sales per employee), capital expenditure and output (as measured by total sales) increased significantly after the privatization. However, there are significant differences in these post-privatization improvements across geographic regions. In particular, companies from Africa and the Middle East experience the smallest changes in profitability, efficiency and output. Boubakri et al. found that trade liberalization increases the post-privatization improvements in profitability, output and capital expenditure. In addition, stock market liberalization and development as well as the quality of law have a positive impact on output. Boubraki et al. explained the positive effect of the stock market by its monitoring role. Finally, they also found that if the government gives up control after the privatization, improvements in profitability, efficiency and output are significantly larger.

Juliet D'Souza, William Megginson and Robert Nash documented similar post-privatization improvements for 129 privatized companies from 23 developed OECD countries.[21] However, contrary to Boubakri et al., they found that government ownership retained after the privatization has a positive impact on capital expenditure. Further, both government and foreign ownership have a negative effect on employment. D'Souza et al. argued that foreign shareholders are less likely to be concerned by local social and political concerns and are therefore more likely to reduce excess employment in the former SOEs. However, they noted that the negative effect of government ownership on employment is somewhat surprising. They explained this negative effect by the government's incentive in part-privatizations to reduce the excess work force in order to maximize the sales price of its remaining stake. Also in contrast to Boubakri et al., they did not find that trade liberalization and law have an effect on post-privatization outcomes. This suggests that institutional factors are important in developing markets, but less so in developed economies.

Further, Narjess Boubakri, Jean-Claude Cosset and Walid Saffar found that for 245 privatized firms from 27 emerging economies and 14 developed economies the higher the percentage of ownership retained by the government after the privatization the higher is the likelihood that politicians and ex-politicians sit on the firm's board of directors.[22] In contrast, the likelihood of politicians and ex-politicians being on the board decreases with the size of foreign ownership. These relationships hold for both strategically important industries and

[19]Gul, F.A., Kim, J.-B. and Qiu, A.A. (2010), 'Ownership Concentration, Foreign Shareholding, Audit Quality, and Stock Price Syncronicity: Evidence from China', *Journal of Financial Economics* 95, 425–42.

[20]Boubakri, N., Cosset, J.-C. and Guedhami, O. (2005), 'Liberalization, Corporate Governance and the Performance and Privatized Firms in Developing Countries', *Journal of Corporate Finance* 11, 767–90.

[21]D'Souza, J., Megginson, W. and Nash, R. (2005), 'Effect of Institutional and Firm-specific Characteristics on Post-Privatization Performance: Evidence from Developed Countries', *Journal of Corporate Finance* 11, 747–66.

[22]Boubakri, N., Cosset, J.-C. and Saffar, W. (2008), 'Political Connections in Newly Privatized Firms', *Journal of Corporate Finance* 14, 654–73.

those that are not. The likelihood of having politicians on the board of directors of newly privatized firms is also higher in countries with less judicial independence.

Table 9.2 shows the importance of firms with political connections across 47 developed and emerging economies. Emerging economies where politically connected firms represent more than 10 per cent of the market capitalization include Indonesia, Malaysia, the Philippines, Russia and Thailand. Developed economies that fulfil the same criterion include Belgium, Ireland, Italy, Taiwan and the UK. The question that then arises is whether political connections are good or bad for firm performance.

Table 9.2 Firms from 47 countries with political connections

	No. of firms with available data	No. of firms connected with a minister or MP	% of firms connected with a minister or MP	No. of firms connected through close relationships	% of firms connected with a minister or MP, or a close relationship	% of top 50 firms connected with a minister or MP, or a close relationship	Connected firms as % of market capitalization
Argentina	38	0	0.00	0	0.00	0.00	0.00
Australia	287	2	0.70	0	0.70	0.00	0.32
Austria	110	1	0.91	0	0.91	2.00	0.25
Belgium	157	6	3.82	0	3.82	8.00	18.77
Brazil	167	0	0.00	0	0.00	0.00	0.00
Canada	534	7	1.31	0	1.31	2.00	2.53
Chile	89	2	2.25	0	2.25	4.00	1.43
Colombia	32	0	0.00	0	0.00	0.00	0.00
Czech Rep.	63	0	0.00	0	0.00	0.00	0.00
Denmark	228	7	3.07	0	3.07	6.00	2.52
Finland	132	2	1.52	0	1.52	0.00	0.14
France	914	16	1.75	4	2.19	10.00	8.03
Germany	840	11	1.31	2	1.55	2.00	1.20
Greece	153	1	0.65	0	0.65	0.00	0.09
Hong Kong	405	3	0.74	5	1.98	6.00	2.33
Hungary	27	1	3.70	0	3.70	3.85	2.81
India	323	9	2.79	0	2.79	2.00	1.83
Indonesia	154	12	7.79	22	22.08	24.00	12.76
Ireland	82	2	2.44	0	2.44	4.00	22.83
Israel	55	2	3.64	0	3.64	4.26	8.13
Italy	233	24	10.30	0	10.30	16.00	11.27
Japan	2,395	31	1.29	1	1.34	2.00	1.34
Luxembourg	23	1	4.35	0	4.35	4.55	10.48
Malaysia	445	23	5.17	65	19.78	44.00	28.24
Mexico	94	6	6.38	2	8.51	12.00	8.14
Netherlands	238	1	0.42	0	0.42	0.00	0.01
New Zealand	50	0	0.00	0	0.00	0.00	0.00

Table 9.2 (*Continued*)

	No. of firms with available data	No. of firms connected with a minister or MP	% of firms connected with a minister or MP	No. of firms connected through close relationships	% of firms connected with a minister or MP, or a close relationship	% of top 50 firms connected with a minister or MP, or a close relationship	Connected firms as % of market capitalization
Norway	206	0	0.00	0	0.00	0.00	0.00
Peru	37	0	0.00	0	0.00	0.00	0.00
Philippines	114	1	0.88	4	4.39	8.00	16.16
Poland	57	0	0.00	0	0.00	0.00	0.00
Portugal	101	3	2.97	0	2.97	4.00	2.00
Russia	25	3	12.00	2	20.00	36.36	86.75
Singapore	229	18	7.86	0	7.86	4.00	2.59
South Africa	212	0	0.00	0	0.00	0.00	0.00
South Korea	313	7	2.24	1	2.56	4.00	8.95
Spain	200	3	1.50	0	1.50	0.00	0.82
Sri Lanka	18	0	0.00	0	0.00	0.00	0.00
Sweden	280	3	1.07	0	1.07	4.00	1.02
Switzerland	243	6	2.47	0	2.47	4.00	0.69
Taiwan	237	2	0.84	6	3.38	10.00	12.74
Thailand	279	23	8.24	19	15.05	34.00	41.62
Turkey	84	1	1.19	0	1.19	0.00	0.14
UK	2,149	154	7.17	0	7.17	46.00	39.02
US	7,124	6	0.08	8	0.20	6.00	4.94
Venezuela	18	0	0.00	0	0.00	0.00	0.00
Zimbabwe	8	0	0.00	0	0.00	0.00	0.00
All countries	20,202	400	1.98	141	2.68	6.92	7.72

Notes: No. of firms connected with a minister or MP is the number of firms with a shareholder controlling at least 10 per cent of the votes or a top officer who is a member of parliament or government, excluding close relationships. % of firms connected with a minister or MP is the number of firms connected with a minister or MP as a proportion of the total number of firms in a given country. No. of firms connected through close relationships is the number of firms with a shareholder controlling at least 10 per cent of the votes or a top officer who is a member of parliament or government, plus all identified cases of close relationships. % of firms connected with a minister or MP, or a close relationship is the number of all connected firms as proportion of the total number of firms in a particular country. % of top 50 firms connected with a minister or MP, or a close relationship is the number of connected firms as proportion of the largest 50 firms (based on end of 1997 market capitalization) in a particular country. For countries with fewer than 50 firms in the sample, this fraction is computed based on the available companies.

Source: Faccio, M. (2006), 'Politically Connected Firms', *American Economic Review* 96, table 2.

There are two views on this. The first view, as held by Andrei Shleifer and Robert Vishny, can be described as the 'grabbing hand' of government.[23] According to this view, politicians sitting on boards of directors pursue their own objectives, in particular winning votes from their electorate. One way of winning votes is to force the firms on whose boards they sit to employ more people than would be efficient, thereby reducing shareholder

---

[23]Shleifer, A. and Vishny, R. (1994), 'Politicians and Firms', *Quarterly Journal of Economics* 109, 995–1025. Shleifer, A. and Vishny, R. (1998), *The Grabbing Hand: Government Pathologies and their Cures*, Cambridge, MA: Harvard University Press.

value. Hence, according to this view politicians seek rents and the latter come at the expense of the firms' shareholders. A slightly different spin on this view is that even if there are benefits from political connections, politicians will appropriate all of these via bribes and other favours they obtain from the firms concerned. Mara Faccio found evidence in support of this argument: political connections are more prevalent in countries that are considered to be highly corrupt and there is no significant market reaction to the appointment of politicians to boards of directors.[24] The second view is about the 'helping hand' of government. Government and political connections bring about favours and privileges such as government subsidies and government procurement orders. Raymond Fisman studied the value of political connections for Indonesian firms during the Suharto regime.[25] President Suharto, the second president of Indonesia, was in power from 1967 until 1998. At the height of its power, the Suharto family allegedly controlled a total of 417 quoted and unquoted companies via several business groups headed by the children and other relatives, as well as business partners of President Suharto; many of whom were also government officials.[26] Fisman's estimate suggests that firms which had the closest connection to Suharto would have lost about 23 per cent more in stock value than firms with no connection at the announcement of the death of President Suharto. While this may be a rough estimate its magnitude nevertheless suggests that political connections can be very valuable. Simon Johnson and Todd Mitton found similar evidence about the value of political connections for the case of Malaysian firms.[27] They reported that at the start of the Asian crisis, in August 1998, nine per cent of the drop in the market value of firms with political connections due to the Asian financial crisis can be attributed to the decrease in the expected amount of government subsidies for these firms. A month later when capital controls were introduced, the stock market bounced back: 32 per cent of the estimated $5 billion gain in market value for these firms can be attributed to the introduction of these capital controls.

Finally, Mara Faccio and David Parsley studied the stock price reaction to the sudden death of politicians for firms headquartered in the hometowns of these politicians.[28] Their study covered 35 developed and less developed economies. The authors claimed that their use of geographic ties rather than board ties enabled them to measure the value of more informal ties of companies with politicians. They found great variation in the market reaction across the 35 countries. Political ties are worth more than 10 per cent of a firm's market value in Pakistan and Zimbabwe compared to only one per cent in France, two per cent in the UK and about four per cent in the USA (see Table 9.3). Surprisingly, in almost a third of the countries studied, political ties seem to destroy rather than create firm value. For example, in Argentina and in Russia firm value increases on average by almost 12 per cent and 6.35 per cent, respectively, after the sudden death of a locally based politician. They also explored the factors that explain the value of political connections. They found that political connections are more valuable for family controlled firms, firms with high growth, small firms, firms operating in the industry directly under the influence of the politician and firms from more corrupt countries.

To summarize, there are studies that suggest that the overall effect of politicians sitting on corporate boards is zero, given that politicians manage to extract the value they create. However, there are also studies that suggest political connections are highly valuable and that they cause substantial increases in firm value. What can we conclude as to the validity of the two views – the 'grabbing hand' and the 'helping hand' of government? Returning to Mara Faccio's study, her results also suggested that when a business person becomes a politician there

[24]Faccio, M. (2006), 'Politically Connected Firms', *American Economic Review* 96, 369–86.

[25]Fisman, R. (2001), 'Estimating the Value of Political Connections', *American Economic Review* 91, 1095–102.

[26]Claessen, S., Djankov, S. and Lang, L.H.P. (2000), 'The Separation of Ownership and Control in East Asian Corporations', *Journal of Financial Economics* 58, 81–112.

[27]Johnson, S. and Mitton, T. (2003), 'Cronyism and Capital Controls: Evidence from Malaysia', *Journal of Financial Economics* 67, 351–82.

[28]Faccio, M. and Parsley, D.C. (2009), 'Sudden Deaths: Taking Stock of Geographic Ties', *Journal of Financial and Quantitative Analysis* 44, 683–718.

Table 9.3 The effect of sudden deaths of politicians on firm value

Country	Sudden deaths	Firms	Average change in firm value	Median change in firm value
Argentina	1	11	11.78%	4.41%
Australia	3	456	−1.81%	−0.84%
Austria	1	33	0.50%	−0.23%
Belgium	1	51	0.97%	−0.20%
Brazil	1	79	−1.38%	3.31%
Canada	5	126	1.97%	1.11%
Colombia	1	8	−1.29%	0.01%
Egypt	1	14	3.05%	1.82%
France	2	265	−1.08%	−0.57%
Ghana	1	1	−0.23%	−0.23%
Greece	1	48	−3.82%	−7.50%
Hungary	1	9	−5.60%	−9.31%
India	6	76	−1.50%	−1.23%
Israel	1	26	−3.14%	−2.48%
Italy	5	15	1.55%	1.83%
Japan	2	3,192	−1.46%	−1.20%
Luxembourg	1	27	2.25%	2.19%
Malaysia	2	6	3.90%	2.19%
Mexico	1	32	−0.77%	0.03%
Netherlands	1	8	0.69%	1.64%
Norway	2	77	−0.05%	−1.12%
Pakistan	1	1	−10.04%	−10.04%
Philippines	1	70	−3.01%	−5.66%
Poland	1	11	−2.07%	−2.20%
Portugal	1	41	3.07%	3.35%
Russia	11	107	6.31%	0.55%
Singapore	1	5	−1.67%	0.05%
South Africa	3	34	1.95%	−1.47%
Spain	2	2	−1.55%	−1.55%
Sri Lanka	8	156	−0.43%	−0.43%
Sweden	2	163	2.46%	2.16%
Switzerland	1	1	−1.10%	−1.10%
UK	10	1,812	−2.05%	−1.52%
USA	37	1,207	−4.19%	−1.02%
Zimbabwe	3	21	−10.24%	−6.93%
Total	122	8,191	−1.68%	−0.97%

Notes: The change in firm value is measured as the difference between the stock return for the firm and the return on the Datastream stock market index of the firm's home country over the period starting with the day before the sudden death and ending ten trading days after the sudden death.

Source: Faccio, M. and Parsley, D.C. (2009), 'Sudden Deaths: Taking Stock of Geographic Ties', *Journal of Financial and Quantitative Analysis* 44, table 1.

is a significant stock price increase, suggesting that rent seeking is less of a problem in such a case. Finally, Mara Faccio's paper with David Parsley implied that firm characteristics as well as the country's level of corruption also have an impact on the value of political ties.

9.5 The design of corporate governance in former SOEs

Based on a review of the corporate governance literature and the literature on privatization, Ravi Dharwadkar, Gerard George and Pamela Brandes made a series of recommendations about how to design the corporate governance of privatized SOEs in emerging markets.[29] They made two sets of recommendations. The first set concerns the optimal ownership and control of the former SOEs. The second one concerns the types of management, organizational form and managerial contracts as well as the capital structure.

The first set consists of the following three recommendations:

1 Given that managers and other employees with experience of competitive markets are scarce in emerging economies, managerial and employee ownership is not an effective device for the mitigation of the principal-agent problem. In addition, managerial and employee ownership is unlikely to foster the risk-taking behaviour that is needed to restructure the former SOEs. Indeed, managers and employees tend to be risk-averse and this tendency is further amplified by stock ownership.

2 Since investor rights in emerging markets are not well protected, control by large shareholders (other than the management) – rather than dispersed ownership and control – will be more efficient as it prevents the shareholders from being expropriated by the management.

3 Out of local individuals or families, local institutional investors and foreign investors, it is foreign investors that are the preferred type of large shareholder. While control by local individuals or families reduces the principal-agent problem and improves managerial risk-taking incentives, it also increases the danger of minority-shareholder expropriation. This danger may be amplified by the appointment of family members to top management posts and the use of ownership pyramids (see also Section 3.7 of Chapter 3). Local institutional investors are also not the most appropriate type of large shareholder given weaknesses in their own corporate governance and the local financial system. These weaknesses are likely to increase the risk of minority-shareholder expropriation. Foreign investors are likely to both mitigate the principal-agent problem and reduce the risk of minority-shareholder expropriation for at least two reasons. First, foreign investors are more likely to be independent of the local government and therefore more likely to get scrutinized by the latter than local investors that may have close ties with the local government. Second, foreign investors are likely to benefit from economies of scale in terms of their monitoring due to their experience and their greater size.

The second set consists of the following four recommendations:

1 There needs to be a change in management, as the incumbent management team is likely to underperform compared to firms with a new management for at least two reasons. First, the incumbent managers are unlikely to restructure the firm in ways that improve its performance given their lack of experience and knowledge. Second, the government is likely to carry on exercising a strong influence over the privatized firm if the incumbent management stays in place and/or the government carries on appointing the

[29]Dharwadkar, R., George, G. and Brandes, P. (2000), 'Privatization in Emerging Economies: An Agency Theory Perspective', *Academy of Management Review* 25, 650–69.

management team after the privatization, reducing the likelihood of performance-improving restructuring and increasing the likelihood of shareholder expropriation.

2 Multi-divisional structures, so-called M-form structures,[30] are the optimal organizational structure for the former SOEs as they increase the efficiency of the monitoring of the management, thereby reducing the principal-agent problem and substituting for other weak corporate governance mechanisms. M-forms also create internal capital markets which may substitute for underdeveloped external capital markets and the disciplining role exerted by the latter.

3 As to the design of managerial contracts, two aspects of work can be monitored. These are work outcomes and the behaviours that create them. As outcomes are highly uncertain due to the weak political, economic and social institutions prevailing in emerging markets and a lack of benchmarks to which to compare outcomes, behaviour-based contracts will be more efficient and easier to enforce than outcome-based contracts.

4 While high levels of debt may reduce Jensen's free cash flow problem in developed economies (see e.g. Section 8.10 of Chapter 8), Dharwadkar et al. argued that the disciplinary role of debt is unlikely to be effective in emerging markets where law enforcement, including that of bankruptcy law, tends to be weak. They cited the example of South Korea where firms typically carry on being run by the incumbent management after the bankruptcy proceedings and are barely affected in other ways too. Hence, more debt increases the agency problem of debt rather than reducing the free cash flow problem. The former SOEs' capital structure should therefore include as little debt as feasible.

9.6 Conclusions

Developing economies typically have weak laws as well as underdeveloped capital markets. While a substantial body of the corporate governance literature asserts that strong investor rights are a necessary condition for large equity markets to develop in a country and that, in turn, such markets are a necessary and sufficient condition to guarantee strong economic growth, there are some dissenting voices that claim this is not the case. One argument is that some countries, such as China, have experienced strong economic growth without strong laws and enforcement. Further, the separation of ownership and control in UK firms predates the strong protection that investors enjoy nowadays. Hence, there is evidence that formal and informal mechanisms as well as market and non-market mechanisms can overcome weak institutions and the absence of well-regulated capital markets. Another argument is that stock markets may cause more harm via increased economic volatility and concentrating wealth and income with a small fraction of the population.

Are large stock markets a necessary and sufficient condition for economic development?

Apart from weak law, emerging economies are also frequently plagued by so-called crony capitalism. One form of crony capitalism is inherited wealth, which stifles entrepreneurship as well as preventing trade and financial liberalization via its grip on the political classes. The empirical evidence suggests that countries where inherited wealth is relatively important and entrepreneur wealth is

Inherited wealth and economic growth

[30]See Williamson, O.E. (1975), *Markets and Hierarchies*, New York: Free Press.

relatively unimportant, suffer from poor economic growth due to the entrenchment of old money combined with bad management.

Another form of crony capitalism is the tight links between corporations and
politicians sitting on boards of directors. Whereas overall the empirical evidence
suggests that political connections are valuable, there is nevertheless evidence out
there that suggests politicians extract bribes and other favours from their firms at
the expense of the other stakeholders. The value of political connections has also
been shown to depend on firm characteristics. In particular, family controlled
firms, high-growth firms, small firms, firms operating in the industry under the
influence of politicians and those from highly corrupt countries benefit the most
from political ties.

Political connections and firm
value

Finally, the design of the corporate governance of newly privatized SOEs is an
important issue. First, it makes sense for the former SOEs to be controlled by a
large foreign shareholder with experience of competitive markets and independence from the local government. The latter will ensure that the local government will monitor the controlling shareholder to avoid the expropriation of the
minority shareholders. Second, the incumbent management should be replaced
by new management to ensure competence as well as independence from the
government, the firm should be organized along several divisions to improve the
monitoring of the management, managerial contracts should focus on behaviour
rather than outcome, and high levels of debt should be avoided. Last but not least,
it is also important for emerging countries to learn from the mistakes made by
developed countries. While the UK was the first country in Europe to privatize
its railways, it also now has the most expensive passenger rail system in the world,
costing taxpayers substantially more money in subsidies than during national
ownership.[31]

The design of corporate governance in former SOEs

9.7 Discussion questions

1   Are stock markets and strong investor rights
necessary and sufficient to ensure economic
development?

2   What are the political, institutional and economic
implications if wealth within a country is

mostly inherited rather than created by
entrepreneurs?

3   Discuss the theory and evidence on the value of
firms' political connections.

Reading list

Key reading

Allen, F. (2005), 'Corporate Governance in Emerging
Economies', *Oxford Review of Economic Policy* 21,
164–77.

Allen, F. (2012), 'Trends in Financial Innovation and their
Welfare Impact: An Overview', *European Financial
Management* 18, 493–514.

---

[31]Department for Transport and the Office of Rail Regulation (2011), *Realising the Potential of GB Rail: Final Independent Report of the
Value for Money Study*, London: Department for Transport and the Office of Rail Regulation.

Boubakri, N., Cosset, J.-C. and Saffar, W. (2008), 'Political Connections in Newly Privatized Firms', *Journal of Corporate Finance* 14, 654–73.

Dharwadkar, R., George, G. and Brandes, P. (2000), 'Privatization in Emerging Economies: An Agency Theory Perspective', *Academy of Management Review* 25, 650–69.

Faccio, M. (2006), 'Politically Connected Firms', *American Economic Review* 96, 369–86.

Faccio, M. and Parsley, D.C. (2009), 'Sudden Deaths: Taking Stock of Geographic Ties', *Journal of Financial and Quantitative Analysis* 44, 683–718.

Fisman, R. (2001), 'Estimating the Value of Political Connections', *American Economic Review* 91, 1095–102.

Franks, J., Mayer, C. and Rossi, S. (2009), 'Ownership: Evolution and Regulation', *Review of Financial Studies* 22, 4009–56.

Morck, R., Stangeland, D. and Yeung, B. (2000), 'Inherited Wealth, Corporate Control and Economic Growth: The Canadian Disease?', in R. Morck (ed.), *Concentrated Corporate Ownership*, National Bureau of Economic Research and University of Chicago Press, 319–69.

Mueller, D.C. (2006), 'The Anglo-Saxon Approach to Corporate Governance and its Applicability to Emerging Markets', *Corporate Governance: An International Review* 14, 207–19.

Shleifer, A. and Vishny, R. (1994), 'Politicians and Firms', *Quarterly Journal of Economics* 109, 995–1025.

Singh, A., Glen, J., Zammit, A., De-Hoyos, R., Singh, A. and Weisse, B. (2005), 'Shareholder Value Maximisation, Stock Market and New Technology: Should the US Corporate Model be the Universal Standard?', *International Review of Applied Economics* 19, 419–37.

Further reading

Bottazzi, L. and Da Rin, M. (2002), 'Venture Capital in Europe and the Financing of Innovative Companies', *Economic Policy* 17, 229–69.

Boubakri, N., Cosset, J.-C. and Guedhami, O. (2005), 'Liberalization, Corporate Governance and the Performance and Privatized Firms in Developing Countries', *Journal of Corporate Finance* 11, 767–90.

D'Souza, J., Megginson, W. and Nash, R. (2005), 'Effect of Institutional and Firm-specific Characteristics on Post-Privatization Performance: Evidence from Developed Countries', *Journal of Corporate Finance* 11, 747–66.

Khanna, T. and Palepu, K. (2000), 'Is Group Affiliation Profitable in Emerging Markets? An Analysis of

Diversified Indian Business Groups', *Journal of Finance* 55, 867–91.

Mayer, C., Schoors, K. and Yafeh, Y. (2005), 'Sources of Funds and Investment Activities of Venture Capital Funds: Evidence from Germany, Israel, Japan and the United Kingdom', *Journal of Corporate Finance*, 11, 586–608.

O'Sullivan, M. (2000), *Contests for Corporate Control*, Oxford, UK: Oxford University Press.

Shiller, R.J. (2005), *Irrational Exuberance*, Princeton, NJ: Princeton University Press, 2nd edition.

Shleifer, A. and Vishny, R. (1998), *The Grabbing Hand: Government Pathologies and their Cures*, Cambridge, MA: Harvard University Press.

Additional resources

The OECD developed its 'OECD Guidelines on Corporate Governance of State-Owned Enterprises' in 2005. The Guidelines were revised in 2015 and can be found at:

www.oecd.org/corporate/guidelines-corporate-governance-SOEs.htm.

10 Contractual corporate governance

Chapter Aims

Firms that are highly dependent on equity financing and are based in economies with underdeveloped capital markets may face financial constraints, i.e. a high cost of capital. This chapter discusses the ways that enable firms to overcome the absence of highly liquid local capital markets and to tap into more developed foreign capital markets. These ways include foreign cross-listings, (re)incorporations and cross-border mergers. The chapter also discusses whether competition among regulatory systems is good or bad for investors.

Learning Outcomes

After reading this chapter, you should be able to:

1 Demonstrate how different contractual devices may enable firms from countries with weak corporate governance to improve the level of shareholder protection they offer

2 Assess how firms can reduce their cost of capital by tapping into more developed foreign capital markets

3 Critically review the arguments on both sides of the debate on whether regulatory competition causes a race to the top or a race to the bottom

10.1 Introduction

Chapter 4 on the taxonomies of corporate governance systems and Chapter 5 on corporate governance, types of financial systems and economic growth suggest:

- There is a link between a country's political and legal setting and the size and development of its capital market.
- Specific industries are highly dependent on equity and may only thrive in the presence of a highly developed capital market whereas others are less reliant on equity.

Concerning the link between the institutional setting and the size and development of the capital market, a firm's access to capital may be determined by:

- the quality of law, in particular investor protection, as well as the enforcement of law in its home country.
- the way social peace is maintained, including the political orientation of the country's government.
- the type of electoral system (majoritarian or proportional voting systems).

So how can firms in countries with underdeveloped stock markets improve their access to capital? More generally, how can a firm based in a country with weak corporate governance standards exceed those standards credibly and attract new investors? A firm can do so by using specific types of contractual devices or arrangements such as cross-border mergers and acquisitions, (re)incorporations and cross-listings. Each of these devices enables the firm to choose its preferred level of investor protection and regulation. This is what contractual corporate governance is about. In other words, these devices provide companies with the choice to deviate from their national corporate governance standards by (partially) opting into another system. Within this context, Henry Hansmann and Reinier Kraakman proposed a Darwinian theory of corporate law and regulation.[1] They argued that firms that do not adopt a shareholder-oriented approach will be punished via a higher cost of capital and will eventually fail given their competitive disadvantage.

What all three of the above-mentioned devices have in common is that they consist of a firm subjecting itself voluntarily to the law and regulation of *another* country. So are there any *domestic* alternatives for improving corporate governance? There are two potential such alternatives. However, neither is satisfactory and likely to achieve the intended outcome of convincing outside investors that the firm is committed to better corporate governance.

These two alternatives are as follows. First, it may be simpler and quicker for the firm to improve its corporate governance by adding provisions to its articles of association that bring about positive changes.[2] Such provisions may, e.g. prohibit the use of anti-takeover devices which may be perfectly permissible according to national law. This would then signal to outside shareholders that the firm's management commits itself not to expropriate the shareholders by entrenching itself and by opposing value-creating takeover bids. Similarly, a firm with a large, controlling shareholder may improve its corporate governance by, e.g. adding a provision to its articles of association requiring a certain number of non-executive directors to sit on the firm's board who are independent of the controlling shareholder. However, outside investors may give little credence to these changes. Indeed, while the management or the large shareholder in the above examples may have good intentions, investors may not believe that these changes to the firm's statutes are credible given the weak local law and the lack of law and contract enforcement. In other words, the firm may very well offer its shareholders a valuable contractual clause, but the shareholders may have every reason to believe that it is likely that the firm will break the clause sometime in the future. Hence, the stock market may refuse to believe that these changes are credible signals. So what makes a signal credible? In order to be credible, a signal must be costly. If the firm breaks its commitment to provide better corporate governance, there needs to be a penalty and the penalty needs to exceed the benefits generated from breaking the contractual commitment. A credible way for the firm to commit itself to better corporate governance is to subject itself to the better regulation and enforcement of another country. If the firm breaks the contract, there will be legal consequences and costs. The mere threat of the legal consequences and costs would then prevent the firm from breaking the contract, a threat that may not exist in the firm's home country.

The second alternative consists of the firm petitioning its local political representative or even better the government directly to change the law and improve investor protection. However, this is easier said than done. First, legal reforms and especially radical ones take time. Second, path dependence and a country's belonging to a broad legal family (see Chapter 4) may significantly reduce the magnitude and effectiveness of any legal reform. Hence, neither of the two domestic alternatives may improve the firm's corporate governance. We shall now review each of the above three contractual corporate governance devices.

---

[1]Hansmann, H. and Kraakman, R. (2001), 'The End of History for Corporate Law', *Georgetown Law Journal* 89, 439–68.
[2]Graeme Acheson, Gareth Campbell and John D. Turner reported that during Victorian times investor protection provided by company law was virtually non-existent. They found that UK firms then provided as much investor protection via their articles of association as is provided by modern company law. Acheson, G.G., Campbell, G. and Turner, J.D. (2016), 'Common Law and the Origin of Shareholder Protection', Queen's University Centre for Economic History Working Paper Series, available at www.quceh.org.uk/uploads/1/0/5/5/10558478/wp16 -04.pdf.

10.2 Cross-border mergers and acquisitions

Firms may improve their corporate governance and access to capital via cross-border mergers and acquisitions. The questions that then arise are as follows:

- Does the target benefit from the stronger corporate governance of the bidder or does the bidder benefit from the stronger corporate governance of the target?
- Do bidders with weak corporate governance harm targets with better corporate governance?

In order to answer these questions, one needs a conceptual framework distinguishing between the various possible effects of cross-border mergers and acquisitions on corporate governance. Marina Martynova and Luc Renneboog distinguished between three possible effects of cross-border mergers and acquisitions.[3] The first two assume that the target adopts the corporate governance of the bidder rather than the converse. The first of these two effects is the so-called positive spillover effect. There is a positive spillover effect if a bidder with better corporate governance improves the corporate governance of the target. The second one is the negative spillover effect. There is a negative spillover effect if a bidder with weaker corporate governance reduces that of the target. In contrast to the two previous effects, the third effect assumes that the bidder adopts the corporate governance of the target. This is the so-called bootstrapping effect[4] which consists of a bidder with weaker corporate governance adopting the stronger corporate governance of the target company. Bootstrapping is voluntary in the case of a full acquisition, but in the case of a partial acquisition the bidder has to honour the corporate governance regulation that the target is subject to. This is the so-called extraterritoriality principle. This is a principle embedded in international law which enables a host country to subject a foreign-owned sub-sidiary to its own law and regulation given that the subsidiary is domiciled within its jurisdiction. For example, the partially owned French subsidiary of a British company will still be subject to French corporate law and, if it is listed on the French stock market, it will also be subject to French stock-market regulation. The rationale behind the extraterritoriality principle is to protect the local minority shareholders from being expropriated by a large, foreign shareholder.

Stefano Rossi and Paolo Volpin found that compared to bidders, targets tend to be from countries with weaker shareholder protection.[5] They found evidence of a positive spillover effect. Further, they found that the positive effect from a cross-border takeover by a bidder with better corporate governance benefits the target's entire industry. Indeed, bidders with stronger corporate governance have a positive effect on takeover volume and the size of bid premiums. Arturo Bris, Neil Brisley and Christos Cabolis focused on the industry-wide effects of cross-border mergers and acquisitions.[6] They found that the value of an entire industry increases as a result of one of its firms being taken over by a bidder with better corporate governance. Alongside the study by Rossi and Volpin, this paper provided further evidence of an industry-wide positive spillover effect.

Laura Starks and Kelsey Wei assumed that the target always ends up adopting the corporate governance of the bidder.[7] They argued that for acquisitions where the means of payment is the bidder's equity shares, the bid

[3]Martynova, M. and Renneboog, L. (2008), 'Spillover of Corporate Governance Standards in Cross-Border Mergers and Acquisitions', *Journal of Corporate Finance* 14, 200–23.

[4]Boots are strapped by starting at the bottom of the boots and then working oneself gradually up to the top of the boots. As an analogy to the way laces are tied on boots, bidders with weak corporate governance may gradually improve their corporate governance by taking over targets with increasingly better corporate governance.

[5]Rossi, S. and Volpin, P. (2004), 'Cross-Country Determinants of Mergers and Acquisitions', *Journal of Financial Economics* 74, 277–304.

[6]Bris, A., Brisley, N., and Cabolis, C. (2008), 'Adopting Better Corporate Governance: Evidence from Cross-Border Mergers', *Journal of Corporate Finance* 14, 224–40.

[7]Starks, L. and Wei, K. (2005), 'Cross-Border Mergers and Differences in Corporate Governance', Working paper, University of Texas, Austin.

premium is higher for bidders with lower corporate governance as the target shareholders are concerned about the increased risk from the reduction in corporate governance. They found evidence for their hypothesis as the shareholders of US target companies taken over by bidders from countries with weaker corporate governance earn higher announcement returns.

Similar to Rossi and Volpin, Marina Martynova and Luc Renneboog also found that bidders tend to have better corporate governance.[8] They found evidence of a positive spillover effect, but no evidence of a negative spillover effect. They reported that for bidders with weaker corporate governance, the returns to both the bidder and target shareholders are higher. This suggests that there is a bootstrapping effect whereby bidders benefit from adopting the better corporate governance of the target. The bootstrapping effect is mainly observed for partial acquisitions. This is in line with what one expects given that the extraterritoriality principle subjects bidders conducting partial acquisitions to the law and regulation of the target's home country.

To conclude, the empirical evidence on the corporate governance effects of cross-border mergers and acquisitions suggests the following. First, the targets in cross-border acquisitions tend to be from countries with weak corporate governance. Second, targets with better shareholder protection require a higher premium when they are taken over by bidders with weaker governance. Third, there is evidence of a positive spillover effect, including evidence suggesting an industry-wide positive spillover effect. Fourth, there is also evidence of a bootstrapping effect whereby bidders with weaker corporate governance adopt the corporate governance of their targets. However, in line with the extraterritoriality principle, this effect is mainly found for partial acquisitions. Finally, while targets tend to benefit from being taken over by a bidder with better governance, there is some evidence that bidders lose value when taking over weaker targets.

10.3 (Re)incorporations

Given the focus of this chapter and the aim of contractual corporate governance, this section focuses on incorporations and reincorporations in *foreign* countries or *other* federal states for the case of US companies. A reincorporation consists of a firm, which is already incorporated in one country (or federal state), moving its legal seat to another country (or federal state). The main motives behind reincorporations are:

- putting in place takeover defences.
- reducing directors' liability.
- the move to a jurisdiction with more flexible corporate law.
- savings on tax or franchise fees.
- the reconciliation of the legal and operating domicile of the firm.
- the facilitation of cross-border mergers and acquisitions.

Among these six motives, the adoption of takeover defences and reducing directors' liability are the most popular ones driving reincorporation proposals.

There are two principles in law applying to incorporations and reincorporations. These are the real seat principle and the incorporation principle. According to the real seat principle, the law applying to the firm is that of the geographic location of its headquarters or main activities. Hence, according to this principle firms are subject to the law of their *real* seat. In contrast, according to the incorporation principle the law that applies to a firm is that of its country of incorporation, independent of whether the latter is its real seat or not. Hence,

---

[8]Op. cit. footnote 3.

whereas the former principle makes it onerous and expensive for a firm to move to another country, the latter makes it fairly easy.

Most Continental European countries have adopted the real seat principle whereas Ireland, the UK and the USA have adopted the incorporation principle. Until recently, only US firms could change relatively easily the state of their incorporation, whereas corporate mobility was significantly restricted in Europe. However, recent rulings by the European Court of Justice (ECJ) have increased corporate mobility for incorporations, but not as yet for reincorporations.[9]

The question that arises is whether managers choose locations for their (re)incorporations that pursue shareholder interests rather than their own interests, or whether the converse is the case. There are two schools of thought on this. The first school argues that competition between jurisdictions leads to better-quality corporate law given that firms will choose jurisdictions that provide legal services at the lowest cost and that suit their needs the best. This is the cost-avoidance hypothesis as advanced by Ralph Winter[10] and Roberta Romano.[11] This school argues that regulatory competition results in a race to the top, with firms moving to legal regimes with better law to reduce their costs of doing business, which is in the interests of the shareholders. The second school argues that in order to maximize the revenues from incorporations, jurisdictions will compete in ways to provide laws that cater for managerial rather than shareholder interests. This is the shareholder-exploitation hypothesis as proposed by William Cary.[12] This school predicts that there will be a race to the bottom, which will harm economic efficiency. A study by Stephen Ferris, Robert Lawless and Gregory Noronha provided evidence which supports the shareholder-exploitation hypothesis.[13] This study found that US managers choose the federal state to incorporate their firm according to the discretion that that state's law provides them with. Again, this suggests that regulatory competition is bad as it results in a race to the bottom and a gradual weakening of law protecting investor interests.

So, does this mean that regulatory competition is always bad and should be avoided at all costs? The answer is not necessarily affirmative as in turn Cary's argument about the race to the bottom has been challenged. Some argue that jurisdiction shopping is indispensable to guarantee competition between jurisdictions and is therefore not necessarily against shareholder interests. There is also evidence that the US Federal State of Delaware which attracts most US (re)incorporations commands higher stock prices.[14] However, others report that the higher share prices for Delaware-incorporated firms only apply to the pre-1997 period[15] and that the main reason why managers decide to move their firms to Delaware is to set up anti-takeover devices.[16] As a large body of empirical studies suggests that there is a negative stock-market reaction to the adoption of takeover defences, this provides evidence supporting the shareholder-exploitation hypothesis.

[9]Gelter, M. (2017), 'EU Law Stories: Centros, the Freedom of Establishment for Companies, and the Court's Accidental Vision for Corporate Law', in F. Nicola and B. Davies (eds), *EU Law Stories. Comparative and Contextual Histories of European Jurisprudence*, Cambridge, UK: Cambridge University Press.

[10]Winter, R.K. (1977), 'State Law, Shareholder Protection, and the Theory of the Corporation', *Journal of Legal Studies* 6, 251–92.

[11]Romano, R. (1985), 'Law as a Product: Some Pieces of the Incorporation Puzzle', *Journal of Law, Economics, and Organization* 1, 225–83.

[12]Cary, W.L. (1974), 'Federalism and Corporate Law: Reflections upon Delaware', *Yale Law Journal* 83, 663–705.

[13]Ferris, S.P., Lawless, R.M. and Noronha, G. (2006), 'The Influence of State Legal Environments on Firm Incorporation Decisions and Values', *Journal of Law, Economics and Policy*, 2, 1–28.

[14]See Dodd, P. and Leftwich, R. (1980), 'The Market for Corporate Charters: "Unhealthy Competition" versus Federal Regulation', *Journal of Business* 53, 259–83; Romano, R. (1985), 'Law as a Product: Some Pieces of the Incorporation Puzzle', *Journal of Law, Economics, and Organization* 1, 225–83; Netter, J. and Poulsen, A. (1989), 'State Corporation Laws and Shareholders: The Recent Experience', *Financial Management* 18, 29–40.

[15]See e.g. Bebchuk, L. and Cohen, A. (2003), 'Firm's Decisions Where to Incorporate', *Journal of Law and Economics* 46, 383–425.

[16]Heron, R.A. and Lewellen, W.G. (1998), 'An Empirical Analysis of the Reincorporations Decision', *Journal of Financial and Quantitative Analysis* 33, 549–68.

Hence all in all, it is as yet unclear whether regulatory competition is good or bad. To some extent, the existing empirical evidence seems to suggest that there is some validity to Hansmann and Kraakman's Darwinian theory of corporate law and regulation. While the outcome of this regulatory competition is as yet uncertain and may not necessarily lead to the universal adoption of the shareholder-oriented approach, the existing evidence seems to suggest that corporations may at times go down dead-ends similar to what has happened with evolution of life on Earth. Indeed, while the dinosaurs dominated Earth for more than 165 million years, they eventually died out.

Nevertheless, regulators are still happy to experiment. For example, in recent years a series of rulings by the ECJ has reaffirmed the principle of freedom of establishment within the EU. Some scholars have predicted lots of incorporations of foreign companies in the UK. Recent trends suggest that this prediction has become a reality. Indeed during 2002–5, the number of new private limited companies from other EU member states established in the UK was already over 55,000. Mathias Siems and colleagues estimated that this number increased to about 227,000 in 2016.[17] Still, Brexit may put a stop to this trend or even reverse it.

10.4 Cross-listings

A cross-listing consists of a firm listing on a foreign stock exchange at the time of its domestic IPO or thereafter. According to John Coffee's bonding hypothesis, firms from weaker corporate governance regimes cross-list on the US market in order to commit themselves not to expropriate their minority shareholders.[18] If the bonding hypothesis holds, cross-listed firms trade at a premium. Virtually all of the finance literature focuses on firms cross-listing in the USA. However, the bonding hypothesis can also be extended to other stock markets with strong regulation and high corporate governance standards.

Returning to the USA, firms seeking a US cross-listing can do so in two different ways. First, they can cross-list via the issue of American Depository Receipts (ADRs). Except for Canadian and Israeli firms which can list their equity shares directly on a US stock exchange, firms from other countries have to cross-list indirectly by depositing some of their shares with an American bank, the depository bank, which will then issue the ADRs which will trade on a US stock exchange. Second, they can cross-list via Global Registered Shares. However, this option is normally only used by very large firms as it involves a simultaneous cross-listing on several foreign stock markets.

Empirical evidence by William Reese and Michael Weisbach showed that firms from French civil law countries were more likely to be cross-listed in the USA (10.5 per cent of French firms have a US cross-listing) than firms from common-law countries (6.7 per cent of firms).[19] This provided support for the bonding hypothesis: firms from weaker legal systems are more likely to cross-list in order to opt into a better legal system. They also found that cross-listed firms from civil law countries are more likely to place subsequent equity issues *outside* the USA. This provided further support for the bonding hypothesis: firms by cross-listing bond themselves

[17]Siems, M., Schuster, E., Mucciarelli, F. and Gerner-Beuerle, C. (2016), 'Why Do Businesses Incorporate in other EU Member States? An Empirical Analysis of the Role of Conflict of Laws Rules', working paper, available at www.kcl.ac.uk/law/newsevents/eventrecords/Siems -Why-Do-Businesses-Incorporate-in-other-EU-Member-States-002.pdf.
[18]Coffee, J.C. Jr. (1999), 'The Future as History: The Prospects for Global Convergence in Corporate Governance and its Implications', Columbia Law School Center for Law and Economic Studies Working Paper No. 144. Coffee, J. (2002), 'Racing Towards the Top? The Impact of Cross-listings and Stock Market Competition on International Corporate Governance', *Columbia Law Review* 102, 1757–831.
[19]Reese, W.A. Jr. and Weisbach, M.S. (2002), 'Protection of Minority Shareholder Interests, Cross-Listings in the United States, and Subsequent Equity Offerings', *Journal of Financial Economics* 66, 65–104.

not to expropriate their shareholders and, in turn, improve their access to capital within their national capital market.

Craig Doidge examined whether the cross-listing has an impact on the voting premium.[20] The voting premium is defined as the ratio of the price of the voting right to the price of the cash flow right. As discussed in Section 3.8 of Chapter 3, the voting premium is a measure for private benefits of control. The higher the latter, the higher is the expected premium on the voting shares. In line with the bonding hypothesis, Doidge found that firms with a US cross-listing have lower voting premiums than those without. In other words, firms from countries with weak investor rights may choose to cross-list in the USA to commit themselves to curtail the private benefits of control of the management or the large shareholder.

Craig Doidge, in another study with Andrew Karolyi and René Stulz, examined the effect of a US cross-listing on firm value.[21] They expected a US cross-listing to result in a reduction in the firm's cost of capital and hence an increase in its value for the following four reasons:

- The cross-listing increases the shareholder base and risk is therefore shared among more shareholders.
- The cross-listing increases the liquidity of the firm's shares.
- The higher disclosure standards reduce the information asymmetry between insiders and outsiders.
- The cross-listing leads to higher scrutiny and monitoring by the financial press.

They argued that the large shareholder faces a trade-off when cross-listing the firm. The trade-off is between the reduction in the cost of capital, which increases the ability to finance growth opportunities, leading to higher future cash flows, and the reduction in the private benefits of control due to improved minority-shareholder protection. Hence, only firms with significant growth opportunities will cross-list as for these firms the benefits from cross-listing accruing to the large shareholder outweigh the costs from the reduction in the latter's private benefits of control. Doidge et al. measured growth opportunities by the Tobin's q, i.e. the ratio of market value of equity over book value of equity. In line with their hypothesis, they found that the Tobin's q of cross-listed firms is higher – by 16.5 per cent – than for firms from the same country that are not cross-listed.

Finally, Wissam Abdallah and Marc Goergen examined the decision about the choice of the host market for a sample of 175 firms cross-listing on 19 different foreign stock exchanges.[22] They argued that there are at least three reasons why a firm's ownership and control may influence this decision. First, and similar to Doidge et al., the large shareholder faces a trade-off between the benefits from dispersed ownership (liquidity and risk diversification) and the private benefits from retaining control. The large shareholder will only be willing to give up control if the benefits from doing so outweigh the private benefits of control. If this is the case, it makes sense to cross-list the firm on a market with greater shareholder protection, bringing about a higher valuation. Second, owners of high-risk firms prefer to cross-list on a market with greater diversification potential, which in turn has been shown to be linked to investor protection. Finally, while the current ownership and control structure itself is likely to have an impact on the decision, the form of the link is however a priori not clear. Abdallah and Goergen found that a firm's ownership and control structure does indeed have an impact on this decision. However, contrary to their expectations, firms with substantial private benefits of control cross-list on markets with better investor protection. This relationship is particularly pronounced for firms where control is concentrated

[20]Doidge, C. (2004), 'U.S. Cross-Listings and the Private Benefits of Control: Evidence from Dual-Class Firms', *Journal of Financial Economics* 72, 519–53.

[21]Doidge, C., Karolyi, A.G. and Stulz, R.M. (2004), 'Why are Foreign Firms Listed in the U.S. Worth More?' *Journal of Financial Economics* 71, 205–38.

[22]Abdallah, W. and Goergen, M. (2008), 'Does Corporate Control Determine the Cross-listing Location?' *Journal of Corporate Finance* 14, 183–99.

in the hands of a single shareholder. Further, firms with significant minority shareholders are more likely to cross-list on a better market whereas those with several large shareholders are more likely to cross-list on a market with similar or worse investor protection. This suggests that those firms where the danger of expropriation by the large shareholder is most pronounced are more likely to choose a market for their cross-listing with better regulation, thereby bonding themselves not to expropriate their minority shareholders. Similar to the above studies, this study is in line with Coffee's bonding hypothesis.

To conclude, there is strong empirical support for the bonding hypothesis, as firms based in countries with weak investor protection tend to cross-list on better markets to commit themselves not to expropriate their minority shareholders. However, the US Sarbanes-Oxley Act of 2002 seems to have changed investors' and academics' views on the benefits of cross-listings. While the Act may have benefitted some firms, it also seems to have generated significant costs, outweighing in many cases the benefits from a US cross-listing (see also Section 6.3 of Chapter 6).

10.5 Conclusions

Access to finance for firms from countries with weak institutions and under-developed capital markets may be severely limited. The weakness of local institutions, such as law and its enforcement, may make local as well as foreign investors wary of investing in the country's corporations. Indeed, investors may be worried about being expropriated by the management or the large, controlling shareholder once they have invested their funds in the firms. Hence, the firms may only have little access to external financing or its cost may be prohibitive, significantly reducing their competitive advantage relative to firms from countries with highly liquid capital markets. One way whereby firms can improve their access to capital as well as reduce their cost of capital is via a range of contractual devices that enable them to opt into another country's legal and regulatory system. Such devices include cross-border mergers and acquisitions, (re)incorporations and cross-listings.

Concerning the first device, two questions emerge. First, does the target adopt the corporate governance of the bidder or is the converse the case? Second, do bidders with weak corporate governance reduce the corporate governance of the target? In order to answer these questions, we distinguished between three different potential effects of cross-border mergers and acquisitions on corporate governance. The first two effects assume that the target adopts the corporate governance of the bidder. The positive spillover effect consists of the target benefitting from the better corporate governance of the bidder, whereas the negative spillover effect consists of the former seeing a reduction in its corporate governance via the bidder's weaker corporate governance. Finally, the third effect, the bootstrapping effect, consists of the bidder adopting the better corporate governance of the target. Existing empirical studies provide consistent support for the positive spillover effect. Further, some studies also support the existence of an industry-wide positive spillover effect whereby an entire industry benefits from one of its member firms being taken over by a bidder from a country with better

Contractual corporate governance

Cross-border mergers

corporate governance standards. However, there is little evidence of a negative spillover effect. One reason why there is no such effect is that bidders tend to be from countries with better corporate governance than the targets. Finally, there is evidence of the bootstrapping effect, but only for partial acquisitions which are subject to the extraterritoriality principle. According to this principle, which is enshrined in international law, a country is allowed to subject a foreign-owned subsidiary to its law and regulation.

The second contractual device that may improve a firm's access to capital consists of incorporations and reincorporations in other countries or federal states of the same country. Enabling corporate mobility creates competition between national and federal regulators. However, a priori it is not clear whether such competition is beneficial or not. One school of thought advocates regulatory competition and predicts that such competition will result in a race to the top, as corporations will move to the jurisdiction which provides legal services at the lowest cost (the cost-avoidance hypothesis). In contrast, the other school of thought predicts that competition between regulators will result in a race to the bottom, as national regulators will compete for (re)incorporations by catering for managers' needs rather than shareholders' needs. As it stands, the empirical literature does not as yet provide evidence which is broadly consistent with only one school of thought.

(Re)incorporations

Finally, cross-listings are yet another way whereby companies can bridge the deficiencies of their national institutional system, improve their access to outside capital and reduce their cost of capital. According to the bonding hypothesis, companies cross-list in stock markets with more stringent rules to commit not to expropriate their minority shareholders. A growing body of empirical studies provides strong and consistent support for the bonding hypothesis.

Cross-listings

10.6 Discussion questions

1 How can firms located in countries with weak corporate governance standards credibly improve their corporate governance?

2 Critically review the evidence on the validity of the bonding hypothesis.

3 'Competition between national legislators and regulators should be avoided at all costs as it will result in a furious race to the bottom, dragging all concerned to the lowest common denominator'. (Anonymous)

Discuss the validity of the above statement.

Reading list

Key reading

Cary, W.L. (1974), 'Federalism and Corporate Law: Reflections upon Delaware', *Yale Law Journal* 83, 663–705.

Coffee, J. (2002), 'Racing Towards the Top? The Impact of Cross-listings and Stock Market Competition on International Corporate Governance', *Columbia Law Review* 102, 1757–831.

Doidge, C. (2004), 'U.S. Cross-Listings and the Private Benefits of Control: Evidence from Dual-Class Firms', *Journal of Financial Economics* 72, 519–53.

Martynova, M. and Renneboog, L. (2008), 'Spillover of Corporate Governance Standards in Cross-Border Mergers and Acquisitions', *Journal of Corporate Finance* 14, 200–23.

Romano, R. (1985), 'Law as a Product: Some Pieces of the Incorporation Puzzle', *Journal of Law, Economics, and Organization* 1, 225–83.

Winter, R.K. (1977), 'State Law, Shareholder Protection, and the Theory of the Corporation', *Journal of Legal Studies* 6, 251–92.

Further reading

Abdallah, W. and Goergen, M. (2008), 'Does Corporate Control Determine the Cross-listing Location?', *Journal of Corporate Finance* 14, 183–99.

Bebchuk, L. and Cohen, A. (2003), 'Firm's Decisions Where to Incorporate', *Journal of Law and Economics* 46, 383–425.

Bris, A., Brisley, N. and Cabolis, C. (2008), 'Adopting Better Corporate Governance: Evidence from Cross-Border Mergers', *Journal of Corporate Finance* 14, 224–40.

Doidge, C., Karolyi, A.G. and Stulz, R.M. (2004), 'Why are Foreign Firms Listed in the U.S. Worth More?', *Journal of Financial Economics* 71, 205–38.

Hansmann, H. and Kraakman, R. (2001), 'The End of History for Corporate Law', *Georgetown Law Journal* 89, 439–68.

Reese, W.A. Jr. and Weisbach, M.S. (2002), 'Protection of Minority Shareholder Interests, Cross-Listings in the United States, and Subsequent Equity Offerings', *Journal of Financial Economics* 66, 65–104.

Rossi, S. and Volpin, P. (2004), 'Cross-Country Determinants of Mergers and Acquisitions', *Journal of Financial Economics* 74, 277–304.

11 Corporate governance in initial public offerings

Chapter Aims

When a firm goes public, typically there is a substantial reduction in the entrepreneur's incentives to maximize shareholder value as he/she no longer owns 100 per cent of the equity, but still has significant control over the firm. Hence, the initial public offering (IPO) calls for a redesign of the firm's corporate governance arrangements. In addition, IPO firms also frequently suffer from greater asymmetry of information between the insiders and outsiders than more mature firms. They also often have financing provided by venture capitalists, which comes with its own benefits but may also cause conflicts of interests. Hence, IPO firms are likely to have corporate governance needs that differ substantially from those of more mature firms.

Learning Outcomes

After reading this chapter, you should be able to:

1 Evaluate the conflicts of interests that prevail in IPO firms

2 Assess the ways whereby IPO firms can mitigate conflicts of interests between their insiders and outsiders as well as mitigate other problems arising from asymmetric information

3 Explain the benefits from the presence of venture capitalists as well as the conflicts of interests they may cause

4 Discuss the corporate governance needs of IPO firms and how these may differ from those of more mature firms

11.1 Introduction

Asymmetric information is about different actors holding different levels of information. In corporate governance, asymmetric information typically refers to the management having better information about the firm's value and quality as well as their own effort than outsiders such as shareholders and debtholders (see Chapter 1). Asymmetric information implies that complete contracts, which specify what the managers have to do in each future contingency of the world and the distribution of profits in each contingency, are not possible (see also Section 1.3 of Chapter 1). Hence, conflicts of interests cannot be entirely prevented and corporate governance remains an important issue.

While corporate governance is a key issue for mature, publicly listed companies, it is even more so for firms going through or having recently gone through their IPO. This is the case for at least four reasons. First, when a firm goes public it experiences, at least to some degree, a separation of ownership and control. Indeed, while frequently before the IPO the entrepreneur or founding family owns 100 per cent of the firm's equity, after the IPO their ownership will be reduced while their control remains substantial. Hence, the entrepreneur's or the founder's incentives will be affected. Second, IPO firms tend to suffer more substantially from problems of asymmetric information than more mature firms. In particular, very little is known about a firm at the time of its IPO. This creates uncertainty as to the quality and value of the firm as well as its prospects. In addition, the entrepreneur is also typically an untested quantity unless he or she has already successfully taken firms public in the past, which is unlikely. The question arises as to how IPO firms can mitigate problems of asymmetric information and signal their superior quality to potential investors. Third, the power of CEOs in IPO firms and newly listed firms is high compared to more mature firms. This may give rise to problems and conflicts of interests in IPO firms that do not arise in mature firms. One such conflict of interests has resulted in a practice called the 'spinning' of the IPO. Finally, IPO firms frequently involve venture capitalists that are not present in more mature firms. Venture capitalists are often directly involved in the design of the IPO firm's governance. Hence, they frequently have a positive impact on firm value and performance. However, they may also be subject to conflicts of interests that reduce shareholder value. Readers are also referred to Section 16.4 of Chapter 16 for a more general description of conflicts of interests affecting investment banks and their clients.

This chapter will review the above five issues. The issue pertaining to the separation of ownership and control in IPOs will be looked at in the wider context of asymmetric information and the pricing of IPOs given that there is a clear link between all three. The chapter will discuss the ways of mitigating problems of asymmetric information and improving corporate governance in IPOs. Such ways include managerial remuneration contracts as well as so-called lock-in agreements.

Finally, the chapter will also highlight more generally how the corporate governance needs of IPO firms differ from those of more mature firms. This implies that what might be value-destroying for mature firms may be value-enhancing for IPO firms, and vice-versa. The following caveat applies. IPOs can range from SOEs[1] to tech 'unicorns' to private equity sales to highly speculative natural resources or biotech companies. The governance issues raised in this chapter are common to most varieties of IPO. A discussion of the governance issues affecting specific types of company or sellers would go beyond the remit of an introductory textbook on corporate governance.

11.2 Asymmetric information, pricing anomalies and the separation of ownership and control in IPOs

As part of the process of going public, the firm normally appoints an investment bank (the so-called sponsor in the UK), which will help with the issuing and sale of the equity shares as well as their pricing. Pricing mechanisms do vary across countries and stock markets. However, broadly speaking, they consist of offers at a fixed price and so-called book-building offers.[2] In an offer at a fixed price, the price of the shares to be issued is determined by the investment bank after due consideration of the fundamentals of the issuing firm. Once the investment bank has priced the issue, investors will be invited to subscribe for the shares at the so-called offer price. In a book-building offer, the pricing is more complex. It involves three separate stages. In the first stage, the investment bank approaches major clients, such as institutional investors, and asks them whether they are

---

[1]Section 9.5 of Chapter 9 discusses the challenges associated with the design of the governance of SOEs that are being (part-)privatized.
[2]One of the other pricing mechanisms includes an auction such as the Dutch auction used for the Google IPO in the USA. A Dutch auction starts with the auctioneer quoting a high price which is then reduced gradually until one of the bidders accepts the current price or the reserve price is achieved. In the UK, offers for sale by tender were relatively popular in the 1980s. They consisted of investors making applications consisting of the quantity of shares they were willing to buy and the maximum price they were willing to pay. The issuer would then rank the applications according to the price stated by them and then determine a strike price. Investors who had bid at a price equal or higher to the price would then be allocated shares.

interested in subscribing to the planned equity issue and, if yes, at what price and for how many shares. While these expressions of interest are not legally binding, they nevertheless help the bank assess the demand for the equity issue and help with its pricing. At the end of this stage, the bank typically determines the price range (consisting of a minimum and maximum price) within which investors have to apply for the shares. The second stage then consists of the actual book-building. Investors will be asked to apply for the shares by specifying the maximum price (within the price range) they are willing to pay as well as the quantity of shares they want. These offers are legally binding. In the final stage, the bank goes through the book and determines the offer or strike price. Investors that have bid at a price equal to or higher than the offer price will get shares in the IPO; all others will leave empty handed. As the average IPO is oversubscribed, i.e. the demand for the shares exceeds the supply, investors that have been successful will typically get fewer shares than they applied for. This allows for a discretionary allocation of shares which may discriminate in favour of or against certain applications.[3]

Three pricing anomalies have been observed for IPOs. These are the initial underpricing of IPO shares, their subsequent bad performance over the long term and the cycles in the number of IPOs as well as their initial returns (the so-called phenomenon of hot-issue markets). All three phenomena are pricing anomalies because they violate one of the key assumptions in finance which is the efficient market hypothesis (EMH) (see also Chapter 12). According to the EMH, there should be no persistent and predictable patterns in the prices of securities. As hot-issue markets are driven by more general cycles in markets, in what follows we shall concentrate on the other two pricing anomalies, i.e. IPO underpricing and the bad long-term performance of IPOs. Indeed, the latter two have been linked to firm characteristics, including the governance of firms.

Most IPOs are oversubscribed and on average the offer price tends to be lower than the closing price on the first day or week of trading. This implies that the average IPO is underpriced. This pricing pattern has been observed for a large number of countries, including developed as well as emerging economies. Average IPO underpricing ranges from a minimum of 3.3 per cent in Russia to a maximum of 239.8 per cent in Saudi Arabia (see Figure 11.1). Although an abundance of theoretical reasons has been advanced to explain the existence of IPO underpricing, there is as yet no single theory that explains all of the IPO underpricing and has empirical support across both different types of firms and markets.[4]

It is worthwhile mentioning the explanation of underpricing advanced by Michael Brennan and Julian Franks as it directly relates to corporate governance or more precisely the allocation of power between insiders and outsiders after the IPO.[5] Brennan and Franks argued that the incumbent owners of IPO firms deliberately underprice their firm's shares in the IPO in order to keep control over the firm. By underpricing the shares in the IPO, the incumbent owners ensure that the IPO is oversubscribed. The oversubscription then enables the incumbents to discriminate in favour of small investors in the allocation of the shares, thereby reducing the concentration of outside ownership. Brennan and Franks found support for their argument for a sample of UK IPOs. In detail, they found that:

- There is a positive link between underpricing and the rate of oversubscription.
- There is a positive link between underpricing and the dispersion of outside ownership after the IPO.
- Most of the cost of underpricing is borne by venture capitalists selling out in the IPO whereas the directors only sell a small proportion of their shares in the IPO.

---

[3]In the UK, the London Stock Exchange allows for applications being discriminated against on the basis of their size, but not on the basis of the type of applicant. See Brennan, M.J. and Franks, J. (1997), 'Underpricing, Ownership and Control in Initial Public Offerings of Equity Securities in the UK', *Journal of Financial Economics* 45, 391–413.

[4]See e.g. Ritter, J.R. (2003), 'Investment Banking and Securities Issuance', in G. Constantinides, M. Harris and R. Stulz (eds.), *Handbook of the Economics of Finance*, Amsterdam: Elsevier, 253–304.

[5]See op. cit. footnote 3.

Figure 11.1 Average initial IPO returns for 48 countries
Notes: see source for details of country studies.
Source: Professor Jay Ritter's IPO data website, site.warrington.ufl.edu/ritter/ipo-data/, accessed on 9 February 2017.

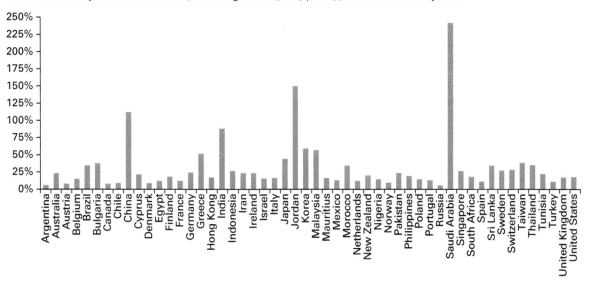

While IPO firms are initially underpriced, they have also been shown to underperform over the long term relative to other firms that have been on the stock market for a while and are of a similar size (see Figure 11.2). Although compared to IPO underpricing there are fewer theoretical explanations of the bad long-term performance of IPOs, the latter has also been linked to corporate governance. Bharat Jain and Omesh Kini as well as Wayne Mikkelson, Megan Partch and Kshitij Shah investigated whether there is a link between long-term performance and ownership for US IPOs.[6] They based themselves on Michael Jensen and William Meckling's (1976) principal-agent theory that, as managerial ownership decreases, the managers experience a reduction in their incentives and hence they are less likely to run the firm in the interests of all the shareholders (see Chapter 1).[7] The IPO, more than any other corporate event, typically brings about the separation of ownership and control as described by Adolf Berle and Gardiner Means.[8] The two studies have contradictory conclusions. While Jain and Kini detected a positive relationship between ownership retention by managers and post-IPO performance, Mikkelson et al. did not find such a link. However, Jain and Kini measured managerial ownership by the percentage of shares retained by all pre-IPO shareholders immediately after the IPO. Hence, they ignored the possibility that some of the pre-IPO shareholders are not part of the management and that insider ownership may experience further changes after the IPO. Conversely, Mikkelson et al. measured managerial ownership directly and tracked its changes over time. They did not find a link between firm value and financial performance over the ten years following the IPO. Similarly, Marc Goergen and Luc Renneboog failed to find evidence of a link between ownership and control of shares held by family shareholders and long-term performance for German and UK IPOs over the six years after the IPO.[9]

[6]Jain, B.A. and Kini, O. (1994), 'The Post-Issue Operating Performance of IPO Firms', *Journal of Finance* 49, 1699–726; and Mikkelson, W.H., Partch, M.M. and Shah, K. (1997), 'Ownership and Operating Performance of Companies that Go Public', *Journal of Financial Economics* 44, 281–307.
[7]Jensen, M. and Meckling, W. (1976), 'Theory of the Firm. Managerial Behavior, Agency Costs and Capital Structure', *Journal of Financial Economics* 3, 305–60.
[8]Berle A. and Means, G. (1932), *The Modern Corporation and Private Property*, New York: Macmillan.
[9]Goergen, M. and L. Renneboog (2007), 'Does Ownership Matter? A Study of German and UK IPOs', *Managerial Finance* 33, 368–87.

Figure 11.2 Percentage returns of US IPOs from 1980–2014 over the first five years after the issue compared to firms of a similar size

Notes: The returns are equally-weighted average returns for all IPOs on Nasdaq, the Amex and the NYSE at the start of a period. For each year, the portfolios are rebalanced to equal weights. If an issuing firm is delisted within a year, its return for that year is calculated by compounding the CRSP value-weighted market index for the rest of the year. The size-matched returns are obtained by matching each IPO with the non-issuing firm of the same or next higher market capitalization (based on the closing market price on the first day of trading for the IPO, and the market capitalization at the end of the previous month for the matching firms). The sample size is 8,061 IPOs from 1980–2014. IPOs with an offer price of less than US$5.00, American Depository Receipts, real estate investment trusts, acquisition funds, closed-ended funds, banks and S&Ls, small best efforts deals, oil and gas partnerships and unit offers have been excluded. See source for further details.

Source: Professor Jay Ritter's IPO data website, site.warrington.ufl.edu/ritter/ipo-data/, accessed on 9 February 2017.

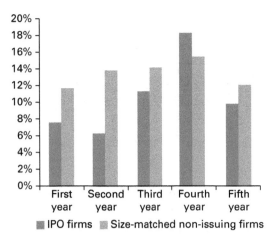

■ IPO firms   ■ Size-matched non-issuing firms

Hence, the existing empirical evidence suggests that there is no link between ownership and control held by the incumbent management and other pre-IPO shareholders after the IPO and post-IPO performance. While there does not seem to be a link between ownership and control on the one side and financial performance on the other for IPO firms, Marc Goergen and Luc Renneboog nevertheless found that the evolution of ownership and control in British and German IPOs can be explained by firm characteristics such as risk, growth, size and performance.[10] They also found that the likelihood of an IPO firm being taken over by a bidder that is ultimately widely held or a bidder that has a controlling shareholder depends on firm characteristics. They reported that UK firms are more likely to be taken over by a widely held bidder if they are large, have a high growth rate and are profitable. Further, UK firms with poor performance and high risk are more likely to be taken over by a concentrated bidder. German firms with high risk, but in contrast to UK firms German firms with high profitability, are more likely to be taken over by concentrated bidders, whereas high growth and low profitability increase the likelihood of being taken over by a dispersed bidder. This evidence suggests that post-IPO ownership and control are a result of firm characteristics, providing a possible explanation of why studies on the long-term performance of IPOs have not found a link with ownership and control. In other words, it seems that ownership and control are influenced by firm characteristics, including (past) performance, rather than the converse (see also Section 8.8 of Chapter 8).

[10]Goergen, M. and Renneboog, L. (2003), 'Why are the Levels of Control (So) Different in German and UK Companies? Evidence from Initial Public Offerings', *Journal of Law, Economics, and Organization* 19, 141–75.

11.3 Problems of asymmetric information and how to mitigate them

At the time of its IPO, very little is known about the firm as well as the incumbent management or the entrepreneur who frequently carries on running the firm after it has gone public. Although most stock exchanges require firms seeking a listing to have a minimum age, this minimum is often very low, such as three years for the Official List (the main stock-market segment) of the London Stock Exchange. Hence, potential investors will have little information on the firm, including a severely reduced financial track record, to rely on at the time of the IPO. So what are the likely consequences of the pronounced asymmetry of information characterizing IPO firms?

In 2001, George Akerlof received the Nobel Prize in Economics for his work – in particular his 1970 paper – on the consequences of asymmetric information.[11] The focus of the paper that earned him the Nobel Prize was the market for second-hand cars. One important characteristic of this market is that it is very difficult for buyers (unless maybe they are qualified mechanics) to judge the quality of a second-hand car they are interested in. The danger here is that once a buyer has bought a second-hand car, the car may end up being a lemon (American slang for a bad quality second-hand car) and the buyer may find it difficult or impossible to get his money back. The main consequence of the difficulty of assessing the quality of a good in a market, such as the second-hand car market, is that the prices in the market will reflect the *average* quality of the goods in that market. This will have severe consequences for sellers of *above-average* goods in that market as the price they will be able to receive for their goods will be too low.

Returning to the IPO market, the quality of firms going public is also difficult to assess for prospective investors. The consequence will be that entrepreneurs with above-average quality firms will receive a price for their firm which is too low. So how can entrepreneurs of such firms credibly signal to the market that their firm is of superior quality? They can do so via third-party certification such as via the use of a highly reputable investment bank to underwrite their IPO (see Section 16.2 of Chapter 16)[12] or via the use of venture capital financing. As venture capitalists (VCs) are repeat investors, they are better equipped to assess the quality of a firm and, similar to underwriters, they also have reputation capital at stake. In addition to third-party certification, entrepreneurs can also signal their superior quality via the ownership they retain in the firm after the IPO. Hayne Leland and David Pyle's model predicts that outside investors will perceive the percentage of ownership retained by the entrepreneur as a credible signal of firm quality.[13] The higher this percentage the higher will be the perceived quality, i.e. the expected future value of the firm. The signal is credible as it is costly for the entrepreneur to retain a large stake in the firm given the amount of his wealth locked up in the firm and the lack of diversification for his investment portfolio. Obviously, one can argue that by retaining a large stake in his firm, the entrepreneur prevents or at the very least slows down the separation of ownership and control. Still, by issuing new shares and/or selling

---

[11]Akerlof, G.A. (1970), 'The Market for "Lemons": Quality Uncertainty and the Market Mechanism', *Quarterly Journal of Economics* 84, 488–500.

[12]See e.g. Chemmanur, T.J. and Fulghieri, P. (1994), 'Investment Bank Reputation, Information Production, and Financial Intermediation', *Journal of Finance* 49, 57–79. While in the USA there was a negative relationship between IPO underpricing during the 1980s, the relationship became positive in the 1990s. See e.g. Ritter, J. and Loughran, T. (2004), 'Why Has IPO Underpricing Changed Over Time?', *Financial Management* 33, 5–37.

[13]Leland, H.E. and Pyle, D.H. (1977), 'Informational Asymmetries, Financial Structure and Financial Intermediation', *Journal of Finance* 32, 371–87.

some of his existing shares in the IPO, the entrepreneur's incentives have worsened as he no longer owns all of the equity.

In addition to retaining a large stake in the IPO, the entrepreneur may also commit himself not to sell his shares after the IPO for a specific period. Such a commitment is called a lock-in agreement (lock-up agreement in the USA). While some stock markets prescribe minimum lock-in periods, others do not. However, even in those stock markets that require minimum lock-in periods, these requirements are frequently voluntarily exceeded by the incumbent shareholders (see Box 11.1 for an example of lock-ins).[14] There is some evidence

Box 11.1
Lock-in agreement in Fitbit Inc.

We, all of our directors and officers, and the holders of substantially all of our outstanding equity securities have agreed or will agree that, without the prior written consent of Morgan Stanley & Co. LLC on behalf of the underwriters, we and they will not, for 180 days after the date of this prospectus:

- offer, pledge, sell, contract to sell, sell any option or contract to purchase, purchase any option or contract to sell, grant any option, right, or warrant to purchase, lend, or otherwise transfer or dispose of, directly or indirectly, any shares of Class A common stock, Class B common stock, or any securities convertible into or exercisable or exchangeable for shares of Class A common stock or Class B common stock;
- enter into any swap or other arrangement that transfers to another, in whole or in part, any of the economic consequences of ownership of Class A common stock or Class B common stock, whether any such transaction described in these first two bullet points is to be settled by delivery of Class A common stock, Class B common stock, or such other securities, in cash or otherwise;
- in the case of our directors, officers, and security holders, make any demand for or exercise any right with respect to, the registration of any shares of Class A common stock, Class B common stock, or any securities convertible into or exercisable or exchangeable for Class A common stock or Class B common stock;
- in our case, file any registration statement with the SEC relating to the offering of any shares of Class A common stock, Class B common stock, except for the filing of registration statements on Form S-8 with respect to the employee benefit plans described in this prospectus; or
- in our case, make any public announcement of any intention to do any of the foregoing.

Source: Fitbit Inc. (2015), 'Form S-1 Registration Statement', p. 134.

[14]See Goergen, M., Renneboog, L. and Khurshed, A. (2006), 'Explaining the Diversity in Shareholder Lockup Agreements', *Journal of Financial Intermediation* 15, 254–80, for evidence on France and Germany where there are compulsory lock-in periods. See Espenlaub, S., Goergen, M. and Khurshed, A. (2001), 'IPO Lock-in Agreements in the UK', *Journal of Business Finance and Accounting* 28, 1235–78, for evidence on the UK where there are no compulsory lock-in periods. In contrast, while US stock markets do not impose minimum lock-in periods, in most firms the incumbent shareholders are subject to lock-in periods of 180 days. See e.g. Mohan, N J and Chen, C R (2001), 'Information Content of Lock-up Provisions in Initial Public Offerings', *International Review of Economics and Finance* 10, 41–59, for evidence on the USA.

from France that firms with more stringent lock-in agreements have less underpricing, suggesting that the former act as signals of firm quality,[15] as well as evidence from the UK that hi-tech firms that tend to be characterized by more uncertainty, have more stringent lock-in agreements.[16] This suggests that the characteristics of lock-in agreements, including the fraction of ownership locked in, depend on firm characteristics.

Armando Gomes extended the Leland and Pyle model from a static context to a dynamic one.[17] He argued that especially in countries with weak investor protection, the founder can reduce problems of asymmetric information, in particular moral hazard, at the time of going public by holding a large stake in his firm after the IPO, thereby gradually building up a reputation as a manager who does not expropriate the minority shareholders. If the manager were to engage in moral hazard by extracting private benefits of control from the firm, at the expense of the minority shareholders, the latter would discount the firm's share price. As a result, the manager would then be punished by the reduction in the value of his remaining stake in the firm. Gomes's model predicts that the reduction in the manager's stake over time is negatively related to the magnitude of the moral hazard problem. His model also provides a justification for the use of dual-class shares and pyramids of ownership (see Chapter 3) as these enable the manager to divest some of his equity without losing control, thereby giving the manager more time and opportunity to build up a reputation as a manager who does not succumb to moral hazard.

11.4 The power of the CEO

The CEO typically assumes a key position in the firm and even more so in IPO firms. Sydney Finkelstein[18] proposed the following four dimensions of CEO power[19]:

- structural power
- ownership power
- expert power
- prestige power

Structural power is the power the CEO derives from her position within the firm's hierarchy or organizational structure. This structural power enables the CEO to control the behaviour and actions of her subordinates, thereby reducing uncertainty within the firm. This power may enable the CEO to push through decisions in the event that the top management is split down the middle about what to do. Structural power may also have more indirect manifestations. For example, the CEO may hold more information on the firm's future than some or all of her subordinates.

Ownership power is derived from the CEO's ownership stake in the firm. Ownership power tends to increase with the size of the CEO's stake. If the CEO is the founder of the firm or is related to the founder, this may further amplify her ownership power over her subordinates as well as other board members.

The CEO's expert power stems from her firm-specific human capital, such as her knowledge about the technologies the firm uses and her ability to deal with the firm's stakeholders (such as customers, suppliers,

[15]Goergen, M., Renneboog, L. and Khurshed, A. (2006), 'Explaining the Diversity in Shareholder Lockup Agreements', *Journal of Financial Intermediation* 15, 254–80.

[16]Espenlaub, S., Goergen, M. and Khurshed, A. (2001), 'IPO Lock-in Agreements in the UK', *Journal of Business Finance and Accounting* 28, 1235–78.

[17]Gomes, A. (2000), 'Going Public without Governance: Managerial Reputation Effects', *Journal of Finance* 55, 615–46.

[18]Finkelstein, S. (1992), 'Power in Top Management Teams: Dimensions, Measurement, and Validation', *Academy of Management Journal* 35, 505–38.

[19]Finkelstein focused not just on the CEO, but extended his four dimensions to the entire top management of the company.

employees, competitors and the government) as well as the other environmental factors that the firm faces. At the extreme, the CEO's skills set may make her indispensable to the firm and put in danger the survival of the latter should the CEO die or leave the firm.

Finally, another dimension or source of CEO power is prestige power. This power is derived from the CEO's reputation and status within the institutional environment she operates. The CEO's prestige power increases with her stakeholders' perception of her influence. For example, CEOs who sit on the boards of other firms are likely to have high prestige power. CEOs with high prestige power may be part of managerial elites that are admired and whose actions are copied by less prestigious managers. The firm's legitimacy is also, at least to some extent, likely to depend on the CEO's prestige power. The CEO's prestige power may also benefit the firm via the information the CEO is able to collect through her contacts within the institutional environment.

In addition to Finkelstein's four dimensions of power, Salim Chahine and Marc Goergen proposed a fifth source of power, which is control power.[20] Control power measures how pivotal the CEO is in the voted decision, i.e. how often she will be part of a winning coalition. For example, assume that a company has three large shareholders: shareholder A who holds 40 per cent of the votes, shareholder B who holds 30 per cent of the votes and the CEO who holds 25 per cent of the votes. The remaining five per cent of the votes are held by a large number of small shareholders. None of the three large shareholders has enough votes to push through a decision that requires a majority. Hence, each of the three large shareholders will need to form a coalition with at least one of the other two large shareholders to win a voted decision. While the CEO has the smallest percentage of votes, there are three winning coalitions she can form with at least one of the other two large shareholders. These winning coalitions are: A and CEO (65 per cent), B and CEO (55 per cent), and A, B and CEO (95 per cent). The only other winning coalition, and which does not include the CEO, is A and B (70 per cent). Hence, in this example the CEO is pivotal in three out of four winning coalitions and her control power index is therefore 0.75. The latter index is the so-called Shapley value, derived from the John Milnor and Lloyd Shapley power index for oceanic games. It is used in the empirical literature to determine the pivotal role of a shareholder.[21] The concept of oceanic games is particularly suitable for corporate governance within large corporations as it assumes that the voted decision is mainly dominated by a few large shareholders and that the minority shareholders are typically irrelevant when one or several of the large shareholders intend to form a winning coalition.

While CEOs in general tend to have high levels of power across one or several of the above five dimensions, the power of CEOs of IPO firms is likely to be even more concentrated. In particular, CEOs of IPO firms are likely to have a lot of expert power as they may have developed the technology or innovation (including possible patents) behind the firm. Such CEOs may be intrinsically linked to the firm and their departure may seriously put in danger the survival of the firm. To allay investor concerns about this danger, in practice CEOs signal their commitment to their firm by keeping large stakes of equity in the firm and frequently also agree to lock in their ownership over the long term via a voluntary lock-in contract. Jonathan Arthurs and colleagues argue that the dependence of new ventures on their CEO, more specifically the founder CEO, can be seen from two theoretical perspectives: principal-agent theory and the resource dependence theory.[22] From a

[20]Chahine, S. and Goergen, M. (2011), 'VC Board Representation and Performance of US IPOs', *Journal of Business Finance and Accounting* 38, 413–45.

[21]Milnor, J.W. and Shapley, L.S. (1978), 'Values of Large Games II: Oceanic Games', *Mathematics of Operations Research* 3, 290–307.

[22]Arthurs, J.D., Busenitz, L.W., Hoskisson, R.E. and Johnson, R.A. (2009), 'Firm-Specific Human Capital and Governance in IPO Firms: Addressing Agency and Resource Dependence Concerns', *Entrepreneurship Theory and Practice* 33, 845–65.

principal-agent perspective, even before the firm goes public, it may have to rely on external capital such as business angel finance and venture capital. Such financiers will normally insist on putting in place corporate governance arrangements to protect their investments. The firm is likely to undergo further changes in its governance just before going public. Arthurs et al. find that ownership by outsiders is typically greater and pay-performance sensitivity is higher when the firm is more dependent on its CEO. Concerning the resource dependence theory perspective, they find that the more critical the skills of the CEO are to the firm the greater is the likelihood that the firm will have in place involuntary departure arrangements – essentially life insurance policies on the CEO – which will provide the firm with money to cover the costs of finding a replacement CEO with similar firm-specific skills.

CEOs of IPO firms are also likely to have high ownership and control power given that they frequently remain the largest shareholder in their firm following the IPO (see Section 2.2. of Chapter 2). They also tend to have high structural power given that they are often the founders of the firm or part of the founder's family. However, it is less likely that they have prestige power given the smaller size and visibility of firms that have recently conducted their IPO compared to more mature firms. In the next section, we shall discuss the 'spinning' of IPOs, which is a particular manifestation of the conflicts of interests a CEO may be facing at the time of the IPO.

11.5 Spinning of IPOs

Jay Ritter discussed the practice of 'spinning' initial public offerings (IPOs) in the USA during the 1990s.[23] Shares issued in IPOs tend to be underpriced, i.e. the shares are issued at a price, the offer price, which on average is lower than the price at the end of the first day of trading on the stock exchange (see also Chapter 12). If there is sufficient competition between investment banks taking companies public, one would expect that underpricing would not exist or at the very least be much lower than the average 17 per cent observed in the case of US IPOs. Ritter found evidence that investment banks used the underpriced shares as bribes. The underpriced shares were allocated to clients of the investment banks to obtain further fee-earning business from them in the future. The underpriced shares were also allocated to the executives of the underpriced IPO firms. In a study he conducted with Xiaoding Liu, Jay Ritter found the following:[24] First, firms with executives that had been 'spun' were more underpriced (by 23 per cent (!) on average). Second, these firms were less likely to switch investment banks in the future. Only six per cent of executives of 'spun' IPOs switched lead underwriters compared to 31 per cent for the other IPOs. Some of the data on 'spinning' of IPOs were used to prosecute the chief executive of Credit Suisse First Boston (CSFB), Frank Quattrone. Accounts of executives who were 'spun' were referred to as 'Friends of Frank' (see Box 11.2). Most other major investment banks had also been involved in the practice.

[23]Ritter, J.R. (2008), 'Forensic Finance', *Journal of Economic Perspectives* 22, 127–47.
[24]Liu, X. and Ritter, J.R. (2010), 'The Economic Consequences of IPO Spinning', *Review of Financial Studies* 23, 2024–59. The figures in Ritter (2008) refer to an earlier version: Liu, X. and Ritter, J.R. (2007), 'Corporate Executive Bribery: An Empirical Analysis', Unpublished University of Florida working paper. The figures used in this chapter are the updated figures in Liu and Ritter (2010).

Box 11.2
Spinning of initial public offerings

Silicon Valley's onetime top technology financier, Frank Quattrone, has won a third round in his battle for legal vindication now that an industry regulator has dropped all charges related to allocation of hot IPO shares to clients during the internet boom era.

The dismissal, issued by the National Association of Securities Dealers, which originally brought the charge, means that Quattrone has now prevailed against all charges and penalties brought by the securities regulatory group. He still faces a possible trial – the third – on a federal charge of obstructing justice.

Quattrone and his attorneys announced their latest victory in a news release. 'Throughout my 23-year career, I have upheld high standards of integrity and professional conduct in my work and complied with the rules and regulations', Quattrone said in the release. 'I am pleased that justice has been done, and truly grateful for the support of my family, friends and clients who stood by me during these challenges'.

The dismissal issued Wednesday cleared Quattrone of the charge of 'spinning' – or helping to award shares of hot initial public offerings to executives of client companies, including some Silicon Valley companies, so they could sell them for a quick profit. The original investigation that led to this charge also produced a list of about 300 executives, including many in the Bay Area, known as 'Friends of Frank', who allegedly received IPO shares of young technology companies.

The decision issued Wednesday by NASD Hearing Officer Dennis M. FitzGerald also dismissed a charge of conflict of interest in Quattrone's alleged involvement in supervising investment research at his former firm, Credit Suisse First Boston.

In March, Quattrone also won a decision from the Securities and Exchange Commission overturning a separate NASD order that would have banned him for life from working in the securities industry.

The dismissal continues a string of legal victories for Quattrone, who has steadfastly maintained his innocence while being variously portrayed as a hero, villain or scapegoat.

'CLEAN UP' FILES

In March, a federal court set aside his criminal conviction on a charge of obstructing justice during an investigation of Credit Suisse, where he ran the technology investment banking unit. The charge arose from an e-mail Quattrone forwarded to co-workers in 2000 urging them to 'clean up' files on stock deals. After his first trial ended in a deadlocked jury, a second trial led to Quattrone's conviction on the obstruction charge in 2004. On appeal, that conviction was set aside.

Quattrone still faces the possibility that federal prosecutors could bring him to trial for a third time. A spokesman for the U.S. Attorney in New York said no decision has been made on a retrial.

Quattrone's defenders contend that the investment banker was targeted by overly aggressive regulators and prosecutors seeking a high-profile target in the aftermath of the dot-com crash. In an interview, the lawyer who handled Quattrone's case before the NASD, Kenneth Hausman, said 'the withdrawal of charges is vindication and a complete exoneration for Mr Quattrone. It cleared his name of all the substantive charges'.

Quattrone's supporters include many valley venture capitalists and executives who worked with him during his 23 years as an investment banker. By his own estimation, Quattrone has raised more than $65 billion and helped launch IPOs for 175 firms, including Cisco Systems, Netscape and Amazon.com, according to the news release his lawyers issued Thursday.

Arguably the valley's most important financier in his heyday, Quattrone is also credited with advising on 425 mergers and acquisitions with a value of more than $500 billion, according to the news release.

In his first trial, prosecutors showed the jury a list of 208 executives – including Meg Whitman of eBay, KLA-Tencor's Kenneth Levy, Stratton Sclavos of VeriSign and others from Phone.com and Ascend Communications – that had allegedly been given accounts to receive IPO shares.

The order issued Wednesday by the NASD's FitzGerald withdrew the March 2003 allegations by the NASD that accused Quattrone of 'spinning', alleging that his actions permitted allocations of IPO shares to banking clients that violated its existing rules against gifts and gratuities. Spinning was alleged to be a way to win their companies' banking business.

Quattrone, Hausman said, sought an immediate hearing on the charges in a bid to clear his name, only to have the case drag out from delays sought by the NASD. 'That's why they never brought it to a hearing. They would have lost. They were accusing him of violations of rules that were enacted after the conduct at issue', the attorney said.

AFTER THE FACT

Quattrone's attorneys argued that Quattrone was being held to standards that didn't exist when the alleged wrongdoing occurred. Bob Chlopak, a spokesman for Quattrone spokesman, said in a news release that 'NASD did not propose rules addressing the longstanding and widespread industry practices challenged in its action against Mr. Quattrone until 2002, well after the period at issue in this case'.

Quattrone's legal battle could end if the U.S. Attorney's Office in New York decides against a third trial. Both the prosecutor who initially brought charges against Quattrone and the two prosecutors who won the conviction have since left the office – a fact in Quattrone's favour, one former federal prosecutor said.

Source: Norris, F. (2003), 'Inside the Workings of a Money Machine', *New York Times*, p. 1.

11.6 The role of venture capitalists in IPO firms

VCs provide risk capital to young firms, in particular hi-tech firms with few tangible assets, that may find it difficult to tap into other sources of finance, including bank loans.[25] However, they do not just limit their role to providing finance as they also provide management guidance – including commercial and technical advice – as well as networking opportunities indispensable for forming strategic alliances with other firms.[26] They also frequently help firms build their management teams, attract key staff, design their organizational structure and establish their market share.[27]

Thomas Hellmann argued that after a certain stage has been reached in the firm's life cycle, VCs frequently call for the replacement of the entrepreneur by a professional manager, as the latter is thought to add value to the firm whereas the former is likely to act in her own interests.[28] However, the entrepreneur is likely to be against her replacement as she may be personally attached to her firm and may consider her replacement to be humiliating and to harm her professional reputation. Nevertheless, the replacement of founder CEOs is a frequent occurrence and it becomes more likely over time. For Silicon Valley firms, the likelihood of the CEO founder being replaced is only 10 per cent over the first 20 months of the firm's life time, but then quadruples after 40 months and then doubles after 80 months to reach 80 per cent.[29] So how do VCs manage to replace the entrepreneur? They do so via the voting rights they hold and frequently the latter are amplified by being represented on the board of directors. They also often have shareholder agreements and employment contracts which enable them to terminate the

---

[25]See Gompers, P. and Lerner, J. (1999), *The Venture Capital Cycle*, Cambridge, MA: MIT Press for a discussion about the types of firms that are unlikely to find access to bank financing.
[26]See e.g. Hellmann, T. and Puri, M. (2002), 'Venture Capital and the Professionalization of Start-up Firms: Empirical Evidence', *Journal of Finance* 57, 169–97; Hochberg, Y.V., Ljungqvist, A. and Lu, Y. (2007), 'Venture Capital Networks and Investment Performance', *Journal of Finance* 62, 251–301; and Sorensen, M. (2007), 'How Smart is Smart Money? A Two-sided Matching Model of Venture Capital', *Journal of Finance* 62, 2725–62.
[27]See Hellmann and Puri (2002), op. cit. footnote 26.
[28]Hellmann, T. (1998), 'The Allocation of Control Rights in Venture Capital Contracts', *RAND Journal of Economics* 29, 57–76.
[29]Hellmann cites the study by Hannan et al. (1996) and notes that they do not distinguish between forced replacements and voluntary ones. Hannan, M.T., Burton, M.D. and Baron, I.N. (1996), 'Inertia and Change in the Early Years: Employment Relations in Young, High-technology Firms', *Industrial and Corporate Change* 5, 503–35.

founder's ownership and employment. Shareholder agreements specify the percentage of shares held by the entrepreneur, the other managers and the investors. Frequently, the entrepreneur's shares are vested. Vested shares are shares that are held by the firm on behalf of the entrepreneur and the latter obtains legal ownership over the shares only after specific conditions have been met. The employment contract specifies the employment terms of the entrepreneur, including the reasons that may justify the termination of the CEO founder's employment and the severance pay. In practice, severance pay is very low.

Hellmann formulates a theoretical model which explains why in practice entrepreneurs are willing to transfer control over the firm to the VCs, including the decision to appoint the CEO, and why they are happy to accept vesting of their shares and modest severance pay. The model makes the following three predictions:

1 The smaller the entrepreneur's equity in the firm and the smaller his overall wealth the more likely he is willing to give up control.
2 The entrepreneur is more likely to give up control the lower his business skills and experience of running the firm.
3 The higher the supply of professional managers and the higher their quality, the higher the likelihood that the entrepreneur is willing to transfer control over the firm to the VCs.

VCs also typically provide their financing to the firm in the form of stage financing. Stage financing is financing that is provided gradually as the firm achieves specific performance milestones. The milestones are typically linked to major stages in the firm's life cycle such as the development of a prototype, the launch of the production based on an economically viable prototype and the first profit.

Francesca Cornelli and Oved Yosha studied the role of convertible securities and stage financing in venture capital financing from a theoretical point of view.[30] Convertible securities are debt securities that can be converted into a fixed number of equity shares. Stage financing incorporates the option to abandon for the VC: if the firm's management does not achieve the agreed milestones, the VC has the right to stop financing the firm. To prevent the VC from exiting the firm and hence causing its liquidation, the entrepreneur is likely to engage in creative accounting, thereby boosting short-term profits. Cornelli and Yosha's theoretical model predicts that the VC can prevent such window dressing by financing the firm via the purchase of convertible securities rather than via the purchase of the firm's debt and equity securities. Indeed, the threat of conversion will reduce the entrepreneur's tendency to boost profits artificially as the conversion will change the firm's capital structure, i.e. its debt-equity mix, via the increase in the VC's ownership of the firm. The increased ownership will then enable the VC to appropriate an increased share of the firm's value.

To sum up, there is evidence that VCs create value via the support, the expertise and the networks they offer the firm. They are also frequently seeking a successor to the founder who is expected to improve the firm's value. Finally, they also tend to be involved in the design of the firm's governance structure and the improvement of the founder CEO's incentives.

However, there is also evidence that suggests that VCs, in particular young VCs, may be subject to conflicts of interests, i.e. they may pursue their own interests rather the maximization of the firm's value. Paul Gompers advanced the grandstanding hypothesis whereby young VCs, intent on establishing their reputation within the venture capital industry, take their portfolio firms public early in order to create a track record of successful investments.[31] Venture capital firms are frequently in the form of partnerships with the silent partners, typically institutional investors, providing all the funding. Young venture capital partnerships may find it difficult to obtain further funding unless they have succeeded in getting at least one of their portfolio firms to the stock

[30]Cornelli, F. and Yosha, O. (2003), 'Stage Financing and the Role of Convertible Securities', *Review of Economic Studies* 70, 1–32.
[31]Gompers, P.A. (1996), 'Grandstanding in the Venture Capital Industry', *Journal of Financial Economics* 42, 133–56.

exchange. Gompers argued that future access to financing can be ensured by young VCs rushing their firms to the stock market. The cost of doing so is more pronounced underpricing at the IPO; the empirical literature shows consistent evidence that underpricing is inversely related to the issuing firm's age. However, this cost will be shared by all the pre-IPO shareholders and not just the VC, whereas the benefits from taking the firm public early accrue only to the VC.

Bearing in mind that CEOs of IPO firms frequently hold shares in their firm, the question then arises as to how VCs convince CEOs to take their firm public early, given the cost of higher underpricing. Michelle Lowry and Kevin Murphy argued that VCs grant CEOs stock options just before the IPO with an exercise price which is set equal to the deliberately low offer price.[32] These IPO options then more than compensate the CEOs for the losses they may suffer from the shares they sell in the IPO at the too low offer price. However, Lowry and Murphy did not find any evidence of a link between IPO underpricing and the expected gains from the IPO stock options held by the CEO.

In contrast, Salim Chahine and Marc Goergen found evidence of such a link, but only when they adjusted for the power of the VC, the power of the CEO as well as the power of the board of directors.[33] They measured CEO and VC power along the four dimensions proposed by Finkelstein, augmented by a fifth dimension, i.e. control power (see Section 11.4). They reported strong evidence of a link between underpricing and the ex ante gains from the CEO IPO options for firms with powerful VCs as well as powerful CEOs. This link is more positive the more powerful the VC or the CEO. Finally, they found that this perverse effect of stock options only holds for firms with weak boards of directors. Conversely, for firms with highly independent boards of directors the positive link between IPO underpricing and CEO IPO stock options is reversed and becomes negative. This suggests that stock options only work properly as incentivizing devices in the presence of strong corporate governance (as measured by strong boards), whereas otherwise they become devices enabling VCs and CEOs to expropriate the other shareholders (see also Section 8.8 of Chapter 8).

The question arises as to whether – overall – VCs create value (the so-called management support hypothesis) or whether they expropriate the other pre-IPO shareholders (the grandstanding hypothesis). Salim Chahine and Marc Goergen[34] studied the impact of the power of VCs – along the same five dimensions used to measure CEO power as reviewed in Section 11.4 – on the likelihood of VC board representation as well as the impact of the latter on IPO underpricing and value creation.[35] They find that the likelihood of the VC being on the board of directors increases with VC power. In turn, the latter has a positive effect on both IPO underpricing as well as value creation. This evidence is consistent with *both* the management support hypothesis and the grandstanding hypothesis.

11.7 The corporate governance needs of IPO firms

IPO firms are a good illustration that the dictum that 'one size fits all' does not apply to corporate governance. For example, the board of directors has two main functions: monitoring the management and providing the latter with advice. As ownership and control is more likely to be concentrated in IPO firms than mature firms, the agency problem tends to be less severe. At the same time, the management of IPO firms tends to be less experienced than the management of mature firms.[36] Hence, IPO firms are more likely to require advice rather than monitoring

[32]Lowry, M. and Murphy, K.J. (2007), 'Executive Stock Options and IPO Underpricing', *Journal of Financial Economics* 85, 39–65.
[33]Chahine, S. and Goergen, M. (2011), 'The Two Sides of CEO Option Grants at the IPO', *Journal of Corporate Finance* 17, 1116–31.
[34]See op. cit. 20.
[35]The latter is measured by the so-called IPO premium, i.e. the ratio of the difference between the offer price and the book value of the IPO shares to the offer price.
[36]Field, L.C., Lowry, M. and Mkrtchyan, A. (2013), 'Are Busy Boards Detrimental?', *Journal of Financial Economics* 109, 63–82.

from the board of directors. In turn, this requires a friendly board rather than a strong and independent board as Renée Adams and Daniel Ferreira theorized.[37] Salim Chahine and Marc Goergen provided evidence in support of this argument.[38] They found that IPO firms whose top management team (TMT) has social ties to the board of directors perform better than those without such ties. In contrast, Byoung-Hyoun Hwang and Seoyong Kim found that social ties between the TMT and the board destroy firm value for mature firms.[39]

Similarly, evidence is emerging that anti-takeover devices, staggered boards, dual-class shares and incorporations in Delaware may act as a means to protect manager-specific skills, innovation and the long-term business relations of the firm. Empirical evidence suggests that such devices or arrangements can create value for the case of IPO firms.[40] In contrast, these devices are typically associated with the 'quiet life' hypothesis or the preservation of private benefits of control for more mature firms.[41]

11.8 Conclusions

Before its IPO the firm's equity is fully or mainly owned by the founder or entrepreneur who also runs the firm. Hence, the principal and the agent are identical and there are no agency costs. At the time of its IPO, the firm then faces the challenge of designing its governance in order to convince potential investors to subscribe for its shares. Importantly, the IPO is normally the first occasion on which there is a substantial separation of ownership and control. While the existing empirical literature does not suggest that ownership and control have an impact on post-IPO performance, there is evidence that the incumbent shareholders use underpricing in order to avoid the emergence of large outside shareholders and to stay in control of their firm.

The separation of ownership and control in IPO firms

The issue as to the design of the firm's governance is intrinsically linked to the broader issue of asymmetric information, which is particularly pronounced in IPO firms. As little is known about the firm at the time of its IPO, the IPO market is a lemons, market where the equilibrium price of newly issued IPO shares reflects the average quality of IPO firms. In order to achieve a better, fairer price for the shares of their firm, the incumbent shareholders of superior IPO firms face the challenge of signalling the above-average quality of their firm to the stock market. A signal of firm quality is the percentage of shares retained by the incumbent shareholders after the IPO. This signal is credible as it is costly for a shareholder to hold a large stake in the firm given that this ties down most or all of his wealth in a single investment and results in an undiversified and highly risky investment portfolio. Given the cost attached to this signal, it is unlikely

Asymmetric information and firm quality

---

[37]Adams, R. and Ferreira, D. (2007), 'A Theory of Friendly Boards', *Journal of Finance* 62, 217–50. See also Section 7.4 of Chapter 7.
[38]Chahine, S. and Goergen, M. (2013), 'The Effects of Management-Board Ties on IPO Performance', *Journal of Corporate Finance* 21, 153–79.
[39]Hwang B.H. and Kim, S. (2009), 'It Pays to Have Friends', *Journal of Financial Economics* 93, 138–58.
[40]Johnson, W.C., Karpoff, J.M. and Yi, S. (2015), 'The Bonding Hypothesis of Takeover Defenses: Evidence from IPO Firms', *Journal of Financial Economics* 117, 307–32; see section 8 of Lowry, M., Michaely, R. and Volkova, E. (2017), 'Initial Public Offering: A Synthesis of the Literature and Directions for Future Research', available at SSRN: ssrn.com/abstract=2912354, for a review of this literature.
[41]See also Section 6.3 of Chapter 6.

that owners of bad firms will be able to afford it. The signal can be further re-inforced via lock-in contracts whereby the incumbent shareholders agree not to dispose of further shares in their ownership during a specific period.

Even though IPO firms experience a separation of ownership and control, typically the CEO is still very powerful after the flotation on the stock market. Finkelstein proposes four dimensions of CEO power. The first one is structural power, defined as the power of the CEO within the firm's hierarchy or organizational structure. The second dimension is ownership power, the power the CEO derives from her ownership of the firm's equity. If the CEO is the founder of the firm, this may further amplify her ownership power. Given that IPO firms are frequently high-growth, high-tech firms, the CEO may also have expert power stemming from her knowledge of cutting-edge technologies. Finally, the CEO may also derive prestige power from her membership of management elites and her recognition and reputation within the wider business world. However, given that IPO firms tend to be less visible and have less recognition than more mature, stock-market listed firms, CEOs of IPO firms are unlikely to have much prestige power while scoring relatively higher on the former three dimensions. A fifth dimension is control power, which measures how pivotal the CEO is in the voted decision. As discussed in Chapter 3, some firms violate the principle of one-share one-vote and these are the firms where the control power of the CEO may be substantially greater than her ownership power.

Finkelstein's dimensions of CEO power applied to IPO firms

In the recent past, some investment banks have been found to 'spin' IPOs, by using the underpriced shares as bribes and allocating them to their clients to generate further fee-earning business from them in the future. The underpriced shares were also allocated to the executives of the underpriced IPO firms to ensure their loyalty.

'Spinning' of IPOs

IPO firms also often tend to have VCs among their shareholders. Overall, the empirical literature suggests that VCs create value via the management support, the industry expertise and the network opportunities they offer to their portfolio firms. They also frequently call for the replacement of the founder CEO by a professional manager with the aim of increasing firm value. Apart from replacing the founder CEO, VCs may also be involved in the firm's governance in other ways such as making further financing contingent on the firm's management achieving certain milestones. This is called stage financing. In that context, theory recommends that VCs finance their portfolio firms by buying convertible debt securities from the firm rather than by buying a mix of debt and equity securities. The advantage of the former over the latter is that it addresses the tendency of the management to overstate the firm's achievements in order to avoid liquidation. Indeed, if the management engages in window dressing, the VC may convert the debt securities into equity, replacing debt by equity and thereby reaping the increase in firm value. However, while VCs are frequently associated with value creation, there is empirical evidence which suggests that young VCs grandstand by taking their portfolio firms public early in order to improve their reputation and ultimately their access to further financing. While there are net

The role of VCs in IPO firms: value creation versus conflicts of interests

benefits from grandstanding, these accrue to the VCs whereas the costs via the higher underpricing are shared by all the shareholders.

Finally, IPO firms are a good example illustrating that when it comes to corporate governance 'one size does not fit all'. An emerging literature suggests that devices that are normally used by managers of mature firms to preserve their private benefits of control or to ensure a quiet life help IPO firms to focus on the long term, thereby creating value and enhancing their performance.

One size does not fit all

11.9 Discussion questions

1 Discuss the use of IPO underpricing by CEOs and VCs in the pursuit of their own interests.

2 Review the various dimensions of CEO power.

3 Discuss the practice of 'spinning' IPOs.

4 What is the role of VCs in the design of IPO firms' corporate governance?

5 Explain the conflicts of interests certain VCs may suffer from.

Reading list

Key reading

Akerlof, G.A. (1970), 'The Market for "Lemons": Quality Uncertainty and the Market Mechanism', *Quarterly Journal of Economics* 84, 488–500.

Brennan, M.J. and Franks, J. (1997), 'Underpricing, Ownership and Control in Initial Public Offerings of Equity Securities in the UK', *Journal of Financial Economics* 45, 391–413.

Finkelstein, S. (1992), 'Power in Top Management Teams: Dimensions, Measurement, and Validation', *Academy of Management Journal* 35, 505–38.

Goergen, M. and Renneboog, L. (2003), 'Why are the Levels of Control (So) Different in German and UK Companies? Evidence from Initial Public Offerings', *Journal of Law, Economics, and Organization* 19, 141–75.

Gompers, P.A. (1996), 'Grandstanding in the Venture Capital Industry', *Journal of Financial Economics* 42, 133–56.

Jain, B.A. and Kini, O. (1994), 'The Post-Issue Operating Performance of IPO Firms', *Journal of Finance* 49, 1699–726.

Leland, H.E. and Pyle, D.H. (1977), 'Informational Asymmetries, Financial Structure and Financial Intermediation', *Journal of Finance* 32, 371–87.

Mikkelson, W.H., Partch, M.M. and Shah, K. (1997), 'Ownership and Operating Performance of Companies that Go Public', *Journal of Financial Economics* 44, 281–307.

Ritter, J.R. (2008), 'Forensic Finance', *Journal of Economic Perspectives* 22, 127–47.

Further reading

Arthurs, J.D., Busenitz, L.W., Hoskisson, R.E. and Johnson, R.A. (2009), 'Firm-Specific Human Capital and Governance in IPO Firms: Addressing Agency and Resource Dependence Concerns', *Entrepreneurship Theory and Practice* 33, 845–65.

Chahine, S. and Goergen, M. (2011), 'The Two Sides of CEO Option Grants at the IPO', *Journal of Corporate Finance* 17, 1116–31.

Chahine, S. and Goergen, M. (2011), 'VC Board Representation and Performance of US IPOs', *Journal of Business Finance and Accounting* 38, 413–45.

Cornelli, F. and Yosha, O. (2003), 'Stage Financing and the Role of Convertible Securities', *Review of Economic Studies* 70, 1–32.

Espenlaub, S., Goergen, M. and Khurshed, A. (2001), 'IPO Lock-in Agreements in the UK', *Journal of Business Finance and Accounting* 28, 1235–78.

Goergen, M. and Renneboog, L. (2007), 'Does Ownership Matter? A Study of German and UK IPOs', *Managerial Finance* 33, 368–87.

Goergen, M., Renneboog, L. and Khurshed, A. (2006), 'Explaining the Diversity in Shareholder Lockup

Agreements', *Journal of Financial Intermediation* 15, 254–80.

Gomes, A. (2000), 'Going Public without Governance: Managerial Reputation Effects', *Journal of Finance* 55, 615–46.

Johnson, W.C., Karpoff, J.M. and Yi, S. (2015), 'The Bonding Hypothesis of Takeover Defenses: Evidence from IPO Firms', *Journal of Financial Economics* 117, 307–32

Liu, X. and Ritter, J.R. (2010), 'The Economic Consequences of IPO Spinning', *Review of Financial Studies* 23, 2024–59.

Lowry, M., Michaely, R. and Volkova, E. (2017), 'Initial Public Offering: A Synthesis of the Literature and Directions for Future Research', available at SSRN: ssrn.com/abstract=2912354.

Lowry, M. and Murphy, K.J. (2007), 'Executive Stock Options and IPO Underpricing', *Journal of Financial Economics* 85, 39–65.

Mohan, N.J. and Chen, C.R. (2001), 'Information Content of Lock-up Provisions in Initial Public Offerings', *International Review of Economics and Finance* 10, 41–59, for evidence on the USA.

12 Behavioural biases and corporate governance

Chapter Aims

This chapter introduces you to biases in human behaviour. It outlines how these biases may limit human rationality, reduce the quality of corporate governance and more generally cause bad decision making. Importantly, the chapter revisits the classic principal-agent problem by making explicit reference to the lack of loyalty of executives to their shareholders. In turn, excessive loyalty of board members to the CEO is advanced as a possible reason why empirical studies have not found a relation between board structure and firm value or performance. The chapter also reviews, among other biases, overconfidence and hubris by managers as well as attitudes towards risk taking and collective intelligence according to gender and age.

Learning Outcomes

After reading this chapter, you should be able to:

1 Perform a critique of the key assumption in finance and economics that humans (always) act rationally

2 Evaluate the potential impact of biases in human behaviour on managerial decision making

3 Explain the link between human psychology and agency problems

4 Discuss how lack of loyalty can be used to describe the classic principal-agent problem and how excessive loyalty can be used to identify a second type of agency problem

5 Assess the usefulness and limitations of possible solutions to behavioural biases

6 Appraise how gender and age differences may affect risk preferences

12.1 Introduction

While the corporate governance theory, such as the principal-agent model, reviewed in Chapter 1 predicts that conflicts of interests between economic actors result in value destruction or expropriation, this theory nevertheless assumes that all economic actors concerned behave *rationally*, i.e. they maximize their own utility. More generally, economics and finance assume that individuals are value-maximizing rational decision makers that make optimal decisions in an uncertain world based on all the information available at the time of the decision. In particular, the efficient market hypothesis (EMH), which is central to finance and essential to securities valuation models such as the capital asset pricing model (CAPM) and the arbitrage pricing theory (APT) model, states that securities prices always fully reflect all available information. Hence, market prices of securities are always a true and fair reflection of their value. This implies that mispricings, i.e. overvaluations and under-valuations, do not occur. Nevertheless, the occurrence of short-term mispricings does not necessarily call for the rejection of the EMH. Indeed, it seems reasonable to allow for the odd 'accident' or anomaly in the short run while expecting the hypothesis to be upheld over the long run. However, occurrences of persistent, i.e. long-term mispricings would provide a strong case for the rejection of the EMH.

The question that then arises is whether there are such incidences of persistent mispricings. The answer to this question seems straightforward (see also Section 9.2 of Chapter 9). The internet stock market bubble of the late 1990s and the ensuing global stock market crash of 2001–2 is just one case where stock markets got valuations wrong over the long run. At first, investors were overly optimistic about the valuations of internet stock. This was followed by the realization that stock prices had deviated too much from what could be considered their fair value. There are other more regularly occurring incidences of persistent mispricings. Such examples include pricing anomalies observed around IPOs (see Section 2.2 of Chapter 2 for a discussion of the IPO process). As discussed in Chapter 11, there is now ample and consistent empirical evidence from across the world that on average firms go public at a price, the offer price, which is too low when compared to the closing price on the first day of trading on the stock exchange. This suggests a clear, predictable pattern in stock prices around the IPO. Such predictable patterns violate the EMH. Indeed, if the EMH were valid, then such predictable patterns should not persist in the long term as investors would trade on these mispricings and quickly push securities prices back to their fair value. In addition, while IPO firms seem to be a good investment in the short run, they seem to underperform over the long term relative to other firms that have been on the stock market for a while and are of a similar size. Again, there is a clear, predictable pattern in prices here which violates the EMH.

The existence of persistent mispricings, such as those mentioned above as well as others, has urged academics and practitioners to seek possible explanations. Proponents of the EMH argue that these pricing anomalies are in actual fact only due to mismeasurement, in particular mismeasurement of the risk of the securities concerned. Hence, they are not true pricing anomalies. However, others argue that the reason for persistently mispriced securities can be found in human psychology. In other words, contrary to what classical economics and finance assume, humans may not always be fully rational. This limited or bounded rationality would then explain why markets get prices wrong and why such mispricings persist in the long run.

12.2 Bounded rationality

While economists and finance scholars started only in the 1980s with a systematic analysis of the effect of limited rationality of humans on decision making, the concept of bounded rationality had already been formalized in 1947 by Herbert Simon.[1] Humans are typically not able to analyze all the information available to them due to time constraints as well as limits to their cognitive resources. Limits to cognitive resources include limits to our intelligence or processing power, limits to our memory and limits to our attention span. Hence, given the time and cognitive constraints, humans frequently do not make optimal decisions, but make do with the best possible choice given these constraints.

Further, human evolution has wired our brains in such ways that we are able to deal with these constraints and the complex environment that surrounds us. As a result, we use rules of thumb to simplify the

---

[1]Simon, H.A. (1947), *Administrative Behavior*, New York: Free Press.

complexity of our environment.[2] These rules of thumb are also called heuristics, algorithms and mental modules. As this heuristic simplification is used by all humans, this may cause biases in human behaviour, resulting in systematic mistakes such as long-run mispricings in capital markets. However, heuristic simplification is only one possible source of systematic biases in human behaviour. There are at least five other such sources. These are:

- emotions
- social interactions
- self-deception
- risk taking and decision making according to gender and age
- reflexive loyalty

We shall now review all six of the above potential sources of biases in human behaviour and their likely impact on managerial and investor decision making.[3] While there is now a sizeable body of research on the impact of human psychology on decision making, research on the effects of behavioural biases on corporate governance is as yet limited. As the focus is on those behavioural biases that have been explicitly linked to corporate governance or should be so linked, this chapter does not claim to provide an exhaustive discussion of behavioural effects that influence decision making.

12.3 Heuristic simplification

As stated above, heuristic simplification is the way human evolution has hardwired our brains to enable us to make decisions in a complex environment, as we typically do not have sufficient time and sufficient cognitive resources to analyze decision problems in an optimal way. Given the limited time and cognitive resources:

- We focus on subsets of the information available.
- We analyze problems in isolation.
- We focus on similarities.
- We only slowly change our beliefs.

We shall now review the effects caused by each of the above consequences from our limited time and cognitive resources in detail.

12.3.1 FOCUSING ON SUBSETS OF INFORMATION

The effects caused by focusing on subsets of the information available rather than all of the information include the halo effect. The halo effect consists of admiring an exceptional characteristic of an individual and then widening this positive assessment to all the other characteristics of this individual. The halo effect may explain why in certain corporations everybody, including the members of the board of directors, is in awe of the CEO. While the CEO may have truly exceptional characteristics, this does not of course mean that he or

---

[2]Simon, H.A. (1956), 'Rational Choice and the Structure of Environments', *Psychological Review* 63, 129–38.
[3]Parts of this chapter are based on the excellent literature survey on behavioural finance by Hirshleifer, D. (2001), 'Investor Psychology and Asset Pricing', *Journal of Finance* 56, 1533–97. Readers who want to know more about human psychology and its effects on capital markets are strongly encouraged to read this survey article. Most of the examples and exercises in this chapter are taken from and/or adapted from the literature survey by Hilton, D.J. (2001), 'The Psychology of Financial Decision-Making: Applications to Trading, Dealing, and Investment Analysis', *Journal of Psychology and Financial Markets* 2, 37–53.

she is infallible. At worst, the halo effect may prevent other constituencies within the firm, such as the board of directors, from challenging the decisions of the CEO and ultimately lead to the corporation's failure.

12.3.2 ANALYZING PROBLEMS IN ISOLATION

Typically, we analyze decision problems in isolation, ignoring the broader context or environment surrounding them. In other words, we tend to compartmentalize decision problems or package or frame them in a narrow way. This can be done easily and safely for most problems. However, there is a danger of so-called narrow framing or packaging. This danger consists of the fact that the way the information is presented to the decision maker may influence the actual decision. Narrow framing may be caused purposefully. For example, a junior manager may present information about an investment opportunity in such a way that the investment's risk is difficult to assess by the senior management team in charge of approving new projects. Similarly, the CEO, the most senior executive in the corporation, may present information to the board of directors in a way that makes it cognitively costly to analyze and understand. This purposefully cognitively costly packaging of information may then make it difficult for the non-executive directors to scrutinize the information properly and to monitor the CEO's decision making.

Examples of compartmentalization or narrow framing or packaging include:

- mental accounting
- the disposition effect
- loss aversion
- the house money effect

Mental accounting consists of most investors keeping two separate accounts in their brains: one for the gains from their investments and another one for the losses. This kind of narrow framing may explain the so-called disposition effect. Empirical studies suggest that investors tend to sell winners, i.e. stock that has appreciated in value, too soon, but then hold on to losing stock for too long. The reason why investors treat losses differently from gains may be due to the fact that losses are perceived to be painful as they damage one's self-esteem, whereas gains create exactly the opposite effect. Hence, investors may postpone selling losers to avoid the painful realization of a loss. However, as a consequence, the eventual losses tend to be even more pronounced than they would have been had the stock been sold much earlier.

Another example of narrow packaging is loss aversion, which consists of the fact that most people are very risk averse and shy away even from very small risks. Loss aversion may be explained by the fact that we tend to turn a continuous return from an investment into a discrete return (see Figure 12.1) by distinguishing between two regions, i.e. the region for losses and that for gains, both of which are clearly separated by the break-even point. The fact that humans tend to simplify the continuous return from an investment, which could be situated anywhere on the horizontal bold line, by turning it into a dichotomous variable (a loss or a gain) may explain why most people do not like risks, even minor risks.

Figure 12.1 **Turning a continuous return into a discrete one**

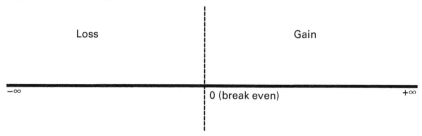

Finally, the house money effect is the greater willingness of people to gamble with money that they have recently won, e.g. in a casino. This behavioural pattern may be explained by the fact that the recent positive sensation of a gain may cancel out – or at least reduce – the possible future painful sensation of a loss. In a corporate context, a manager may be more willing to take on unnecessary risk after having had one or more highly successful projects.

12.3.3 FOCUSING ON SIMILARITIES

We tend to give too much attention to information that is perceived to be similar. In other words, we tend to be obsessed about creating stereotypes, often based on flimsy evidence. Two examples of our focus on similarities are the representativeness heuristic and gambler's fallacy. The representativeness heuristic consists of determining the probability of an event based on information judged to be typical or similar to that event. At first sight, there is nothing wrong with this heuristic. Essentially, this is what statistical analysis frequently is about: it involves the study of a sample of data in order to identify similarities within the sample and then to draw inferences from the sample for the population as a whole. However, in practice, most people tend to draw inferences from small samples that are too strong given the small sample size whereas the inferences they draw from large samples tend to be too weak. This implies that there is a systematic bias which can be predicted by the sample size or the number of observations.

Gambler's fallacy consists of mistakenly reading patterns into random events that are clearly independent of each other. The classic example of gambler's fallacy is that a lot of lottery players, when choosing the numbers to play, tend to avoid those numbers that have come up in recent draws. This implies that they turn a random event, the impending lottery draw, into a conditional event whose outcome depends on the outcomes from previous lottery draws. The main consequence will be that the lottery players in question will underestimate the probability of a given number coming up in the impending draw. For example, people who suffer from gambler's fallacy will avoid playing number 12 if that number has come up in recent lottery draws. However, the fact that number 12 has come up recently does not imply that its probability of being drawn tonight is reduced (or affected in any other way). Using statistical terminology, gambler's fallacy consists of mistakenly taking unconditional probabilities for conditional probabilities, thereby underestimating or underweighting the probability of an event. This is also referred to as base-rate underweighting.

12.3.4 WE ONLY SLOWLY CHANGE OUR BELIEFS

In certain circumstances, we tend to be conservative, i.e. we tend to change or update our beliefs less frequently than would be rational. This bias is exactly the opposite of the one we have just reviewed. While base-rate underweighting is about *overreacting* to information, conservatism is about *underreacting* to information. In other words, base-rate underweighting is about excessive reliance on the strength of an information signal (i.e. how extreme it is) whereas conservatism is about underreliance on the weight (i.e. the reliability) of the information. Given these contrasting biases, which one is likely to prevail? Evidence suggests that we are more likely to suffer from conservatism if the information we are dealing with is cognitively costly to analyze. Examples include statistical and abstract information such as sample size.

12.4 Emotions

Emotions, such as anger, resentment and love, are another reason why humans do not always act rationally. At worst, our emotions may be so strong in certain circumstances that we end up suffering from a loss of self-control, i.e. our emotions take over and our intelligence takes second place.

Evidence from experiments suggests that people who are in a good mood are less critical and spend less time analyzing the information they are presented with than people who are in a bad mood. More generally, there is some empirical evidence that stock market prices are affected by a medical condition called seasonal affective disorder (SAD) which consists of an individual suffering from clinical depression during the winter months when the days are short and the amount of daylight is very limited compared to the summer months. Some empirical studies suggest that there is a correlation between the amount of daylight across the seasons and stock returns: stock returns are higher during the dark winter months than during the brighter summer months in the Northern hemisphere and the increase in stock returns during the winter months is more pronounced in countries that are closer to the North Pole.[4] The higher stock returns in winter may then compensate for the increased risk aversion among the population of investors due to SAD.

Again, it is important to put all of the above into context. Indeed, according to neurologist Antonio Damasio, rational decision making is not just driven by the mind, but also by our emotions and body.[5] In other words, there may also be something called emotional intelligence.[6] For example, we may have the gut feeling that one possible alternative is definitely bad and should not be chosen. This would then leave us with fewer alternatives to choose from and simplify the decision problem at hand.

12.5 Social interactions

An individual's behaviour and decisions are influenced by the interactions the individual has with other members of his or her social group. In particular, people tend to conform to the beliefs and behaviours of others. However, this so-called conformity effect (or herding) also depends on an individual's country, including the country's culture, religion and history. Some cultures are more conformist (e.g. Japan and China) whereas others are more individualistic (e.g. the UK and USA).[7] However, similar to the other behavioural patterns reviewed so far, the conformity effect is not all bad and it has been wired into human brains by evolution to deal with the limited amounts of time and cognitive resources we have. In other words, I may dress like everybody else in my social circle as this will give me more time and energy to spend on activities I perceive to be more interesting and worthwhile.

An important means of social interaction is conversation. However, conversation tends to be a poor means of communication for at least three reasons. First, the subject of most conversations tends to be information which is already known to all the participants to the conversation rather than information which is only known by one of the participants. Second, conversations are subject to time constraints. Third, the type and complexity of information conveyed via a conversation are also limited. In order to deal with these constraints, information conveyed via conversations tends to be sharpened and oversimplified. As a result, listeners in a conversation might end up shifting their beliefs to extremes.

Other effects caused by social interactions include the fundamental attribution error, the false consensus effect and the curse of knowledge. The fundamental attribution error consists of underestimating external factors and overestimating the importance of a person's mindset when explaining that person's actions. For example, the non-executive directors may think that the CEO has decided to grant himself as well as the other executives stock options to improve the executive directors' incentives to maximize firm value. However, the real reason for

---

[4]See Kamstra, M.J., Kramer, L.A. and Levi, M.D. (2003), 'Winter Blues: A SAD Stock Market Cycle', *American Economic Review* 93, 324–43.
[5]Damasio, A.R. (1994), *Descartes' Error: Emotion, Reason, and the Human Brain*, New York: Putnam Publishing.
[6]The concept of emotional intelligence (EI) is more far reaching than *using* of emotions in decision making. According to the four-branch model, EI also refers to *perceiving*, *understanding* and *managing* our own emotions as well as those of others. See e.g. Salovey, P. and Grewal, D. (2005), 'The Science of Emotional Intelligence', *Current Directions in Psychological Science* 14, 281–5.
[7]See the sociologist Geert Hofstede's website on the degree of conformity or individualism in various countries: www.geert-hofstede.com/. Hofstede's work on the links between national cultures and organizational cultures is highly recognized.

granting the stock options is that the CEO believes that the firm's stock is undervalued and that its price will inevitably rise in the future, making the stock options highly valuable. The **false consensus effect** consists of people having a tendency to assume that others share their opinions more than they actually do. Finally, the **curse of knowledge** consists of assuming that others who have less knowledge have more similar beliefs than they actually have. It is important for the members of the board of directors as well as the members of board committees, such as the remuneration, nomination and audit committees, to be aware of these possible effects as they are likely to bias their assessment of the performance and the intentions of the executive team.

12.6 Self-deception

The two main forms of self-deception are **overconfidence** and **confirmatory bias**. Most of us suffer from overconfidence. Overconfidence is the tendency of overestimating one's skills, abilities and knowledge. Men tend to suffer more from overconfidence than women and the difference in overconfidence between genders is higher for tasks that are perceived to be more masculine.[8] Experts also tend to suffer from overconfidence in situations where the information to be treated is opaque and highly complex. CEOs have also been shown to be more prone to overconfidence than other executives.[9] For overconfidence to persist in the long run, it needs to be coupled with another effect. Indeed, an individual who is a rational learner will discover over time that he has been wrong more often than he expected to be. This other effect is biased self-attribution. **Biased self-attribution** consists of imputing positive outcomes to one's own doing and imputing negative outcomes to external factors. Whereas rational learning would make an individual less overconfident over time, biased self-attribution increases overconfidence over time.

Richard Roll argued that managerial overconfidence, or what he calls hubris, explains why so many mergers and acquisitions fail to realize the expected gains or synergies.[10] **Hubris** would here consist of the bidding managers overestimating the gains from mergers. While the majority of mergers and acquisitions are unsuccessful, individual bidding managers may believe that their skills are superior to those of other managers, preventing them from following the same fate as the majority (see Box 12.1). Mathew Hayward and Donald Hambrick tested Roll's hubris hypothesis for a sample of 106 large US acquisitions.[11] They used four different measures of CEO hubris, or what they called exaggerated self-confidence. The first one is the acquiring firm's recent performance. The second one is recent praise in the media of the CEO. The third one is the CEO's self-importance proxied by the amount of the CEO's salary relative to the salaries of the other executives. Finally, they also used a measure which aggregates the previous three measures. Hayward and Hambrick found that on average acquisitions destroy shareholder value for the acquiring firm, confirming the results obtained by other studies on the wealth effects of mergers and acquisitions. However, more importantly, they found evidence that all four measures of CEO hubris increase the wealth loss to the shareholders of the acquirer and that the impact of the former on the latter is even more pronounced for acquirers with weak corporate governance. Their proxies for weak corporate governance are the absence of board independence and CEO-chairman duality. Apart from bad acquisition decisions, CEO overconfidence has also been shown to result in overinvestment, financial constraints (as reflected by a heightened sensitivity of investment to cash flows) and reduced dividends.[12] In turn, CEO overconfidence reduces firm value and performance.

---

[8] See also Section 7.6 of Chapter 7 for a discussion of the evidence on differences in risk taking between genders.
[9] Goel, A.M. and Thakor, A.V. (2008), 'Overconfidence, CEO Selection, and Corporate Governance', *Journal of Finance* 63, 2737–84; Graham, J.R., Harvey, C.R. and Puri, M. (2013), 'Managerial Attitude and Corporate Actions', *Journal of Financial Economics* 109,103–21.
[10] Roll, R. (1986), 'The Hubris Hypothesis of Corporate Takeovers', *Journal of Business* 59, 197–216.
[11] Hayward, M.L.A and Hambrick, D.C. (1997), 'Explaining the Premiums Paid for Large Acquisitions: Evidence of CEO Hubris', *Administrative Science Quarterly* 42, 103–27.
[12] See Malmendier, U. and Tate, G. (2005), 'CEO Optimism and Corporate Investment', *Journal of Finance* 60, 2661–700; Malmendier, U., Tate, G. and Yan, J. (2011), 'Overconfidence and Early-life Experience: The Effect of Managerial Traits on Corporate Financial Policies', *Journal of Finance* 66, 1687–733; Banerjee, S., Humphery-Jenner, M. and Nanda, V. (2015), 'Restraining Overconfident CEOs through Improved Governance: Evidence from the Sarbanes-Oxley Act', *Review of Financial Studies* 28, 2812–58.

Box 12.1
Hubris, overarching vanity and how one man's ego brought banking to the brink

The arrogance of the disgraced former boss of the Royal Bank of Scotland, Sir Fred Goodwin, always has been his most striking feature.

He was a banker who always knew better than anyone else, was contemptuous of his competitors on the High Street and had convinced himself that when it came to takeovers – whether they were in Britain, the United States, China or, finally, Holland – there was no one to match his genius.

Now, we all know differently. His bank has moved from being among the world's largest lenders to corporate dunce.

The loss of GBP28 billion we now know it ran up over the past year is the biggest ever made by a British company and consigns RBS to the fate of public ownership for years, if not decades, to come.

Yet to the very end, when he was finally removed from office by the Treasury in November, Goodwin behaved as if he still walked on water. The former chief executive described the process under which the Government poured in new capital in November as 'more like a drive-by shooting than a negotiation'.

This despite the fact that his bank was in desperate trouble and almost certainly would have collapsed without the initial slug of GBP20 billion of taxpayers' money injected by Gordon Brown in October 2008.

This, however, was typical Goodwin. When he was once asked at a press conference whether he had any interest in taking over any of the former building societies, he ruthlessly retorted that he was 'more likely to be involved in mercy killings'.

Goodwin had begun to believe in his own myths. As a result of his success in turning around the ailing NatWest, he came to believe that no deal was beyond his capacity.

It was this extraordinary overconfidence, fuelled by macho rivalry with Barclays, which led Goodwin into the merger with Dutch bank ABN Amro in October 2007 when the credit crunch – as exemplified by the run on Northern Rock – had already begun.

Yet Goodwin, unchallenged by a board of Scottish panjandrums, looked to be blissfully ignorant of the fact that the world was changing dramatically.

Even after RBS had turned to shareholders in June 2008, raising GBP12 billion from the nation's pension fund and insurers amid the International Monetary Fund's warnings of the worst financial crisis since the Great Depression, his self-assurance was unshaken.

In late July last year, I was Goodwin's guest for lunch at the group's towering City of London headquarters on Broadgate. Mistakenly, the taxi had dropped me next door at ABN Amro's former London headquarters, which had already been re-badged as the Royal Bank of Scotland.

The Edinburgh bank, it seemed, had not just one City headquarters but two, not to mention its glittering corporate citadel north of the border. It had doubled up on office space in much the same way as it would double up on balance sheet losses.

Over his starter of pigeon salad, Goodwin openly mocked journalists and analysts like myself who had dared question the wisdom of a GBP50 billion banking takeover at a time when the American subprime mortgage crisis had caused devastation to global finance.

The RBS share of the deal, he explained, would be a mere GBP10billion after disposals. Profits, he boasted, would be boosted in 2008 by GBP600 million as a result of the deal and eventually by an estimated GBP3 billion a year.

'Fred the Shred', as he was known after the management bloodbath he oversaw at NatWest, would be taking his meat cleaver to costs at ABN Amro – among the highest in global banking.

When I questioned him about the potential liabilities that RBS and ABN Amro were exposed to on the wholesale money markets – where we know both banks suffered massively – he suggested that the scale of the losses was

(Continued)

containable and that adequate provision had been made for them in the balance sheet. He even suggested that the money would come back.

His self-belief was infectious.

It is of course natural for businessmen, when talking to the financial press, to put the best gloss on matters. The hope is always that we will return to our offices and write nice things about the company concerned.

But after a three-course meal accompanied by fine wine, a two hour teach-in on the brilliance of the ABN Amro deal and how it would help make RBS the top bank in India and the Far East – where it was well developed – the deal still seemed to me to be daft.

If the bidding for ABN Amro had become too heady for Goodwin's rival John Varley, the chief executive of Barclays, then surely RBS should have had pause too?

Looking back at that lunch, with the benefit of knowing what has happened since, there seems to me that there are only two possibilities. Either Goodwin was lying through his teeth, which I somewhat doubt, or he was actually delusional.

Banks, like politicians, like to put the best complexion on events. This is particularly important for financial institutions where confidence is crucial. Clearly, I could not have expected the RBS chief to say he had made a dreadful mistake, that RBS shareholders and the taxpayers were in for record-breaking losses and the bank's independence was doomed.

However, the scale of his naivety, in the light of all that was happening in the banking world and the collapse of the American housing market (to which RBS was exposed through its Citizens offshoot in the United States), was, in retrospect, breathtaking.

The downward spiral since that meeting in July 2008 has been astonishing in its speed. A bank which can trace its origins back to 1727, when it was set up as a commercial rival to the 'Jacobite' Bank of Scotland, is now all but nationalised, with the Government owning 70 per cent.

Just days after my conversations with Goodwin, the bank revealed a loss of GBP691million, after writing down bad loans of GBP5.9 billion, a loss which has now ballooned to an astonishing GBP28 billion.

What is really worrying is that despite putting a new team in charge, which has sought to clear out the mess, the skeletons keep tumbling out of the cupboard.

In addition to its exposure to toxic 'sub-prime' mortgages, the bank has bad loans outstanding to failed Russian oligarchs and property around the world, at a time when real estate values are in freefall.

None of this, or the huge losses taken by investors including the Government, should affect Sir Fred's retirement.

He may no longer have his suite at the Savoy Hotel in London or be able to enjoy fresh scallops from the kitchens of the bank's folie de grandeur HQ on the outskirts of Edinburgh.

But any hardship should be cushioned by the GBP4.2million paycheck he collected in 2007, his last full year at the helm, and a pension pot worth GBP8.37 million. Nor, according to highly placed sources, need he fear legal action from shareholders.

Goodwin's strategy of rapid growth in the credit-fuelled years of the past decade led him confidently into a merger with ABN Amro which was doomed to failure because of its appalling timing. But he cannot take the blame alone.

He was loyally supported by a board of directors which refused to put brakes on the person they regarded as a financial maestro.

Moreover, he was egged on by City adviser Merrill Lynch and others who earned a great payday from the takeover deal.

Most significantly, however, it was his own ego which, ultimately, was his downfall. It made him delusional about the direction of the world economy and his ability to create value when everyone else was losing faith in the credit bubble.

As a result of Goodwin's and the bank's hubris, the prosperity not only of the RBS but the whole nation has been betrayed.

Source: Brummer, A. (2009), 'Hubris, Overarching Vanity and How One Man's Ego Brought Banking to the Brink', 20 January, *Daily Mail*, no page number given.

Finally, most people also tend to suffer from confirmatory bias, i.e. they tend to spend too little time on evidence that contradicts their beliefs and discard it as bad luck or bad data. This is potentially a very dangerous bias to suffer from for CEOs having invested in novel projects such as new products and services. While market feedback may be negative suggesting that the project is likely to fail, the CEO may discard these signals as bad data and carry on with the project rather than abandon it.

12.7 Gender and age

Evidence from empirical studies as well as economics experiments[13] suggests the following differences in preferences between genders:

- Women are more risk averse than men and more cautious in their investment decisions. However, there is also evidence that this gender difference in risk preferences only applies to whites but not to other ethnic groups. Melissa Finucane and colleagues termed this the 'white male' effect.[14] Renate Schubert and colleagues have also found that framing matters: when lotteries are framed as losses rather than gains, men become more risk averse than women.[15] There is evidence from the finance literature that women are more risk averse as to their investment decisions and also more conservative in terms of financial reporting.[16]
- Social preferences include altruism, envy, inequality aversion and reciprocity. Experiments indicate that gender differences in social preferences vary across different studies and settings. For example, in some settings women have been shown to be more trusting than men. The reason for this seems to be that women react more strongly to social cues which change across experimental designs and implementations.
- Women are less likely to engage in competition, such as auctions, bargaining and tournaments, than men. In addition to increased male participation in competitions, male performance is also enhanced in competitive settings whereas female performance is reduced. Importantly, these differences in the willingness to engage in competitive behaviour can be both explained by nurture and by nature. This suggests that training might be a way forward to mitigate this gender difference.

John Coates and Joe Herbert found evidence that human biology and, in particular, gender differences in hormones drive risk-taking behaviour.[17] Their research suggested that testosterone in male stock-exchange traders has two contrasting effects. At first, an increase in testosterone has a positive impact on traders'

---

[13]See Croson, R. and Gneezy, U. (2009), 'Gender Differences in Preferences', *Journal of Economic Literature* 47, 1–27, for a review of this literature.

[14]Finucane, M.L., Slovic, P., Mertz, C.K., Flynn, J. and Satterfield, T.A. (2000), 'Gender, Race, and Perceived Risk: The "White Male" Effect', *Health, Risk and Society* 2, 159–72.

[15]Schubert, R., Brown, M., Gysler and Brachinger, H.W. (1999), 'Financial Decision-Making: Are Women Really More Risk-Averse?' *American Economic Review* 89, 381–5.

[16]See e.g. Krishnan, G. and Parsons, L. (2008), 'Getting to the Bottom Line: An Exploration of Gender and Earnings Quality', *Journal of Business Ethics* 78, 65–76; Barua, A., Davidson, L., Rama, D. and Thiruvadi, S. (2010), 'CFO Gender and Accruals Quality', *Accounting Horizons* 24, 25–39; Faccio, M., Marchica, M.T. and Mura, R. (2016), 'CEO Gender, Corporate Risk-Taking, and the Efficiency of Capital Allocation', *Journal of Corporate Finance* 39, 193–209.

[17]Coates J.M. and Herbert, J. (2008), 'Endogenous Steroids and Financial Risk Taking on a London Trading Floor', *Proceedings of the National Academy of Sciences of the United States of America* 105, 6167–72.

performance as it makes them more persistent, more willing to take on risk and seek novelty. However, if testosterone continues to increase and takes on persistently high levels, rational decision making may suffer, and risk that does not increase expected performance but only creates more volatility may be sought. Testosterone has also been shown to decline significantly with age, suggesting that excessive risk-taking behaviour is mainly an issue with younger males.[18]

Another study by Yuping Jia, Laurence van Lent and Yachang Zeng suggested that there is a link between facial masculinity and financial misreporting.[19] As highlighted by the above study, testosterone affects behaviour. However, it has also been shown to influence the development of the facial shape. This might explain why the facial shape of a male executive is correlated with the likelihood of the executive engaging in financial misreporting.

Research by Anita Woolley and Thomas Malone suggested that the collective intelligence of a team increases with the percentage of women being part of the team while it does not increase with the intelligence quotients (IQs) of the individuals forming the team.[20] Woolley and Malone administered standard intelligence tests to randomly formed teams, which included decision making as well as complex problem solving. They found that teams with more women managed to earn higher collective IQs than teams with fewer women and that the members of teams dominated by very intelligent people were unlikely to listen to each other and engage in constructive criticism.

Finally, there is an emerging literature which suggests that differences in age between the board members, in particular between the CEO and the chairman, have corporate governance consequences as well as valuation consequences. For example, Marc Goergen, Peter Limbach and Meik Scholz found that a greater age difference between the CEO and the chairman increases the monitoring intensity of the board and improves firm value for firms with greater monitoring needs.[21]

Although this research is still at an early stage, it nevertheless suggests that board diversity, in relation to both gender and age, may be good in terms of risk management, i.e. in terms of avoiding unnecessary and excessive risk taking (see also Section 7.6 of Chapter 7).

12.8 How can these behavioural issues be addressed?

One way to increase awareness of these behavioural issues and to reduce their impact on corporate decision making is to improve managers' education. However, this may be easier said than done. It is also likely that those suffering the most from behavioural biases, such as overconfidence, are the least likely to engage in life-long training and learning. Another way to mitigate psychological biases is to ensure that boards of directors are effective and that they rein in bad decision making by managers, in particular the CEO. However, from Section 7.4 of Chapter 7 we know that there is little evidence that independent directors are effective monitors.

[18]Ferrini, R.L. and Barrett-Connor, E. (1998), 'Sex Hormones and Age: A Cross-sectional Study of Testosterone and Estradiol and Their Bioavailable Fractions in Community-dwelling Men', *American Journal of Epidemiology* 147, 750–4.

[19]Jia, Y., van Lent, L. and Zeng, Y. (2014), 'Masculinity, Testosterone, and Financial Misreporting', *Journal of Accounting Research* 52, 1195–246.

[20]Woolley, A. and Malone, T. (2011), 'What Makes a Team Smarter? More Women', *Harvard Business Review* 89, 32–3.

[21]Goergen, M., Limbach, P. and Scholz, M. (2015), 'Mind the Gap: The Age Difference between the CEO and the Chair', *Journal of Corporate Finance* 35, 136–58.

Why is there little evidence of a link between board independence and firm performance and value? One possible answer, which was provided in Chapter 7, is that the current board composition, including the percentage of non-executives, is not exogenous and is likely to be the result of past performance and corporate governance issues. For example, if a firm performed badly in the past, executives may have been put under pressure by the shareholders to appoint more independent directors. Hence, that firm may have good current performance, but may now have a large number of independent directors on its board given its bad past performance whereas another firm with equally good current performance may have a much lower number given that its past performance has always been good. The next section will revisit the issue as to the lack of evidence on the effectiveness of non-executives.

A somewhat different way of addressing behavioural issues – or at the very least reducing the likelihood of bad decisions – is to conduct for each project what Gary Klein called a *pre-mortem*.[22] Klein defined a pre-mortem as the hypothetical opposite of a post-mortem. A medical post-mortem is conducted to find out the reasons for the death of a patient. Everybody benefits from the post-mortem, except for the patient who is already dead. Similarly, in a business setting the focus tends to be on finding the reasons why a project has failed. However, at this stage the damage has been done and all one can do is draw lessons from this failure. Klein argued that to reduce the likelihood of a project failing, before starting a project, executives should go through the scenario that the project has failed badly and come up with reasons why it has failed. Once everybody has stated their reasons for the disastrous failure of the project, the project leader should then go back to the drawing board. Klein argued that this will avoid cognitive biases such as confirmatory bias whereby the proposer of the project discards possible weaknesses of the project as bad data.

12.9 Reflexive loyalty

Randall Morck proposed another possible reason for the observed lack of a relationship between corporate performance and board composition.[23] He argued that there are two distinct principal-agent problems rather than just one as suggested by the Jensen and Meckling principal-agent theory (see Chapter 1).[24] Each of these can be described by making reference to loyalty. The **type I agency problem** is the classic, Jensen and Meckling agency problem between the managers and the shareholders. It is caused by the managers acting in their own interests rather than performing their duty of looking after the shareholders' interests. It consists of managers being disloyal to their principals, i.e. the shareholders. The **type II agency problem** is caused by excessive loyalty to one's principal (the CEO or large shareholder) rather than a lack of loyalty. Morck argued that corporate scandals such as Enron, Hollinger and Worldcom have been caused by misplaced loyalty of directors to powerful CEOs (see also Box 12.1 earlier). This problem is caused by a behavioural bias which consists of a reflex for loyalty to figures of authorities.

[22]Klein, G. (2007), 'Performing a Project *Premortem*', *Harvard Business Review* (September), 18–19.
[23]Morck, R. (2008), 'Behavioral Finance in Corporate Governance: Economics and Ethics of the Devil's Advocate', *Journal of Management and Governance* 12, 179–200.
[24]Jensen, M. and Meckling, W. (1976), 'Theory of the Firm. Managerial Behavior, Agency Costs and Capital Structure', *Journal of Financial Economics* 3, 305–60.

Morck derived his type II agency problem from the experiments on human subjects conducted during the 1960s by Stanley Milgram, professor of social psychology at Yale.[25] The subjects were recruited via newspaper ads and paid for their participation. They were told that the experiments were about the effects of punishment on learning and memory. Each subject would act as a 'teacher' who would ask questions to a 'learner'. The subject would then administer an electric shock of a certain voltage to the learner for every wrong answer. Unbeknown to the subject, the learner was a professional actor and the machine administering the electric shock a fake. The electric switches on the machine were labelled from 15V to 450V and were also labelled with the intensity of the pain ('slight' through 'very strong' through 'danger: severe' and 'XXX'). Each time the learner would give a wrong answer, the severity of the electric shock would increase and the actor feign increasing levels of pain. A psychologist would be present at the experiments. Milgram found that more than 60 per cent of the American subjects were happy to go all the way to 450V. Milgram's experiments were repeated across other countries and cultures and the results were similar. The results were also similar across genders suggesting that women were not more compassionate than men.

Milgram followed up with his subjects and asked them why they had behaved the way they had. Many were very upset about the experience, but justified it with words such as 'loyalty' and 'duty'. Milgram concluded that humans have a reflex for loyalty, i.e. loyalty is hardwired into human brains. Prehistoric men who were loyal to their tribal leader were more likely to survive. Through evolution this resulted in loyalty being hardwired into the human brain.

Morck argued that in the boardroom directors have a tendency to be loyal to their leader, the CEO, rather than to ask probing questions and challenge his/her decisions. This may explain why studies that look at the effects of boards on corporate performance (see Chapter 7) have found little evidence of any effects.

The question that then arises is how this reflex for loyalty can be mitigated and how boards of directors can be encouraged to be more critical of the CEO. Milgram performed many variants of his experiment. One consisted of having three 'teachers', two dissenting teachers plus the actual subject. At 150V, the first fake teacher would walk out in protest. The second fake teacher would then walk out at 210V. The two 'dissenting peers' caused a huge increase in disobedience. While in the basic version of the experiment, more than 60 per cent of subjects had gone all the way to 450V, in the experiment with the two dissenting 'teachers' this percentage dropped to 10 per cent.

Morck argued that boards of directors should be designed in ways that promote disloyalty to the CEO (or the large shareholder), i.e. in ways that prevent type II agency problems. Both the US Sarbanes-Oxley Act and the UK Higgs Report, as well as the Guidance on Board Effectiveness by the UK's Financial Reporting Council (FRC) issued in March 2011, seem to have adopted that approach by stressing the role of non-executives on the board of directors as well as the importance of their independence. One way of avoiding type II agency problems would then be to reduce the dominance of the CEO. Remember the framing effect we discussed in Section 12.3. The CEO may influence the board's decision by the way he/she presents the information discussed during the board meetings. The Higgs Report recommended that the CEO should not chair board meetings. However, this also has costs as it may give too much power to less well-informed outsiders who may then dominate the boardroom discussions and make corporate decision making more difficult and less effective. Hence, there is a trade-off between keeping the power of the CEO in check and ensuring the effectiveness of executive decision making.

[25]Milgram, S. (1963), 'Behavioral Study of Obedience', *Journal of Abnormal and Social Psychology* 67, 371–8; and Milgram, S. (1974), *Obedience to Authority*, New York: Harper & Row.

12.10 Conclusions

While the concept of bounded human rationality was formalized by Herbert Simon in the late 1940s, finance and economics research has been slow to admit that humans may not always be guided by rationality. The potential sources for biases in human behaviour are as follows:

Bounded rationality

- heuristic simplification
- emotions
- social interactions
- overconfidence or hubris
- reflexive loyalty or the type II agency problem

Heuristic simplification relates to the fact that humans use rules of thumb to simplify the complex environment they deal with and to make decisions under cognitive and time constraints. While heuristics usually work well, they may nevertheless, under certain circumstances, cause systemic biases in human behaviour.

Heuristic simplification

Another possible source of bias in human decision making is emotions. Emotions such as love, envy and anger may prevent us from making rational decisions. For example, experiments suggest that people in a good mood tend to be less critical than those in a bad mood. In addition, empirical research suggests that seasonal affective disorder (SAD) drives share prices and explains why there is a positive correlation between stock returns and the lack of daylight in winter.

Emotions

The actions and decisions of human beings are also influenced by their social interactions. For example, humans tend to conform to other members of their social group or culture. However, the degree of this conformity effect depends on a country's culture, history and religion.

Social interactions

In addition, most of us tend to overestimate our own knowledge, abilities and skills, i.e. we are overconfident. Anecdotal evidence as well as the consistent empirical evidence on the lacklustre performance of corporate mergers and acquisitions suggest that CEOs of bidding firms may be subject to hubris or overconfidence when making their acquisition decisions.

Overconfidence and hubris

Randall Morck proposed a second agency problem, the type II agency problem. While the classical principal-agent problem, which he referred to as the type I agency problem, stems from a lack of loyalty of the executives to their shareholders, the type II agency problem is caused by the excessive loyalty of the board members to the CEO. Humans have this excessive loyalty to figures of authority hardwired into their brains given that throughout human evolution the survival of humans loyal to their tribal leader has been greater than that of disloyal humans.

Reflexive loyalty

While it may be relatively easy to be aware of these behavioural issues, it is much less easy to address them properly and to mitigate the adverse effects they may have on corporate decision making. Reducing the dominance of the CEO may be one way forward. However, this may then increase the power of less well-informed outsiders (e.g. non-executives and institutional investors) who may be subject to their own agency problems. More generally, board meetings should be

Reducing behavioural biases

conducted in such a way that they are not dominated by the CEO and that the non-executive directors have ample opportunities to question and scrutinize the validity of the decisions and policies proposed by the executives. Executives should also consider carrying out a so-called pre-mortem before embarking on major projects.

12.11 Discussion questions

1 In 1984, the magazine *The Economist* asked four ex-finance ministers of OECD countries, four chairmen of multinationals, four Oxford University economics students and four dustbin men to predict several economic factors for the OECD ten years ahead. The factors to be predicted included the average growth rate, the average inflation rate, the price of petrol in 1994 and when Singapore's GDP would exceed that of Australia. In 1994, the magazine revisited the predictions of each of the above four groups and checked their accuracy against the actual numbers. The winners were jointly the businessmen and the dustbin men, followed by the students and the last were the ex-finance ministers. What behavioural bias does the result of this experiment illustrate?

2 How can boardrooms be turned into forums for constructively discussing and challenging the CEO's proposed strategic choices rather than places that just rubber-stamp the latter?

3 'Misplaced loyalty lies at the heart of virtually every recent scandal in corporate governance'. (Morck, R. (2008), 'Behavioral Finance in Corporate Governance: Economics and Ethics of the Devil's Advocate', *Journal of Management and Governance* 12, p.180.)

Discuss the above statement with particular relevance to the arguments advanced by Morck (2008).

12.12 Exercises

1 You are forced to enter the following gamble which is characterized as follows. There is:

- a 75 per cent chance of losing £7,600 and
- a 25 per cent chance of winning £2,400

You are now offered £100 before you are told the outcome of the gamble. If you accept the £100, your total payoff after the gamble will be:

- a 75 per cent chance of losing £7,500 and
- a 25 per cent chance of winning £2,500

(a) Does it make sense to accept the £100?

(b) You now face the following two *concurrent* decision problems. You need to choose between A and B *as well as* between C and D.

Option A consists of a sure gain of £2,400 and option B is a gamble characterized by a 25 per cent chance

of winning £10,000 and a 75 per cent chance of winning nothing. So, choose between A and B. Option C is a sure loss of £7,500 and option D consists of a gamble characterized by a 75 per cent chance of losing £10,000 and a 25 per cent chance of losing nothing. Choose between C and D.

2 Imagine 100 bags. The bags are opaque and there is no way of determining the exact content of each bag without turning the bag upside down and shaking out its contents, which is not allowed. Each bag contains 1,000 tokens. Forty-five of the bags contain 700 black and 300 red tokens, i.e. a majority of black tokens. The remaining 55 bags contain 300 black and 700 red tokens, i.e. a majority of red tokens. One bag is selected at random.

(a) What is the probability that this bag contains mostly black tokens?

(b) Twelve tokens are drawn from this bag, *with replacement*. This means that after a token has been drawn and its colour has been recorded, it is placed back in the bag. As a result, there are always 1,000 tokens in the bag before each draw. The result of the 12 draws is eight black tokens and four red tokens. Based on this new information, what is the probability that this randomly selected bag is one of the bags with mostly black tokens?

3 There are four cards in front of you and you can only see the side of each card facing you:

Please test the validity of the following hypothesis
  'All cards with a vowel on one side have an even number on the other side'
  by turning over the card(s) and only those that will determine its validity.

Reading list

Key reading

Croson, R. and Gneezy, U. (2009), 'Gender Differences in Preferences', *Journal of Economic Literature* 47, 1–27.

Hirshleifer, D. (2001), 'Investor Psychology and Asset Pricing', *Journal of Finance* 56, 1533–97.

Morck, R. (2008), 'Behavioral Finance in Corporate Governance: Economics and Ethics of the Devil's Advocate', *Journal of Management and Governance* 12, 179–200.

Roll, R. (1986), 'The Hubris Hypothesis of Corporate Takeovers', *Journal of Business* 59, 197–216.

Woolley, A. and Malone, T. (2011), 'What Makes a Team Smarter? More Women', *Harvard Business Review* 89, 32–33.

Further reading

De Jong, A. (2009), 'Irrational Executives and Corporate Governance', *International Journal of Corporate Governance* 1, 285–97.

Forbes, W. (2009), *Behavioural Finance*, Chichester, UK: John Wiley & Sons.

Goel, A.M. and Thakor, A.V. (2008), 'Overconfidence, CEO Selection, and Corporate Governance', *Journal of Finance* 63, 2737–84.

Goergen, M., Limbach, P. and Scholz, M. (2015), 'Mind the Gap. The Age Difference between the CEO and the Chair', *Journal of Corporate Finance* 35, 136–58.

Graham, J.R., Harvey, C.R. and Puri, M. (2013), 'Managerial Attitude and Corporate Actions', *Journal of Financial Economics* 109, 103–21.

Hayward, M.L.A and Hambrick, D.C. (1997), 'Explaining the Premiums Paid for Large Acquisitions: Evidence of CEO Hubris', *Administrative Science Quarterly* 42, 103–27.

Hilton, D.J. (2001), 'The Psychology of Financial Decision-Making: Applications to Trading, Dealing, and Investment Analysis', *Journal of Psychology and Financial Markets* 2, 37–53.

Kent, D., Hirshleifer, D. and Teoh, S.H. (2002), 'Investor Psychology in Capital Markets: Evidence and Policy Implications', *Journal of Monetary Economics* 49, 139–209.

Klein, G. (2007), 'Performing a Project Premortem', *Harvard Business Review* (September), 18–19.

Milgram, S. (1963), 'Behavioral Study of Obedience', *Journal of Abnormal and Social Psychology* 67, 371–8.

Milgram, S. (1974), *Obedience to Authority*, New York: Harper & Row.

Salovey, P. and Grewal, D. (2005), 'The Science of Emotional Intelligence', *Current Directions in Psychological Science* 14, 281–5.

Shefrin, H. (1999), *Beyond Greed and Fear*, Financial Management Association Survey and Synthesis Series, Cambridge, MA: Harvard Business School Press.

Corporate governance
and stakeholders

PART IV

13 Corporate social responsibility and socially responsible investment

Chapter Aims

In the context of the diminishing role of governments and increasing economic globalization, large corporations are under pressure from various stakeholder groups to reassess the impact their activities have on the environment and society at large. Badly handled cases of environmental accidents, product failures, etc. can have a substantial impact on the firm's value and its market share for decades to follow. However, the literature shows that not all types of corporate policies of stakeholder management pay off. Indeed, some policies destroy rather than create firm value. The chapter reviews this literature. It also reviews the increasing importance of indices of corporate social responsibility as well as socially responsible investment.

Learning Outcomes

After reading this chapter, you should be able to:

1 Critically review the studies that investigate the impact of corporate social responsibility (CSR) on firm value and vice-versa

2 Describe some of the CSR indices that are available from commercial providers and evaluate their usefulness

3 Discuss the definitions of CSR and socially responsible investment (SRI) and how these may change with an investor's set of values

4 Assess the evidence on whether investors pay a price for SRI

13.1 Introduction

'Did you ever expect a corporation to have a conscience, when it has no soul to be damned, and no body to be kicked?'

EDWARD, FIRST BARON THURLOW 1731–1806, LORD CHANCELLOR DURING KING GEORGE III'S REIGN

CSR is also sometimes referred to as environmental, social and governance (ESG) issues. In this book, we shall adopt the former term. Craig Carter, Rahul Kale and Curtis Grimm defined CSR as follows[1]: '[Corporate] social responsibility deals with the managerial consideration of non-market forces or social aspects of corporate activity outside of a market or regulatory framework and includes consideration of issues such as employee welfare, community programs, charitable donations, and environmental protection'.

[1]Carter, C.R., Kale, R. and Grimm, C.M. (2000), 'Environmental Purchasing and Firm Performance: An Empirical Investigation', *Transportation Research Part E: Logistics and Transportation Review* 36, 219–28.

The two sides of the debate on CSR are best illustrated by the following two quotes:

There is one and only one social responsibility of business – to use its resources and engage in activities designed to increase its profits so long as it stays within the rules of the game, which is to say, engages in open and free competition without deception or fraud. Milton Friedman[2]

The idea that business is about maximizing profits for shareholders is outdated and doesn't work very well, as the recent global financial crisis has taught us. The 21st Century is one of 'Managing for Stakeholders'. The task of executives is to create as much value as possible for stakeholders without resorting to tradeoffs. Great companies endure because they manage to get stakeholder interests aligned. R. Edward Freeman[3]

Milton Friedman's quote suggests that while CSR may be in the interests of the targeted recipients, it is less clear a priori whether it is in the interests of the company's shareholders. At worst, CSR may just be a manifestation of the principal-agent problem whereby the management wastes shareholder funds on causes that are close to their heart, but generate few or no benefits for the shareholders. This chapter will attempt to answer the question of whether CSR is in the interests of the shareholders.

We shall also review the other side of social responsibility, which is the investors' side, i.e. socially responsible investment. Socially responsible investment (SRI) is 'an investment process that considers the social and environmental consequences of investments, both positive and negative, within the context of rigorous financial analysis.'[4]

13.2 CSR and financial performance

As the Perrier case study in Box 13.1 illustrates (see also the Samsung case in Box 13.2), a lack of CSR or bad stakeholder management can cost a company dearly, may even be exploited by the company's competitors or at the very least may generate bad publicity.

Box 13.1
Perrier and Benzene

Benzene is a chemical which occurs naturally in crude oil. In laboratory tests on animals, it has been found to cause cancer. It is also believed to cause cancer in humans. Perrier was the number one mineral water, charging premium prices based on its reputation of the 'champagne of bottled water'. In early February 1990, traces of benzene were found in Perrier bottles in North Carolina, USA. Perrier initially seemed to hush up the incident, shifting from explanation to explanation and delaying any action. It finally recalled 160 million bottles worldwide at a cost of £150m. By 1995, its market share in the USA had dropped by half. Its market share in the UK fell from 60 per cent to nine per cent. La Source Perrier S.A. was bought in 1992 by Nestlé S.A. The Perrier debacle was happening as other (cheaper) rival brands were entering the UK and US markets and gaining market share.

[2]Friedman, M. (1962), *Capitalism and Freedom*, Chicago, IL: University of Chicago Press.
[3]redwardfreeman.com/stakeholder-management/, accessed on 9 February 2017.
[4]Social Investment Forum (2001), *2001 Report on Socially Responsible Investing Trends in the United States*, Washington, DC: Social Investment Forum Foundation and Social Investment Forum.

Box 13.2
Samsung suspends one of its Chinese suppliers over alleged child labour

In July 2014, Samsung Electronics Co. from South Korea suspended its business ties with Dongguan Shinyang Electronics Co, one of its Chinese suppliers, following allegations of child labour. Samsung was reacting to allegations made by New York-based China Labor Watch (chinalaborwatch.org) that Shinyang had hired at least five children under the age of 16. Following undercover investigations, China Labor Watch had found evidence that the children were employed for 11 hours, but only paid for 10 hours. Apart from child labour, the report also found evidence of unpaid overtime as well as the absence of health and safety training. In addition, temporary workers, accounting for more than 40 per cent of the workforce in the Shinyang factory, did not have social insurance. Samsung stated that, if Chinese officials were to confirm evidence of child labour, it will cancel all business ties with Shinyang.

Source: Lee, Y. (2014), 'Samsung Suspends China Supplier over Child Labor', *The Associated Press, Business News*, 14 July 2014.

The academic literature has investigated the link between financial performance and CSR. The early studies have found mixed and inconsistent evidence as to the presence of a link between financial performance and CSR as well as with the nature of this link. For example, Stanley Vance found a negative link, suggesting that CSR is a net cost to the firm.[5] In contrast, Jean McGuire, Alison Sundgren and Thomas Schneeweis as well as Richard Wokutch and Barbara Spencer found a positive link.[6] Finally, Gordon Alexander and Rogene Buchholz found no relationship between the two.[7]

However, apart from McGuire et al., none of the above studies raises the issue as to the direction of causality between the two. Interestingly, McGuire et al. found that past performance has a stronger positive link with the current level of CSR than future performance, suggesting that companies with good performance have more funds to spend on CSR than those with bad performance. Apart from ignoring the issue about the direction of causality, the early studies also faced the challenge of measuring CSR due to the lack of CSR indices at that time. Hence, McGuire et al. used Fortune survey data on the perceived CSR of US companies, whereas most of the earlier studies used an evaluation of the degree of CSR of 67 firms undertaken by Milton Moskowitz.[8] Finally, apart from McGuire et al., the earlier studies used either accounting or stock performance as measures of company performance, but not both, hence failing to adjust for the potential shortcoming of either type of performance measure. Indeed, most studies that were based on accounting performance found a positive link between the former and CSR, but then also failed to adjust for other firm characteristics such as age and risk. When these latter characteristics were taken into account, accounting performance was no longer positively affected by CSR.

[5]Vance, S.G. (1975), 'Are Socially Responsible Corporations Good Investment Risks?' *Management Review* 64, 18–24.
[6]McGuire, J.B., Sundgren A. and Schneeweis, T. (1988), 'Corporate Social Responsibility and Firm Financial Performance', *Academy of Management Journal* 31, 854–72. Wokutch, R.E. and Spencer, B.A. (1987), 'Corporate Saints and Sinners: The Effects of Philanthropic and Illegal Activity on Organizational Performance', *California Management Review* 29, 77–88.
[7]Alexander, G.J. and Buchholz, R.A. (1978), 'Research Notes Corporate Social Responsibility and Stock Market Performance', *Academy of Management Journal* 21, 479–86.
[8]Moskowitz, M. (1972), 'Choosing Socially Responsible Stocks', *Business and Society Review* 1, 71–5.

However, while McGuire et al. acknowledged that the direction of causality may flow both from CSR to performance and vice-versa, the way they tested this was fairly basic. Indeed, they limited themselves to measuring the statistical correlation between current levels of CSR and past performance and the correlation between current performance and past levels of CSR. Sandra Waddock and Samuel Graves performed a more thorough analysis of the direction of causality between CSR and performance.[9] They argued that higher levels of CSR may cause higher levels of financial performance and vice-versa. The reason why the direction of causality should flow from CSR to financial performance is that CSR is part of good management and part of having good relationships with the firm's stakeholders. The reason why the direction of causality should flow from financial performance to CSR is given by Michael Jensen's free cash flow problem (see Chapter 1). Free cash flow is the total cash stock of the firm minus the cash component of working capital, minus cash necessary for all compulsory payments (debt, payables, tax), minus cash invested in positive net present value (NPV) projects. Managers who have access to significant amounts of free cash flow may divert some of this to social causes.[10]

Waddock and Graves measure of CSR is based on the Kinder, Lydenberg and Domini (KLD) index which rates US firms according to several aspects of CSR (e.g. community relations and workforce relations; see Section 13.3 for the full details). They first tested whether current levels of CSR depend on past financial performance, i.e. performance from the previous year. They found that there is such a link for each of their three measures of performance (return on assets (ROA), return on equity (ROE) and return on sales) and that the link is positive. This suggests that the free cash flow hypothesis is valid in the context of CSR. They also tested whether current financial performance depends on past levels of CSR. They found that there is such a link for ROA and return on sales and that it is positive. This provides support for the hypothesis of good management. In other words, Waddock and Graves found that the direction of causality between CSR and performance flows both ways: firms with better past profitability have more funds to spend on CSR and firms with higher levels of CSR perform better.

The main limitation of the Waddock and Graves study is that it gives only a partial answer to the question as to whether CSR is in the interests of the company's shareholders. In particular, the study does not provide clear recommendations as to when CSR destroys shareholder value and as to when it creates shareholder value. The study by Amy Hillman and Gerald Keim established a theoretical framework to answer this question.[11] Their theoretical model proposed that there are two components of CSR. One component relates to improving the firm's relationships with its primary stakeholders. They called this stakeholder management (SM). SM is expected to have a positive impact on firm performance. The other component relates to the firm's involvement with social issues that do not improve the relationships between the firm and its primary stakeholders. They called this social issue participation (SIP). This component is expected to reduce financial performance. As in the Waddock and Graves study, Hillman and Keim also used the KLD index to measure CSR. They measured SM by the various attributes that measure a company's relationship with its stakeholders, whereas they measured SIP by the KLD exclusionary screens such as alcohol and tobacco (see Section 13.3). To some extent, Hillman and Keim's SM and SIP components reflect Waddock and Graves stakeholder management hypothesis and free cash flow hypothesis, respectively. However, in contrast to Waddock and Graves, Hillman and Keim clearly split CSR into two components, i.e. SM which is expected to create shareholder value and

[9]Waddock, S. and Graves, S. (1997), 'The Corporate Social Performance-Financial Performance Link', *Strategic Management Journal* 18, 303–19.

[10]Masulis, Ron W. and Reza, S.W. (2015), 'Agency Problems of Corporate Philanthropy', *Review of Financial Studies* 28, 592–636, found that corporate philanthropy or charity giving is a form of diverting shareholder money to social causes.

[11]Hillman, A.J. and Keim, G.D. (2001), 'Shareholder Value, Stakeholder Management, and Social Issues: What's the Bottom Line?' *Strategic Management Journal* 22, 125–39.

SIP which is expected to destroy it. They found that financial performance depends positively on SM and negatively on SIP. However, contrary to Waddock and Graves, they did not find that the levels of SM and SIP depend on past financial performance.[12]

A more recent study by Allen Ferrell, Hao Liang and Luc Renneboog took a somewhat different approach to the above studies to identify the relation between CSR and firm value. They argued that the effect of CSR on firm value depends on the incentives of the management. In other words, firms with good corporate governance would be more likely to engage in value-enhancing CSR, whereas firms with bad corporate governance would be more likely to engage in value-destroying CSR. Based on a sample of companies from 59 different countries, they found that companies with good corporate governance typically engage more in CSR.[13] This suggests that CSR is not a reflection of agency problems. Importantly, the study also finds a positive link between CSR and firm value. Finally, in another study, Luc Renneboog and Hao Liang found that a firm's CSR rating and the legal family to which its country of origin belongs are correlated.[14] Firms from common law countries have lower CSR ratings than those from civil law countries, with firms from Scandinavian countries having the highest CSR ratings.

To summarize, while there has been a long debate in the academic literature about the value implications of CSR, more recent research suggests that CSR and good corporate governance go hand in hand and that CSR is value-enhancing. Finally, similar to studies on the impact of managerial ownership (see Section 8.9 of Chapter 8) and board independence on firm value and performance (see Section 7.4 of Chapter 7), studies on the link between CSR and firm performance may suffer from endogeneity issues.

13.3 CSR indices

CSR indices (e.g. FTSE Kinder, Lydenberg and Domini (KLD) 400 Social Index) tend to be based on exclusionary screens as well as strengths (and/or weaknesses) along the lines of a series of attributes. **Exclusionary screens** consist of excluding firms from the index with significant involvement in, for example:

- Alcohol
- Gambling
- Tobacco
- Firearms
- Military weapons
- Pornography
- Nuclear power

Exclusionary screens are also sometimes referred to as excluding sin industries.
Attributes include, for example:

- Community relations

  - Support for education and social housing, etc.

---

[12]More recent studies which find that CSR is a reflection of agency problems include: Masulis, R.W. and Syed W. Reza (2015), 'Agency Problems of Corporate Philanthropy', *Review of Financial Studies* 28, 592–636; Cronqvist, H. and Yu, F. (2017), 'Shaped by Their Daughters: Executives, Female Socialization, and Corporate Responsibility', forthcoming in *Journal of Financial Economics*.
[13]Ferrell, A., Liang, H. and Renneboog, L. (2016), 'Socially Responsible Firms', *Journal of Financial Economics* 122, 585–606.
[14]Renneboog, L. and Liang, H. (2017), 'On the Foundations of Corporate Social Responsibility', *Journal of Finance* 72, 853–910.

- Diversity

  - The firm has policies in place to promote gender equality and to ensure equal opportunities for minorities.

- Employee relations

  - Relationships with trade unions, employee profit sharing schemes, etc.

- Environment

  - Policies aiming to reduce or prevent pollution, carbon neutrality, recycling, etc.

- Product

  - Quality, innovation, product safety, antitrust, policies enabling socially disadvantaged groups to benefit from the firm's products and services, etc.

- Corporate governance

  There are now indices which cater for investors concerned about, for example:

- Catholic values (KLD)
- Sustainability (KLD)
- Islamic values (S&P Dow Jones)

13.4 Socially responsible investment

SRI funds apply a set of exclusionary and/or inclusionary screens to select their investments. However, the definition of SRI and the choice of exclusionary and/or inclusionary screens may change depending on the values of the investor or index. For example, Islamic and Jewish funds will not invest in companies that use or process pork meat. Further, the FTSE KLD Catholic Values 400 Index excludes companies that are involved in or support:

- Abortion
- Contraceptive products
- The use of embryonic stem cells and foetal tissue

SRI has ancient roots. For example, the Jewish Torah has strict rules on how to invest money. In particular, Exodus 22:25 states that 'If you lend money to my people, to the poor among you, you are not to act as a creditor to him; you shall not charge him interest' and Deuteronomy 23:19 states that 'You shall not charge interest to your countrymen: interest on money, food, or anything that may be loaned at interest. You may charge interest to a foreigner, but to your countrymen you shall not charge interest, so that the Lord your God may bless you in all that you undertake in the land which you are about to enter to possess'. Other religions such as Islam, Christianity and Buddhism equally condemn so-called usury, historically defined as charging interest on a loan, i.e. requiring the borrower to pay back an amount of money which exceeds the initial amount of the loan. Christianity was even more zealous in its condemnation of usury. In the eighth century, Charlemagne turned usury into a criminal offence. This was followed in the fourteenth century by Pope Clement V's total ban on usury and his declaration that any secular law permitting usury was null and void. It was only in the early 1600s that in Christendom usury became a matter for each individual's conscience rather than an offence. Finally, the

Holy Qur'an, Surat Al-Baqarah 2:275, states the following: 'Those who consume interest cannot stand [on the Day of Resurrection] except as one stands who is being beaten by Satan into insanity. That is because they say, "Trade is [just] like interest". But Allah has permitted trade and has forbidden interest. So whoever has received an admonition from his Lord and desists may have what is past, and his affair rests with Allah. But whoever returns to [dealing in interest or usury] – those are the companions of the Fire; they will abide eternally therein'.

In the seventeenth century, Quakers ('Society of Friends') who settled in America refused to benefit from the weapons and slave trade. The first fund to use exclusionary screens was the Pioneer Fund, which was set up in 1928. Its investment policy was not to invest in alcohol and tobacco. The Pax Fund was created in 1971 in the US by two Methodists who were opposed to the Vietnam War and militarism in general. It refused to invest in weapons contracting. The 1980s then saw increased awareness by the general public of racism (e.g. the apartheid regime in South Africa) and environmental issues (e.g. Chernobyl and the Exxon Valdez oil-spill disaster).

More recently, the United Nations issued their Principles of Responsible Investment (PRI) in 2006. The UN PRI are aimed at institutional investors, and the signatories to the UN PRI commit themselves to the following six principles:

1 To include CSR issues in their investment analysis and decision-making processes
2 To be active shareholders and to include CSR issues in their ownership practices and policies
3 To request their investee firms to disclose their CSR issues
4 To promote the Principles within the investment industry
5 To work together to improve the effectiveness of the implementation of the Principles
6 To report on their progress and activities towards reporting the implementation of the Principles

The question that arises is whether there is a price for SRI or whether SRI funds outperform other funds. Luc Renneboog, Jenke ter Horst and Chendi Zhang found that SRI funds from Europe, North America and the Asia-Pacific region underperformed compared to the market by between −2.2 per cent and −6.5 per cent as measured by risk-adjusted returns.[15] However, SRI funds do not generally perform worse than conventional funds from the same country. Indeed, conventional investment funds have also been shown to underperform the market.

13.5 Conclusions

This chapter has reviewed the literature investigating whether corporate social responsibility (CSR) has an effect on firm performance. While earlier studies did not find consistent evidence on the presence of such a link as well as on the nature of this link, more recent studies suggest that CSR affects firm performance. However, the recent studies also suggest that it is important to take into account the type of CSR as there are two different types, with contrasting effects on performance. The first type of CSR concerns the firm's relationships with its primary stakeholders, such as customers and employees. This research suggests that having good stakeholder relationships improves firm performance. The second type concerns the firm's relationships with wider social issues. Funds and efforts spent

The link between CSR and firm performance

[15]Renneboog, L., ter Horst, J. and Zhang, C. (2008), 'The Price of Ethics: Evidence from Socially Responsible Mutual Funds around the World', *Journal of Corporate Finance* 14, 302–22.

on these relationships have been shown to reduce rather than increase firm profitability and value. More recent research suggests that CSR and good corporate governance go hand in hand and that CSR increases firm value.

There is also some evidence that socially responsible investment (SRI) does not come at a price, as the performance of SRI funds is not lower than that of conventional investment funds. However, both SRI funds and conventional funds underperform the market as a whole.

The performance of SRI funds

Further, it is important to bear in mind that there is no generally accepted definition of CSR and SRI. The definition of both depends on an investor's ethical values, religion and culture. Hence, what may be acceptable to one investor may be unacceptable to another investor. For example, Catholic life insurance companies may refuse to cover unmarried couples and/or same-sex couples, believing that both types of couples live in sin given the teachings of the Bible, whereas others may take offence at such behaviour and believe it to be discriminatory.

How do you define SRI?

Finally, while there are contrasting views as to whether companies should engage in it, CSR may be an important means of achieving economic development and improving social equality in countries with weak governments and corrupt or ineffective institutions. More generally, CSR in general and sustainable development in particular are in the interests of the long-term survival of any business.

13.6 Discussion questions

1 'Advocates of CSR argue that firms should pursue the "triple bottom line": not only profits, but also environmental protection and social justice. This notion, if taken seriously, is "incomprehensible", says Ms Bernstein [the head of a South African think-tank called the Centre for Development and Enterprise]. Profits are easy to measure. The many and often conflicting demands of a local community are not. A business that is accountable to all is in effect accountable to no one, says Ms Bernstein'. (*The Economist*, 'Companies Aren't Charities', 23 October 2010, p. 82)

Discuss the above statement in the context of what you have learnt in this chapter.

2 'Corporate social responsibility is a waste of shareholders' money and is just another way the classic agency problem between the managers and the shareholders manifests itself'.

Discuss the above statement based on academic evidence as to the effect of corporate social responsibility on firm value and performance.

3 'Corporate social responsibility (CSR) can only be afforded by companies with good financial performance. Hence, studies that investigate the link between financial performance and CSR need to rethink the direction of causality between the two'. (Anonymous)

Discuss the validity of the above statement by referring to the existing empirical literature.

4 What is the empirical evidence on the effects of corporate social responsibility (CSR) on firm performance?

5 Is there a price for socially responsible investment or do SRI funds outperform other funds?

6 How do you feel about Samsung potentially permanently stopping doing business with Shinyang (see Box 13.2)? Do you think their walking away from their supplier, if found guilty of using child labour, makes sense? What would you have done in this situation?

Reading list

Key reading

Ferrell, A., Liang, H. and Renneboog, L. (2016), 'Socially Responsible Firms', *Journal of Financial Economics* 122, 585–606.

Hillman, A.J. and Keim, S.D. (2001), 'Shareholder Value, Stakeholder Management, and Social Issues: What's the Bottom Line?' *Strategic Management Journal* 22, 125–39.

Renneboog, L. and Liang, H. (2017), 'On the Foundations of Corporate Social Responsibility', *Journal of Finance* 72, 853–910.

Renneboog, L., ter Horst, J. and Zhang, C. (2008), 'The Price of Ethics: Evidence from Socially Responsible Mutual Funds around the World', *Journal of Corporate Finance* 14, 302–22.

Waddock, S. and Graves, S. (1997), 'The Corporate Social Performance-Financial Performance Link', *Strategic Management Journal* 18, 303–19.

Further reading

Aras, G. and Crowther, D. (2010), *The Gower Handbook of Corporate Governance and Social Responsibility*, Farnham, UK: Gower.

Masulis, R.W. and Reza, S.W. (2015), 'Agency Problems of Corporate Philanthropy', *Review of Financial Studies* 28, 592–636.

Servaes, H. and Tamayo, A. (2013), 'The Impact of Corporate Social Responsibility on the Value of the Firm: The Role of Customer Awareness', *Management Science* 59, 1045–61.

Visser, W.A.M. and Macintosh, A. (1998), 'A Short Review of the Historical Critique of Usury', *Accounting, Business & Financial History* 8, 175–89.

Additional resources

UN Principles of Responsible Investment (PRI): www.unpri.org.

14 Debtholders

Chapter Aims

The aim of this chapter is twofold. First, the chapter elaborates on the potentially important role that debtholders may play in corporate governance. This role pertains to their monitoring function as well as to the alleviation of problems of asymmetric information between the management and investors. Second, the chapter aims to review the conflicts of interests that debtholders face and are likely to benefit from as well as those they may be the victim of within the corporations they finance. The main conflict of interests that debtholders may create relates to situations where they provide not only debt financing, but also equity financing. Such situations are frequent in the bank-based system, i.e. a corporate governance system with universal banks. Another important conflict of interests that banks may create is via their use of proxy votes. The chapter also provides a detailed discussion of the agency problem of debt (which was briefly introduced in Chapter 1) via examples of debtholder expropriation by the shareholders. Such incidences include leveraged buy-outs and acquisitions by hedge funds.

Learning Outcomes

After reading this chapter, you should be able to:

1 Assess the role of debtholders in corporate governance

2 Understand the conflicts of interests that large debtholders, in particular banks, may face and benefit from

3 Identify situations where debtholders risk being expropriated by the corporation's shareholders

4 Evaluate the risk to bondholders from changes in control of the issuing corporation

14.1 Introduction

Chapter 8 (in particular Section 8.11) reviewed the role of large creditors in corporate governance, in particular the bank-based corporate governance system. Given the amount of funds they have lent their borrowers, they have strong incentives, similar to large shareholders, to monitor the management of the firm. In addition, large creditors, such as banks, also frequently hold equity in the firms to which they have granted loans. Although the equity stakes they hold in corporations tend to be small (see Chapter 2), frequently banks' influence is amplified by their representation on the board of directors of their investee firms and/or the exercise of proxy votes at the AGM.

However, the fact that banks in the bank-based system are frequently not only large creditors to corporations but also shareholders, may create conflicts of interests with other shareholders, debtholders and corporate stakeholders. Finally, the chapter returns to the agency problem of debt, which was introduced in Chapter 1, by reviewing the empirical evidence on the expropriation of debtholders by the firm's shareholders.[1]

14.2 Benefits and costs from relationship-based banking

An important characteristic of some corporate governance systems, in particular the bank-based system (see Chapter 4), is close and long-term lending relationships. For example, the German corporate governance system has traditionally been described by the close relationship of firms with their house bank (*Hausbank*). Ralf Elsas studied the determinants of house bank status versus normal banking relationships for the case of five major German universal banks. He found two types of major determinants.[2] The first type relates to the access the bank has to information as well as its influence over the borrowing firm's management. In particular, the bank's likelihood of having house bank status increases with its share in the firm's debt. The second one is the competition in the local market. He finds a U-shaped relation between competition in the local market and the likelihood of the bank having house bank status. Finally, although the duration of the bank-firm relationship has frequently been considered to be a valid proxy for house bank status, Elsas did not find a link between duration and the likelihood of house bank status. The house bank also often provides equity finance. Frequently, it is also represented on the supervisory board and its voting power may be further amplified by proxy votes (see Chapter 2). In addition, Christoph Memmel, Christian Schmieder and Ingrid Stein found that young, small and R&D-intensive firms typically have a house bank.[3]

The main reason why firms have close relationships with their banks is to overcome problems of asymmetric information which may limit their access to external financing. In relation to this, banks are also thought to mitigate the free-rider problem which exists in debt markets with many small lenders that lack the incentives to monitor the borrower. In other words, banks are thought to provide the monitoring that may be absent in markets of tradable debt securities, such as bond markets, and benefit from economies of scale due to the large number of lenders with which they deal (see Chapter 4). They may also provide monitoring in widely held firms where there is no monitoring of the management by the shareholders. There is empirical evidence from the Netherlands[4] and Japan[5] that firms with close ties to a bank are less dependent on internal funds for their investments. This suggests that banks alleviate financing constraints by improving access to external funds, thereby reducing the reliance on internal funds.

[1]Section 16.5 of Chapter 16 will discuss the issue as to whether industry regulation, including bank regulation, acts as substitute or complement for corporate governance.

[2]Elsas, R. (2005), 'Empirical Determinants of Relationship Lending', *Journal of Financial Intermediation* 14, 32–57.

[3]Memmel, C., Schmieder, C. and Stein, I. (2007), 'Relationship Lending. Empirical Evidence for Germany', *Deutsche Bundesbank Discussion Paper Series 2: Banking and Financial Studies* 14/2007.

[4]Van Ees, H. and Garretsen, H. (1994), 'Liquidity and Business Investment: Evidence from Dutch Panel Data', *Journal of Macroeconomics* 16, 613–27; and Degryse, H. and De Jong, A. (2006), 'Investment and Internal Finance: Asymmetric Information or Managerial Discretion?', *International Journal of Industrial Organization* 24, 125–47.

[5]Hoshi, T., Kashyap A. and Scharfstein, D. (1991), 'Corporate Structure, Liquidity, and Investment: Evidence from Japanese Industrial Groups', *Quarterly Journal of Economics* 106, 33–60.

However, the information on the firm that the bank acquires via its monitoring also increases its bargaining power. Stuart Greenbaum, George Kanatas and Itzhak Venezia's theoretical model predicts that if the bank obtains private, non-transferable information from its close relationship with the firm, the bank will end up with a monopoly, resulting in a higher cost of borrowing to the firm.[6] Hence, as proposed by Raghuram Rajan, there may be a trade-off between the improved access to finance that a close relationship with a bank may provide and the rents, via increased interest rates, that banks may extract from their close relationships with firms.[7]

This trade-off may explain why studies on the impact of banks on the financial performance of firms have found a somewhat inconsistent link between the two. For example, a number of studies on Germany have found conflicting results as to the effect of bank relationships on firm performance (see Section 8.10 of Chapter 8). Similarly, studies on other countries have found mixed effects: they have found no effect whatsoever, or a negative effect, or a positive one. Apart from Rajan's rent-extraction argument, the other reason why no consistent effect has been found may be that banks are typically more risk averse than the firms' shareholders and may therefore prevent firms from investing in some shareholder-value increasing projects. In addition, studies on the effect of bank ownership on firm performance have also failed to find a consistent link between the two (see also Section 8.11 of Chapter 8).

Similarly, the evidence as to the effects of board representation of banks is as yet inconclusive. On the one hand, there is some evidence that firms where banks have board representation perform better than other firms. Banks also seem to call for board representation in firms with weak performance or financial difficulties. After the bankers have been appointed to the board, there is evidence of a slight increase in firm performance. Apart from financial distress and poor performance, other factors that increase the likelihood of bank representation on the board of directors include a need for long-term debt rather than short-term financing as well as a relatively low proportion of intangibles on the firm's balance sheet. In line with the greater importance of banks in the German and Japanese systems of corporate governance, bank representation on the board is also more important in these two countries compared to, e.g. the USA. Indeed, 75 per cent of large firms in Germany and 53 per cent of large firms in Japan have a commercial banker sitting on their board compared to only 32 per cent of large US firms.[8] On the other hand, there are studies which suggest that bankers sitting on corporate boards do not monitor the management and pursue the banks' interests rather than those of the firm. In particular, Ingolf Dittmann, Ernst Maug and Christoph Schneider found that for Germany bankers on the board promote their bank as a lender as well as an advisor on mergers and acquisitions (M&As).[9] Nevertheless, they still found evidence that banks fund firms in difficult times.

While Raghuram Rajan in another paper with Mitchell Petersen conceded that for the USA the house bank may charge above-market interest rates, the reason for doing so is to smooth interest rates over the life-cycle of the firm.[10] Indeed, when firms are young, there is a lot of uncertainty about their future. Hence, they may be charged disproportionately high interest rates in the market. As a result, some firms may be deprived of outside financing. In contrast, a lender with monopoly power may charge the firm a lower interest rate during its early stages than would be the case in a competitive market. The monopolistic position then enables the lender to

[6]Greenbaum, S.I., Kanatas, G. and Venezia, I. (1989), 'Equilibrium Loan Pricing under the Bank-client Relationship', *Journal of Banking and Finance* 13, 221–35.

[7]Rajan, R. (1992), 'Insiders and Outsiders. The Choice between Relationship and Arms Length Debt', *Journal of Finance* 47, 1367–400.

[8]Kroszner, R.S. and Strahan, P.E. (2001), 'Banker on Boards: Monitoring, Conflicts of Interest, and Lender Liability', *Journal of Financial Economics* 62, 415–52.

[9]Dittmann, I., Maug, E. and Schneider, C. (2010), 'Bankers on the Boards of German Firms: What They Do, What They Are Worth, and Why They Are (Still) There', *Review of Finance* 14, 35–71.

[10]Petersen, M.A. and Rajan, R.G. (1995), 'The Effect of Credit Market Competition on Lending Relationships', *Quarterly Journal of Economics* 110, 407–43.

share in future increases in firm value by charging above-market interest rates. However, countries with competitive banking sectors may constrain such long-term banking relationships (see also Chapter 5). In contrast, Ralf Elsas and Jan Pieter Krahnen did not find any evidence of intertemporal interest rate smoothing for the case of Germany.[11] They justified this absence of interest rate smoothing by the fact that the house bank does not normally have an *exclusive* relationship with the firm, but that the firm also sources some of its debt from banks with which it does not have a close relationship. However, Elsas and Krahnen still found a behavioural difference between the house bank and the other banks of the firm. Indeed, when the firm experiences a downgrading of its credit rating, the house bank increases its share of the firm's bank debt whereas the other banks decrease their share. This suggests that the house bank provides an insurance function in difficult times when the firm's access to financing may be restricted.

However, a caveat is in order. While Germany is typically characterized as a bank-based system, large German firms have been reported to be no less dependent on bank loans and other types of bank financing than UK and US firms that are thought to operate in a market-based corporate governance system (see also Section 5.3 of Chapter 5). Indeed, Jeremy Edwards and Klaus Fischer dispelled some of the myths about the German system in their 1994 book.[12] First, there is no evidence that firms with a close relationship with a bank have better access to bank loans or equity. Second, banks are only influential enough to exercise a sizeable degree of control in the very largest German firms which also tend to be widely held compared to the smaller-sized firms which have concentrated control, which is typically associated with the German system of corporate control. However, the banks' incentives to monitor these firms are also reported to be lower than it is often assumed.

Nevertheless, this does not imply that Germany is not a bank-based corporate governance system. Indeed, as Richard Deeg qualified, German banks are important as providers of both finance and management advice to small- and medium-sized enterprises (SMEs), the so called *Mittelstand* firms.[13] As SMEs in Germany are comparatively more important in terms of employment than in e.g. the UK and the USA, banks still assume a significantly more important role in the German corporate governance system than in other economies. As there is still a reluctance of German *Mittelstand* firms to go public, banks assume the important role of providing long-term financing and management support. It is thought that this is the main difference with the German corporate governance system compared to the market-based system.

Since the early 1990s, Germany has started reforms and policies aimed at promoting the development of its stock markets. One of the main initiatives was the creation of a new stock-market segment at the Frankfurt bourse, the *Neuer Markt*, which is similar to the US-based Nasdaq aimed at providing equity finance to young, hi-tech and high-growth firms. However, although the *Neuer Markt* experienced remarkable growth until 2000, blatant violations of insider trading legislation and stock-market regulation as well as share price manipulations forced it to close down in 2002–3. Another major reform in 2001 encouraged workers to save more for their retirement by investing in private pension funds. Finally, the tax reform of 2002 enabled banks to sell their stakes in corporations without incurring capital gains tax.

While all these steps have resulted in a decrease in bank ownership of equity, the cornerstones of the German bank-based corporate governance system are still pretty much intact for at least four reasons. First, while bank ownership of equity securities has decreased, this has affected mainly the largest firms whose shares banks have traditionally held. Second, the decrease in ownership by banks has been accompanied by an increase in

[11]Elsas, R. and Krahnen, J.P. (1998), 'Is Relationship Lending Special? Evidence from Credit-file Data in Germany', *Journal of Banking & Finance 22*, 1283–316.

[12]Edwards, J. and Fischer, K. (1994), *Banks, Finance and Investment in Germany*, Cambridge, UK: Cambridge University Press.

[13]Deeg, R. (1998), 'What Makes German Banks Different', *Small Business Economics* 10, 93–101.

ownership by foreign institutional investors, such as UK and US investors.[14] Third, Ingolf Dittmann, Ernst Maug and Christoph Schneider reported that while bank ownership of corporate equity has fallen, bank representation on corporate boards has not.[15] Finally, the importance of close bank relationships has stayed fairly constant since the mid-1990s.[16]

14.3 Addressing conflicts of interests created by bank ownership and bank board representation

Ignoring conflicts of interests between different types of shareholder, the agency problem of debt will be mitigated if an investor, such as a bank, is both a creditor and a shareholder. However, the dual role of a bank as a creditor and shareholder may create conflicts of interests with other shareholders, debtholders and corporate stakeholders. Indeed, the bank's debt and equity claims tend to require different decisions in case one of its investee-cum-debtor firms enters financial distress. While the bank's debt claims may call for winding up the firm and recovering the assets as soon as possible, its equity claims may call for revolving its existing loans to the firm.

These conflicts of interests may be exacerbated in corporate governance systems with strong networks and links between firms and banks, as the bank's decisions are likely to be influenced by the objectives of the network rather than those of the firm in question. Bank board representation may give the bank sufficient power to further its own objectives to the detriment of the firm's shareholders and other stakeholders. The above-mentioned study by Dittmann et al. (see Section 14.2) provides some evidence in favour of this argument, as German bankers on corporate boards seem to pursue their bank's interests as a lender and M&A advisor rather than those of the firm on whose board they sit.

In addition, Mitchell Berlin, Kose John and Anthony Saunders argued that equity ownership may incentivize the bank to side with the firm's shareholders to expropriate its fixed-claim stakeholders such as long-term suppliers and customers with significant costs of switching their business to another firm.[17] As stated above, banks have lower costs of monitoring than dispersed debtholders. In addition, they can also perform monitoring at cheaper costs and more regular intervals than long-term suppliers and customers. Hence, the latter may rely on the firm's bank to carry out the monitoring of the firm's management and to disclose whether the firm is in financial distress. However, if the bank holds equity claims, the long-term stakeholders may be less willing to rely on the bank monitoring the firm. Indeed, the fact that it holds shares in the firm may push the bank to collude with the firm in order to expropriate the long-term stakeholders (see also Section 1.7 of Chapter 1). Still, the stakeholders are also likely to be suspicious of the bank if it only holds debt claims as these will have priority over the stakeholders' fixed claims. Indeed, if the firm is in financial distress, it is in the interest of the bank to collude with the firm to convince the stakeholders that the firm is in good health. Given that the bank's debt claims are more senior to the stakeholders' claims, the bank will then be able to reap all the revenues to the detriment of the stakeholders. While an easy solution to this conflict of interests would be to make the bank's

[14]Vitols, S. (2005), 'Changes in Germany's Bank-based Financial System: Implications for Corporate Governance', *Corporate Governance: An International Review* 13, 386–96.
[15]See op. cit. footnote 9.
[16]See op. cit. footnote 3.
[17]Berlin, M., John, K. and Saunders, A. (1996), 'Bank Equity Stakes in Borrowing Firms and Financial Distress', *Review of Financial Studies* 9, 889–919.

claims subordinate to those of the long-term stakeholders, it is likely that the bank would breach this order of seniority given the superior information about the firm it acquires via its monitoring.

Berlin et al.'s theoretical model predicts that it is optimal for the long-term stakeholders that the bank holds debt as well as equity claims. First, to avoid the bank colluding with the healthy firm to expropriate the long-term stakeholders by claiming the firm is in financial distress thereby obtaining concessions from the long-term stakeholders, the bank should hold either a negligible stake or virtually all of the equity. In other words, the bank should not hold an *intermediate* stake, i.e. a stake somewhere between the afore-mentioned two extremes, as an intermediate stake incentivizes it to collude with the healthy firm and to pretend that the latter is facing financial distress in order to expropriate the long-term stakeholders. Second, to avoid the bank siding with the financially distressed firm by pretending that the firm is healthy, a sufficient percentage of the bank's debt claims should be subordinated to those of the long-term stakeholders. As the bank may find it difficult to convince the long-term stakeholders that its debt claims are indeed subordinated in practice, the bank needs to hold an equity stake in the healthy firm.

14.4 Expropriation of debtholders

Chapter 1 introduced the agency problem of debt, which consists of the shareholders gambling with the debtholders' funds once the firm is in financial distress and it is unlikely for the shareholders to recoup their initial investment in the firm. If the high-risk investments pay off, the shareholders will benefit from most of the gains as the debtholders' claims are capped, i.e. at best the debtholders will be paid any interest due as well as the debt principal. Conversely, if these investments fail, the debtholders will lose out as the remaining funds of the firm will have been spent whereas the shareholders will be no worse off.

There is evidence of debtholder expropriation from particular types of changes in control or acquisitions, i.e. leveraged buy-outs and purchases of equity stakes by hedge funds. Leveraged buy-outs (LBOs) normally consist of the sale of a division of a company or the sale of a whole company. In contrast to regular M&As, LBOs are mainly financed by debt – hence the term leveraged buy-out – and are frequently undertaken by institutional or specialist investors. LBOs are normally taken private for a period of 3–5 years and then taken public again (via a reverse LBO). The shareholders of the firms targeted via LBOs earn large premiums on their shares, typically in the region of 40 to 60 per cent. Some empirical studies suggest that at least part of this wealth gain to the target shareholders consists of a wealth transfer from other stakeholders, such as the bondholders (see Box 14.1 for an example).[18] As the amount of debt increases substantially, at least part of the increase in the value of the firm's equity may be derived from the drop in the value of the existing bonds. Indeed, bond covenants do not always succeed in protecting bondholders from changes in control. Also, the new debt may not be subordinated to the existing debt and may be due for repayment earlier than the existing debt. In addition, in bankruptcy proceedings, the absolute seniority of debt is not always respected. The evidence shows that at the announcement of the LBO, bondholders experience negative returns in the region of −3 to −7 per cent.

Similarly, there is evidence of wealth transfers from the bondholders to the shareholders in firms where hedge funds have bought a stake of the equity. Indeed, April Klein and Emanuel Zur reported that bondholders suffer an average abnormal return of −3.9 per cent on the filing date of the purchase of the stake by the

---

[18]Asquith, P. and Wizman, T. (1990), 'Event Risk, Covenants, and Bondholder Returns in Leveraged Buyouts', *Journal of Financial Economics* 27, 195–213. Warga, A. and Welch, I. (1993), 'Bondholder Losses in Leveraged Buyouts', *Review of Financial Studies* 6, 959–82.

hedge fund and suffer another −4.5 per cent over the remaining year after the filing date.[19] Klein and Zur also found that the negative returns to the bondholders are larger if the hedge fund obtains a board seat within the year following the filing date. The reasons for the negative abnormal returns to the bondholders are a decrease in collateral (via a reduction in the firm's assets and cash holdings) as well as an increase in debt. Klein and Zur also found direct evidence of bondholder expropriation by the shareholders, as the abnormal returns earned by the bondholders are negatively correlated with the short-term and long-term returns earned by the shareholders.

There is also evidence that corporate restructuring in the form of equity carve-outs, spin-offs and asset sell-offs may result in bondholder expropriation. An equity carve-out consists of a parent firm selling one of its subsidiaries via an IPO. A spin-off is the sale of a subsidiary by issuing free shares in the subsidiary to the parent firm's shareholders pro rata to their holdings in the latter. An asset sell-off consists of the sale of a subsidiary to a third party via a private transaction. There is frequently bondholder expropriation via corporate restructuring, as the latter often results in an uneven reallocation of debt between the parent firm and the subsidiary. In addition, corporate restructuring by refocusing the parent firm's activities reduces the insurance effect on debt provided by diversified firms and cross-subsidizing across the various subsidiaries.[20]

Finally, there is more evidence of bondholder expropriation by the shareholders via large dividend payments. Upinder Dhillon and Herb Johnson found that the bond price reaction to large dividend payments is negatively correlated to the share price reaction.[21]

Box 14.1
Wealth transfers from bondholders to shareholders in LBOs

The US-based Caesars Entertainment Group, owner of casinos and hotels, seems to be a textbook example of wealth transfers from bondholders to shareholders. Caesars is owned by the private equity houses, TPG and Apollo. Caesars has suffered from lacklustre financial performance, partly due to its failure to invest in Macau, a growing market, and the slow recovery of the US market. This is not helped by the fact that Caesars took out $25bn before the 2008 financial crisis. While its net book value is negative (as it has more debt than its book value), somewhat surprisingly the market value of its listed equity is not zero as it amounts to $2bn.

Following the LBO, Caesars extended some of the debt maturities. However, it gets worse. It then sold casinos as well as intangible assets owned by its subsidiary, Caesars Entertainment Operating Company (CEOC). Most of the debt sits with CEOC. In contrast, the assets were sold to affiliates of the Caesars Entertainment Group that are mostly owned by the shareholders. Creditors allege that these sales were made at unfair prices. It gets even worse as Caesars is alleged to have reduced a guarantee it had issued on CEOC's debt.

Source: Anonymous (2016), 'Caesars: The House Always Wins', *Financial Times*, 26 December 2014.

[19]Klein, A. and Zur, E. (2011), 'The Impact of Hedge Fund Activism on the Target Firm's Existing Bondholders', *Review of Financial Studies* 4, 1735–71.
[20]See Renneboog, L. and Szilagyi, P.G. (2008), 'Corporate Restructuring and Bondholder Wealth', *European Financial Management* 14, 792–819.
[21]Dhillon, U.S. and Johnson, H. (1994), 'The Effect of Dividend Changes on Stock and Bond Prices', *Journal of Finance* 49, 281–9.

14.5 Conclusions

Large debtholders, such as banks, may potentially play an important role via reducing problems of asymmetric information. They may also play an important corporate governance role. More specifically, their monitoring of the firm's management may generate value via the mitigation of the principal-agent problem, which is particularly severe in widely held firms. While the monitoring performed by banks may create value for the shareholders as well as other stakeholders, it may also result in monopolistic power for the bank which may charge the firm above-market interest rates. However, there is also evidence that banks with close relationships to firms smooth interest rates over time by charging below-market interest rates to firms when they are young and have limited access to outside funding, and then participating in the surplus generated by the firms as they mature by charging above-market interest rates. This intertemporal smoothing of interest rates charged by house banks may explain why studies that analyze the link between bank influence and firm performance have found conflicting results. While the support for interest rate smoothing is somewhat scant, studies tend to agree that house banks seem to provide financial support when a firm is in financial difficulties.

The jury is still out as to the impact of bank influence on firm profitability. Similarly, the evidence on the effects on firm value and performance of bankers on corporate boards is as yet inconclusive. While there is evidence that bankers are appointed to the board of directors when the firm enters financial distress and that the firm's performance increases after these board appointments, there is also evidence that suggests bankers pursue the bank's own interests, as a lender and advisor on M&As, in normal times.

While situations where banks hold both debt and equity claims or have board representation may create conflicts of interests, theory suggests that the optimal mix of debt and equity claims to be held by the bank to protect long-term, fixed-claim stakeholders, such as suppliers and customers, depends on the financial health of the firm. If the firm is healthy, then the bank should hold equity claims in the firm to commit itself not to mislead the stakeholders by claiming the firm is in financial distress to reduce the claims of the latter. If the firm is in financial difficulties, the bank should avoid holding an intermediate stake and rather hold either a negligible stake or virtually all of the equity.

Finally, there is evidence of debtholder expropriation via acquisitions involving LBO investors and hedge funds as well as via large dividend payments. All three have been shown to cause significant drops in the value of debt securities in the targeted firms, while equity securities experience an increase in value. There is also evidence of debtholder expropriation caused by corporate restructuring, i.e. the selling-off of subsidiaries via asset sell-offs, spin-offs and equity carve-outs.

Benefits and costs from relationship-based banking

The effects of bank influence and board representation

Conflicts of interests created by bank ownership and board representation

Evidence of debtholder expropriation around changes in ownership

14.6 Discussion questions

1 Review the theoretical and empirical literature on the advantages and disadvantages of close lender relationships. What, if anything, do you conclude?

2 What evidence is there about the expropriation of debtholders by shareholders?

Reading list

Key reading

Berlin, M., John, K. and Saunders, A. (1996), 'Bank Equity Stakes in Borrowing Firms and Financial Distress', *Review of Financial Studies* 9, 889–919.

Dittmann, I., Maug, E. and Schneider, C. (2010), 'Bankers on the Boards of German Firms: What They Do, What They Are Worth, and Why They Are (Still) There', *Review of Finance* 14, 35–71.

Elsas, R. (2005), 'Empirical Determinants of Relationship Lending', *Journal of Financial Intermediation* 14, 32–57.

Kroszner, R.S. and Strahan, P.E. (2001), 'Banker on Boards: Monitoring, Conflicts of Interest, and Lender Liability', *Journal of Financial Economics* 62, 415–52.

Petersen, M.A. and Rajan, R.G. (1995), 'The Effect of Credit Market Competition on Lending Relationships', *Quarterly Journal of Economics* 110, 407–43.

Rajan, R. (1992), 'Insiders and Outsiders. The Choice between Relationship and Arms Length Debt', *Journal of Finance* 47, 1367–400.

Renneboog, L. and Szilagyi, P.G. (2008), 'Corporate Restructuring and Bondholder Wealth', *European Financial Management* 14, 792–819.

Vitols, S. (2005), 'Changes in Germany's Bank-Based Financial System: Implications for Corporate Governance', *Corporate Governance: An International Review* 13, 386–96.

Further reading

Asquith, P. and Wizman, T. (1990), 'Event Risk, Covenants, and Bondholder Returns in Leveraged Buyouts', *Journal of Financial Economics* 27, 195–213.

Degryse, H. and De Jong, A. (2006), 'Investment and Internal Finance: Asymmetric Information or Managerial Discretion?', *International Journal of Industrial Organization* 24, 125–47.

Dhillon, U.S. and Johnson, H. (1994), 'The Effect of Dividend Changes on Stock and Bond Prices', *Journal of Finance* 49, 281–9.

Edwards, J. and K. Fischer, K. (1994), *Banks, Finance and Investment in Germany*, Cambridge, UK: Cambridge University Press.

Hoshi, T., Kashyap A. and Scharfstein, D. (1991), 'Corporate Structure, Liquidity, and Investment: Evidence from Japanese Industrial Groups', *Quarterly Journal of Economics* 106, 33–60.

Van Ees, H. and Garretsen, H. (1994), 'Liquidity and Business Investment: Evidence from Dutch Panel Data', *Journal of Macroeconomics* 16, 613–27.

Warga, A. and Welch, I. (1993), 'Bondholder Losses in Leveraged Buyouts', *Review of Financial Studies* 6, 959–82.

15 Employee rights and voice across corporate governance systems

Chapter Aims

This chapter focuses on a key corporate stakeholder, i.e. employees. The chapter reviews how various theories on corporate governance assess the impact on firm value of improvements in workers' rights. Other topics reviewed in this chapter include the level of investments in employee training, the strength of employee representation and voice across corporate governance systems, and possible breaches of trust via takeovers of implicit contracts managers have with their employees.

Learning Outcomes

After reading this chapter, you should be able to:

1 Contrast the views of the law and finance literature and the varieties of capitalism (VOC) literature on how improvements in workers' conditions and rights affect firm performance and investor rights

2 Compare the comparative advantages and disadvantages of economies based on networks and strong employee voice with those of economies based on flexible and highly liquid markets

3 Assess how investment in human capital varies across corporate governance systems

4 Evaluate the degrees of employee voice and representation across corporate governance systems and their impact on firm performance and productivity

5 Critically review the literature on employee ownership

6 Appraise the existing evidence on breaches of trust of implicit contracts with workers

15.1 Introduction

In the previous chapters, the focus has been on the providers of finance, i.e. shareholders and debtholders. Much of the corporate governance literature focuses on the latter two, their relationship as well as the relationships they have with the firm's management. However, corporations also deal with other important but non-financial stakeholders, such as employees, gatekeepers, customers, suppliers and local citizens. This chapter will focus on the relationships of the firm with its employees while the next chapter will study the firm's dealings with its gatekeepers.

The strength of employee rights in each country is intrinsically linked to the generally accepted objective of the firm in that country. This link has already been discussed in Chapter 1. However, as a reminder it is important to illustrate how managers from different countries perceive their priorities with regard to maintaining dividends and avoiding employee lay-offs. Figure 15.1 suggests that stakeholder considerations, including the safeguarding of existing jobs within the firm, are more important in France, Germany and Japan whereas shareholder value is the focus in the UK and the USA.

Figure 15.1 Dividend cuts or employee lay-offs
Notes: The number of firms surveyed is 68 for France, 105 for Germany, 68 for Japan, 75 for the UK and 83 for the USA.
Source: Yoshimori, M. (1995), 'Whose Company is It? The Concept of the Corporation in Japan and the West', *Long Range Planning* 28, figure 2.

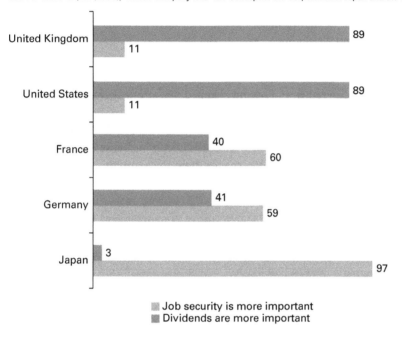

Returning to the taxonomies of corporate governance systems, the law and finance literature assumes that the relationship between shareholders and employees is a zero-sum game, i.e. the rights of one party can only be improved by weakening the rights of the other one. Conversely, the varieties of capitalism (VOC) literature argues that it is possible to combine strong investor rights with strong employee rights.

More generally, the rights of employees as well as their voice vary across corporate governance systems. In some countries, virtually all workers are members of a trade union whereas in some other countries trade unions are illegal. However, in most developed countries trade unions do play some role and the degree of their role is determined by institutional, legal and corporate governance characteristics. Further, employer-employee dependency, such as job security and training, are also likely to vary across corporate governance systems.

Apart from revisiting the taxonomies of corporate governance while adopting a different angle, this chapter also reviews the literature on employee ownership as well as employee board representation and the efficiency of such arrangements in terms of productivity and performance. Finally, this chapter concludes by reviewing the evidence as to breaches of trust of implicit employment contracts.

15.2 The law and finance literature

Most of the law and finance literature is based on the premise that institutions act as either constrainers or facilitators on rational, profit-maximizing individuals. The focus of this literature tends to be on the level of property rights, i.e. investor protection, as well as law enforcement. As discussed in Chapter 1, the two influential academics Andrei Shleifer and Robert Vishny defined corporate governance as 'the ways in which suppliers of finance to corporations assure themselves of getting a return on their investment'.[1] The reason why suppliers of finance, and in particular shareholders, are thought to be paramount is that they are the only corporate stakeholders who have invested sunk funds in the firm. If the firm fails, shareholders will lose all of their money while other stakeholders walk away relatively *unscathed*. Further, given the key importance it attaches to the role of owners or shareholders, the law and finance literature argues that there is a clear hierarchy of corporate governance systems, with those systems that provide strong investor rights being clearly superior to those with weak property rights. Ultimately, the level of investor protection dictates the size of a country's capital market and, in turn, its levels of economic growth and development.

Mark Roe's theory on the political determinants of corporate governance (see also Chapter 4) is the only theory from the law and finance literature which does not advocate the superiority of corporate governance systems that provide strong investor rights. Nevertheless, Roe still assumed that strong investor rights cannot be combined with strong employee protection. Roe argued that different countries have found different ways of ensuring social peace. While the social democracies of Continental Europe have maintained social peace by granting their workers strong rights, other countries such as the UK and the USA have focused on ensuring that investors in companies are well protected. From a corporate governance angle, the main consequence of strong worker rights is the absence of a separation of ownership and control. Both will stay concentrated, as this is the only way shareholders can protect themselves from a powerful workforce and strong managers.

Compared to Roe, who focused on the political orientation of governments in power, Marco Pagano and Paolo Volpin concentrated on electoral systems, i.e. proportional versus majoritarian systems.[2] They argued that political parties under proportional systems focus on social groups with homogenous preferences such as workers and managers, whereas political parties under majoritarian or first past the post systems focus on the pivotal voting district. As the latter is assumed to be inhabited by investors, political parties in majoritarian systems will cater for this social group by promising to improve property rights in their political manifesto. In contrast, in proportional systems political parties will promise to improve worker rights to the detriment of investor rights in order to capture the votes of employees and managers. Again, Pagano and Volpin assumed that there is a zero-sum game between investor protection and employee rights and that strengthening one of them necessarily implies weakening the other one.

Similarly, Rafel La Porta, Florencio Lopez-de-Silanes, Robert Vishny and Andrei Shleifer argued that weak law, in particular weak investor rights, make it easier for corporate stakeholders, such as managers and employees, to expropriate the shareholders.[3] Again, improving the rights of these stakeholders can only result in weakening the rights of the owners of the corporation. Juan Botero, Simeon Djankov, Rafael La Porta, Florencio Lopez-de-Silanes and Andrei Shleifer went further in terms of assessing the consequences of strong employee rights.[4] Their study looked at the regulation of labour markets in 85 countries. They analyzed the following three areas of labour market regulation: employee protection, laws on collective relations and social security.

[1]Shleifer, A. and Vishny, R.W. (1997), 'A Survey of Corporate Governance', *Journal of Finance* 52 (2), 737–83.
[2]Pagano, M. and Volpin, P. (2005), 'The Political Economy of Corporate Governance', *American Economic Review* 95, 1005–30.
[3]La Porta, R., Lopez-de-Silanes, F., Shleifer, A. and Vishny, R. (1997), 'Legal Determinants of External Finance', *Journal of Finance* 52, 1131–50. La Porta, R., Lopez-de-Silanes, F., Shleifer, A. and Vishny, R. (1998), 'Law and Finance', *Journal of Political Economy* 106, 1113–55.
[4]Botero, J.C., Djankov, S., La Porta, R., Lopez-de-Silanes, F. and Shleifer, A. (2004), 'The Regulation of Labor', *Quarterly Journal of Economics* 119, 1339–82.

The results from their study suggested that countries with more strongly regulated labour markets have higher unemployment rates, especially for younger workers, and lower participation rates, i.e. lower proportions of the population participating in the labour market. While they found that countries with left-wing governments tend to have more labour market regulation in place, legal families are better at explaining differences in labour market regulation across countries. They concluded that legal families are better at explaining differences in the degree of labour market regulation than the political orientation of governments.

15.3 The varieties of capitalism literature

While the law and finance literature attributes a central role to law, government and electoral systems and is firmly grounded in path dependence, the varieties of capitalism (VOC) literature allows for institutions to co-evolve over time and to adjust to the changing and evolving environment. Importantly, the VOC literature is based on the concept of complementarities. Two institutions have complementarities if their joint existence increases the efficiency and productivity of one or both of them. It also focuses on relationships, i.e. it is embedded in patterns of expectations and activities that reflect not just norms and rules, but also attitudes and values. In contrast, the law and finance literature is much more mechanistic as well as more fatalistic given its strong emphasis on path dependence and history.

Chapter 4 reviewed the two broad varieties of capitalism proposed by Peter Hall and David Soskice.[5] They are the liberal market economies (LMEs) and the coordinated market economies (CMEs). The main difference between the two varieties is the way they tackle economic coordination problems. LMEs resolve economic coordination problems via markets. Hence, markets – including capital markets and labour markets – in LMEs are highly developed, liquid and flexible, and regulation is kept to a minimum to avoid constraining market forces. Firms will invest in generic assets that can be easily sold off if the need to do so arises. Downsizing of the workforce will be common practice in economic downturns given the flexibility of labour markets and the relatively low levels of employment protection and employee voice. However, flexible labour markets also enable workers to switch easily between companies or even industries. Firms will be unwilling to invest heavily in training given the risk that competitors may free-ride on their efforts by poaching their employees once they have been fully trained. In contrast, CMEs rely on complex networks to address economic coordination problems. The role and size of markets will be limited compared to LMEs, and heavy regulation will prevent their development. Firms will invest in specific, less generic assets given the lack of liquid markets. The heavily regulated labour market will make it relatively difficult for firms to reduce their workforce, and employees will also find it more difficult to 'shop around' for a better-paid job. Hence, firms will be willing to provide industry-specific training and any attempt by their competitors to poach their highly-trained workers will be kept to a minimum by powerful employer associations policing entire industries.

Again, it is important to understand that the VOC literature does not claim that one system is superior compared to all others (see also Chapter 4).[6] It is rather based on the concept of complementarities, i.e. that two institutions operating together may be more efficient and achieve better outcomes than if they were to exist

[5]Hall, P.A. and Soskice, D. (2001), *Varieties of Capitalism: The Institutional Foundations of Comparative Advantage*, Oxford, UK: Oxford University Press.

[6]Hall and Soskice's work needs to be seen as the culmination of a long tradition of work by Dore and by Lincoln and Kalleberg. Contrary to Hall and Soskice, who did not advocate the superiority of one variety of capitalism, Dore, Lincoln and Kalleberg argued that more stakeholder-oriented varieties of capitalism are superior to other varieties and they based their conclusion at least in part on the better economic performance of Germany and Japan compared to the UK and the USA in the 1980s. See e.g. Dore, R. (2000), *Stock Market Capitalism: Welfare Capitalism*, Cambridge, UK: Cambridge University Press; and Lincoln, J. and Kalleberg, A. (1990), *Culture, Control and Commitment: A Study of Work Organization in the United States and Japan*, Cambridge, UK: Cambridge University Press.

and operate in isolation. Further, this school of thought also predicts that institutions that are dysfunctional are unlikely to persist and form a distinct variety of capitalism. Hence contrary to the law and finance literature, the VOC literature concedes that different institutional setups may produce very similar economic outcomes.

One of the limitations of the dichotomous approach of the VOC literature is that because it focuses on the role of markets, it ignores other institutional differences between capitalist systems. Some of these differences concern the operation of labour markets and employment practices more generally. However, there are more complex taxonomies of capitalist systems in the VOC literature involving more than two varieties of systems. One such taxonomy has been proposed by Richard Whitley.[7] He distinguished between six different types of capitalism or business systems. These are 'compartmentalized' (LMEs), 'collaborative' (Western European type CMEs), 'industrial districts' (a type developed to explain regional synergies found in parts of Italy), and three others, which largely describe business systems found in the Far East. These three other business systems include 'fragmented' (as in Hong Kong), 'state organized' (as in Korea, but also France) and 'highly coordinated' business systems (as in Japan where the government is less interventionist and intermediary associations are more important). Two of the shortcomings of Whitley's approach are that it ignores the peculiarities of Mediterranean capitalism (apart from Italy) and that it does not distinguish between 'Rhineland' and Scandinavian economies despite the marked differences in job protection, wage bargaining and financial systems.

In contrast to Whitley's a priori approach, Bruno Amable's taxonomy is systematically grounded on comparative empirical, rather than sometimes anecdotal case study, evidence. Amable proposed five different types of capitalist systems which do a better job in terms of considering differences across Europe.[8] His types of capitalism included 'Asian capitalism' (e.g. Japan) and 'market-based economies' (or LMEs), but most importantly also three distinct European varieties of capitalism, i.e. 'social democratic economies' (Scandinavia), 'Continental European capitalism' (France, Germany, Benelux) and 'south European capitalism' (Italy, Greece, etc.).

Indeed, within the broader group of the CMEs, there are significant differences between Scandinavia and many Rhineland economies. While Germany, Austria, Switzerland and Sweden can be characterized as high job-security CMEs, countries such as Denmark and Norway operate so-called flexicurity policies, which combine job-market *flexi*bility with some degree of job se*curity*. Flexicurity policies reduce job security, but they also give a greater role to the government in the development of skills as well as the retraining of employees in declining industries, and unemployment benefits are better than in LMEs. South European capitalism has features of both LMEs and Continental European capitalism. Similar to LMEs, its corporations compete on price. However, in common with Continental European capitalism, its corporations are characterized by concentrated control. While workers of large corporations typically have good job security, those working for smaller companies are less well protected and the enforcement of employment law is also weaker. France and Italy share many features of CMEs, such as the relatively small size of their stock markets and the high levels of job security. However, in recent years France has moved closer to Anglo-Saxon type capital markets. Similarly, Italy is a capitalist system with somewhat ambiguous characteristics, with its Northern region sticking out given the relatively large proportion of small firms that use skilled labour.

There are also marked differences in terms of training and education between the different varieties of capitalism. As stated above, the flexibility of labour markets reduces the provision of vocational training by employers in LMEs to a minimum as they are reluctant to invest in training given the risk that their competitors may free-ride on their efforts. In the UK, the government has focused on the provision of good quality generic tertiary, vocational training. This ensures that firms have access to cheap, short-term labour. In turn, employees

[7]Whitley, R. (1999), *Divergent Capitalisms: The Social Structuring and Change of Business Systems*, Oxford, UK: Oxford University Press.
[8]Amable, B. (2003), *The Diversity of Modern Capitalism*, Oxford, UK: Oxford University Press.

can use their generic skills in various jobs and organizational settings, enabling them to switch jobs quickly should the need arise. This also facilitates the distribution of ideas and knowledge to a greater extent than would otherwise be possible in contexts of high competition. The USA, another LME, is often characterized by the dualistic nature of employment and work practices, with at one extreme mass production of standardized products and basic services requiring cheap and unskilled workers, and at the other extreme a highly skilled labour force working in highly innovative industries such as the software and biotech industries.

The high job-security CMEs of e.g. Austria, Germany and Sweden rely heavily on employees with firm-specific skills and strong vocational training. Good job tenure provides employees with the right incentives to acquire firm-specific skills as well as ensuring that the employer's investments in employee training are less likely to be reaped by its competitors. A highly developed state welfare system operates as a safety net to support workers made redundant in an economic downturn. In contrast, firms in LMEs will concentrate on basic induction training and spend relatively large amounts of money on this training given the high staff turnover. Given the nature of the training, some or all of it may be contracted out to external providers that benefit from significant economies of scale and are therefore more likely to provide the training at a reduced cost.

15.4 Employee stock ownership[9]

According to the National Center for Employee Ownership (NCEO), approximately 32 million US workers own shares in their employers and the total asset value of employee stock ownership exceeds one trillion US dollars (see Table 15.1).[10] Table 15.2 shows the equivalent figures for Europe.

Table 15.1 Employee stock ownership in the USA in 2016

Type of plan	Number of plans	Number of participants (million)	Employer securities (US$ billion)	Total assets (US$ billion)
Standalone ESOPs	5,533	1.77	115.5	131
KSOPs[1]	1,184	12.28	155	1,200
ESOP-like plans[2]	2,898	1.1	23.5	64
Total for ESOP and ESOP-like plans	9,615	15.1	294	1,400

Notes: [1]Combination of a 401(k) plan and an ESOP (a 401(k) plan is a type of retirement plan); [2]ESOP-like plans are profit sharing, stock bonus and other defined contribution plans that are at least 20 per cent invested in employer stock and have at least five participants.

Source: National Center for Employee Ownership (NCEO) (www.nceo.org/articles/statistical-profile-employee-ownership), accessed on 8 February 2017

There are two contrasting views about the consequences of employee equity ownership of their companies. According to the first view, whose supporters included Peter Drucker[11] and Masahiko Aoki,[12] employee stock ownership should be encouraged as it aligns the interests of the workers with those of the shareholders. In turn, this will not only improve corporate performance but also increase the monitoring of the management. Given that employees are both shareholders and workers of the corporation, they will have the incentives to monitor

---

[9]As the focus of this book is on corporate governance and in particular corporate governance relating to stock corporations, this section omits reviewing another important organizational form involving employee ownership, which is worker cooperatives. Readers interested in employee financial participation more generally as well as its practice across Europe should read the excellent survey paper by Poutsma, E. and De Nijs, W. (2003), 'Broad-based Employee Financial Participation in the European Union', *International Journal of Human Resource Management* 14, 863–92.

[10]National Center for Employee Ownership (NCEO), www.nceo.org/articles/statistical-profile-employee-ownership, accessed on 18 March 2017.

[11]Drucker, P.F. (1978), *The Future of Industrial Man. A Conservative Approach*, New York: The John Day Company.

[12]Aoki, M. (1984), *The Cooperative Game Theory of the Firm*, Oxford, UK: Oxford University Press.

the management as well as have better information than other shareholders, which should facilitate the monitoring of the management. Conversely, Michael Jensen and William Meckling had a different view according to which employee equity ownership entrenches employees, just like management ownership may entrench managers.[13] This will not only make it difficult to remove employees but it will also push the latter to maximize their own utility, including increasing their wages beyond the current market rates. Hence, employee equity ownership will reduce rather than increase corporate performance.

Table 15.2 **Employee stock ownership in Europe**

	2010	**2011**	**2012**	**2013**	**2014**	**2015**
Employee owners (million)	8.446	8.541	8.389	8.130	8.028	8.021
Employees' share in ownership structure (%)	2.88	2.95	2.84	3.05	3.07	3.09
Capitalization held by employees (billion euro)	202	240	204	271	310	367
Percentage of European companies with employee ownership (%)	87.3	88.2	89.4	90.8	92.4	93.3
Percentage of European companies with broad-based plans (%)	46.8	47.7	48.7	49.4	50.8	52.8
Percentage of European companies with stock option plans (%)	58.3	59.3	60.3	60.7	61.7	63.1
Percentage of European companies having launched new plans (%)	26.9	29.8	28.6	27.8	28.7	29.4

Notes: Table 15.2 is based on 2,596 European companies which includes (a) all listed companies whose stock market capitalization was at least 200 million euro in May of the years 2010 to 2015 and (b) non-listed companies with more than 100 employees and whose employees own 50 per cent or more of the company. The countries covered include Austria, Belgium, Bulgaria, Croatia, Cyprus, Czech Republic, Denmark, Estonia, Finland, France, Germany, Greece, Hungary, Iceland, Ireland, Italy, Latvia, Lithuania, Luxembourg, Malta, the Netherlands, Norway, Poland, Portugal, Romania, Slovak Republic, Slovenia, Spain, Sweden, Switzerland and the UK.

Source: European Federation of Employee Share Ownership (www.efesonline.org), accessed on 8 February 2017.

Importantly, both of the above views implicitly assume that employee stock ownership comes hand in hand with employee voting power. However, this is not necessarily the case as executive directors frequently exercise the votes from the employee shares. For example, in the UK, employee shares are often held by trusts whose trustees are the executive directors. Hence, rather than entrenching the employees, employee ownership may further entrench the management.

The empirical evidence as to the effect of employee ownership on firm performance and employee productivity is as yet inconclusive. Event studies (i.e. studies measuring stock market response to a specific corporate event) on the adoption of US employee stock option plans (ESOPs) report either positive abnormal returns[14]

[13]Jensen, M.C. and Meckling, W.H. (1979), 'Rights and Production Functions: An Application to Labor-Managed Firms and Codetermination', *Journal of Business* 52, 469–506.

[14]See e.g. Chang, S. (1990), 'Employee Stock Ownership Plans and Shareholder Wealth: An Empirical Investigation', *Financial Management* 19, 48–58; Faria, H.J., Trahan, E. and Rogers, R.C. (1993), 'ESOPs in Public Companies: Firm Characteristics, Shareholder Wealth, and Impact on Performance', *Journal of Employee Ownership Law and Finance* 5, 75–92.

or insignificant abnormal returns.[15] Olumbunmi Faleye, Vikas Mehrotra and Randall Morck explained the lack of conclusive results by the characteristics of US ESOPs.[16] From a tax point of view, an ESOP is treated as a defined contribution retirement plan and therefore creates tax breaks for the company that introduces the plan. Hence, the positive stock market reaction to the announcement of a new ESOP may be due to the reduction in the company's tax liability and/or the expected increase in employee productivity. In addition, ESOPs may also be used by the management of takeover targets either to strengthen the support against an unwelcome takeover offer or to increase the shareholder returns from a takeover contest. Hence, a priori it is not clear what the stock market reaction to the adoption of an ESOP should be. Similarly, studies on the improvements in productivity and financial and accounting performance brought about by ESOPs are inconclusive.[17] Further, the study by Faleye et al. reported negative effects of ESOPs across the board: decreases in shareholder value, sales growth, job creation and reduced investment as evidenced by lower capital expenditure and spending on R&D.

However, Joseph Blasi, Richard Freeman, Christopher Mackin and Douglas Kruse argued that it is important to consider the whole set of employment practices of a company when assessing the effects of employee ownership.[18] Based on survey evidence from 14 companies employing more than 41,000 workers at 320 sites and offering a range of employee ownership instruments as well as stock options, Blasi et al. reported that employee ownership lowers employee turnover and increases loyalty as well as increases the willingness to work hard, especially when combined with low levels of supervision, high-performance policies and fixed pay at or above market rates. These beneficial effects are particularly strong for profit-sharing programmes, stock options and ESOPs, which are relatively low risk and keep employee concerns about risking their own capital at bay.

15.5 Employee board representation

Table 15.3 provides information on employee representation in Europe. The countries that have a legal requirement for employee representation on the board of directors (frequently subject to a minimum firm size) include Austria, Denmark, Finland, Germany, Luxembourg and Sweden. In addition, board representation of employees in Norway exists in a significant percentage of private sector firms, and in France and the Netherlands employee representatives have a consultative capacity. The German Co-determination system is the most generous one as it grants employee representatives 50 per cent of the supervisory board seats, i.e. half of the non-executive board seats (see also Section 7.2 of Chapter 7) in companies with more than 2,000 workers. In comparison, other countries that have employee board representation typically limit the proportion of workers on the board to one-third, except for Finland where the proportion is one-fifth and Sweden where it is less than a half.

---

[15]Gordon, L. and Pound, J. (1990), 'ESOPs and Corporate Control', *Journal of Financial Economics* 27, 525–55.

[16]Faleye, O., Mehrotra, V. and Morck, R. (2006), 'When Labor Has a Voice in Corporate Governance', *Journal of Financial and Quantitative Analysis* 41, 489–510.

[17]See e.g. Bloom, S. (1986), 'Employee Ownership and Firm Performance', PhD dissertation, Harvard University, USA, who found no improvement in productivity, whereas Beatty, A. (1995), 'The Cash Flow and Informational Effects of Employee Stock Ownership Plans', *Journal of Financial Economics* 38, 211–40, found a significant increase in productivity. See also e.g. Park, S. and Song, M.H. (1995), 'Employee Stock Ownership Plans, Firm Performance, and Monitoring by Outside Blockholders', *Financial Management* 24, 52–65, who found an increase in performance compared to Lougee, B. (1999), 'An Empirical Investigation of the Implications of Employee Ownership for the Agency Problem and the Information Content of Earnings', PhD dissertation, Cornell University, USA.

[18]Blasi, J.R., Freeman, R.B., Mackin, C. and Kruse, D.L. (2010), 'Creating a Bigger Pie? The Effects of Employee Ownership, Profit Sharing, and Stock Options on Workplace Performance', in Kruse, D.L., Freeman, R.B. and Blasi, J.R. (eds.), *Shared Capitalism at Work: Employee Ownership, Profit and Gain Sharing, and Broad-based Stock Options*, Chicago, IL: University of Chicago Press, pp. 139–65.

Table 15.3 Employee representation in Europe

Country	Type of employee representation	Statutory provisions/ collective agreements	Public sector board-level representation only	Type of regulation: legislation, collective agreement or other
Austria	Austrian companies have supervisory boards which oversee the action of the executive board, which runs the business on a day-to-day basis. The works council has the right to choose one-third of the representatives of the supervisory board in companies with at least 40 employees.	Yes	No	1965 Stock Act; 1974 Labour Constitution Act; 1974 Directive on Employee Representation on Supervisory Boards.
Belgium	In Belgium, there is no system for the representation of employees on the management, supervisory or administrative bodies of private companies, whatever their structure, in the strict sense of the term. Employee representation to management is provided by works councils and workplace health and safety committees. However, in some public service companies such as railways, public transport and universities, employees have seats on the boards.	No	–	No regulation by law or collective agreements.
Denmark	Employees in Danish companies employing at least 50 employees are entitled (though not obliged) to elect at least two representatives on the board of directors and up to one-third of the total number of members.	Yes	No	Two separate laws, one concerning joint stock companies (A/S) and one concerning companies with limited liabilities (ApS).
Finland	In companies with 150 and more staff, employees have the right to board-level representation. Much of the detail, however, is left to local negotiation between the employer and the trade unions. There must be between one and four employee representatives, who should make up one-fifth of the body in which they sit.	Yes	No	1990 Act on Personnel Representation in the Administration of Undertakings.
France	In private sector companies, the law provides for two or four representatives of the works council (depending on the number of managers employed) to attend meetings of the board of directors or supervisory board in a consultative capacity. In public sector organizations, elected employee representatives constitute up to one-third of the board and act as full members. Furthermore, in all limited companies, the shareholders may voluntarily decide to include elected employee representatives on the board.	Yes	No	A 1946 decree provides for the consultative participation of members of the works council on the board of directors or the supervisory board. A 1983 law on the democratization of the public sector provided for elected employees on the boards of all government-run companies. A 1986 decree allows for companies to opt for board-level employee representation. Additional collectively agreed provisions exist, but do not improve upon statutory measures.

Country	Type of employee representation	Statutory provisions/ collective agreements	Public sector board-level representation only	Type of regulation: legislation, collective agreement or other
Germany	Employees in companies with 500 employees or more have representation on the supervisory board. The proportion of worker representatives varies from one-third, in companies with between 500 and 2,000 employees, to one-half, in companies with more than 2,000 workers. In these larger companies, the chair in effect represents the shareholders and has the casting vote. The one exception is the larger coal or iron and steel companies where the chair is independent. In the coal, iron and steel industries, the employee representatives can also appoint the 'labour director', who is part of the management board.	Yes	No	1951 Coal, Iron and Steel Industry Co-determination Act; 1952 Works Constitution Act; 1976 Co-determination Act. A number of collectively agreed provisions exist in the private sector.
Greece	Employee representation on the board exists only in the 'socialized sector', such as public utilities and transport, where there are two levels of worker participation. The highest level in each company is the 'representative assembly of social control', which sets broad policy objectives. Employee representatives constitute up to one-third of this group, with another third from consumer groups and local authorities and one-third from the government. Below this there is the board of directors, where again one-third of the members are elected by the workforce.	Yes	Yes	Law 1365/1983 on 'socialization of state-run undertakings and utilities' of 1983.
Ireland	There is no statutory requirement for board-level representation in the private sector in Ireland. In a number of state-owned companies, employee representatives have one-third of the seats on the main boards.	Yes	Yes	Worker Participation (State Enterprise) Acts of 1977 and 1988.

(Continued)

Table 5.3 (*Continued*)

Country	Type of employee representation	Statutory provisions/ collective agreements	Public sector board-level representation only	Type of regulation: legislation, collective agreement or other
Italy	Although the Italian Constitution recognizes 'the rights of workers to participate in management, in the manner and within the limits prescribed by law', this has never led to legislation which provides for board-level representation in Italy, which is largely absent. However, some company-level agreements provide for the participation of employee representatives in management boards or supervisory boards, usually through forms of employee share-ownership programmes.	No	–	Neither legislation nor comprehensive collective agreements. Some company-level agreements.
Luxembourg	Employees have representation on the boards of companies which are more than 25 per cent state-owned or which receive state aid for their main business, and of all companies with more than 1,000 employees. In the latter case, the employee representatives make up one-third of the board, while in the former there is one employee representative for every 100 employees with a minimum of three employee representatives and a maximum of one-third of the total board.	Yes	No	1915 Companies Act; Law of 6 May 1974 introduced workers' representation at board and auditors' level.
Netherlands	Companies with more than 100 employees, a works council and a set amount of capital must set up a supervisory board. The supervisory board elects its own members and the shareholders, the works council and the executive board have the right to recommend new members. There is no fixed proportion of employee representatives on the board: a works council may use its right of recommendation, but employees do not necessarily have a real representative on the board. According to the Civil Code, members of the supervisory board must take the interest of the company and the undertaking as a whole into account in the fulfilment of their duties; they are not employee representatives as such.	Yes	No	1971 'Structure Law'; Civil Code (Dutch company law).

Country	Type of employee representation	Statutory provisions/ collective agreements	Public sector board-level representation only	Type of regulation: legislation, collective agreement or other
Norway	A significant proportion of private sector enterprises are regulated by legislation that safeguards employee representation on company boards – usually one-third of the total. In some, but far from all, state and municipal institutions, political authorities have decided that employees should be entitled to be represented on the boards. Similar voluntary arrangements may be found in companies that are not covered by the traditional legal framework.	Yes	No	1976 Companies Act; 1980 Foundations Act; and 1985 Act on general and limited partnerships. No uniform set of rules regulating employees' rights to board-level representation in the public sector. Only in a few cases is the right to board representation regulated by national collective agreements, e.g. that for cooperatives. Improvements by collective agreement are rare.
Portugal	The appointment of employees' representatives to the governing bodies of state corporations or other public entities is provided for expressly by the Constitution and by the Law on Workers' Committees. The legislation on public corporations also provides for the appointment of an employees' representative to each of the governing bodies: board of directors and supervisory board. However, this legislation is not complied with in practice. There are, in fact, no known cases in which employees' representatives have been appointed to a corporation's governing bodies. In the private sector, the law expressly states that recognition of this right depends exclusively on the wishes of the parties involved. In practice, there are no known cases of any significance in which this right has been recognized.	Yes	Yes	Portuguese Constitution; 1979 Law on Workers' Committees; 1976 and 1984 legislation on public corporations. NB – legislation not implemented in practice.
Spain	There is no statutory right for employees to have any representation at board level. However, as a result of tripartite agreements, there is some union representation on the boards of the largest public sector companies. There is also regulation of board-level employee representation in institutions with a special legal status. This is the case for savings banks, which are subject to specific regulations because they are foundations of a private nature with 'charitable' aims that act according to market criteria.	Yes	Yes	No legislation. Some tripartite agreements and specific regulations on board representation in certain types of public companies and in organizations with a special legal status.

(Continued)

Table 15.3 *(Continued)*

Country	Type of employee representation	Statutory provisions/ collective agreements	Public sector board-level representation only	Type of regulation: legislation, collective agreement or other
Sweden	Board-level representation is widespread in Sweden. In almost all companies with more than 25 employees, employees have the right to two board members. In companies with more than 1,000 employees engaged in at least two types of businesses, this rises to three board members. The employee representatives can never be in a majority.	Yes	No	1987 Act on Board Representation for Private Sector Employees (original legislation dates from 1973).
United Kingdom	There is no legal right for workers to have any representation at board level. There are very few examples of the existence of 'worker directors' except in the area of management buy-outs of particular companies, mostly in the recently privatized or deregulated areas of the economy, e.g. the transport industry.	No	–	No legal right for workers to have any representation at board level.

Source: Adapted from Schulten, T. and Zagelmeyer, S. (1998), *Board-Level Employee Representation in Europe*, European Industrial Relations Observatory (EIRO).

Box 15.1 shows the composition of the supervisory board of the German company, Siemens AG. Siemens AG has 20 members on its supervisory board and half of these are employee representatives. Three of the employee representatives are from IG Metall, the German trade union for metalworkers. All other employee representatives are employees of Siemens AG or its subsidiaries.

Box 15.1
The composition of the supervisory board of Siemens AG

Name	Occupation	Date of birth	Member since
Reinhard Hahn*	Trade Union Secretary of the Managing Board of IG Metall	June 24, 1956	January 27, 2015
Bettina Haller*	Chairwoman of the Combine Works Council of Siemens AG	March 14, 1959	April 1, 2007
Hans-Jürgen Hartung*	Chairman of the Works Council of Siemens Erlangen Süd, Germany	March 10, 1952	January 27, 2009
Robert Kensbock*	Deputy Chairman of the Central Works Council of Siemens AG	March 13, 1971	January 23, 2013
Harald Kern*	Chairman of the Siemens Europe Committee	March 16, 1960	January 24, 2008
Jürgen Kerner*	Executive Managing Board Member of IG Metall	January 22, 1969	January 25, 2012
Nicola Leibinger-Kammüller, Dr. phil.	President and Chairwoman of the Managing Board of TRUMPF GmbH + Co. KG	December 15, 1959	January 24, 2008
Gérard Mestrallet	Chairman of the Board of Directors of ENGIE S.A.	April 1, 1949	January 23, 2013
Norbert Reithofer, Dr.-Ing. Dr.-Ing. E.h.	Chairman of the Supervisory Board of Bayerische Motoren Werke Aktiengesellschaft	May 29, 1956	January 27, 2015
Güler Sabancı	Chairwoman and Managing Director of Hacı Ömer Sabancı Holding A.Ş.	August 14, 1955	January 23, 2013
Nathalie von Siemens, Dr. phil.	Managing Director and Spokesperson of Siemens Stiftung	July 14, 1971	January 27, 2015
Michael Sigmund*	Chairman of the Committee of Spokespersons of the Siemens Group; Chairman of the Central Committee of Spokespersons of Siemens AG	September 13, 1957	March 1, 2014

(Continued)

Name	Occupation	Date of birth	Member since
Jim Hagemann Snabe	Supervisory Board Member	October 27, 1965	October 1, 2013
Sibylle Wankel*	General Counsel, Managing Board of IG Metall	March 3, 1964	April 1, 2009
Gerhard Cromme, Dr. iur. Chairman	Chairman of the Supervisory Board of Siemens AG	February 25, 1943	January 23, 2003
Birgit Steinborn* First Deputy Chairwoman	Chairwoman of the Central Works Council of Siemens AG	March 26, 1960	January 24, 2008
Werner Wenning Second Deputy Chairman	Chairman of the Supervisory Board of Bayer AG	October 21, 1946	January 23, 2013
Olaf Bolduan*	Chairman of the Works Council of Siemens Dynamowerk, Berlin, Germany	July 24, 1952	July 11, 2014
Michael Diekmann	Supervisory Board Member	December 23, 1954	January 24, 2008
Hans Michael Gaul, Dr. iur.	Supervisory Board Member	March 2, 1942	January 24, 2008

Note: Employee representatives are marked with an asterisk.

Source: Siemens 2016 annual report, pp. 126–7.

Employee representation on the board of directors potentially has a dual informational role. First, it may democratize working life as well as provide valuable information for the management. Such information includes information on work practices within the firm, experience of workers as well as workers' attitudes towards specific company policies or strategies. This information is valuable to the directors as it is likely to help them run the firm more efficiently. Second, employee representation on the board may enable employees to gather information that is valuable to them. In particular, employees may use information gathered on the firm's value and profitability to extract rents from the firm, such as salaries that exceed the going rate, or to protect their jobs within the firm. In turn, this will affect firm performance and productivity in a negative way. Hence, a priori it is not clear what the effect of employee board representation on performance and productivity will be. This is reflected in the empirical evidence which is not conclusive either.

Felix FitzRoy and Kornelius Kraft studied the impact of the German Co-determination Law of 1976 which required firms with more than 2,000 workers to have 50 per cent of employee representatives on their supervisory board. Previously, the proportion of employee representatives had to be only one-third.[19] They studied the performance, productivity and wage costs for a sample of 68 large companies and 44 smaller firms for 1975 and 1983. They found a negative impact on both productivity and performance of the change in law, but no effect

[19]FitzRoy, F.R. and Kraft, K. (1993), 'Economic Effects of Codetermination', *Scandinavian Journal of Economics* 95, 365–75.

on wage costs. Similarly, Gary Gorton and Frank Schmid found that firms subject to the Co-determination Law have lower performance than firms that are not.[20]

In contrast, Larry Fauver and Michael Fuerst found a positive effect of employee board representation on firm performance.[21] They found that this positive effect is particularly strong in industries where coordination and information sharing are important. In addition, managerial perks are also reduced via employee board representation, suggesting that workers monitor managerial excesses and reduce principal-agency costs. However, these results do not hold for employee board seats held by union representatives who are not employees of the firm.

The above studies on the impact of employee representation on the board are all based on Germany. As a result, a major limitation of these studies is the lack of a suitable control group. In other words, given that employees have the right to appoint a third of the supervisory board members in firms with between 500 and 2,000 workers and half in firms with more than 2,000 workers, the only control group of firms without employee board representation that is available is very small firms, i.e. firms with fewer than 500 workers. However, the performance and productivity of these firms may be very different compared to those with employee board representation for reasons that have *nothing* to do with worker representation.

Øvind Bøhren and Øystein Strøm studied the impact of employee board representation on the value of Norwegian firms. Compared to Germany, not all Norwegian firms have to have worker representation on the board of directors.[22] In addition, board members representing the employees have to be employees of the firm and cannot therefore be union representatives as is often the case with German firms. Bøhren and Strøm found a negative effect of employee board representation on firm value. Edith Ginglinger, William Megginson and Timothée Waxin studied employee representation on the boards of French firms.[23] According to French law, employees have the right to elect two types of directors: employees can elect directors by right of employment and employee-shareholders can elect a director if they hold at least three per cent of the equity. Ginglinger et al. found that directors elected by employees are value neutral while directors elected by employee-shareholders increase firm value and profitability.

While the empirical evidence is as yet inconclusive as to the impact of employee board representation on firm performance and productivity, it nevertheless is appropriate to conclude that it is important to take into account the type of employee representative as well as the industry in which the firm operates. Indeed, while employees of the firm that sit on the board increase firm profitability, employee representation via trade union officials not employed by the firm does not seem to have such a positive effect. This suggests that employees on the board provide valuable information to the managers, enabling them to run the firm more efficiently, whereas trade union officials are unlikely to convey information to the managers about the inner workings of the firm. This information sharing role of employee representatives also seems to be more important in some industries than in others.

[20]Gorton, G. and Schmid, F. (2000), 'Universal Banking and the Performance of German Firms', *Journal of Financial Economics* 58, 29–80.
[21]Fauver, L. and Fuerst, M.E. (2006), 'Does Good Corporate Governance Include Employee Representation? Evidence from German Corporate Boards', *Journal of Financial Economics* 82, 673–710.
[22]Bøhren, Ø. and Strøm, R.Ø. (2010), 'Governance and Politics: Regulating Independence and Diversity in the Board Room', *Journal of Business Finance and Accounting* 37, 1281–308.
[23]Ginglinger, E., Megginson, W. and Waxin, T. (2011), 'Employee Ownership, Board Representation, and Corporate Financial Policies', *Journal of Corporate Finance* 17, 868–87.

15.6 Breaches of trust and employee expropriation

Section 1.7 of Chapter 1 already reviewed one of the ways whereby the owners of a corporation may expropriate the employees. This section introduces another way (see also Section 5.3 of Chapter 5 where this way was briefly discussed in the context of the disadvantages of the market-based system). According to Andrei Shleifer and Lawrence Summers, changes in ownership via takeovers are a means of expropriating the employees via breaches of trust which result in breaking the implicit contracts the incumbent management has with the workforce.[24] For example, while the incumbent management promised lifetime employment in return for workers investing in skills valuable to the firm, the new management may be tempted to break this promise and to reduce the workforce by dismissing employees close to retirement age that are perceived to be less productive.

However, the existing empirical research provides little support for the Shleifer and Summers breach of trust hypothesis for both friendly and hostile takeovers[25] as well as management buy-outs.[26] Nevertheless, there is evidence emerging from research that clearly distinguishes private equity acquisitions from other types of acquisitions, and which finds that certain types of private equity acquisitions tend to experience a reduction in employment that cannot be explained by an equivalent increase in productivity and profitability.[27]

15.7 Conclusions

Most of the law and finance literature argues that workers are assets like any others that should be highly liquid and that the firm should be able to dispose of should the need arise. Hence, improving worker rights can only result in reduced investor rights. In other words, the relationship between the former and the latter is a zero-sum game. Some of the law and finance literature has even more extreme conclusions, arguing that greater employee rights reduce overall employment rates and penalize young job seekers. The varieties of capitalism (VOC) literature adopts a somewhat different approach. Improving worker rights can have clear benefits to the owners or shareholders of corporations in terms of workers' greater loyalty and willingness to invest in their human capital. The VOC literature argues that strong employee rights may be part of a greater set of institutional features and that such a set may generate similar economic outcomes and performance to a set of institutional features based on frictionless markets.

The contrasting views of the law and finance literature and the VOC literature on the consequences of improving workers' rights

[24]Shleifer, A. and Summers, L. (1988), 'Breach of Trust in Hostile Takeovers', in A.J. Auerbach (ed.), *Corporate Takeovers: Causes and Consequences*, Chicago, IL: University of Chicago Press.

[25]See e.g. Denis, D. (1994), 'Evidence on the Effects of Hostile and Friendly Tender Offers on Employment', *Managerial and Decision Economics* 15, 341–57, for the USA; Conyon, M.J., Girma, S., Thompson, S. and Wright, P. (2001), 'Do Hostile Mergers Destroy Jobs?' *Journal of Economic Behaviour and Organization* 45, 427–40, as well as Beckman, T. and Forbes, W. (2004), 'An Examination of Takeovers, Job Loss, and Wage Decline within UK Industry', *European Financial Management* 10, 141–65, for the UK; and Gugler, K. and Yurtoglu, B.B. (2004), 'The Effects of Mergers on Company Employment in the USA and Europe', *International Journal of Industrial Organization* 22, 481–502, for a cross-country study.

[26]See e.g. Lichtenberg, F.R. and Siegel, D. (1990), 'The Effects of Leveraged Buyouts on Productivity and Related Aspects of Firm Behaviour', *Journal of Financial Economics* 27, 165–94, for the USA; and Amess, K. and Wright, M. (2012), 'Leveraged Buyouts, Private Equity, and Jobs', *Small Business Economics* 38, 419–30, for the UK.

[27]Goergen, M., O'Sullivan, N. and Wood, G. (2014), 'The Employment Consequences of Private Equity Acquisitions: The Case of Institutional Buy-Outs', *European Economic Review* 71, 67–79.

When workers' rights and training are considered, the diversity of practices and rules across countries increases and the simple, dichotomous version of the VOC literature fails to take into account that diversity. Indeed, the group of coordinated market economies (CMEs) becomes such a disparate group, with at one extreme high job-security countries, such as Austria and Germany, and at the other extreme the flexicurity countries of Northern Europe, which show some of the characteristics of liberal market economies (LMEs) but also major differences which make them distinct from the latter.

The limits of the dichotomous version of the VOC literature

The empirical evidence on the consequences of employee equity ownership on firm performance is as yet inconclusive with some studies finding a positive effect, others a negative effect and yet others an insignificant effect. However, there is some evidence suggesting that employee equity ownership has positive effects if it is part and parcel of a larger set of human resource management policies that aim to motivate employees and increase their commitment to the firm.

The effect of employee ownership on firm performance

Overall, there is little evidence that employees are expropriated after a change in ownership via breaches of trust resulting in the violation of implicit contracts they have with the incumbent management. The lack of evidence applies to both takeovers in general as well as management buy-outs (MBOs) more specifically. However, evidence suggests that certain types of private equity acquisitions are different from other types of acquisition in the sense that they cause employment to fall after the acquisition and that this reduction cannot be explained by an equivalent increase in profitability or productivity.

Breaches of trust and employee expropriation

Finally, while several studies suggest a negative effect of employee board representation on performance and productivity, a recent study by Larry Fauver and Michael Fuerst suggested that employees on the board increase financial performance whereas union representatives on the board do not have such an effect. The positive effect of employee board representation is particularly strong in those industries where information and coordination problems matter.

The impact of employee board representation on firm value

15.8 Discussion questions

1 'Employee rights and investor rights are a zero-sum game. You can only improve the rights of one of these social groups by weakening the rights of the other group'. (Anonymous)

Critically discuss the above statement by referring to the relevant academic literature on corporate governance and capitalist systems.

2 Discuss the limitations of the dichotomous version of the VOC literature when it comes to categorizing labour markets, work practices and employee training across Europe.

3 Download the figures for the level of employment rights and social security used in the Botero et al.

(2004) paper from Professor Andrei Shleifer's website (scholar.harvard.edu/shleifer/publications) for your country. How do you feel about the characterization of your country by Botero et al., taking into account your country's economic performance over the last few decades? Do you agree with their conclusions?

4 What, if anything, can we conclude about the effects of employee ownership and employee board representation on firm performance and productivity? What are the likely limitations of the existing studies in the field? How, if at all, can these limitations be addressed?

Reading list

Key reading

Amable, B. (2003), *The Diversity of Modern Capitalism*, Oxford, UK: Oxford University Press.

Blasi, J.R., Freeman, R.B., Mackin, C. and Kruse, D.L. (2010), 'Creating a Bigger Pie? The Effects of Employee Ownership, Profit Sharing, and Stock Options on Workplace Performance', in Kruse, D.L., Freeman, R.B. and Blasi, J.R. (eds.), *Shared Capitalism at Work: Employee Ownership, Profit and Gain Sharing, and Broad-based Stock Options*, Chicago, IL: University of Chicago Press, pp. 139–65.

Botero, J.C., Djankov, S., La Porta, R., Lopez-de-Silanes, F. and Shleifer, A. (2004), 'The Regulation of Labor', *Quarterly Journal of Economics* 119, 1339–82.

Fauver, L. and Fuerst, M.E. (2006), 'Does Good Corporate Governance Include Employee Representation? Evidence from German Corporate Boards', *Journal of Financial Economics* 82, 673–710.

Shleifer, A. and Summers, L. (1988), 'Breach of Trust in Hostile Takeovers', in A.J. Auerbach (ed.), *Corporate Takeovers: Causes and Consequences*, Chicago, IL: University of Chicago Press.

Whitley, R. (1999), *Divergent Capitalisms: The Social Structuring and Change of Business Systems*, Oxford, UK: Oxford University Press.

Further reading

Beatty, A. (1995), 'The Cash Flow and Informational Effects of Employee Stock Ownership Plans', *Journal of Financial Economics* 38, 211–40.

Bøhren, Ø. and R.Ø. Strøm (2010), 'Governance and Politics: Regulating Independence and Diversity in the Board Room', *Journal of Business Finance and Accounting* 37, 1281–308.

Chang, S. (1990), 'Employee Stock Ownership Plans and Shareholder Wealth: An Empirical Investigation', *Financial Management* 19, 48–58.

Faria, H.J., Trahan, E. and Rogers, R.C. (1993), 'ESOPs in Public Companies: Firm Characteristics, Shareholder Wealth, and Impact on Performance', *Journal of Employee Ownership Law and Finance* 5, 75–92.

FitzRoy, F.R. and Kraft, K. (1993), 'Economic Effects of Codetermination', *Scandinavian Journal of Economics* 95, 365–75.

Ginglinger, E., Megginson, W. and Waxin, T. (2011), 'Employee Ownership, Board Representation, and Corporate Financial Policies', *Journal of Corporate Finance* 17, 868–87

Goergen, M., Brewster, C. and Wood, G. (2009), 'Corporate Governance Regimes and Employment Relations in Europe', *Relations Industrielles/Industrial Relations* 64, 620–40.

Goergen, M., Brewster, C. and Wood, G. (2009), 'Corporate Governance and Training', *Journal of Industrial Relations* 51, 459–87.

Gordon, L. and Pound, J. (1990), 'ESOPs and Corporate Control', *Journal of Financial Economics* 27, 525–55.

Park, S. and Song, M.H. (1995), 'Employee Stock Ownership Plans, Firm Performance, and Monitoring by Outside Blockholders', *Financial Management* 24, 52–65.

Poutsma, E. and De Nijs, W. 'Broad-based Employee Financial Participation in the European Union', *International Journal of Human Resource Management* 14, 863–92.

16 The role of gatekeepers in corporate governance

Chapter Aims

While regulators have been gradually reinforcing the importance of gatekeepers, such as auditors and credit rating agencies, to ensure that companies are well governed, the Enron scandal and the 2007–8 bank failures suggest that gatekeepers often lack the necessary degree of independence, judgement, competence and power to prevent corporate fraud and failure. This chapter aims at assessing the role of gatekeepers in corporate governance. Such gatekeepers include among others stock-market listing authorities, auditors, credit rating agencies and bank regulators. The chapter also reviews the role of corporate governance in regulated industries, including the financial sector.

Learning Outcomes

After reading this chapter, you should be able to:

1 Evaluate the role of gatekeepers in ensuring that companies are run in the interests of their shareholders and other stakeholders

2 Critically assess the independence of gatekeepers – such as auditors and credit rating agencies – vis-à-vis their client firms

3 Gauge the effectiveness of gatekeepers in preventing corporate fraud

4 Evaluate the danger of capture of gatekeepers by the economic actors they are supposed to supervise

5 Judge the existing empirical evidence as to whether regulation acts a substitute or a complement for corporate governance

16.1 Introduction

This chapter reviews the role of gatekeepers and regulation in corporate governance. Gatekeepers, such as auditors and credit rating agencies, play an important role in corporate governance as they provide monitoring and certification services which are useful to investors. However, various gatekeepers tend to suffer from a lack of incentives or conflicts of interests and hence the monitoring they provide may be limited and the certification they offer may be biased. As a result, it is unlikely that investors will be able to rely on a single type of gatekeeper. Instead, they may have to rely on a range of gatekeepers to help them monitor and assess the quality of their investee firms.

While corporate governance regulation has already been the focus of Chapter 6, this chapter looks at regulation more generally, i.e. industry regulation. Regulated industries include the financial sector such as banks and insurance companies. In most countries, they also include utilities such as water, gas, telephony and electricity companies. This chapter will review the extant empirical evidence as to whether industry regulation acts as substitute or a complement for corporate governance.

Finally, while this chapter covers formal mechanisms of third-party certification, such as credit rating agencies, Chapter 11 focused on more informal third-party certification, such as certification by venture capitalists and investment banks, for the specific case of IPOs.

16.2 The role and duties of gatekeepers

John Coffee defines the role of gatekeepers as 'assess[ing] and vouch[ing] for the corporate client's own statements about itself or a specific transaction'.[1] Hence, gatekeepers provide a certification role of information released by the company and/or its processes by risking their own reputational capital. Gatekeepers may be particularly important in corporate governance systems where there is a lack of shareholder monitoring of corporate managers and hence where principal-agency problems may be particularly severe. However, gatekeepers may also play a role in corporate governance systems with dominant, large shareholders as there may be a need to monitor related-party transactions. Gatekeepers include:

- auditors
- investment banks
- lawyers
- financial analysts
- credit rating agencies
- corporate governance rating agencies
- commercial banks and other creditors
- insurers of directors' and officers' liability (D&O insurers)
- stock markets
- securities exchange regulators

In his discussion of gatekeeper liability, Reinier Kraakman argues that gatekeepers should only be made liable if the primary sources of liability, i.e. corporate and managerial liability, prove to be insufficient.[2] Third-party liability by gatekeepers, such as auditors and lawyers, is justified if the gatekeepers are connected in such a way with the firm that this connection creates some degree of responsibility in the event that the firm fails. However, according to Kraakman, gatekeeper liability raises at least three issues. First, it may be difficult to justify gatekeeper liability as it may be very costly for the gatekeeper to discharge the legal duties. Second, the gatekeeper may not have sufficient incentives to fulfil its legal duties and may even be tempted to collude with the firm. Indeed, gatekeepers such as auditors may provide a range of non-audit services to the firm and may therefore prefer to keep good relations with the firm to ensure future business. Third, enforcement of gatekeeper liability may be difficult as this depends not only on the type of gatekeeper and the nature of its legal duties, but also on the degree of culpability. Hence, gatekeeper liability may be costly and complex to enforce. The question that then arises is whether there is a need to regulate gatekeepers given that they put their reputational capital at stake when dealing with clients.

[1] Coffee, J. (2002), 'Understanding Enron: "It's about the Gatekeepers, Stupid"', *Business Lawyer* 57, 1403–20.
[2] Kraakman, R.H. (1984), 'Corporate Liability Strategies and the Costs of Legal Controls', *Yale Law Journal* 93, 857–98.

The spectacular failures of Enron and Worldcom in the USA renewed interest in gatekeeper liability and in particular auditor liability. They also called for regulating gatekeepers as the risk of the latter losing their reputational capital has done little to prevent corporate failures and conflicts of interests. One of the main features of the Enron case was that its auditor, Arthur Andersen, ignored irregularities in the company's accounting practices as its main concern was the loss of lucrative consulting income. John Coffee blames the failure of Enron on the commodification of auditing services, the auditor's capture by its client and more generally the lack of competition among auditors.[3] Capture refers to the influence that the client or firm may have over its auditor (or other gatekeepers) and may push the latter to serve the interests of the client rather than preventing malpractice and wrong-doing. In addition, the lack of competition may reduce the risk of reputational damage caused by client failure, calling for regulation of gatekeepers' roles and duties. Apart from Enron's auditor, another type of gatekeeper that failed to police Enron and hence failed investors was the financial analysts that kept on issuing buy recommendations for Enron's stock, thereby fuelling further increases in the company's stock price as well as sustaining investor frenzy.

Other countries such as the Netherlands and Italy have had their own Enron-style corporate failures. For example, Italy saw its dairy firm Parmalat fail spectacularly. Similar to the Enron collapse, the Parmalat debacle can be blamed on its auditor and financial analysts, but also its creditors. Again, there was capture of gatekeepers by a large client as well as over-optimism on behalf of financial analysts that failed to spot worrying signals. Finally, the 2008 subprime mortgage crisis which has caused a global economic depression can be blamed on the failure of another gatekeeper, i.e. credit rating agencies. CalPERS (the California Public Employees' Retirement System), one of the largest public pension funds in the USA, sued the three credit rating agencies, Moody's, Standard & Poor's and Fitch, having invested in mortgage-backed securities during the subprime mortgage boom and claiming to have lost US$1 billion because of inaccurate ratings. CalPERS settled with Moody's for $130m in 2016 and with Standard & Poor's for $125m in 2015, while Fitch denied liability.[4]

While there has clearly been failure by gatekeepers in recent corporate scandals, national as well as international regulators have responded by reinforcing the role and duties of gatekeepers rather than thinking about viable alternatives. For example, in the USA, the response to Enron has been the Sarbanes-Oxley Act (SOX) of 2002 (see also Chapter 6). The Act includes a range of provisions regulating the roles of auditors, lawyers and financial analysts. For example, SOX reinforces the need for independent auditors and exposes auditors to increased penalties in the event of audit failures. Section 404 requires the management and the auditors to prepare an internal control report and to comment on the soundness of the company's internal control over financial reporting. Auditors are regulated by the Public Company Accounting Oversight Board (PCAOB), which has disciplinary power over the accounting profession (Sections 101–108). Under the Act, audit firms also need the approval of the firm's audit committee before they are allowed to provide non-audit services (Section 202). Finally, the lead audit partner and the audit partner responsible for reviewing the audit (rather than the audit firm itself) have to be rotated every five fiscal years (Section 203).

The Act also requires lawyers acting on behalf of the firm to report any material violations of securities laws and any breaches of fiduciary duties by the senior management. Such violations and breaches have to be reported in the first instance to the firm's chief legal counsel or CEO. If the latter fail to act appropriately, then the lawyers have to inform the audit committee, the board of directors or the independent (non-executive)

[3]Coffee, J. (2004), 'What Caused Enron? A Capsule Social and Economic History of the 1990s', *Cornell Law Review* 89, 269–310; Coffee, J. (2006), *Gatekeepers*, Oxford, UK: Oxford University Press.
[4]See www.bloomberg.com/news/articles/2016-03-09/calpers-says-moody-s-to-pay-130-million-to-settle-ratings-case, accessed on 18 March 2017.

directors on the board (Section 307). The Act also obliges stock exchanges to regulate financial analysts and to request the latter disclose any conflicts of interests they may be facing (Section 501).

Finally, the 2010 Dodd-Frank Wall Street Reform and Consumer Protection Act in the USA specifically addresses the issue of capture, i.e. capture of the US securities exchange regulator, the Securities Exchange Commission (SEC), in Title IX, Subsection A, by setting up the Office of the Investor Advocate.

The 2008 financial crisis has pushed US and EU regulators to consider regulating credit rating agencies, further strengthening the role, duties and liability of gatekeepers in the context of corporate governance. The question arises as to what the ideal attributes of a gatekeeper are. The next section will attempt to answer this question.

16.3 The ideal attributes of a gatekeeper

A gatekeeper should ideally have the following seven attributes. It should be *independent* of the companies it is to supervise. This implies that there should be little or no risk of capture of the gatekeeper by its supervisees. If the gatekeeper's duties consist of having a close relationship with its supervisees, then periodic rotation of the gatekeeper may be advisable.

The gatekeeper also needs to have *access to the information required* to carry out its duties and it should be able to obtain information on the firm's dealings that is unbiased and accurate.

The gatekeeper should not be subject to major *conflicts of interests* that may prevent it from carrying out its duties. If there are potential conflicts of interests, these should be disclosed to third-party users of the gatekeeper's services and mechanisms should be put in place to mitigate these conflicts of interests.

The gatekeeper should have the necessary *skills*, in particular the necessary judgement and competence, to perform its duties. Hence, the gatekeeper should have access to highly qualified staff, with skills and competencies comparable to those of the staff of the supervisee companies.

The gatekeeper should also have the right *incentives* to fulfil its duties. Incentives may include reputation at stake and legal liability. However, there is only likely to be a risk of reputational loss if the gatekeeper operates in a competitive industry and reputational damage results in a loss of market share, benefitting its competitors.

Importantly, the gatekeeper has to have sufficient *power* to force its supervisees to disclose any information it requires to fulfil its duties and to force them to put a stop to malpractice and wrong-doing. It should also have the power and authority to penalize supervisees that fail to meet its requests. Alternatively, if the gatekeeper provides services to the firm such as directors' and officers' liability insurance, the gatekeeper may derive power from refusing its services to firms it deems do not comply with its standards and from the negative signal emitted by this refusal.

Following from the previous six attributes, gatekeepers should provide meaningful and reliable *third-party certification* to investors and other users. The certification and any related information should enable users to assess the quality of the firm's governance and to identify any conflicts of interests that the firm may suffer from.

Finally, and more generally, John Coffee argues that it is important to bear in mind that different corporate governance systems are subject to different types of corporate scandals.[5] A corporate governance system such as the US system, characterized by dispersed ownership and control, is likely to be subject to scandals involving excessive earnings management by the executives (e.g. Enron). In contrast, companies from Continental Europe, where control is concentrated, are more likely to be subject to scandals involving the extraction of

---

[5]Coffee, J.C. Jr. (2005), 'A Theory of Corporate Scandals: Why the USA and Europe Differ', *Oxford Review of Economic Policy* 21, 198–211.

private benefits of control (e.g. Parmalat). Given that different corporate governance systems are likely to suffer from different types of corporate scandals, this suggests that regulators need to focus on different types of gatekeepers. In addition, the type of corporate governance system may also affect how the ideal attributes of a given gatekeeper can be achieved. For example, to ensure the independence of auditors in a corporate governance system characterized by strong control, the auditors may have to be appointed by the minority shareholders rather than the large shareholder.

16.4 Types of gatekeepers and limitations to their role

Recent corporate governance reforms, such as SOX, have put a lot of emphasis on auditors as corporate gatekeepers. However, the efficiency of auditors as gatekeepers may be severely limited for at least two reasons. First, auditors rely on the information that the company provides to them and this information may be biased, incomplete and/or untruthful. Hence, they may not be able to perform efficient monitoring of the management. Second, auditors may suffer from conflicts of interests as they may be more concerned about maintaining their business relationship with the company as well as securing future business rather than alerting outsiders about any inaccuracies and malpractices in relation to the company's accounts. These conflicts of interests may be amplified if the auditors provide non-audit services to the firm and may therefore call for auditors to be appointed and paid for by outsiders to the company rather than by the company. Auditors may issue so-called qualified audit reports if they have detected deviations from the generally accepted accounting principles (GAAP) or were unable to audit one or several areas of the financial accounts. Auditors only rarely issue qualified audit reports and even fewer issues of such qualified audits make it into the press. While in general qualified audit reports do not cause a negative stock price reaction, those that the financial press report on do so.[6] Hence, auditors are likely to have the necessary power to penalize wrongdoers and to fulfil a role of third-party certification.

Given the close relationships they have with companies and the amount of information they collect via the provision of services, such as underwriting securities issues and consultancy, investment banks are a likely gatekeeper. Both the theoretical and empirical literature suggest that investment banks are gatekeepers as they certify the quality of new issues of equity shares by underwriting such issues and thereby put at stake their reputational capital (see Chapter 11). In some countries, such as the USA and most of Europe, underwriters are also signatories to the prospectus that is published shortly before the securities issue and are jointly liable with the directors for any material information that has been omitted from the prospectus. However, the subprime mortgage crisis of 2008 and the subsequent events suggest at least two reasons why it is unlikely that investment banks will be perceived to be credible gatekeepers (see also Chapter 14). First, investment banks may be subject to conflicts of interests because of client capture, similar to auditors, or because of internal conflicts of interests. Section 11.5 of Chapter 11 describes the technique of 'spinning' IPOs whereby investment banks bribed CEOs of IPO firms via the allocation of underpriced shares to ensure future fee-earning business. In addition, internal conflicts of interests may exist between a bank's underwriting department and its research department. The latter may be put under internal pressure to issue a strong buy recommendation for an issue underwritten by the former. Second, some legal scholars, such as Hilary Sale, also doubt that investment banks will ever be credible gatekeepers as they are strong lobbying groups that have been successful in keeping regulation of their

---

[6]Dopuch, N., Holthausen, R.W. and Leftwich, R.W. (1986), 'Abnormal Stock Returns Associated with Media Disclosures of "Subject to" Qualified Audit Opinions', *Journal of Accounting and Economics* 8, 93–117.

activities at bay.[7] Even after the subprime mortgage crisis, in countries such as the USA and the UK there has been little focus by policy makers on regulating investment banks in a meaningful way.[8] For example, in the UK much of the recent political debate and government initiatives have concentrated on reducing social benefits and preventing benefit fraud rather than curtailing conflicts of interests in the financial industry and reducing white-collar fraud. Finally, US President Donald Trump is likely to take a step back as he has stated that he is going to roll back parts of the 2010 Dodd-Frank Act, which improves the protection of consumers of financial products and services.[9]

Moving onto lawyers, this type of gatekeeper comes in two versions. They may be in-house legal counsels or outside lawyers dealing with specific, more specialized and/or one-off transactions of the firm such as an equity issue. While in-house counsels are likely to be well informed about the firm's processes and dealings, they may be too close to the firm and therefore suffer from capture and possibly behavioural biases. Such behavioural biases may include considering appropriate practice or 'normal' something that is happening on a regular basis within the firm (see also Chapter 12). For example, it may be practice in a highly hierarchical firm not to question the judgement of the CEO. If the in-house counsel also suffers from this behavioural bias, she may condone malpractice by the CEO, including severe wrong-doing, rather than raise it as an issue that needs to be redressed and prevented in the future. While in-house counsels may possess a lot of information on the firm, they may also lack sufficient independence to be objective gatekeepers. In contrast, outside lawyers may not have enough information on the firm to detect wrong-doing.

The main role of financial analysts is to predict the future performance of firms as well as to value the securities the latter are about to issue or have already outstanding. Financial analysts study the firm's fundamentals, such as earnings, sales and dividends, forecast these for the near future and then issue buy, sell or hold recommendations based on these forecasts. However, financial analysts may suffer from conflicts of interests as they may be part of the same investment bank that is also underwriting the firm's new equity issue. Hence, they may be under internal pressure to issue buy recommendations while their valuation of the firm and their forecasts of its future performance suggest otherwise. There is an entire section of SOX (Section 501) that covers such conflicts of interests. While in the past investment banks have set up so-called Chinese walls that prevent communication between their financial analysts and their underwriting department, in practice these have not worked. Financial analysts may also be driven by the same psychological biases, such as overconfidence (see Chapter 12), as other investors.

The role of credit rating agencies is to issue ratings about the creditworthiness of debt securities such as government and corporate bonds. However, similar to auditors, credit rating agencies are paid by the clients, i.e. the issuers themselves. This, combined with the fact that issuers seek the highest possible rating to make their securities more attractive to potential investors, may severely limit the role of credit rating agencies as credible gatekeepers. The 2008 subprime mortgage crisis has highlighted these shortcomings. As stated in Section 16.2, one of the largest public pension funds in the USA (CalPERS) has been suing three credit rating agencies, Moody's, Standard & Poor's and Fitch, for what they perceive to be erroneous and misleading ratings for collateralized debt obligations. The 2008 financial crisis is not the first time credit rating agencies got things totally wrong. Indeed, they also failed to predict the Asian crisis of 1997. In addition, Giovanni Ferri, Li-Gang Liu and

[7]Sale, H.A. (2003), 'Gatekeepers, Disclosure, and Issuer Choice', *Washington University Law Quarterly* 81, 403–16.
[8]See e.g. Bebchuk, L.A. and Spamann, H. (2010), 'Regulating Bankers' Pay', *Georgetown Law Journal* 98, 247–87.
[9]See Jopson, B. and Leatherby, L. (2017), 'FT Explainer: Dodd-Frank Picked to Pieces. Wholesale Abolition is Unlikely But Parts of the Act Are More Vulnerable than Others', *Financial Times* March 13, www.ft.com/content/915666b6-f928-11e6-bd4e-68d53499ed71, accessed on 18 March 2017.

Joseph Stiglitz found evidence that credit rating agencies tried to compensate for failing to foresee the crisis by issuing ratings after the crisis that were perceived to be too conservative (see also Box 16.1).[10]

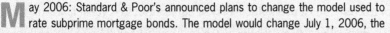

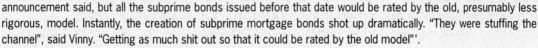

Box 16.1
Credit rating agencies and the subprime mortgage crisis

'**M**ay 2006: Standard & Poor's announced plans to change the model used to rate subprime mortgage bonds. The model would change July 1, 2006, the announcement said, but all the subprime bonds issued before that date would be rated by the old, presumably less rigorous, model. Instantly, the creation of subprime mortgage bonds shot up dramatically. "They were stuffing the channel", said Vinny. "Getting as much shit out so that it could be rated by the old model"'.

Source: Lewis, M. (2010), *The Big Short*, London: Allen Lane, p. 94.

Also, similar to the auditing industry, the credit rating industry is highly concentrated and there are also similar doubts as to whether reputational loss is still an issue in such a concentrated industry. For example, Frank Partnoy disputes that credit rating agencies provide credible signals about the quality of debt issues by putting at stake their reputational capital.[11] He argues that credit rating agencies merely fulfil a regulatory requirement. In the aftermath of the 2008 financial crisis, both the USA and the European Union introduced regulations requiring credit rating agencies to register with regulators and to monitor the methodologies used to rate specific debt securities issues.

While corporate governance ratings agencies are still a relatively recent phenomenon, the industry has been developing fast, and a range of corporate governance indices is now available to assess the corporate governance of individual firms as well as the corporate governance standards of entire countries. Existing corporate governance rating agencies include Deminor, which tends to concentrate on Europe, Standard & Poor's and MSCI Governance Metrics International (GMI). While these ratings have some use in informing interested parties about the quality of the governance of corporations, they also have their limitations. Typically, these indices are in the form of counters which are incremented by a value of one if a specific corporate governance device is present (sometimes the value is weighted to take into account the importance of that particular corporate governance device relative to other devices). However, the indices do not normally make a detailed assessment about the governance issues or conflicts of interests that prevail in a particular firm. Hence, they tend to treat a widely held firm which suffers mainly from the classic principal-agent problem in the same way as a firm which is controlled by a large shareholder and which is more likely to suffer from conflicts of interests between the latter and the minority shareholders. Those indices that exist for a range of countries also frequently do not take into account differences in the national institutional setting. To sum up, these indices typically assume that 'one size fits all' and that there is one '"best" measure of corporate governance'.[12] Another criticism relates to the direction of causality. Kenneth Lehn, Sukesh Patro and Mengxin Zhao found evidence that the direction of causality runs

[10]Ferri, G., Liu, L.G. and Stiglitz, J.E. (1999), 'The Procyclical Role of Rating Agencies: Evidence from the East Asian Crisis', *Economic Notes* 28, 335–55.

[11]Partnoy, F. (1999), 'The Siskel and Ebert of Financial Markets: Two Thumbs Down for the Credit Rating Agencies', *Washington University Law Quarterly* 77, 619–712.

[12]Bhagat, S., Bolton, B. and Romano, R. (2008), 'The Promise and Peril of Corporate Governance Indices', *Columbia Law Review* 108, 1803–82.

from firm value to governance indices and not the converse as advanced by the providers of these indices. They found that firms that had low market-to-book values during the period preceding the launch of the corporate governance indices put in place takeover defences which subsequently damaged their governance ratings.[13]

Commercial banks and other creditors may also act as gatekeepers. Similar to (large) shareholders, it is in the interests of banks and other debtholders to monitor corporate managers to prevent expropriation by the latter and they may therefore fulfil the role of gatekeeper. Section 8.11 of Chapter 8 has already reviewed the monitoring role of banks and other debtholders and the empirical evidence on the effectiveness of this type of monitoring. In addition, Chapter 5 has compared the advantages and shortcomings of the bank-based system with those of the market-based system. Hence, we shall not return to these issues in this section. Finally, Chapter 14 reviewed in detail the conflicts of interests which debtholders may be subject to. However, it is worth mentioning that large debtholders, via their close relationship with the firm and the information they collect on the firm, may acquire a monopoly position and end up charging the firm above-market interest rates.

Information about the directors' and officers' liability (D&O) insurance taken out by a firm, assuming this information is disclosed either mandatorily or voluntarily, may act as a powerful signal conveying information to outsiders about the likely future behaviour of the firm and in particular its board of directors and top management. More specifically, the insured amount as well as the reputation of the insurers may provide valuable information to the market about the risk investors face as to director and officer liability.

Stock markets are another important gatekeeper. They impose entry requirements on firms seeking a stock-market listing as well as imposing continuing obligations on firms that are already listed. For example, the London Stock Exchange imposes the UK Corporate Governance Code on the firms that are listed on it. These firms are required to comply with the Code's recommendations of best practice or explain the reasons why they do not comply with specific recommendations. In addition, stock markets frequently have different segments targeting particular types of firms and enabling investors to distinguish between more mature, safer firms and riskier, younger firms. For example, the London Stock Exchange's Official List targets large and mature firms whereas the Alternative Investment Market (AIM) has less stringent entry requirements and ongoing obligations, making it easier for smaller and younger firms to list. Similarly, in the USA, larger firms are listed on the New York Stock Exchange (NYSE) whereas young, hi-tech and high-growth firms are listed on the Nasdaq.

Finally, securities exchange regulators, such as the Securities Exchange Commission (SEC) in the USA, are likely to play an important role given the lack of independence and incentives as well as the conflicts of interests that the above gatekeepers may suffer from. For example, James Fanto argues that in the USA, the SEC should take on the role of the ultimate gatekeeper and perform much closer monitoring of corporations similar to what the regulator does in the banking industry.[14] However, this would then require the securities exchange regulator to monitor all sorts of areas of corporate activity for which other gatekeepers may have greater competence. Another limitation to the role of securities exchange regulators as ultimate gatekeepers is that typically the law provides judicial immunity to the regulator.[15]

Hence, ultimately, investors and other corporate stakeholders may have to rely on a range of corporate gatekeepers rather than a single gatekeeper, bearing in mind that all gatekeepers suffer – at least to some

[13]Lehn, K., Patro, S. and Zhao, M. (2007), 'Governance Indices and Valuation: Which Causes Which?', *Journal of Corporate Finance* 13, 907–28. Lehn et al. suggested two possible reasons for this practice. First, firms with low market-to-book ratios are likely to be badly run and hence managers may want to adopt takeover defences to protect themselves from hostile takeovers. Second, low market-to-book ratios may signal low growth opportunities which would again make the firm attractive as a takeover target. Managers may prevent such takeovers by putting in place takeover defences.

[14]Fanto, J. (2006), 'Paternalistic Regulation of Public Company Management: Lessons from Bank Regulation', *Florida Law Review* 58, 859–919.

[15]Readers should consult Section 6.3 of Chapter 6 for a discussion of the substantially different approach to corporate governance regulation adopted in the UK as compared to the USA.

degree – from a lack of independence, power and access to information, as well as incentive problems, conflicts of interests and limitations to their monitoring skills. Box 16.2 illustrates the frequently complex relationships between regulators and those they are supposed to regulate. Table 16.1 summarizes the above discussion on the different types of gatekeepers by stating for each gatekeeper those ideal gatekeeper attributes – from those listed in Section 16.3 – it has and those it lacks.

Box 16.2
Why is it so difficult to rein in Wall Street?

Reforming Wall Street has become a key issue in the ongoing presidential primaries.

Bernie Sanders in particular has used his rival's close ties to the financial industry, including speaking fees and political donations, to suggest Hillary Clinton wouldn't rein in Wall Street. At the same time, Sanders has tried to highlight his own independence, declaring:

If I were elected president, the foxes would no longer guard the henhouse.

Clinton has tried to dispel the notion that Wall Street donations affect her judgment or independence, claiming her regulatory plan is actually tougher than Sanders'.

These exchanges underscore a crucial point: almost a decade after the 2008 financial crisis, the reforms that many Americans have demanded remain incomplete. Claims of independence, including by Republicans such as Donald Trump, are one way for candidates to suggest that they would be able to bring about real change.

Who would be the best candidate to do so is an important question. But first we must understand this underlying dilemma: why has it been so difficult to reform Wall Street following the worst financial crisis since the Great Depression?

This led us to a more fundamental question: whose voice matters most in determining how the financial industry should be run?

Given how much anger there still is at Wall Street, the answer may be surprising.

AN AUTHORITATIVE VOICE

In a forthcoming research paper, we argue that major change has been so difficult because Wall Street's top executives ensure that the authoritative voice on the financial industry remains theirs. In other words, no one else understands how it works, so no one else can tell it what to do.

Consequently, other stakeholders, such as customers, investors, policymakers, academics, other businesses and society at large, have been sidelined.

But how do the executives manage this? Based on systematic analysis of data from the Financial Crisis Inquiry Commission and media, we found that how industry elites use public rhetoric shines some light on this, revealing clear patterns.

First, executives highlight only the positives of their banks to help make strong claims of expertise. A quick glimpse of this can be seen in this 2010 quote from former Bear Stearns CEO James Cayne defending his bank (which nearly collapsed during the crisis before being acquired by JPMorgan Chase):

Our capital ratios and liquidity pool remained high by historical standards … Subsequent events show that Bear Stearns' collapse was not the result of any actions or decisions unique to Bear Stearns … The efforts we made to strengthen the firm were reasonable and prudent.

(Continued)

Second, they work to gain trust by using language that suggests care for stakeholders, including clients but also society. As just one example, JPMorgan CEO James Dimon told the commission why he and his bankers should be trusted:

> Throughout the financial crisis, we continued to support our clients' financing and liquidity needs. For example, we helped provide state and local governments financing to cover cash flow shortfalls ... JPMorgan Chase is also at the forefront in doing everything we can to help families meet their mortgage obligations.

Complementing this, they focus on discrediting others – whether regulators or other market players – by forcefully questioning their expertise and trustworthiness. For example, former Morgan Stanley CEO John Mack projected blame on the state to question its expertise:

> From a policy perspective, (the financial crisis) made clear that regulators simply didn't have the tools or the authority to protect the stability of the financial system as a whole.

Similarly, the judgment and motives of market players are questioned to deflect blame, as in this statement from Richard Fuld, former chief of the famously bankrupt Lehman Brothers:

> Lehman's demise was caused by uncontrollable market forces and the incorrect perception and accompanying rumors ... Those same forces threatened the stability of other banks – not just Lehman ... This loss of confidence, although unjustified and irrational, became a self-fulfilling prophecy and culminated in a classic run on the bank.

ESSENTIAL ACTORS IN A COMPLEX SYSTEM

In summary, industry elites rhetorically construct themselves as essential actors in the field due to their expertise in managing their organizations in a complex system and their trustworthiness in terms of caring for multiple stakeholders. Simultaneously, they sharply critique the failings and motives of others.

This really matters because, in a domain that outsiders find difficult to understand, using such public rhetoric reinforces what social psychologists call 'epistemic authority' – in this case the authority of elite financial industry executives.

The idea is simple: those who are considered to have expertise and are trustworthy rank high on epistemic authority. Their voices carry more weight and acceptance on crucial matters related to their field. And those who are lower down in this hierarchy are unable to pose a credible challenge.

Research from social psychology shows that those with higher epistemic authority on a subject are turned to earlier as a source of information, given priority, inspire higher confidence and are more likely to lead to actions that reflect their wishes.

Hence this is how Wall Street can both be reviled by much of American society yet maintain its status as the primary authority on the financial industry.

Challenging this authority requires strong political will. Campaign donations and lobbying play an augmenting role to ensure we don't even get close to posing a credible challenge. 'The Blob' of regulating agencies (from the Treasury Department to the Securities and Exchange Commission) moves together with an 'army of Wall Street representatives and lobbyists that continuously surrounds and permeates them', according to former Congressional staffer Jeff Connaughton. The result is that no credible challenge is mounted, and the epistemic authority of industry executives prevails.

WHO GETS THE FINAL WORD

After the crisis, the Dodd-Frank Act sent a signal that reform was needed, but it did not go far enough and in fact many parts of it are already under legal challenge from Wall Street.

The diluted nature of these changes shows how much authority industry executives have acquired since the Great Depression. Many of the regulations imposed in its aftermath, such as Glass-Steagall, have been repealed.

To reform the industry, some critics target its internal culture, creating the right incentives and capital requirements. While all these issues are important, how do we get started?

Our research suggests the key obstacle to initiating radical change is that the top executives maintain the final word on 'their' industry, while others whose lives are greatly affected by it have little voice. While other factors such as donations and lobbying certainly also play a role in preventing change, little attention has been paid to the importance of authority.

It is this authority that allows them to reduce the power of the state to regulate their industry by using their perch as 'experts' to question the government's capacity to do so effectively. Fuld, for one, continues to defend the expertise of his Lehman team while blaming the entire crisis and his own bank's collapse on the government. Such rhetoric contributes to an environment where state bodies have little authority to intervene in the industry in the first place, and the donations and lobbying take care of the rest.

The financial industry also undermines tougher rules by taking key jobs at regulatory bodies – a problem known as the 'revolving door' between Wall Street and Washington. Three recent Treasury secretaries, for example, were former executives at Goldman Sachs – hence Sanders' concern about the foxes guarding the henhouse.

Other academics have documented the disproportionate power of the financial industry on other businesses; about a devotion to financial industry practices leading to long-term erosion of investment, competitiveness and prosperity; and more broadly about how its practices have reshaped everyday life in society and contribute to socioeconomic inequality.

But unless we can find a way to overcome the financial industry's epistemic authority so true reform is possible, its negative repercussions on the economy and society will not change.

IT TAKES A TEAM TO REIN IN WALL STREET

And that is perhaps why many voters see presidential candidates' independence from the financial industry as crucial.

Among the many other salient issues, the fact that not much has been done to change things after a financial crisis that damaged so many lives continues to raise hackles. It also likely breeds resentment against a system that has allowed things to continue as if nothing happened. That may lead people to extreme positions against what they perceive as an unfair system and into the hands of outsiders who embody that anger.

As one GOP voter put it: Democrats 'are as eager to see Sanders nominated as I am to see Trump'.

But voters may be confusing simple claims of independence – such as on donations – with actual substantive plans for reform. Beyond the claims, actual change will depend on who is able to challenge the authority of the industry elite.

So here it may be more useful for voters to consider who each candidate would pick to lead the agencies charged with regulating the financial industry and advise the president on these issues. Sanders' assertion that he'd steer clear of resumés that include Goldman Sachs tells us who he wouldn't pick but not who's on the short list.

Thus, the key question is: who would put together the right team to counter the dominance of industry elites? A team comprising those who stand outside the immediate circle of top industry executives (i.e. no conflict of interest) and yet can counter their epistemic authority (i.e. with expertise and trustworthiness)?

That will be tough. But creative ways of building such a team will be needed. Such efforts are essential to challenge the industry, push it to pay more attention to other stakeholders – as opposed to navel gazing – and ultimately lead to a more positive impact on the economy and society.

Source: Riaz, S., Buchanan, S. and Ruebottom, T. (2016), TheConversation.com, 8 March

Table 16.1 **The attributes of the different types of gatekeepers**

Type of gatekeeper	Ideal attributes it has	Ideal attributes it lacks
Auditor	– Skills – Required power – Third-party certification via, e.g. issue of qualified audit report	– Potentially highly dependent on client firm – Possible conflicts of interests via the provision of non-audit services – Access to information is mainly via firm which may make it difficult to detect severe cases of fraud – Lack of incentives as little danger of reputational loss due to high concentration of audit industry
Investment bank	– Skills – Access to information via close relationship with firm – Incentives as there is third-party liability (e.g. via being one of the signatories to the issuing prospectus) and danger of loss of reputation – Required power via refusal of provision of services – Third-party certification via reputation of bank	– Past practices such as IPO 'spinning' suggest that independence may be low and the investment banks may be tempted to focus on safeguarding future fee-earning business from client firms – Conflicts of interests between various departments of investment bank
In-house counsels	– Access to information – Skills	– Highly dependent on firm as directly employed by firm and highly likely to be captured by firm – Conflicts of interests due to employment relation with firm – Few incentives to act as whistle blower as personal costs are high whereas personal benefits are low or even nil – May lack required power – No third-party certification
Outside lawyers	– Independence – No or few conflicts of interests – Skills – Incentives? – Required power?	– Access to information may be highly limited – Third-party certification is limited given the restricted access to information and given that firms tend to deal with multiple outside lawyers in various capacities and over various periods of time
Financial analysts	– Information – Generally, very strong skills, but may suffer from behavioural biases – Third-party certification via analyst reports and buy/sell recommendations	– Lack of independence as they tend to be employed by investment banks – Conflicts of interests and capture if part of an investment bank and bank has firm as its client – Few long-term incentives – Lacks required power to address conflicts of interests

Table 16.1 (*Continued*)

Type of gatekeeper	Ideal attributes it has	Ideal attributes it lacks
Credit rating agencies	– Information – Few conflicts of interests – Required power – Third-party certification	– Lack of independence as paid by the client – Skills have been questioned based on experience from Asian and subprime mortgage crises – Few incentives as highly concentrated industry with little danger of reputational loss
Corporate governance ratings agencies	– Independence – No conflicts of interests – Incentives	– Information mainly from publicly available sources – Skills frequently limited to assessing box ticking by the firm – Third-party certification may be low
Commercial banks and other creditors	– Independence – Information – Skills – Incentives – Required power – Third-party certification	– Conflicts of interests as large creditors may obtain monopoly position and overcharge firm for credit
D&O insurers	– Independence – Information – Few or no conflicts of interests – Skills – Incentives – Required power – Third-party certification as failure to assess firm may result in hefty financial losses and amount of insurance premium may be a function of risks	
Stock markets	– Independence – Few conflicts of interests – Incentives – Required power – Third-party certification for higher stock-market segments	– Information required to supervise properly all aspects of firm dealings would be vast – Skills required to supervise and assess all areas of firm dealings are wide-ranging and extensive
Securities exchange regulators	– Independence – Information – Few or no conflicts of interests – Required power	– Incentives are severely limited due to judicial immunity – Skills – Third-party certification

16.5 Is industry regulation a substitute for corporate governance?

David Becher and Melissa Frye reviewed the existing literature on the link between regulation and corporate governance. Bearing in mind that regulation varies across industries, they argued that regulation has – at the very least – an indirect impact on corporate governance, as the extant research has shown that the deregulation of an industry brings about changes in corporate governance and pushes the firms in that industry to adopt governance structures similar to those of firms from unregulated industries.[16]

However, a priori it is not clear whether regulation is a substitute or complement for corporate governance. On the one hand, regulation may be a substitute for corporate governance given that the regulator monitors the firms under its supervision and hence may reduce the need for corporate governance devices such as independent directors and performance-based compensation for managers. For example, as bank deposits are ultimately guaranteed by the insurance scheme put in place by the bank regulator, such as the Federal Deposit Insurance Corporation (FDIC) in the USA, depositors have little incentive to monitor banks. Given the relatively high debt-equity ratios of banks, in turn shareholders may be more concerned about pushing executives to take on risky projects rather than monitoring the latter. While the bank deposit insurance scheme will bear most of the risk from such projects, shareholders will reap all the benefits if the projects prove to be successful. This is the agency problem of debt (see Section 1.5 of Chapter 1). On the other hand, industry regulators frequently push for improvements in corporate governance, in addition to increased transparency and disclosure. Hence, corporate governance of regulated firms may be better than that of unregulated firms.

While theory does not provide an answer to the question as to whether regulation is a substitute or complement for corporate governance, the existing empirical evidence is also inconclusive. Evidence from studies on the US banking industry suggests that executive compensation changed as a result of the deregulation of the early 1980s as well as that of the 1990s. Before the deregulation of 1982, there was little performance sensitivity of CEO pay (salary plus bonus as well as stock options) in the banking industry whereas the sensitivity increased significantly after 1982.[17] There was also an increase in CEO stock ownership after 1982. The increase in the pay-performance sensitivity is likely to reflect the increase in the importance of managerial input, but also the increase in managerial discretion, both resulting from the reduction in regulation. Similarly, the deregulations of the 1990s brought about further changes in managerial remuneration. While the overall impact on executive compensation was relatively small, the structure of executive pay changed substantially with the importance of variable pay increasing significantly and the importance of the fixed component decreasing. A likely reason for the substantial change in the structure of executive pay is the increase in competition caused by the two deregulations of the 1990s.[18] However, when the pay of bank CEOs is compared to that of non-bank CEOs, the former still receive less incentive-based pay than the latter.[19]

In their study on US CEO pay in regulated and unregulated firms, Paul Joskow, Nancy Rose and Andrea Shepard found that CEOs in regulated industries earn significantly less than CEOs in unregulated industries.[20]

[16]Becher, D.A. and Frye, M.B. (2011), 'Does Regulation Substitute or Complement Governance?', *Journal of Banking and Finance* 35, 736–51.

[17]Crawford, A.J., Ezzell, J.R. and Miles, J.A. (1995), 'Bank CEO Pay-Performance Relations and the Effects of Deregulation', *Journal of Business* 68, 231–56.

[18]Cuñat, V. and Guadalupe, M. (2009), 'Executive Compensation and Competition in the Banking and Financial Sectors', *Journal of Banking and Finance* 33, 495–504.

[19]Becher, D.A., Campbell, T.L. and Frye, M.B. (2005), 'Incentive Compensation for Bank Directors: The Impact of Deregulation', *Journal of Business* 78, 1753–77.

[20]Joskow, P.L., Rose, N.L. and Shepard, A. (1993), 'Regulatory Constraints on CEO Compensation', *Brookings Papers on Economic Activity. Microeconomics* 1, 1–72.

Pay is lowest in those industries where there is price regulation (electricity, gas and communications utilities). Joskow et al. proposed two possible interpretations of their results. First, as a result of political pressure, regulation may keep salaries in regulated industries low to prevent public outrage at what may be perceived to be excessive levels of managerial pay. Second, regulation may have an indirect effect on executive compensation by reducing managerial discretion and therefore reducing the set of managerial actions that may increase firm value. In other words, regulation may reduce the returns to good management and hence the need for incentive-based compensation. While it is impossible to disentangle the direct and indirect effects of regulation on managerial pay, Joskow et al. concluded that the fact that the difference in pay between regulated and unregulated firms is more pronounced for those firms regulated by a single state regulatory agency than for those firms regulated by multiple agencies implies that the direct impact of regulation on executive pay dominates. More generally, the above studies suggest that regulation is a substitute for corporate governance, in particular performance-sensitive executive compensation.

In contrast, other studies conclude that regulation is a complement for corporate governance rather than a substitute. For example, Charles Hadlock, Scott Lee and Robert Parrino studied the turnover of CEOs of electricity and gas utilities. They found that the turnover of CEOs in regulated industries is at least as sensitive to performance as the turnover of CEOs in unregulated industries.[21] While Joel Houston and Christopher James agreed with the above studies that CEO stock holdings and option-based pay in banks are lower than in other industries, they attributed these differences to the fewer investment opportunities in the banking industry, reducing the need for incentive-based pay, rather than regulation.[22] There is also consistent evidence from empirical studies that firms from regulated industries have higher proportions of independent directors.[23]

16.6 Conclusions

Gatekeepers play a potentially important role in corporate governance via the monitoring and certification services they offer. They may be particularly indispensable in corporate governance systems where ownership is dispersed given that they mitigate agency problems caused by the lack of shareholder monitoring. However, in turn, gatekeepers are agents that are expected to act in the best interests of the principals, i.e. investors, but due to incentive problems and conflicts of interests may not do so in practice. This chapter has reviewed the various types of gatekeepers, their roles as well as the likely limitations to the monitoring and certification they provide. While corporate governance regulation, such as the Sarbanes-Oxley Act in the USA, has put further emphasis on the role of gatekeepers, it is however unlikely that gatekeepers will prevent future corporate scandals.

The role of gatekeepers in corporate governance

This chapter has also tried to find an answer to the question of whether industry regulation, such as bank regulation and utilities regulation, improves

Corporate governance and industry regulation

[21]Hadlock, C., Lee, S. and Parrino, R. (2002), 'CEO Careers in Regulated Environments: Evidence from Electric and Gas Utilities', *Journal of Law and Economics* 45, 535–63.

[22]Houston, J.F. and James, C. (1995), 'CEO Compensation and Bank Risk. Is Compensation in Banking Structured to Promote Risk Taking?' *Journal of Monetary Economics* 36, 405–31.

[23]Adams, R. and Mehran, H. (2003), 'Is Corporate Governance Different for Bank Holding Companies?' *FRBNY Economic Policy Review* 9, 123–42. Booth, J.R., Cornett, M.M. and Tehranian, H. (2002), 'Boards of Directors, Ownership, and Regulation', *Journal of Banking and Finance* 26, 1973–96. Roengpitya, R. (2008), 'The Effects of Financial Deregulation on Bank Governance: The Panel Data Evidence of the 1990s', Working Paper, University of Chicago, IL.

corporate governance or reduces the need for corporate governance. Unfortunately, the existing evidence is mixed and therefore there is as yet no straightforward answer to this question. Some of the existing empirical studies suggest that industry regulation reduces the need for corporate governance as the pay-performance sensitivity in regulated industries is absent or at the very least weak compared to unregulated industries. This suggests that industry regulation is a substitute for corporate governance. However, other studies suggest that board independence is higher in regulated industries and that the directors of regulated firms are at least as accountable for their performance as those of unregulated firms. This suggests that regulation is a complement rather than a supplement for corporate governance.

16.7 Discussion questions

1 'Gatekeepers are *the* solution to the principal-agency problem. They provide the monitoring of corporate managers that shareholders are unlikely to provide'.
(Anonymous) Discuss the above statement.

2 Provide examples of incentive problems and conflicts of interests that various gatekeepers may suffer from.

3 What reasons have been advanced to explain the weak pay-performance sensitivity in regulated industries?

Reading list

Key reading

Becher, D.A. and Frye, M.B. (2011), 'Does Regulation Substitute or Complement Governance?', *Journal of Banking and Finance* 35, 736–51.

Coffee, J. (2002), 'Understanding Enron: "It's about the Gatekeepers, Stupid"', *Business Lawyer* 57, 1403–20.

Coffee, J. (2004), 'What Caused Enron? A Capsule Social and Economic History of the 1990s', *Cornell Law Review* 89, 269–310.

Kraakman, R.H. (1984), 'Corporate Liability Strategies and the Costs of Legal Controls', *Yale Law Journal* 93, 857–98.

Further reading

Coffee, J.C. Jr. (2005), 'A Theory of Corporate Scandals: Why the USA and Europe Differ', *Oxford Review of Economic Policy* 21, 198–211.

Coffee, J. (2006), *Gatekeepers*, Oxford, UK: Oxford University Press.

Crawford, A.J., Ezzell, J.R. and Miles, J.A. (1995), 'Bank CEO Pay-Performance Relations and the Effects of Deregulation', *Journal of Business* 68, 231–56.

Fanto, J. (2006), 'Paternalistic Regulation of Public Company Management: Lessons from Bank Regulation', *Florida Law Review* 58, 859–919.

Ferri, G., Liu, L.G. and Stiglitz, J.E. (1999), 'The Procyclical Role of Rating Agencies: Evidence from the East Asian Crisis', *Economic Notes* 28, 335–55.

Goergen, M., Mallin, C., Mitleton-Kelly, E., Al-Hawamdeh, A. and Chiu, I.H.Y. (2010), *Corporate Governance and Complexity Theory*, Cheltenham, UK: Edward Elgar.

Hadlock, C., Lee, S. and Parrino, R. (2002), 'CEO Careers in Regulated Environments: Evidence from Electric and Gas Utilities', *Journal of Law and Economics* 45, 535–63.

Houston, J.F. and James, C. (1995), 'CEO Compensation and Bank Risk. Is Compensation in Banking Structured to Promote Risk Taking?', *Journal of Monetary Economics* 36, 405–31.

Joskow, P.L., Rose, N.L. and Shepard, A. (1993), 'Regulatory Constraints on CEO Compensation', *Brookings Papers on Economic Activity. Microeconomics* 1, 1–72.

Partnoy, F. (1999), 'The Siskel and Ebert of Financial Markets: Two Thumbs Down for the Credit Rating Agencies', *Washington University Law Quarterly* 77, 619–712.

Additional resources

The PwC survey on professional investors' views on the usefulness of external audits:

www.pwc.com/gx/en/services/audit-assurance/publications/investors-views-survey.html.

Conclusions

PART V

17 Learning from diversity and future challenges for corporate governance

Part I of this book introduced the basic concepts of corporate governance. These included the main theoretical model, the principal-agent model. According to this model, as firms grow they experience a separation between ownership and control. The main consequence of this separation is that the managers end up being in control of the firm and the shareholders end up being the residual claimants. The danger here is that the managers do not run the firm in the interests of the shareholders. We also saw in this part that the assumption about the separation of ownership and control is not normally upheld in most countries other than the UK and the USA. Indeed, corporations outside these two countries normally have a large shareholder such as a family, the government or another corporation. Hence, the main corporate governance problem that prevails in most countries of the world is the conflict of interests between the large, dominant shareholder and the minority shareholders. We also saw that it is important to distinguish between ownership and control as for many corporations the rule of one-share one-vote is violated via, e.g. the use of pyramids of ownership and dual-class shares. Such violations typically increase the incentives of the controlling shareholder to expropriate the other shareholders.

Part II focused on the macro aspects of corporate governance. We reviewed the existing taxonomies of corporate governance, starting with those grounded in historical analysis. More recent taxonomies include those that have emerged from the law and finance literature and the varieties of capitalism (VOC) literature. Common to all the taxonomies from the law and finance literature is the assumption that equity markets can only develop under strong property rights. Most of these taxonomies are also normative in the sense they predict that large equity markets are necessary and sufficient to ensure strong economic growth. In contrast, the VOC literature acknowledges that very similar economic outcomes can be achieved by very different institutional setups. Given that there are complementarities between institutions, the economic performance of countries with well-developed and friction-free markets may be very close to that of countries with highly developed informal and formal coordination mechanisms such as networks. Research also suggests that there is a link between the type of financial system that prevails in a country and the types of industries that are likely to emerge and prosper in that country. The bank-based system is likely to give preference to fixed assets that are easy to value and that can serve as collateral, whereas the market-based system tends to prefer intangible assets that are more difficult to price. Finally, recent developments in corporate governance regulation as well as the various regulatory approaches were reviewed. Importantly, the very different approaches to corporate governance adopted by the UK and USA were highlighted. Indeed, whereas successive UK codes of corporate governance have followed the 'comply or explain' approach, the USA has adopted a much more prescriptive approach.

Part III started with a discussion of the role of boards of directors, a governance mechanism of importance to both the insider and outsider systems of corporate governance. Somewhat surprisingly given the corporate governance role that regulators have accorded to boards of directors, there is little conclusive evidence suggesting that boards, including board independence, improve firm value. Nevertheless, it is important to bear in mind that studies analyzing the impact of boards on firm value and performance struggle with the potential endogeneity of board structure. This part also reviewed the various corporate governance devices that may be used to ensure that managers have the right incentives to run the firm in the interests of the shareholders as well as those that may correct managerial failure. We found that given the main conflicts of interests that corporations are suffering from differ across countries, the importance and effectiveness of these devices also vary across countries. An important concept that re-emerged is the potential endogeneity of corporate governance devices. Typically, a firm's governance setup is rooted in its past and not randomly determined. Hence, studies that analyze the impact of a particular corporate governance mechanism on firm value need to adjust for its possible endogeneity, including its possible link with past firm performance. This part also discussed how to improve corporate governance in emerging markets, in individual firms that may have restricted access to outside finance given the weaknesses of their national legal system, and in firms conducting their initial public offering (IPO). Apart from poor investor protection and weak law enforcement, the development of capital markets in emerging economies may also be hampered by crony capitalism. The main forms of crony capitalism include inherited wealth, which slows down economic growth by stifling entrepreneurship, as well as political connections and government interference. While improving corporate governance standards at the national level takes a long time, individual companies can improve their access to outside financing by opting into a better, foreign system. They can do so by cross-listing on a stock exchange with more stringent regulation, by (re)incorporating in another country and via cross-border mergers. There is ample evidence in support of the so-called bonding hypothesis whereby firms from weak national systems cross-list in better systems, thereby committing themselves not to expropriate their (minority) shareholders. There is also evidence of a positive spillover effect of cross-border mergers whereby the target benefits from the better corporate governance of the bidder. In addition, the empirical evidence suggests that there is a bootstrapping effect whereby bidders with weak governance benefit from the better governance of the targets. However, and as one would expect, this bootstrapping effect is only observed for partial acquisitions. While the evidence is fairly consistent as to the beneficial effects of cross-listings and cross-border mergers on corporate governance, it is as yet unclear whether reincorporations result in better or worse corporate governance. This part of the book also explored corporate governance issues in IPOs. IPOs not only suffer from problems caused by the separation of ownership and control but also from greater asymmetry of information between insiders and outsiders. One way of mitigating these problems is via the ownership retained by the incumbent shareholder or entrepreneur after the IPO. The entrepreneur may further show her commitment to the firm by agreeing to lock in her ownership over a given period after the IPO. Other corporate governance issues pertaining to IPOs include the great power of the CEO across four of the five different dimensions of power and the prominent role of venture capitalists (VCs). Whereas VCs frequently create value in their investee firms, they may also be subject to conflicts of interests. In particular, this is likely to be the case for young VCs that may grandstand by taking their portfolio firms public early on, at the cost of greater IPO underpricing, in order to build up their reputation and to ensure future access to funding. Finally, IPO firms are a good illustration that when it comes to corporate governance, 'one size does not fit all'. Part III concluded by investigating biases in investor and manager behaviour. Sources of behavioural biases include heuristics, emotions, social interactions and overconfidence or hubris as well as reflexive loyalty. Humans use heuristics or rules of thumb to deal with limits to their cognitive resources and available time when analyzing decision problems. Typically, heuristics work well but they also create biases in human behaviour such as systematic errors. Emotions may also cloud our judgement and cause us to take actions or make decisions that are not entirely rational. Yet another source of systematic biases in decision making is that humans tend to conform and behave in similar ways to their social circle. Humans also tend to be overconfident, and overconfidence increases rather than decreases with experience. Finally, there is evidence from psychological experiments that we have a reflex for loyalty to figures of authority and that this reflex may explain why non-executives rarely challenge the CEO in the boardroom. This reflexive loyalty is a possible reason for corporate scandals such as Enron, Hollinger, Royal Bank of Scotland and Worldcom that were all characterized by powerful CEOs whose decisions did not face enough scrutiny by their boardroom peers.

The penultimate part of the book, Part IV, explored issues concerning the firm's relationship with its main non-financial stakeholders. Corporate social responsibility (CSR) was analyzed in the context of firm value and performance. Existing research suggests that it is important to distinguish between CSR aimed at the firm's primary stakeholders and CSR aimed at other stakeholders, as the former has been shown to have a positive effect on firm performance whereas the latter has been shown to have a negative effect. This part of the book also investigated corporate governance issues relating to debtholders and employees. While large debtholders such as banks may monitor the management, which benefits the shareholders and other stakeholders, their monitoring may also give them access to private information, thereby conferring on them monopoly power which enables them to charge above-market interest rates to the firm. Debtholders that are also equity holders may also suffer from conflicts of interests. In particular, they may be tempted to side with the shareholders and expropriate the firm's other fixed-claims stakeholders such as long-term customers and suppliers. In a nutshell, there is an optimal mix of debt and equity that the bank should hold to minimize these conflicts of interests. Another important stakeholder is the workforce. Two of the main schools that have proposed taxonomies of corporate governance systems have very different views about the role of employees in corporations. While the varieties of capitalism (VOC) literature argues that strong employee rights are not incompatible with strong economic growth, the law and finance literature is based on the premise that there is a zero-sum game between improving the rights of employees and improving those of investors. In other words, the rights of one group can only be improved at the expense of the other group. Other issues that were discussed include employee stock ownership and employee board representation. While there is still a need for further empirical research in the area, the existing evidence suggests that employee ownership can have positive effects on firm performance as long as it is part of a wider package of policies on human resource management. In turn, employee representation on the board of directors increases firm profitability as long as the representatives are employees of the firm. In contrast, trade union officials who represent the workforce on the board of directors do not increase firm performance. Finally, the corporate governance roles assumed by the various gatekeepers were also reviewed. While gatekeepers have an important role to play, it is unlikely that they will be successful in preventing future corporate scandals. Unfortunately, the existing evidence is as yet inconclusive as to whether industry regulation reduces the need for strong corporate governance or reinforces corporate governance.

In this book, I have tried to convey to the reader the great diversity of corporate governance arrangements across both countries and companies. While since the 1980s national and cross-national policy makers have advocated the superiority of the Anglo-American system of corporate governance, the 2008 subprime mortgage crisis has shown that no one system is infallible and superior in all circumstances. During the late 1980s and early 1990s, Germany and Japan were heralded as the models of good corporate governance that all other countries should follow. At the time, the advantage of both systems of corporate governance was believed to be the existence and prevalence of large and patient shareholders that were committed to their firms over the long run and that were also able to obtain similar long-term commitments from the other stakeholders. This constancy of corporate control and ownership was thought to be one of the main drivers behind the steady economic growth of the German and Japanese economies.

During the second part of the 1990s, the internet as well as other innovations in information technology required managers and firms to be able to react quickly to constant technological changes. It was then that the US economy with its highly developed capital markets – providing easy access to venture capital – took over the rest of the world. Silicon Valley was now the model to follow with its many high-tech start-up firms that were founded by entrepreneurs, many of which had freshly graduated from Ivy League universities, that ben-efitted from funding by VCs and were then taken to the stock exchange a few years later. During the height of Silicon Valley, Asia was hit by the 1997 financial crisis which exposed the so-called crony capitalism thought to prevail in many Asian economies. It was now this crony capitalism that was considered to slow down Asian economies and to enforce the economic, political and social status quo, thereby hampering entrepreneurship.

More than a decade down the line, we have arrived at another crossroads, with UK and US bankers being accused of having brought about global economic meltdown through ruthless casino capitalism and an obses-sion with short-term profits, tacitly condoned by institutional and individual shareholders with little concern for corporate governance and the long-term survival of the business.

During past waves of corporate scandals, politicians have typically been quick to respond by issuing new regulation, often knee-jerk reactions that did little to address the weaknesses and shortcomings in corporate governance. For example, in the UK, successive codes of best practice have tried to mitigate the principal-agent problem – caused by managers being effectively in control of their firm given the passive nature of the firm's many small shareholders – by increasing the role of non-executives and institutional shareholders in corporate governance. However, in turn, non-executives as well as institutional shareholders are merely disinterested agents, acting on behalf of their principals. In other words, regulators have attempted to address the lack of commitment and loyalty of the management to their shareholders by putting in place another link between the former and the latter, i.e. non-executive directors who may be even less committed to the firm. The existing empirical literature provides little support for the effectiveness of independent, non-executive directors, and some research suggests that non-executives tend to side with the CEO rather than to scrutinize and question the validity of the CEO's proposed decisions. Further, UK banks that failed during the subprime mortgage cri-sis had exemplary corporate governance arrangements, at least as evidenced by their full compliance with the Combined Code that was effective at the time.

Hence, one major lesson to be learnt from this book is that no one corporate governance system is infallible. Each system has its strengths as well as weaknesses. It is paramount for policy makers, investors and others concerned with corporate governance to be aware of the weaknesses of their system of corporate governance. Blindly advocating the superiority of one system over all others is not the way forward. Even if at a particular moment in time their system happens to be superior to others in many ways, its unconditional adoption is likely to prevent the system from evolving and adapting to a changing environment. Hence, what may have started off as being superior might end up being less effective than other systems. A second major lesson to be learnt, which is related to the first one, is that diversity in corporate governance is not necessarily bad, but is likely to reflect the fact that 'one size does not fit all'. While it may make perfect sense for a large corporation to have a certain minimum percentage of non-executives on its board of directors, such a requirement may be excessively costly for a small company and may also be entirely unnecessary given the lower dispersion of ownership or the greater need for advice from the board. Although the corporate governance codes of some countries have allowed for flexibility by adopting a 'comply or explain' approach, other countries, including the USA, have gone down the route of prescriptive regulation leaving little or no discretion to firms in terms of choosing the most appropriate governance. However, even for those countries that have chosen the more flexible approach of 'comply or explain', companies often have had little choice but to adopt what is being proclaimed as best practice. One of the dangers of the box-ticking approach is that it lulls shareholders into a false sense of security, further reducing the few incentives they may have to monitor their firm's management.

So what is the way forward? Certainly, educating investors about their *responsibilities* (and not just their *rights*) as well as the risks they are taking by investing in the stock exchange is important. However, corpora-tions should also make it easier and less costly for small shareholders to vote at the annual general meetings (AGMs). Ways forward are internet-based voting and AGMs that are transmitted via the internet. Further, regulation over the last decades has been almost entirely reactive rather than proactive. Regulators, under the pressure from those they are supposed to regulate, have often refrained from intervening in markets while the economy has been doing well. For example, while the Bank of England and the Financial Services Authority (FSA) – now the Financial Conduct Authority (FCA) – were aware of Northern Rock's highly risky business model, they decided not to intervene until it was too late. It was then that the same voices that argued in favour of reducing regulation when the economy was performing well, were accusing governments of not having intervened early enough to prevent the global economic meltdown caused by the subprime mortgage crisis. It will be difficult for regulators to make a case that something that in the eyes of the many 'ain't broke' should be fixed. However, a moderating force is the only way forward to avoid excesses. More generally, gatekeepers need to be much more active and exercise constructive, even if at first sight everything seems to be fine. Moreover, there is also a need for managers' attitudes to change. Managers need to be aware of the wider implications of their actions as well as their responsibilities towards society at large. To some extent, business schools are to blame. Few MBA programmes as well as few other business and management degrees nowadays include modules on business ethics. Frequently, other business and management modules are taught without explicit reference to ethical conduct, and often business ethics has been repackaged as CSR, which absolves individuals from any personal responsibility, leaving it all to impersonal corporations.

Glossary

A

Abnormal returns are returns achieved by a security (e.g. a stock) over and above its risk-adjusted benchmark return. For example, a positive abnormal return to the appointment of a new CEO suggests that the stock market is confident – by reacting positively – that the new CEO will improve firm performance.

Agency costs, see principal-agent problem.

Agency problem, see principal-agent problem, see agency problem of debt.

The **agency problem of debt** consists of the shareholders gambling with the money of the debtholders by investing in highly risky projects when there is very little equity left in the firm. The shareholders will reap the gains from the projects if they are successful whereas most of the risk and losses will be borne by the debtholders.

Agent, see principal-agent problem.

American Depository Receipts (ADRs) are also called American Depository Shares (ADSs). Apart from Canadian and Israeli firms which can list directly on a US stock exchange, all other foreign firms can only do so via ADRs. A foreign firm wanting to list on a US stock exchange deposits some of its shares with an American bank, the depository bank, which will then issue the ADRs that will be trading on a US stock exchange.

The **antidirector rights index** was designed by La Porta et al. It measures how well shareholders are protected against abuses by the management or the large shareholder. It ranges from 0 to 6. It increases by 1 for each of the following criteria that are met: (1) shareholders can mail their proxy votes; (2) shareholders are not required to deposit their shares before the AGM; (3) cumulative voting is allowed; (4) minority shareholders are protected; (5) shareholders have a pre-emptive right to buy newly issued shares; and (6) the percentages of shares required to call an extraordinary shareholders meeting is 10 per cent or less. As an additional measure, one share-one vote is set to 1 if the one share-one vote rule is upheld and 0 otherwise. See also the creditor rights index. (There is also an updated version of the La Porta et al. study which covers 72 countries [Djankov, S., La Porta, R., Lopez-de-Silanes, F. and Shleifer, A., 'The Law and Economics of Self-Dealing', *Journal of Financial Economics* 88, 430–65]. However, this study no longer includes the measure for creditor protection.)

Anti-takeover devices, see takeover defences.

The **arm's length approach** in UK company law prescribes that non-executive directors are to remain independent from particular shareholders or interest groups. Conversely, in the rest of the world large shareholders, suppliers, customers and employees are frequently represented on the board of directors and frequently openly pursue the interests of the party or parties they represent.

An **asset sell-off** consists of a parent firm selling one of its subsidiaries to a third party via a private transaction. See equity carve-out, spin-off.

Asymmetric information refers to situations where one party, typically the one that agrees to carry out a certain duty or agrees to behave in a certain way, i.e. the agent, has more information than the other party, the principal.

B

Bank-based economies are characterized by close and long-term bank ties and debt financing is provided mainly by the banks rather than the bond markets. See market-based economies.

The **Bank Holding Company Act.** In the USA, the Glass-Steagall Act of 1933 and the Bank Holding Company Act of 1956 prevented banks from holding direct equity stakes in companies. See also Glass-Steagall Act.

Base-rate underweighting, see gambler's fallacy.

Benefits of control are benefits derived from having control over a corporation. These benefits come in two forms: security benefits and private benefits. Security benefits are those benefits from large stakes that are shared by *all* the shareholders. These benefits originate from the increase in firm value due to the monitoring of the management carried out by the large shareholder. Given the existence of a large shareholder, the management is less likely to expropriate the shareholders by pursuing their own interests rather than maximizing firm value. The increase in firm value from the reduction in the agency costs benefits all the shareholders. Conversely, private benefits often come at the expense of the minority shareholders. These are the benefits that the large shareholder extracts from the firm and only accrue to him. They include related-party transactions (see related-party transactions), i.e. tunnelling and transfer pricing, as well as nepotism and infighting. Private benefits of control are normally non-transferable, i.e. they are specific to the incumbent controlling shareholder. They are also difficult to observe and measure by outsiders compared to security benefits.

Biased self-attribution, see overconfidence.

The **Big Bang** is the name for the 1986 deregulation of the London Stock Exchange, which was the direct result of the much earlier May Day deregulation of the American stock exchanges. One of the major changes induced by the Big Bang was to remove minimum commissions on stock trades, which brokers had to charge independent of the size of the trade. See also May Day deregulation.

Blocking minority, see control.

Board busyness is typically defined as a board with a majority of non-executive directors who sit on three or more boards. Busy boards as well as busy directors have been associated with weaker corporate governance.

The board of directors consists of the executive directors and the non-executive directors. In some countries (e.g. China and Germany), executives and non-executives sit on separate boards. The executive directors run the company on a day-to-day basis. Some or all of the executives sit on the board of directors, alongside the non-executive directors. The role of the non-executive directors is to look after the interests of all the shareholders as well as sometimes those of other stakeholders such as the corporation's employees or banks. More precisely, the non-executives' roles are to monitor the firm's top management, i.e. the executive directors, as well as providing the latter with advice. See also board independence.

Board independence is normally measured by the percentage of non-executive directors on the board. Boards with a greater percentage of non-executive directors are thought to be stronger, i.e. have greater independence from the executive directors. See also board of directors.

Bonding costs, see principal-agent problem.

The bonding hypothesis states that firms from countries with weak corporate governance standards cross-list on a stock market of a country with better investor protection to commit themselves not to expropriate their (minority) shareholders.

Book building, see initial public offering.

Bounded rationality refers to the fact that humans are typically not able to analyze all the information available to them when facing a decision problem. The reasons why rationality is bounded are time limits and cognitive constraints. Because the time available for making a decision is limited and not all of the available information can be considered, the decision made may not be optimal. In addition, cognitive constraints such as limits to human intelligence, limits to memory and a limited attention span are a further reason why decisions may not be optimal.

The bootstrapping effect consists of a bidder with weak corporate governance adopting the better corporate governance of the target company. Bootstrapping is voluntary in the case of a full acquisition, but in the case of a partial acquisition the bidder has to honour the corporate governance regulation that the target is subject to in line with the extraterritoriality principle. The latter

is a principle embedded in international law which enables a host country to subject a foreign-owned subsidiary to its own law and regulation given that the subsidiary is domiciled within its jurisdiction.

The Bretton Woods agreement established a system of rules as well as new global institutions, including the International Monetary Fund (IMF) and the International Bank for Reconstruction and Development (IBRD), also referred to as the World Bank. The main feature of the Bretton Woods agreement was to put in place a system of fixed currency exchange rates pegged to the dollar, which in turn was pegged to the price of gold.

C

The UK Cadbury Report was published in 1992. It is a code of best practice and companies listed on the London Stock Exchange had to comply with the Code's recommendations or explain why they had chosen not to comply with individual recommendations. The Cadbury Report emphasized the role of the board of directors, in particular non-executive directors, as well as the role of institutional investors in corporate governance.

Capture refers to the influence that the client or firm may have over one of its gatekeepers and may push the latter to serve its own interests rather than preventing corporate malpractice and wrong-doing.

Cash flow rights, see ownership.

A chaebol is a group of Korean companies controlled by a family. Examples of well-known conglomerates include Hyundai, LG and Samsung.

Civic engagement refers to a country's citizens' involvement in public affairs. There are two contrasting views as to the effects of civic engagement. According to Robert Putnam, civic engagement via horizontal rather than vertical, i.e. hierarchical, associations increases trust within society and in turn fosters economic growth. Conversely, Mancur Olson argues that horizontal associations are often self-serving associations, which divert economic resources into their own pockets to the detriment of the rest of society, and reduce trust.

Civil law is law that relies on extensive codes of law and limits the role of judges to interpreting these codes in a court of law. Civil law families include French, German and Scandinavian civil law. See also common law.

Classified board, see staggered board.

The German Co-determination Law of 1976 requires firms with more than 2,000 workers to have 50 per cent of employee representatives on their supervisory board. In addition, firms with no more than 10,000 employees must have a total number of 12 members on the supervisory board, firms with between 10,000 and 20,000 employees must have a total of 16 members and firms with more than 20,000 employees must have 20 members in total.

The Combined Code of 1998 combined the earlier Cadbury, Greenbury and Hampel Reports in a single code. The Code also recommended that a system of internal control should be put in place to ensure that the company is run in the interests of the shareholders and that the directors review the system's effectiveness at least once a year and report back to the shareholders. See Cadbury Report, Greenbury Report, Hampel Report.

Commercial banks are banks that specialize in financial intermediation (i.e. mainly turning small, short-term deposits into large, long-term loans) and payment systems. See also investment banks, universal banks.

Common law is case-based law. Common law relies on judges pronouncing judgements based on the cases that are presented to them in a court of law and these judgements then create precedents for other, similar future cases. Common law is the law prevailing in the UK, the USA and other Commonwealth countries. See civil law.

Common stock, see ordinary shares.

Complementarities relate to sets of institutions that are more efficient and effective than if they were to exist separately. See also coordinated market economies, liberal market economies.

Complete contracts are contracts which specify exactly what the managers must do in each future contingency of the world, and what the distribution of profits will be in each contingency. In practice, they are not feasible.

Confirmatory bias is a form of self-deception consisting of spending too little time on data and other information that contradicts one's beliefs and discarding it as bad data or bad luck. See also overconfidence.

Conflicts of interests exist between the shareholders and the managers; the shareholders and the debtholders; the shareholders and the non-financial stakeholders; as well as different types of shareholders (mainly the large shareholder and the minority shareholders). See also conflicts of interests between owners and customers.

Conflicts of interests between owners and customers are likely to be severe for products and services involving long-term contracts as they may tempt the shareholders to expropriate their customers. Examples of such products and services include mortgages, life insurance and pension savings. For such products and services, the mutual organization is likely to be superior as it merges the functions of owners and customers, thereby avoiding any conflicts between the two.

The conformity effect relates to the tendency of individuals to conform to the beliefs and behaviours of others in their social group or country. The strength of the conformity effect depends on a country's history, religion and culture.

Contractual corporate governance refers to the ways and means by which individual companies can deviate from their national corporate governance standards by increasing (or reducing) the level of protection they offer to their shareholders and other stakeholders.

Control chain, see ownership pyramid.

Control is defined as control rights. They typically stem from voting rights. Voting rights give the holder the right to make certain decisions about the firm and/or vote in favour or against agenda points at the AGM. Such agenda points may include the appointment or dismissal of members of the company's board of directors. A shareholder or group of shareholders may have control over a firm by holding the majority of the shares. For some decisions that cause substantial changes to the nature of the firm (e.g. a merger and the liquidation of the firm), a supermajority, i.e. 75 per cent of the votes, may be required. Hence, a shareholder holding a supermajority has typically uncontested control. For the same decision, a stake of at least 25 per cent of the votes typically constitutes a blocking minority. While a blocking minority does not confer uncontested control to its holder, it nevertheless gives its holder a right to veto any decisions that require a supermajority. Control rights may also stem from channels other than voting rights. For example, the firm's articles of association may include a clause whereby the founder or his/her descendants has the right to appoint a specific number of board members as long as the founding family holds at least one share in the firm. Another channel consists of a so-called golden share, sometimes held by a government in a firm of national importance (e.g. an arms manufacturer) which enables the government to block the takeover of the firm by a foreign investor. Finally, the management may have de facto control in the absence of a large shareholder.

Control rights, see control.

Convertible securities are debt securities that can be converted into a fixed number of equity shares during a specified period. When a debt security is converted into equity shares, the debt security stops existing and the debtholder becomes a shareholder of the firm. It is in the debtholder's interest to convert when the value of the equity shares received from the conversion exceeds the value of the debt security. Convertible debt securities typically earn interest rates that are lower than nonconvertible debt securities.

Coordinated market economies (CMEs) use complex networks to coordinate economic decision problems. Hence, CMEs tend to have inflexible and illiquid capital markets as well as labour markets, and firms tend to specialize in highly specific assets and investments. See also liberal market economies.

Corporate governance devices, see corporate governance mechanisms.

Corporate governance mechanisms are those arrangements that aim to mitigate the conflicts of interests that corporations face. These conflicts of interests are those that may arise between the shareholders and the managers; the shareholders and the debtholders; the shareholders and the non-financial stakeholders; as well as different types of shareholders (mainly the large shareholder and the minority shareholders).

Corporate social responsibility (CSR) 'deals with managerial consideration of non-market forces or social aspects of corporate activity outside of a market or regulatory framework and includes consideration of issues such as employee welfare, community programs, charitable donations, and environmental protection' (Carter, C.R., Kale, R. and Grimm, C.M. (2000), 'Environmental Purchasing and Firm Performance: An Empirical Investigation', *Transportation Research Part E: Logistics and Transportation Review* 36, 219–28.)

The **cost-avoidance hypothesis** and the shareholder-exploitation hypothesis are the two contrasting schools of thought about the impact of regulatory competition on shareholder protection. The cost-avoidance hypothesis states that regulatory competition results in a race to the top, with firms moving to legal regimes with better law to reduce their costs of doing business. The shareholder-exploitation hypothesis states that in order to maximize the revenues from incorporations, jurisdictions will compete in ways to provide laws that cater for managerial rather than shareholder interests and this will cause a race to the bottom, which will harm economic efficiency.

A **credible signal** is a signal used by a firm to convey information about the firm's superior quality to other market players. The signal is credible as it is costly and cannot be used by firms of an inferior quality.

The **creditor rights index** measures how well creditor rights are protected. It ranges from 0 to 4. It increases by 1 for each of the following criteria that are met: (1) secured creditors can withdraw their collateral before the completion of the reorganization; (2) secured creditors have the right to collateral in the reorganization; (3) creditors' approval is needed before managers can file for reorganization; and (4) managers are replaced by a third party appointed by the creditors or the court while the reorganization is pending. See also antidirector rights index.

A **cross-holding** consists of company A holding shares in company B and vice-versa. Frequently, cross-holdings exist in firms with a relatively low concentration of control and aim at protecting the management of each of the two companies involved from a hostile takeover bid.

A **cross-listing** consists of a firm listing on a foreign stock exchange either at the time of its initial public offering on its domestic stock exchange or sometime thereafter.

The **curse of knowledge** consists of assuming that others who have less knowledge have more similar beliefs than they actually have.

D

Demutualization refers to the process whereby, during the 1980s and 1990s, a number of UK mutual building societies changed their legal status to a stock corporation and obtained a stock exchange listing.

Deregulation. Economic and political measures that reduce the scope of regulation in a particular industry and/or economy. See also Big Bang.

Disposition effect, see mental accounting.

Dual-class shares. Firms with dual-class shares have two classes of shares outstanding. One class has voting rights or superior voting rights and the second class has no voting rights or fewer voting rights. See also ordinary shares, preference shares.

Duality refers to the CEO also chairing the board, i.e. the roles of the CEO and chairman are assumed by the same person.

E

The **efficient market hypothesis (EMH)** states that stock markets are efficient and that prices of securities reflect all available information at all times. According to the weak form of the EMH, prices follow a random walk and the future prices cannot be predicted from past prices. Under the semi-strong form of the EMH, prices also reflect all publicly available information such as that contained in company accounts and financial reports, the reports of financial analysts and newspaper articles. Investors will not be able to beat the market by trading on publicly available information as this information is already reflected in the prices. In addition to past prices and publicly available information, under the strong form of the EMH prices also reflect private information. Under this form, even insiders holding private information on their firm would not be able to beat the markets. See also pricing anomalies.

Empire building. One of the main types of agency problems alongside perquisites. See free cash flow problem.

Endogenous, see exogenous.

An **equity carve-out** consists of a parent firm selling one of its subsidiaries via an initial public offering (IPO). Frequently, the parent firm keeps a majority holding in the subsidiary after the IPO. See asset sell-off, spin-off. See also initial public offering.

Exclusionary screens are used by rating agencies that rate companies according to their degree of social responsibility. They are also used by socially responsible investment funds. Exclusionary screens consist of eliminating companies from an index or a pool of possible investment choices because of their involvement with so-called sin industries such as alcohol, gambling, tobacco, firearms, military weapons and pornography as well as nuclear power.

Executive directors, see board of directors.

Exogenous refers to a device, mechanism or action which is determined outside the system whereas endogenous refers to a device, mechanism or action which is determined within the system. A corporate governance device is said to be endogenous if it depends on the company's characteristics such as its past performance. See corporate governance mechanisms.

The expropriation of the minority shareholders consists of the large controlling shareholder (or a group of large shareholders acting in concert) expropriating the minority shareholders. Minority shareholder expropriation can take the form of tunnelling, transfer pricing, nepotism and infighting. Tunnelling consists of transferring assets or profits from the firm to the pockets of its large shareholder, thereby expropriating the firm's minority shareholders. Another way of expropriating the minority shareholders is via transfer pricing. This consists of overcharging the firm jointly owned by the minority shareholders and the large shareholder for services or assets provided by a firm that is fully owned by the large shareholder. Another form of minority shareholder expropriation is nepotism. This form of expropriation stems from family shareholders appointing members of their family to top management positions within their firm rather than the most competent candidates in the managerial labour market. Finally, infighting by the controlling family shareholder may not necessarily be a wilful form of expropriating the firm's minority shareholders, but nevertheless is likely to deflect management time as well as other firm resources.

Extraterritoriality principle, see bootstrapping effect.

F

The false consensus effect consists of people tending to assume that others share their opinions more than they do.

Familism refers to strong family ties which exist in countries such as China and Italy and which dominate most economic activities. Familism may not be directly restricting economic growth, but it does restrict the type of firms, the size of firms as well as the industry sectors that will develop within a country.

Financialization refers to two phenomena. The first one is the increasingly important role of capital markets and the financial services industry at the global level, assuming the key economic role that was previously assumed by the manufacturing industry. The second one is the process of turning any asset which generates cash flows into a tradable financial security or a derivative of a financial security.

First-tier control is control held directly in a firm. See also ultimate control.

Free cash flow is the total cash stock of the firm minus the cash component of working capital, minus cash necessary for all compulsory payments (debt, payables, tax), minus cash invested in positive net present value (NPV) projects.

The free cash flow problem was advanced by Michael Jensen in his influential 1986 paper ('Agency Costs of Free Cash Flow, Corporate Finance, and Takeovers', *American Economic Review* 76, 323–9). The free cash flow problem, also sometimes referred to as empire building, consists of the management pursuing growth rather than shareholder-value maximization. See free cash flow. See also 'quiet life' hypothesis.

The free float is the percentage of shares not held by large shareholders. While there is no universal definition of how to measure the free float, most measures refer to a threshold beyond which a shareholding is considered to be large enough not to be included in the free float. For example, the free float may include all shareholdings of less than 10 per cent of the shares outstanding.

The free-rider problem may occur in firms with dispersed ownership where none of the shareholders has sufficient incentives to monitor the management. If one of the shareholders spends time and effort monitoring the management, the benefits from doing so will be shared by all the shareholders whereas the monitoring shareholder will bear all the costs. Hence, there may be little or no monitoring.

The fundamental attribution error consists of underestimating external factors and overestimating the importance of a person's mindset when explaining that person's actions.

G

Gambler's fallacy consists of mistakenly reading patterns into random events, i.e. events that are independent of each other. It consists of mistakenly replacing unconditional probabilities by conditional probabilities, thereby underestimating or underweighting the probability of an event. This is also referred to as base-rate underweighting.

Glasnost (Russian for publicity or openness) was the policy of transparency, disclosure and openness, about the activities of government in the Soviet Union, combined with freedom of information, introduced by the Soviet leader Mikhail Gorbachev in the second half of the 1980s. See also Perestroika.

The Glass-Steagall Act of 1933 introduced a clear segmentation between commercial banks, which were to specialize in payment and intermediation, and investment banks which were to focus on the securities side. See also commercial banks, investment banks.

Globalization is the gradual integration of national economies and capital markets into a single global market. See also neoliberalism, financialization.

A golden parachute is severance pay that managers receive in the event that they lose their jobs because of, e.g. a takeover or a disciplinary action by the shareholders.

The 'grabbing hand' of government is the view that politicians sitting on boards of directors have their own objectives in mind, in particular winning votes from their electorate. One way of winning votes is to force the firms on whose boards they sit to employ more people than would be efficient, thereby reducing shareholder value. Hence, according to this view politicians seek rents and the latter come at the expense of the firms' shareholders. In contrast, the 'helping hand' of government is the view that government and political connections bring about favours and privileges, such as government subsidies and government procurement orders, which benefit the shareholders.

The US Gramm-Leach-Bliley Act of 1999 practically repealed the 1933 Glass-Steagall Act, enabling banks to engage in both commercial and investment banking and to have their subsidiaries conduct financial activities that the banks themselves were not allowed to carry out. See commercial banking, investment banking, Glass-Steagall Act.

The grandstanding hypothesis states that young venture capitalists (VCs) that still need to establish their reputation within the venture capital industry, take their portfolio firms public early in order to create a track record of successful investments (Gompers, P.A. (1996), 'Grandstanding in the Venture Capital Industry', *Journal of Financial Economics* 42, 133–56). Venture-capital firms are frequently in the form of partnerships with the silent partners, typically institutional investors, providing all the funding. Young venture-capital partnerships may find it difficult to obtain further funding from their silent partners unless they have managed to get at least one of their portfolio firms to the stock exchange. Future access to financing can be achieved by young VCs by rushing their firms to the stock market. The cost from doing so is higher underpricing at the IPO, which will be borne by all the shareholders and not just the VCs. See venture capitalist, initial public offering.

The Greenbury Report was published in July 1995. It was a response to the public outcry about what were perceived to be excessive levels of executive pay. Its main recommendations were that there should be a remuneration committee made up of non-executives, that executive pay should be disclosed on an individual basis, and that executive pay should be linked to company performance and the performance of individual directors.

H

The halo effect is a heuristic simplification which consists of valuing an exceptional characteristic of an individual and then extending this positive assessment to the other characteristics of the individual. Halo effects apply to celebrities, but may also apply to CEOs. The danger of the halo effect is that the subject of the effect may be assumed to be infallible, whereas he or she is clearly not. See heuristic simplification.

The Hampel Report was published in 1998 and it re-emphasized the important role of institutional shareholders in corporate governance.

The 'helping hand' of government, see the 'grabbing hand' of government.

Herding, see conformity effect.

Heuristic simplification is a result of bounded rationality. Human rationality is bounded, and in order to deal with time and cognitive constraints, humans tend to simplify the complex environment that surrounds them by using rules of thumb, also called heuristics, algorithms and mental modules. Evolution has hardwired these rules of thumb into human brains, implying that humans are likely to make the same systematic biases in certain situations where the rules of thumb are unlikely to work well. See bounded rationality.

Hot-issue markets are cycles in the number of firms going public and cycles in the initial returns (e.g. first-month returns) of these firms. Peaks in the number of firms going public typically follow peaks in the initial returns achieved by earlier initial public offerings. Hot-issue markets are one of the three pricing anomalies affecting initial public offerings. See initial public offering, pricing anomalies.

The house money effect is the greater willingness of people to gamble with money that they have recently gained, e.g. in a casino. This behavioural pattern may be explained by the fact that the recent positive sensation of a gain may cancel out the future painful sensation of a loss.

Hubris consists of managers overestimating the gains or synergies from a merger or acquisition. See also over-confidence.

I

Incorporation principle, see reincorporation.

Infighting, see expropriation of the minority shareholders.

The initial public offering (IPO) is the first issue and sale of shares by a firm to the general public, combined with the admission of the issuing firm to the listing of the stock exchange. There are various ways of determining the price of the shares issued in the IPO, i.e. the so-called offer price. If the IPO is an offer at a fixed price, the offer price will be determined by the investment bank and investors will be invited to subscribe for the shares at this price. A book-building offer consists of a much more involved pricing mechanism, including a formal assessment of the demand for the shares to be issued. There are three stages in a book-building offer. The first stage consists of the investment bank obtaining non-binding expressions of interest from its clients, typically large institutional investors. The expressions of interest consist of an indicative price for the shares as well as the number of shares the client in question would in principle be interested in. During the second stage, the investment bank then determines a price range, consisting of a minimum and maximum price. Investors are then invited to apply for the shares by specifying the number of shares they wish to purchase as well as the price (within the price range) they wish to pay. This is the actual book-building stage. The final stage then consists of the investment bank determining a strike price at which the shares will be issued to the investors. Any investor having bid for shares at a price equal to or exceeding the strike price will receive shares in the IPO. All other investors will go empty handed.

The insider system of corporate governance is characterized by concentrated control, underdeveloped stock markets and complex ownership structures, such as ownership pyramids. See ownership pyramids, outsider system.

Interlocked directorships consist of one or several directors of firm A sitting on the board of firm B and vice-versa. Interlocked directorships are thought to entrench management by protecting it from disciplinary actions such as hostile takeovers.

International Bank for Reconstruction and Development (IBRD), see Bretton Woods agreement.

International Monetary Fund (IMF), see Bretton Woods agreement.

Investment banks focus on the securities side of banking. Their activities include advising firms involved in mergers and acquisitions as well as the issue of debt and equity securities. Investment banks also frequently provide underwriting services whereby they underwrite securities issues undertaken by their corporate clients. Underwriting a securities issue consists of bearing the risk that the issue may be undersubscribed, i.e. that the supply of securities issued may exceed the demand. The underwriter agrees to buy any unwanted shares. See also commercial banks, universal banks.

IPO underpricing is one of the three pricing anomalies affecting initial public offerings. Underpricing consists of the offer price being lower than the price at the end of the first day (week or month) of trading on the stock market. Empirical studies for a large number of different stock markets and countries suggest that initial public offerings are on average underpriced. See initial public offering, pricing anomalies.

IPO, see initial public offering.

K

A keiretsu is a group of Japanese companies with ties to a single bank which acts as the principal lender to the group. The bank also has ownership in the group's companies and there are typically cross-holdings between the group companies. See cross-holding. The keiretsus originated from the zaibatsus of the pre-Second World War period. The zaibatsus were groups of industrial companies or conglomerates controlled by families via a holding firm at the top of the group and with a bank as one of the group companies providing the financing.

Keynesian economic policies, called after the British economist John Maynard Keynes (1883–1946), focus on the demand side of the economy. In particular, the government has an important role during economic recessions consisting of reducing unemployment and reviving economic growth. The government's role during recessions is to counteract the slump in demand from the private sector. See also supply-side economics.

Keynesianism, see Keynesian economic policies.

L

The law and finance literature was started by Rafel La Porta, Florencio Lopez-de-Silanes, Andrei Shleifer and Robert Vishny. This literature explains differences in corporate governance as well as corporate control and ownership by institutional differences, including investor protection, the political orientation of governments and types of electoral systems. This literature typically asserts that there is a clear hierarchy of corporate governance systems, with one system being superior to all the other ones. It is also based on the premise that there is a zero-sum game between investors and workers, implying that improving the rights of one of these constituencies automatically reduces the rights of the other one.

Leveraged buy-outs (LBOs) normally consist of the sale of a division of a company or the sale of an entire company. In contrast to standard acquisitions, LBOs are mainly financed by debt and are frequently undertaken by institutional or specialist investors. LBOs are normally taken private for a period of 3–5 years and then taken public again (via a reverse LBO). The shareholders of firms that are the target of LBOs earn large premiums on their shares, typically in the region of 40 to 60 per cent. See also management buy-outs (MBOs).

Liberal market economies (LMEs) are economies that rely on market mechanisms to coordinate economic decision problems. LMEs are characterized by highly developed and frictionless capital markets and labour markets and firms specializing in highly liquid and generic assets. See also coordinated market economies.

A lock-in agreement is an agreement whereby the incumbent shareholders agree not to dispose of any additional shares after the initial public offering for a specific period. See initial public offering.

Lock-up agreement, see lock-in agreement.

Loss aversion is an example of narrow framing or packaging. It consists of the fact that most people are very risk averse and even shy away from very small risks. Loss aversion may be explained by the fact that humans tend to turn a continuous return from an investment into a discrete return by distinguishing between two regions, i.e. the region for losses and that for gains, both of which are clearly separated by the break-even point. The fact that humans tend to turn the continuous return from an investment into a dichotomous variable (a loss or a gain) may explain why they do not like risks, even minor risks.

A loss of self-control consists of one's emotions, such as love and anger, guiding one's actions rather than one's intelligence.

M

Majoritarian electoral systems are those systems where parties have to win a majority of electoral districts to win the election. See also proportional electoral systems.

Majority, see control.

Management board, see two-tier board.

Management buy-outs (MBOs) are a specific type of leveraged buy-out whereby the incumbent management takes the firm private by buying out the existing shareholders and financing the acquisition with mainly debt. See also leveraged buy-outs.

Managerial entrenchment consists of managers shielding themselves from external disciplining such as hostile takeovers and external disciplining by their shareholders. While managerial entrenchment may be a reflection of the principal-agent problem, it may also be the consequence of concentrated family control whereby top management posts within the company are passed from generation to generation of the controlling family. See also principal-agent problem, interlocked directorships, takeover defences.

Managerial risk aversion refers to managers being excessively risk averse, i.e. they are reluctant to invest in risky, but shareholder-enhancing projects given their heavy exposure to firm-specific risk. The latter stems from their human capital being invested in just one firm (i.e. they tend to hold only one job which they will lose if the firm fails) and a large proportion of their personal wealth also being invested in the firm.

Managerial shirking, see 'quiet life' hypothesis.

Market-based economies or systems are economies that rely on well-developed and frictionless capital markets and the issuance of publicly traded securities to finance companies. See bank-based economies.

May Day deregulation refers to the 1 May 1975 when American stock exchanges moved from a system of fixed commissions to negotiated commissions. This reform significantly reduced the cost for foreign firms of cross-listing in the USA, taking away business from other stock markets, such as the London Stock Exchange. See also Big Bang.

Mental accounting consists of keeping two separate accounts in one's brain, one for losses realized on investments and one for gains. Mental accounting is an example of narrow framing or packing. Mental accounting may explain the so-called disposition effect, i.e. the observation that investors tend to dispose of winning stock too quickly and hold onto losing stock for too long.

Monitoring, see principal-agent problem.

Moral hazard consists of the agent behaving badly or at least less responsibly, i.e. in ways that may harm the principal while clearly serving the interests of the agent, once a contract has been signed between the two.

N

The narrow framing effect is a consequence of heuristic simplification which leads humans to analyze decision problems in isolation, i.e. ignore the wider context or environment surrounding the decision problem. Narrow framing is also called narrow packing. The main danger from such compartmentalizing of decision problems is that the way a decision problem may be compartmentalized depends on the way the information has been presented to the decision maker. See heuristic simplification.

Narrow packaging effect, see narrow framing effect.

A negative externality is a cost imposed on others by one's economic activity. Such costs include environmental and noise pollution.

Negative spillover effect, see positive spillover effect.

Neoliberalism (called neo-conservatism in the USA) is the belief that markets are better at allocating resources and ensuring economic efficiency than governments and that individuals are better at making economic choices than governments. See also globalization, financialization.

Nepotism, see expropriation of the minority shareholders.

The net present value (NPV) of an investment project is the difference between the present value of its expected future cash flows and the initial investment outlay. The present value (PV) of the expected future cash flows is obtained by discounting the latter by a rate which takes into account the riskiness of the project as well as the timing of its cash flows, and then summing up the discounted cash flows. An investment project with a positive NPV is expected to increase shareholder value as its projected future cash flows exceed the initial outlay whereas a negative NPV suggests destruction of shareholder value.

New Deal. A series of economic measures undertaken by the US government of President Franklin Delano Roosevelt during 1933 and 1936 to bring down unemployment caused by the Great Depression, a result of the Wall Street crash of 1929.

Non-executive directors, see board of directors.

O

Oceanic games, see Shapley value.

Offer at a fixed price, see initial public offering.

Offer price, see initial public offering.

A one-tier board is a board where both the executives (or officers in the USA) and non-executives (or (independent) directors) sit. The one-tier board system is in place in countries such as Italy, Spain, the UK and the USA. See two-tier board, executive directors, non-executive directors.

Ordinary shares (common stock in American) have one vote each and earn a variable dividend. See also preference shares.

The outsider system has large equity markets, dispersed ownership and control, and an active market for corporate control. See insider system.

Overconfidence is a form of self-deception. It is the tendency of overestimating one's abilities and knowledge. Men tend to be more overconfident than women. Experts also tend to suffer from overconfidence when the information they are presented with is opaque and difficult to understand. CEOs have been shown to suffer more from overconfidence than other executives. For overconfidence to persist, there needs to be biased self-attribution which consists of attributing good outcomes to one's abilities and skills and negative outcomes to external factors. See also hubris, confirmatory bias.

Ownership is defined as cash flow rights. Cash flow rights give the holder a pro rata right to the firm's assets if the firm is liquidated (and after the claims of all the other claimants have been met) and a pro rata right to the firm's earnings, once the claims of all the other claimants have been settled, while the firm remains a going concern.

An ownership pyramid consists of a large shareholder leveraging ownership by putting in place intermediary companies between the target company and itself. Such a pyramid reduces the ownership stake of the large shareholder in the target company while maintaining control. See rule of one-share one-vote.

P

Path dependence is about how the past influences a country's current corporate governance and how these national characteristics persist over time. There are two forms of path dependence. First, structure-driven path dependence is the dependence of the current corporate governance arrangements and current corporate control structures on the structures that were initially in place. Second, rule-driven path dependence relates to how current regulation has been influenced by the corporate structures that were initially in place in the country. In particular, powerful economic actors will resist changes in regulation which will harm their own interests even though these changes would have brought about more efficient regulation.

Perestroika was a political movement around Soviet leader Mikhail Gorbachev aiming at political and economic reform in the Soviet Union. See also Glasnost.

Perquisites is one of the two main types of agency problems, alongside empire building. Perquisites or perks consist of on-the-job consumption by the firm's managers. While the benefits from the perks accrue to the managers, their costs are borne by the shareholders.

A positive spillover effect relates to a bidder with better corporate governance improving the corporate governance of the target. In contrast, there is a negative spillover effect if a bidder with weaker corporate governance reduces that of the target. See also bootstrapping effect.

Preference shares are typically non-voting shares. To compensate their holder for the lack of a voting right, they typically confer preferential dividend rights, such as a guaranteed dividend, and a higher seniority relative to ordinary shareholders. See ordinary shares.

Preferred stock, see preference shares.

Pricing anomalies are regular patterns in the prices of securities which violate the weak form of the efficient market hypothesis. See efficient market hypothesis, hot-issue markets.

Principal, see principal-agent problem.

The principal-agent problem was first formalized by Michael Jensen and William Meckling in 1976 ('Theory of the Firm. Managerial Behavior, Agency Costs and Capital Structure', *Journal of Financial Economics* 3, 305–60). Large widely held firms are run by professional managers, the agents, on behalf of their shareholders, the principals. While the agent is expected to run the firm in the interests of the principal(s), he or she may prefer to pursue his or her own objectives (see also moral hazard). This potential conflict of interests between the agent and principal causes agency costs. Agency costs are the sum of the following three components. The first component consists of the monitoring expenses incurred by the principal. Monitoring not only consists of the principal observing the agent and keeping a record of the latter's behaviour, but it also consists of intervening in various ways to constrain the agent's behaviour and to avoid unwanted actions. The second component is the bonding costs incurred by the agent. Bonding costs are costs incurred by the agent in order to signal credibly to the principal that he or she will act in the interests of the latter. One credible way for the agent to bond him or herself to the principal is to invest in the latter's firm. Finally, the third component is the residual loss. This is the loss incurred by the principal due to the divergence in interests with the agent. In other words, given the conflicts of interests between the principal and the agent, the latter may make decisions that do not maximize the value for the former.

Principal-agent theory, see principal-agent problem.

The principle of shareholder primacy is enshrined in UK and US corporate law. According to this principle, it is the directors' fiduciary duty to run the company in the interest of the shareholders.

Private equity acquisitions are normally undertaken by specialist investors, such as private equity houses and the private equity arms of institutional investors. They are typically leveraged buy-outs financed predominantly by debt as well as a small amount of equity provided by the private equity investor. See also leveraged buyouts.

Private benefits of control, see benefits of control.

Proportional electoral systems are those systems where political parties have to win a majority of votes to come into power. See also majoritarian electoral systems.

Proxy contests, see proxy votes.

Proxy votes are votes exercised by an entity or person on behalf of their holder. In some countries, banks exercise the votes of their customers, who deposit their shares for safe-keeping with the banks, at the AGM. In other countries, the directors may exercise the votes of their shareholders on their behalf. Finally, proxy votes may also be sought to ensure voting success for shareholder-initiated proposals. While such proxy contests are still relatively rare in Continental Europe, they are a frequent occurrence in the USA and also increasingly used in the UK. However, shareholder proposals are not legally binding in the USA and management may therefore resist their implementation whereas in most European countries they are binding.

Q

According to the 'quiet life' hypothesis, managers, if left to their own devices, will avoid cognitively costly activities such as new investments, divestments and improvements in firm efficiency. See also free cash flow problem.

R

Reagonomics is the nickname for US President Ronald Reagan's economic policies, which consisted of keeping inflation low by controlling the supply of money, reducing tax rates and government spending. See also supply-side economics.

Real seat principle, see reincorporation.

Reflex for loyalty or reflexive loyalty refers to humans' reflex for loyalty to their superiors. This reflex is hardwired in human brains as a result of human evolution. In prehistoric times, humans who were loyal to their tribal leader were more likely to survive in a hostile environment. See also type II agency problem.

A reincorporation consists of a firm which is already incorporated in one country (or federal state of a federation such as the USA) moving its legal seat to another country (or federal state). There are two principles in law applying to incorporations and reincorporations. These are the real seat principle and the incorporation principle. According to the real seat principle, the law applying to the firm is that of the geographic location of its headquarters or main activities, i.e. its *real* seat. In contrast, according to the incorporation principle, the law that applies to a firm is that of its country of incorporation, independent of whether the latter is its real seat or not. Hence, whereas the former principle makes it fairly onerous and expensive for a firm to move to another country, the latter makes it fairly easy.

Related-party transactions are transactions carried out with a company by or on behalf of an entity with a close relationship to the company. This entity may be the management, but typically is a large shareholder in control of the company. See expropriation of the minority shareholders.

Relationship-based system, see bank-based economies.

The representativeness heuristic consists of determining the probability of an event based on information judged to be typical or similar to that event. Humans have been shown to draw inferences from small samples that are too strong given the small sample size, whereas the inferences drawn from large samples tend to be too weak. This implies that there is a systematic bias which can be predicted by the sample size, i.e. the number of observations.

Residual claimants, see shareholders.

Residual loss, see principal-agent problem.

Reverse LBO, see leveraged buy-outs.

Rule-driven path dependence, see path dependence.

The rule of one-share one-vote, also known as the principle of one-share one-vote and the optimality of one-share one-vote, was advanced by Sanford Grossman and Oliver Hart in 1988 ('One Share-One Vote and the Market for Corporate Control', *Journal of Financial Economics* 20, 175–202). This rule postulates that it is optimal for firms and their shareholders to have shares that confer one vote each and to avoid violations of this rule. Such violations consist of ownership pyramids, dual-class shares, voting coalitions, voting caps, proxy votes and the conferment via the articles of association of additional votes to long-term shareholders. See dual-class shares, ownership pyramids, voting coalition, voting cap, proxy votes.

S

Seasonal affective disorder (SAD) is a medical condition whereby an individual is suffering from clinical depression during the winter months when the days are short and the amount of daylight is very limited compared to the summer months.

Security benefits of control, see benefits of control.

Separation of ownership and control. Adolf Berle and Gardiner Means were the first to outline this separation of ownership and control in their 1932 book *The Modern Corporation and Private Property* (New York, Macmillan). They argue that most firms start off as small businesses which are fully owned by their founders, typically entrepreneurs. At this stage, there are no conflicts of interests within the firm as the entrepreneur both owns and runs the firm. Hence, if the entrepreneur decides to work harder, all of the additional revenue generated by his or her increased effort will go into his or her own pockets. However, as the firm grows it will reach the point where the entrepreneur is no longer able to provide all the necessary financing and outside equity that needs to be raised. Once outside equity has been raised, the entrepreneur will no longer own all of the firm's equity, reducing his or her incentives to work hard. At the extreme, large firms will be run by professional managers with no or little equity ownership and be owned by shareholders that provide the financing, but have little or no experience in running the firm. See principal-agent problem.

The Shapley value measures how pivotal a shareholder is in a voted decision. A shareholder is pivotal if his or her vote is required to form a particular winning coalition. A shareholder will be more pivotal than others if he or she is more often part of a winning coalition than others. Typically, Shapley values are based on the assumption of oceanic games, i.e. the voted decision is mainly dominated by a few large shareholders and the minority shareholders are typically irrelevant when one or several of the large shareholders intend to form a winning coalition.

Shareholder-exploitation hypothesis, see cost-avoidance hypothesis.

Shareholder proposals are a type of shareholder activism available in the USA. Shareholder proposals are normally submitted under Securities and Exchange Commission Rule 14a-8. This rule allows a shareholder to include a proposal and a 500-word supporting statement in the proxy statement that is distributed to the firm's shareholders in advance of the AGM. The advantage of shareholder proposals is that they are relatively costless to the initiating shareholder, but they also must be submitted at least six months in advance of the AGM.

Shareholders are the residual risk bearers or the residual claimants to the firm's assets. The claims of all the stakeholders other than the shareholders will have to be met first before the claims of the latter can be met.

Shares, see stock corporations.

The Single European Act came into effect in 1992 in the European Union (EU). It removed barriers to capital flows and to the movement of citizens between the member states of the EU. It brought about a liberalization of financial as well as labour markets.

Sin industries, see exclusionary screens.

Single-tier board, see one-tier board.

Social democracies are democracies that combine the principles of social justice with those of capitalism.

Social issue participation (SIP), see stakeholder management.

Socially responsible investment (SRI) is 'an investment process that considers the social and environmental consequences of investments, both positive and negative, within the context of rigorous financial analysis' (Social Investment Forum (2001), *2001 Report on Socially Responsible Investing Trends in the United States*, Washington, DC: Social Investment Forum Foundation and Social Investment Forum).

SOEs, see state-owned enterprises.

A spin-off consists of a parent firm selling one of its subsidiaries by distributing free shares in the subsidiary to its own shareholders, pro rata to their holdings in the parent firm. See asset sell-off, equity carve-out.

Stage financing is venture-capital financing that is provided gradually as the firm achieves certain performance milestones. The milestones tend to be linked to major stages in the firm's life cycle such as the development of a prototype, the launch of the production based on an economically viable prototype and the first profit. Stage financing gives the venture capitalist the option to stop further financing should the firm fail to achieve the agreed milestones. See venture capitalist.

Stagflation consists of high unemployment and economic stagnation combined with high inflation.

A staggered board, also sometimes called a classified board, consists of a board segmented into classes, typically three, with only one class of directors coming up for election in a given year. In the case of a board with three classes of directors, it will take shareholders two elections to replace the majority of directors and three elections to replace all of them.

Stakeholder management (SM) deals with improving the firm's relationships with its primary stakeholders. In contrast, social issue participation (SIP) relates to the firm's involvement with social issues that do not improve the relationships between the firm and its primary stakeholders.

Stakeholders include the corporation's shareholders and debtholders as well as other, non-financial entities that have an interest in the running of the company. These include the corporation's primary stakeholders such as employees, customers, suppliers, local communities and the government as well as more remote stakeholders.

State-owned enterprises (SOEs) are firms that are either fully owned by the government or in the process of being privatized, but still have significant government ownership.

Stock corporations are formed by equity stocks or shares which trade on a recognized stock exchange if the issuing firm is listed. Stocks or shares are certificates of ownership and they also frequently have control rights. The holders of the stocks or shares are the so-called stockholders or shareholders.

Stocks, see stock corporations.

Structure-driven path dependence, see path dependence.

Supermajority, see control.

Supervisory board, see two-tier board.

Supply-side economics is a school of economic thought which argues that governments need to focus on the supply side to foster economic growth. The latter can be achieved by reducing barriers to the supply side of the economy. See Keynesian economic policies, Reagonomics.

T

Takeover defences are devices that prevent hostile raiders from taking over a company without the consent of the management. Hostility in this case is hostility in the eyes of the target company's management whereas the target's shareholders may very well be favourably inclined towards the takeover bid. Takeover defences include voting caps, dual-class shares and staggered boards of directors. See dual-class shares, staggered boards of directors and voting cap. See also golden parachutes.

Theory of property rights. Sanford Grossman, Oliver Hart and John Moore's theory of property rights predicts that employees should be given property rights in their firm if they have to provide investments in human capital which are highly specific to the firm (Grossman, S.J. and Hart, O.D. (1986), 'The Costs and Benefits of Ownership: A Theory of Vertical and Lateral Integration', *Journal of Political Economy* 94, 691–719; Hart, O.D. and Moore, J. (1990), 'Property Rights and the Nature of the Firm', *Journal of Political Economy* 98, 1119–58; Hart, O.D. (1995), *Firms, Contracts, and Financial Structure*, Oxford, UK: Clarendon Press). This prevents conflicts of interests between the owners and the employees in firms where employees make substantial sunk investments in terms of their human capital.

Tobin's q is the ratio of the market value of equity and debt over its book value. A Tobin's q of more than 1 means that the firm creates value as its market value exceeds its book or accounting value or roughly the resale value of its assets. In other words, the firm has valuable growth opportunities. Conversely, a Tobin's q of less than 1 implies that the firm's shareholders would be better off liquidating the firm. Tobin's q is used to measure firm value as well as growth opportunities.

Transfer pricing, see expropriation of the minority shareholders.

The two-tier board exists in countries such as China and Germany as well as some French companies that have opted for a two-tier board rather than the more common one-tier board. The two boards are the supervisory board (in Germany, this is the *Aufsichtsrat*) and the management board (the *Vorstand* in Germany). The non-executive directors, i.e. the shareholder representatives, and also frequently the representatives of other stakeholders, such as trade union and employee representatives, sit on the supervisory board. The top management of the company sit on the management board, which is normally chaired by the chief executive officer (CEO). In France, companies have a choice between the Anglo-American one-tier board (*conseil d'administration*) and the two-tier German board (consisting of the *conseil de surveillance* (the supervisory board)) and the management board (*directoire*)). See also executive directors, non-executive directors.

Tunnelling, see expropriation of the minority shareholders.

Type I agency problem, see type II agency problem.

The type II agency problem is caused by excessive loyalty to one's principal (the CEO or large shareholder) rather than a lack of loyalty. The type I agency problem is the classic agency problem between the managers and the shareholders. It is caused by the managers acting in their own interest rather than performing their duty. It consists of managers being disloyal to their principal, i.e. the shareholders. See principal-agent problem, reflex for loyalty.

U

Ultimate control is defined as the control by the shareholder that ultimately controls a firm via indirect holdings such as a pyramid of ownership (see pyramid of ownership). See also first-tier control.

Unitary board, see one-tier board.

Universal banks are banks that are both commercial and investment banks. See commercial banks, investment banks.

V

The varieties of capitalism (VOC) literature is based on the concept of complementarities. Its simple dichotomous form distinguishes between coordinated market economies and liberal market economies. See complementarities, coordinated market economies, liberal market economies.

A venture capitalist (VC) or venture capital firm finances firms in their early stages, when they are still private companies and not yet listed on a stock exchange. Venture capital tends to be the main form of finance for high-risk, high-growth firms that may have little or no access to bank debt.

Vested shares are shares that are held by the firm on behalf of the entrepreneur and the latter only obtains legal ownership over the shares once certain conditions have been met.

A voting cap is a limit on the percentage of votes a single shareholder can vote at the AGM.

A voting coalition consists of several shareholders agreeing to vote in a concerted way. See also rule of one-share one-vote.

Voting limit, see voting cap.

Voting pool, see voting coalition.

Voting rights, see control rights.

W

World Bank, see Bretton Woods agreement.

Z

Zaibatsu, see keiretsu.

Index